PRACTICAL RELIGION

PRACTICAL RELIGION

BEING PLAIN PAPERS

ON THE DAILY DUTIES, EXPERIENCE, DANGERS, AND

PRIVILEGES OF PROFESSING CHRISTIANS

BY

JOHN CHARLES RYLE, D.D.,

BAKER BOOK HOUSE
Grand Rapids, Michigan

Reprinted 1977 by
Baker Book House

ISBN: 0-8010-7657-9

PHOTOLITHOPRINTED BY CUSHING - MALLOY, INC.
ANN ARBOR, MICHIGAN, UNITED STATES OF AMERICA
1977

CONTENTS

NO.						PAGE
	PREFACE					V
I.	SELF-INQUIRY					1
II.	SELF-EXERTION					23
III.	REALITY					46
IV.	PRAYER					63
V.	BIBLE-READING					97
VI.	GOING TO THE TABLE					140
VII.	CHARITY					165
VIII.	ZEAL					183
IX.	FREEDOM					210
X.	HAPPINESS					230
XI.	FORMALITY					261
XII.	THE WORLD					284
XIII.	RICHES AND POVERTY					312
XIV.	THE BEST FRIEND					336
XV.	SICKNESS					352
XVI.	THE FAMILY OF GOD					375
XVII.	OUR HOME					392
XVIII.	HEIRS OF GOD					403
XIX.	THE GREAT GATHERING					429
XX.	THE GREAT SEPARATION					442
XXI.	ETERNITY					472

PREFACE

————

THE volume now in the reader's hands is intended to be
a companion to two other volumes which I have already
published, entitled "Knots Untied," and "Old Paths."

"Knots Untied" consists of a connected series of papers,
systematically arranged, about the principal points which
form the subject of controversy among Churchmen in the
present day. All who take interest in such disputed
questions as the nature of the Church, the Ministry,
Baptism, Regeneration, the Lord's Supper, the Real
Presence, Worship, Confession, and the Sabbath, will
find them pretty fully discussed in "Knots Untied."

"Old Paths" consists of a similar series of papers about
those leading doctrines of the Gospel which are generally
considered necessary to salvation. The inspiration of

Scripture, sin, justification, forgiveness, repentance, conversion, faith, the work of Christ, and the work of the Holy Spirit, are the principal subjects handled in "Old Paths."

The present volume contains a series of papers about "practical religion," and treats of the daily duties, dangers, experience, and privileges of all who profess and call themselves true Christians. Read in conjunction with another work I have previously put out, called "Holiness," I think it will throw some light on what every believer ought to be, to do, and expect.

One common feature will be found in all the three volumes. I avow it frankly at the outset, and will not keep it back for a moment. The standpoint I have tried to occupy, from first to last, is that of an Evangelical Churchman.

I say this deliberately and emphatically. I am fully aware that Evangelical churchmanship is not popular and acceptable in this day. It is despised by many, and has "no form or comeliness" in their eyes. To avow attachment to Evangelical views, in some quarters, is to provoke a sneer, and to bring on yourself the reproach of being an "unlearned and ignorant man." But none of these things move me. I am not ashamed of my opinions. After forty years of Bible-reading and praying, meditation and theological study, I find myself clinging more tightly than ever to "Evangelical" religion, and more than ever satisfied with it. It wears well: it stands the fire. I know no system of religion which is better. In the faith of it I have lived for the third of a century, and in the faith of it I hope to die.

The plain truth is, that I see no other ground to occupy, and find no other rest for the sole of my foot. I lay no claim to infallibility, and desire to be no man's judge. But the longer I live and read, the more I am convinced and persuaded that Evangelical principles are the principles of the Bible, of the Articles and Prayer-book, and of the leading Divines of the reformed Church of England. Holding these views, I cannot write otherwise than I have written.

I now send forth this volume with an earnest prayer that God the Holy Ghost may bless it, and make it useful and helpful to many souls.

J. C. RYLE,

NOVEMBER, 1878. *Vicar of Stradbroke.*

PRACTICAL RELIGION

I

SELF-INQUIRY

" Let us go again and visit our brethren in every city where we have preached the word of the Lord, and see how they do."— Acts xv. 36.

THE text which heads this page contains a proposal which the Apostle Paul made to Barnabas after their first missionary journey. He proposed to revisit the Churches they had been the means of founding, and to see how they were getting on. Were their members continuing steadfast in the faith? Were they growing in grace? Were they going forward, or standing still? Were they prospering, or falling away?—"Let us go again and visit our brethren, and see how they do."

This was a wise and useful proposal. Let us lay it to heart, and apply it to ourselves in the nineteenth century. Let us search our ways, and find out how matters stand between ourselves and God. Let us "see how we do." I ask every reader of this volume to begin its perusal by joining me in self-inquiry. If ever self-inquiry about religion was needed, it is needed at the present day.

We live in an age of peculiar *spiritual privileges*. Since the world began there never was such an opportunity for a man's soul to be saved as there is in England at this time. There never were so many signs of religion in the land, so many sermons preached, so many services held in churches and chapels, so many Bibles sold, so many religious books and tracts printed, so many Societies for evangelizing mankind supported, so much outward respect paid to Christianity. Things are done everywhere now-a-days which a hundred years ago would have been thought impossible. Bishops support the boldest and most aggressive efforts to reach the unconverted. Deans and Chapters throw open the naves of cathedrals for Sunday evening sermons! Clergy of the narrowest High Church School advocate special missions, and vie with their Evangelical brethren in proclaiming that going to church on Sunday is not enough to take a man to heaven. In short, there is a stir about religion now-a-days to which there has been nothing like since England was a nation, and which the cleverest sceptics and infidels cannot deny. If Romaine, and Venn, and Berridge, and Rowlands, and Grimshaw, and Hervey, had been told that such things would come to pass about a century after their deaths, they would have been tempted to say, with the Samaritan nobleman,—"If the Lord should make windows of heaven might such a thing be." (2 Kings vii. 19.) But the Lord has opened the windows of heaven. There is more taught now-a-days in England of the real Gospel, and of the way of salvation by faith in Jesus Christ, in one week, than there was in a year in Romaine's time. Surely I have a right to say that we live in an age of spiritual privileges. But are we any better for it? In an age like this it is well to ask, "How do we do about our souls?"

We live in an age of peculiar *spiritual danger*. Never perhaps since the world began was there such an immense amount of mere outward profession of religion as there is in the present day. A painfully large proportion of all the congregations in the land consists of unconverted people, who know nothing of heart-religion, never come to the Lord's Table, and never confess Christ in their daily lives. Myriads of those who are always running after preachers, and crowding to hear special sermons, are nothing better than empty tubs, and tinkling cymbals, without a jot of real vital Christianity at home.* The parable of the sower is continually receiving most vivid and painful illustrations. The way-side hearers, the stony-ground hearers, the thorny-ground hearers abound on every side.

The life of many religious professors, I fear, in this age, is nothing better than a continual course of spiritual dram-drinking. They are always morbidly craving fresh excitement; and they seem to care little what it is if they only get it. All preaching seems to come alike to them; and they appear unable to "see differences," so long as they hear what is clever, have their ears tickled, and sit in a crowd. Worst of all, there are hundreds of young unestablished believers who are so infected with the same love of excitement, that they actually think it a duty to be always seeking it. Insensibly almost to themselves, they take up a kind of hysterical, sensational, sentimental Christianity, until they

---

* It is curious and instructive to observe how history repeats itself, and how much sameness there is in the human heart in every age. Even in the Primitive Church, says Canon Robertson, "Many persons were found at church for the great Christian ceremonies, and at the theatres, or even at the temples, for the heathen spectacles. The ritual of the Church was viewed as a theatrical spectacle. The sermons were listened to as the display of rhetoricians; and eloquent preachers were cheered, with clapping of hands, stamping of feet, waving of handkerchiefs, cries of 'Orthodox,' 'Thirteenth Apostle,' and such like demonstrations, which such teachers as Chrysostom and Augustine tried to restrain, that they might persuade their flocks to a more profitable manner of hearing, Some went to Church for the sermon only, alleging that they could pray at home. And when the more attractive parts of the service were over, the great mass of the people departed without remaining for the eucharist."—Robertson's "Church History," B. II., ch. vi., p. 356.

are never content with the "old paths," and, like the Athenians, are always running after something new. To see a calm-minded young believer, who is not stuck up, self-confident, self-conceited, and more ready to teach than learn, but content with a daily steady effort to grow up into Christ's likeness, and to do Christ's work quietly and unostentatiously, at home, is really becoming almost a rarity! Too many young professors, alas, behave like young recruits who have not spent all their bounty money. They show how little deep root they have, and how little knowledge of their own hearts, by noise, forwardness, readiness to contradict and set down old Christians, and over-weening trust in their own fancied soundness and wisdom! Well will it be for many young professors of this age if they do not end, after being tossed about for a while, and "carried to and fro by every wind of doctrine," by joining some petty, narrow-minded, censorious sect, or embracing some senseless, unreasoning, crotchetty heresy. Surely in times like these there is great need for self-examination. When we look around us, we may well ask, "How do we do about our souls?"

In handling this question, I think the shortest plan will be to suggest a list of subjects for self-inquiry, and to go through them in order. By so doing I shall hope to meet the case of every one into whose hands this volume may fall. I invite every reader of this paper to join me in calm, searching self-examination, for a few short minutes. I desire to speak to myself as well as to you. I approach you not as an enemy, but as a friend. "My heart's desire and prayer to God is that you may be saved." (Rom. x. 1.) Bear with me if I say things which at first sight look harsh and severe. Believe me, he is your best friend who tells you the most truth.

(1) Let me ask, in the first place, *Do we ever think about our souls at all*? Thousands of English people, I fear, cannot answer that question satisfactorily. They

never give the subject of religion any place in their thoughts. From the beginning of the year to the end they are absorbed in the pursuit of business, pleasure, politics, money, or self-indulgence of some kind or another. Death, and judgment, and eternity, and heaven, and hell, and a world to come, are never calmly looked at and considered. They live on as if they were never going to die, or rise again, or stand at the bar of God, or receive an eternal sentence! They do not openly oppose religion, for they have not sufficient reflection about it to do so;— but they eat, and drink, and sleep, and get money, and spend money, as if religion was a mere fiction and not a reality. They are neither Romanists, nor Socinians, nor infidels, nor High Church, nor Low Church, nor Broad Church. They are just *nothing at all*, and do not take the trouble to have opinions. A more senseless and un-reasonable way of living cannot be conceived; but they do not pretend to reason about it. They simply never think about God, unless frightened for a few minutes by sickness, death in their families, or an accident. Barring such interruptions, they appear to ignore religion altogether, and hold on their way cool and undisturbed, as if there were nothing worth thinking of except this world.

It is hard to imagine a life more unworthy of an immortal creature than such a life as I have just de-scribed, for it reduces a man to the level of a beast. But it is literally and truly the life of multitudes in England: and as they pass away their place is taken by multitudes like them. The picture, no doubt, is horrible, distressing, and revolting : but, unhappily, it is only too true. In every large town, in every market, on every stock-exchange, in every club, you may see specimens of this class by scores,—men who think of everything under the sun except the one thing needful,—the salvation of their souls. Like the Jews of old they do not "consider their ways," they do not " consider their latter end;" they do not " consider that they do evil." (Isa. i. 3; Hag. i. 7; Deut. xxxii. 29; Eccles. v. i.) Like Gallio they "care for none of these things:" they are not in their way. (Acts xviii. 17.) If they prosper in the world, and get rich, and succeed in their line of life, they are praised, and admired by their contemporaries. Nothing succeeds in England like success! But for all this they cannot live for ever. They will have to die and appear before the bar of God, and be judged; and then what will the end be? When a large class of this kind exists in our country, no reader need wonder that I ask whether he belongs to it. If you do, you ought to have a mark set on your door, as there used to be a mark on a plague-stricken house two centuries ago, with the words, "Lord have mercy on us," written on it. Look at the class I have been describing, and then look at your own soul.

(2) Let me ask, in the second place, *whether we ever do anything about our souls?* There are multitudes in England who think occasionally about religion, but unhappily never get beyond thinking. After a stirring sermon,—or after a funeral,—or under the pressure of illness,—or on Sunday evening,—or when things are going on badly in their families,—or when they meet some bright example of a Christian,—or when they fall in with some striking religious book or tract,—they will at the time think a good deal, and even talk a little about religion in a vague way. But they stop short, as if thinking and talking were enough to save them. They are always meaning, and intending, and purposing, and resolving, and wishing, and telling us that they "know" what is right, and "hope" to be found right at last, but they never attain to any *action*. There is no actual separation from the service of the world and sin, no real taking up the cross and following Christ, no positive *doing* in their Christianity. Their life is spent in playing the part of the son in our Lord's parable, to whom the father said, "Go, work in my

vineyard: and he answered, I go, sir, and went not."
(Matt. xxi. 30.) They are like those whom Ezekiel describes, who liked his preaching, but never practised what
he preached:—" They come unto thee as the people
cometh, and they sit before thee as my people, and they
hear thy words, but they will not do them. . . . . And, lo,
thou art unto them as a very lovely song of one that hath
a pleasant voice, and can play well on an instrument: for
they hear thy words, but they do them not." (Ezek.
xxxiii. 31, 32.) In a day like this, when hearing and
thinking, without *doing*, is so common, no one can justly
wonder that I press upon men the absolute need of self-
examination. Once more, then, I ask my readers to consider the question of my text,—" How do we do about our
souls ? "

(3) Let me ask, in the third place, *whether we are
trying to satisfy our consciences with a mere formal religion?* There are myriads in England at this moment who
are making shipwreck on this rock. Like the Pharisees of
old, they make much ado about the outward part of Christianity, while the inward and spiritual part is totally neglected.
They are careful to attend all the services of their place of
worship, and regular in using all its forms and ordinances.
They are never absent from Communion when the Lord's
Supper is administered. Sometimes they are most strict
in observing Lent, and attach great importance to Saints'
days. They are often keen partisans of their own Church,
or sect, or congregation, and ready to contend with any
one who does not agree with them. Yet all this time
there is no *heart* in their religion. Any one who knows
them intimately can see with half an eye that their
affections are set on things below, and not on things above;
and that they are trying to make up for the want of
inward Christianity by an excessive quantity of outward
form. And this formal religion does them no real good.
They are not satisfied. Beginning at the wrong end, by

making the outward things first, they know nothing of inward joy and peace, and pass their lives in a constant struggle, secretly conscious that there is something wrong, and yet not knowing why. Well, after all, if they do not go on from one stage of formality to another, until in despair they take a fatal plunge, and fall into Popery! When professing Christians of this kind are so painfully numerous, no one need wonder if I press upon him the paramount importance of close self-examination. If you love life, do not be content with the husk, and shell, and scaffolding of religion. Remember our Saviour's words about the Jewish formalists of His day: "This people draweth nigh with their mouth, and honoureth Me with their lips, but their heart is far from Me. In vain do they worship." (Matt. xv. 9.) It needs something more than going diligently to church, and receiving the Lord's Supper, to take our souls to heaven. Means of grace and forms of religion are useful in their way, and God seldom does anything for His church without them. But let us beware of making shipwreck on the very lighthouse which helps to show the channel into the harbour. Once more I ask, "How do we do about our souls?"

(4) Let me ask, in the fourth place, *whether we have received the forgiveness of our sins?* Few reasonable Englishmen would thing of denying that they are sinners. Many perhaps would say that they are not so bad as many, and that they have not been so very wicked, and so forth. But few, I repeat, would pretend to say that they had always lived like angels, and never done, or said, or thought a wrong thing all their days. In short, all of us must confess that we are more or less "*sinners*," and, as sinners, are guilty before God; and, as guilty, we must be forgiven, or lost and condemned for ever at the last day.— Now it is the glory of the Christian religion that it provides for us the very forgiveness that we need,—full, free, perfect, eternal, and complete. It is a leading article in

that well-known creed which most Englishmen learn when they are children. They are taught to say, "I believe in the forgiveness of sins." This forgiveness of sins has been purchased for us by the eternal Son of God, our Lord Jesus Christ. He has purchased it for us by coming into the world to be our Saviour, and by living, dying, and rising again, as our Substitute, in our behalf. He has bought it for us at the price of His own most precious blood, by suffering in our stead on the cross, and making satisfaction for our sins. But this forgiveness, great, and full, and glorious as it is, does not become the property of every man and woman, as a matter of course. It is not a privilege which every member of a Church possesses, merely because he is a Churchman. It is a thing which each individual must receive for himself by his own personal faith, lay hold on by faith, appropriate by faith, and make his own by faith; or else, so far as he is concerned, Christ will have died in vain. "He that believeth on the Son hath everlasting life, and he that believeth not the Son shall not see life, but the wrath of God abideth on him." (John iii. 36.) No terms can be imagined more simple, and more suitable to man. As good old Latimer said, in speaking of the matter of justification, "It is but believe and have." It is only faith that is required; and faith is nothing more than the humble, heartfelt trust of the soul which desires to be saved. Jesus is able and willing to save; but man must come to Jesus and believe. All that believe are at once justified and forgiven: but without believing there is no forgiveness at all.

Now here is exactly the point, I am afraid, where multitudes of English people fail, and are in imminent danger of being lost for ever. They know that there is no forgiveness of sin excepting in Christ Jesus. They can tell you that there is no Saviour for sinners, no Redeemer, no Mediator, excepting Him who was born of the Virgin Mary, and was crucified under Pontius Pilate, dead, and buried. But here they stop, and get no further! They never come to the point of actually laying hold on Christ by faith, and becoming one with Christ and Christ in them. They can say, He is a Saviour, but not 'my Saviour,'—a Redeemer, but not 'my Redeemer,'—a Priest, but not 'my Priest,'—an Advocate, but not 'my Advocate:' and so they live and die unforgiven! No wonder that Martin Luther said, "Many are lost because they cannot use possessive pronouns." When this is the state of many in this day, no one need wonder that I ask men whether they have received the forgiveness of sins. An eminent Christian lady once said, in her old age,—"The beginning of eternal life in my soul, was a conversation I had with an old gentleman, who came to visit my father, when I was only a little girl. He took me by the hand one day, and said, 'My dear child, my life is nearly over, and you will probably live many years after I am gone. But never forget two things. One is, that there is such a thing as having our sins forgiven while we live. The other is, that there is such a thing as knowing and feeling that we are forgiven.' I thank God I have never forgotten his words."—How is it with us? Let us not rest till we "know and feel," as the Prayer-book says, that we are forgiven. Once more let us ask,—In the matter of forgiveness of sins, "How do we do?"

(5) Let me ask, in the fifth place, *whether we know anything by experience of conversion to God.* Without conversion there is no salvation. "Except ye be converted, and become as little children, ye shall not enter into the kingdom of heaven."—"Except a man be born again, he cannot see the kingdom of God."—"If any man have not the Spirit of Christ, he is none of His."—"If any man be in Christ he is a new creature." (Matt. xviii. 3; John iii. 3; Rom. viii. 9; 2 Cor. v. 17.) We are all by nature so weak, so worldly, so earthly-minded, so inclined to sin, that without a thorough change we cannot serve

God in life, and could not enjoy Him after death. Just as ducks, as soon as they are hatched, take naturally to water, so do children, as soon as they can do anything, take to selfishness, lying, and deceit; and none pray, or love God, unless they are taught. High or low, rich or poor, gentle or simple, we all need a complete change,—a change which it is the special office of the Holy Ghost to give us. Call it what you please,—new birth, regeneration, renewal, new creation, quickening, repentance,—the thing must be had if we are to be saved: and if we have the thing it will be *seen*.

Sense of sin and deep hatred to it, faith in Christ and love to Him, delight in holiness and longing after more of it, love to God's people and distaste for the things of the world,—these, these are the signs and evidences which always accompany conversion. Myriads around us, it may be feared, know nothing about it. They are, in Scripture language, dead, and asleep, and blind, and unfit for the kingdom of God. Year after year, perhaps, they go on repeating the words of the Creed, "I believe in the Holy Ghost;" but they are utterly ignorant of His changing operations on the inward man. Sometimes they flatter themselves they are born again, because they have been baptized, and go to church, and receive the Lord's Supper; while they are totally destitute of the marks of the new birth, as described by St. John in his first Epistle. And all this time the words of Scripture are clear and plain,— "Except ye be converted, ye shall in no case enter the kingdom." (Matt. xviii. 3.) In times like these, no reader ought to wonder that I press the subject of conversion on men's souls. No doubt there are plenty of sham conversions in such a day of religious excitement as this. But bad coin is no proof that there is no good money: nay, rather it is a sign that there is some money current which is valuable, and is worth imitation. Hypocrites and sham Christians are indirect evidence that there is such a thing as real grace among men. Let us search our own hearts then, and see how it is with ourselves. Once more let us ask, in the matter of conversion, "How do we do?"

(6) Let me ask, in the sixth place, *whether we know anything of practical Christian holiness?* It is as certain as anything in the Bible that "without holiness no man shall see the Lord." (Heb. xii. 14.) It is equally certain that it is the invariable fruit of saving faith, the real test of regeneration, the only sound evidence of indwelling grace, the certain consequence of vital union with Christ. —Holiness is not absolute perfection and freedom from all faults. Nothing of the kind! The wild words of some who talk of enjoying "unbroken communion with God" for many months, are greatly to be deprecated, because they raise unscriptural expectations in the minds of young believers, and so do harm. Absolute perfection is for heaven, and not for earth, where we have a weak body, a wicked world, and a busy devil continually near our souls. Nor is real Christian holiness ever attained, or maintained, without a constant fight and struggle. The great Apostle, who said "I fight,—I labour,—I keep under my body and bring it into subjection" (1 Cor. ix. 27), would have been amazed to hear of *sanctification without personal exertion*, and to be told that believers only need to sit still, and everything will be done for them!

Yet, weak and imperfect as the holiness of the best saints may be, it is a real true thing, and has a character about it as unmistakable as light and salt. It is not a thing which begins and ends with noisy profession : it will be *seen* much more than *heard*. Genuine Scriptural holiness will make a man do his duty at home and by the fireside, and adorn his doctrine in the little trials of daily life. It will exhibit itself in passive graces as well as in active. It will make a man humble, kind, gentle, unselfish, good-tempered, considerate for others, loving, meek, and forgiving. It will not constrain him to go out of the world, and shut himself up in a cave, like a hermit. But it will make him do his duty in that state to which God has called him, on Christian principles, and after the pattern of Christ. Such holiness, I know well, is not common. It is a style of practical Christianity which is painfully rare in these days. But I can find no other standard of holiness in the Word of God,—no other which comes up to the pictures drawn by our Lord and His Apostles. In an age like this no reader can wonder if I press this subject also on men's attention. Once more let us ask,—In the matter of holiness, how is it with our souls ? " How do we do ? "

(7) Let me ask, in the seventh place, *whether we know anything of enjoying the means of grace?* When I speak of the means of grace, I have in my mind's eye five principal things,—the reading of the Bible, private prayer, public worship, the sacrament of the Lord's Supper, and the rest of the Lord's day. They are means which God has graciously appointed, in order to convey grace to man's heart by the Holy Ghost, or to keep up the spiritual life after it has begun. As long as the world stands, the state of a man's soul will always depend greatly on the manner and spirit in which he uses means of grace. The *manner and spirit,* I say deliberately and of purpose. Many English people use the means of grace regularly and formally, but know nothing of enjoying them : they attend to them as a matter of duty, but without a jot of feeling, interest, or affection. Yet even common sense might tell us that this formal, mechanical use of holy things, is utterly worthless and unprofitable. Our *feeling* about them is just one of the many tests of the state of our souls. How can that man be thought to love God who reads about Him and His Christ, as a mere matter of duty, content and satisfied if he has just moved his mark onward over so many chapters?—How can that man suppose he is ready to meet Christ, who never takes any trouble to

pour out his heart to Him in private as a Friend, and is satisfied with saying over a string of words every morning and evening, under the name of "prayer," scarcely thinking what he is about?—How could that man be happy in heaven for ever, who finds the Sunday a dull, gloomy, tiresome day,—who knows nothing of hearty prayer and praise, and cares nothing whether he hears truth or error from the pulpit, or scarcely listens to the sermon?—What can be the spiritual condition of that man whose heart never "burns within him," when he receives that bread and wine which specially remind us of Christ's death on the cross, and the atonement for sin? These inquiries are very serious and important. If means of grace had no other use, and were not mighty helps toward heaven, they would be useful in supplying a test of our real state in the sight of God. Tell me what a man does in the matter of Bible-reading and praying, in the matter of Sunday, public worship, and the Lord's Supper, and I will soon tell you what he is, and on which road he is travelling. How is it with ourselves? Once more let us ask,—In the matter of means of grace, "How do we do?"

(8) Let me ask, in the eighth place, *whether we ever try to do any good in the world?* Our Lord Jesus Christ was continually "going about doing good," while He was on earth. (Acts x. 38.) The Apostles, and all the disciples in Bible times, were always striving to walk in His steps. A Christian who was content to go to heaven himself, and cared not what became of others, whether they lived happy and died in peace or not, would have been regarded as a kind of monster in primitive times, who had not the Spirit of Christ. Why should we suppose for a moment that a lower standard will suffice in the present day? Why should fig trees which bear no fruit be spared in the present day, when in our Lord's time they were to be cut down as "cumberers of the

ground"? (Luke xiii. 7.) These are serious inquiries, and demand serious answers.

There is a generation of professing Christians now-a-days, who seem to know nothing of caring for their neighbours, and are wholly swallowed up in the concerns of number one,—that is, their own and their family's. They eat, and drink, and sleep, and dress, and work, and get money, and spend money, year after year ; and whether others are happy or miserable, well or ill, converted or unconverted, travelling toward heaven or toward hell, appear to be questions about which they are supremely indifferent. Can this be right? Can it be reconciled with the religion of Him who spoke the parable of the good Samaritan, and bade us "go and do likewise"? (Luke x. 37.) I doubt it altogether.

There is much to be done on every side. There is not a place in England where there is not a field for work, and an open door for being useful, if any one is willing to enter it. There is not a Christian in England who cannot find some good work to do for others, if he has only a heart to do it. The poorest man or woman, without a single penny to give, can always show his deep sympathy to the sick and sorrowful, and by simple good-nature and tender helpfulness, can lessen the misery and increase the comfort of somebody in this troubled world. But alas, the vast majority of professing Christians, whether rich or poor, Churchmen or Dissenters, seem possessed with a devil of detestable selfishness, and know not the luxury of doing good. They can argue by the hour about baptism, and the Lord's supper, and the forms of worship, and the union of Church and State, and such-like dry-bone questions. But all this time they seem to care nothing for their neighbours. The plain practical point, whether they love their neighbour, as the Samaritan loved the traveller in the parable, and can spare any time and trouble to do him good, is a point they never touch with one of their fingers. In too many English parishes, both in town and country, true love seems almost dead, both in church and chapel, and wretched party-spirit and controversy are the only fruits that Christianity appears able to produce. In a day like this, no reader should wonder if I press this plain old subject on his conscience. Do we know anything of genuine Samaritan love to others? Do we ever try to do any good to any one beside our own friends and relatives, and our own party or cause? Are we living like disciples of Him who always "went about doing good," and commanded His disciples to take Him for their "example"? (John xiii. 15.) If not, with what face shall we meet Him in the judgment day? In this matter also, how is it with our souls? Once more I ask, "How do we do?"

(9) Let me ask, in the ninth place, *whether we know anything of living the life of habitual communion with Christ?* By "communion," I mean that habit of "abiding in Christ" which our Lord speaks of, in the fifteenth chapter of St. John's Gospel, as essential to Christian fruitfulness. (John xv. 4—8.) Let it be distinctly understood that union with Christ is one thing, and communion is another. There can be no communion with the Lord Jesus without union first; but unhappily there may be union with the Lord Jesus, and afterwards little or no communion at all. The difference between the two things is not the difference between two distinct steps, but the difference between the higher and lower ends of an inclined plane. Union is the common privilege of all who feel their sins, and truly repent, and come to Christ by faith, and are accepted, forgiven, and justified in Him. Too many believers, it may be feared, *never get beyond this stage!* Partly from ignorance, partly from laziness, partly from fear of man, partly from secret love of the world, partly from some unmortified besetting sin, they are content with a little faith, and a little hope, and a little peace, and a little measure of holiness. And they

live on all their lives in this condition—doubting, weak, halting, and bearing fruit only "thirty-fold" to the very end of their days!

Communion with Christ is the privilege of those who are continually striving to grow in grace, and faith, and knowledge, and conformity to the mind of Christ in all things,—who do not "look to the things behind," and "count not themselves to have attained," but "press toward the mark for the prize of the high calling of God in Christ Jesus." (Phil. iii. 14.) Union is the bud, but communion is the flower: union is the babe, but communion is the strong man. He that has union with Christ does well; but he that enjoys communion with Him does far better. Both have one life, one hope, one heavenly seed in their hearts,—one Lord, one Saviour, one Holy Spirit, one eternal home: but union is not so good as communion! The grand secret of communion with Christ is to be continually "living the life of faith in Him," and drawing out of Him every hour the supply that every hour requires. "To me," said St. Paul, "to live is Christ."—"I live: yet not I, but Christ liveth in me." (Gal. ii. 20; Phil. i. 21.)

Communion like this is the secret of the abiding "joy and peace in believing," which eminent saints like Bradford and Rutherford notoriously possessed. None were ever more humble, or more deeply convinced of their own infirmities and corruption. They would have told you that the seventh chapter of Romans precisely described their own experience. They would have endorsed every word of the "Confession" put into the mouths of true believers, in our Prayer-book Communion Service. They would have said continually, "The remembrance of our sins is grievous unto us; the burden of them is intolerable." But they were ever looking unto Jesus, and in Him they were ever able to rejoice.—Communion like this is the secret of the splendid victories which such men as these won over sin, the world, and the fear of death. They did not sit

still idly, saying, "I leave it all to Christ to do for me,"
but, strong in the Lord, they used the Divine nature He
had implanted in them, boldly and confidently, and were
"more than conquerors through Him that loved them."
(Rom. viii. 37.)   Like St. Paul they would have said, "I
can do all things through Christ which strengtheneth me."
(Phil iv. 13.)—Ignorance of this life of communion is one
among many reasons why so many in this age are hankering
after the Confessional, and strange views of the "real
presence" in the Lord's Supper.   Such errors often spring
from imperfect knowledge of Christ, and obscure views of
the life of faith in a risen, living, and interceding Saviour.

Is communion with Christ like this a common thing ?
Alas ! it is very rare indeed !   The greater part of
believers seem content with the barest elementary knowledge of justification by faith, and half-a-dozen other
doctrines, and go doubting, limping, halting, groaning
along the way to heaven, and experience little either of
the sense of victory or joy.   The Churches of these latter
days are full of weak, powerless, and uninfluential
believers, saved at last, "but so as by fire," but never
shaking the world, and knowing nothing of an "abundant
entrance."   (1 Cor. iii. 15 ; 2 Pet. i. 11.)   Despondency
and Feeble-mind and Much-afraid, in "Pilgrim's Progress,"
reached the celestial city as really and truly as Valiant-
for-the-truth and Greatheart.   But they certainly did not
reach it with the same comfort, and did not do a tenth
part of the same good in the world !   I fear there are
many like them in these days !   When things are so
in the Churches, no reader can wonder that I inquire how
it is with our souls.   Once more I ask,—In the matter of
communion with Christ, "How do we do ?"

(10) Let me ask, in the tenth and last place, *whether
we know anything of being ready for Christ's second
coming?*   That He will come again the second time is as
certain as anything in the Bible.   The world has not yet

seen the last of Him. As surely as He went up visibly, and in the body, on the Mount of Olives, before the eyes of His disciples, so surely will He come again in the clouds of heaven, with power and great glory. (Acts i. 11.) He will come to raise the dead, to change the living, to reward His saints, to punish the wicked, to renew the earth, and take the curse away,—to purify the world, even as He purified the temple,—and to set up a kingdom where sin shall have no place, and holiness shall be the universal rule. The Creeds which we repeat and profess to believe, continually declare that Christ is coming again. The ancient Christians made it a part of their religion to look for His return. *Backward* they looked to the cross and the atonement for sin, and rejoiced in Christ crucified. *Upward* they looked to Christ at the right hand of God, and rejoiced in Christ interceding. *Forward* they looked to the promised return of their Master, and rejoiced in the thought that they would see Him again. And we ought to do the same.

What have we really got from Christ? and what do we know of Him? and what do we think of Him? Are we living as if we long to see Him again, and love His appearing?—Readiness for that appearing is nothing more than being a real, consistent Christian. It requires no man to cease from his daily business. The farmer need not give up his farm, nor the shopkeeper his counter, nor the doctor his patients, nor the carpenter his hammer and nails, nor the bricklayer his mortar and trowel, nor the blacksmith his smithy. Each and all cannot do better than be found doing his duty, but doing it *as a Christian*, and with a heart packed up and ready to be gone. In the face of truth like this no reader can feel surprised if I ask, How is it with our souls in the matter of Christ's second coming? The world is growing old and running to seed. The vast majority of Christians seem like the men in the time of

Noah and Lot, who were eating and drinking, marrying and giving in marriage, planting and building, up to the very day when flood and fire came. Those words of our Master are very solemn and heart-searching,—" Remember Lot's wife."—" Take heed lest at any time your heart be overcharged with the cares of this life, and that day come upon you unawares." (Luke xvii. 32; xxi. 34.) Once more I ask,—In the matter of readiness for Christ's second coming, " How do we do ? "

I end my inquiries here. I might easily add to them; but I trust I have said enough, at the beginning of this volume, to stir up self-inquiry and self-examination in many minds. God is my witness that I have said nothing that I do not feel of paramount importance to my own soul. I only want to do good to others. Let me now conclude all with a few words of practical application.

(a) Is any reader of this paper *asleep and utterly thoughtless about religion?* Oh, awake and sleep no more! Look at the churchyards and cemeteries. One by one the people around you are dropping into them, and you must lie there one day. Look forward to a world to come, and lay your hand on your heart, and say, if you dare, that you are fit to die and meet God. Ah ! you are like one sleeping in a boat drifting down the stream towards the falls of Niagara! " What meanest thou, oh sleeper! Arise and call upon thy God !"—" Awake thou that sleepest, and arise from the dead, and Christ shall give thee light!" (Jonah i. 6; Eph. v. 14.)

(b) Is any reader of this paper *feeling self-condemned, and afraid that there is no hope for his soul?* Cast aside your fears, and accept the offer of our Lord Jesus Christ to sinners. Hear Him saying, " Come unto Me, all ye that labour and are heavy laden, and I will give you rest." (Matt. xi. 28.) "If any man thirst, let him come unto Me and drink." (John vii. 37.) " Him that cometh unto Me I will in no wise cast out." (John vi. 37.)

Doubt not that these words are for you as well as for any one else. Bring all your sins, and unbelief, and sense of guilt, and unfitness, and doubts, and infirmities,—bring all to Christ. "This Man receiveth sinners," and He will receive you. (Luke xv. 2.) Do not stand still, halting between two opinions, and waiting for a convenient season. "Arise: He calleth thee!" Come to Christ this very day. (Mark x. 49.)

(c) Is any reader of this paper a professing believer in Christ, but a *believer without much joy and peace and comfort?* Take advice this day. Search your own heart, and see whether the fault be not entirely your own. Very likely you are sitting at ease, content with a little faith, and a little repentance, a little grace and a little sanctification, and unconsciously shrinking back from extremes. You will never be a very happy Christian at this rate, if you live to the age of Methuselah. Change your plan, if you love life and would see good days, without delay. Come out boldly, and act decidedly. Be thorough, thorough, very thorough in your Christianity, and set your face fully towards the sun. Lay aside every weight, and the sin that doth so easily beset you. Strive to get nearer to Christ, to abide in Him, to cleave to Him, and to sit at His feet like Mary, and drink full draughts out of the fountain of life. "These things," says St. John, "we write unto you that your joy may be full." (1 John i. 4.) "If we walk in the light as He is in the light, we have fellowship one with another." (1 John i. 7.)

(d) Is any reader of this paper *a believer oppressed with doubts and fears,* on account of his feebleness, infirmity, and sense of sin? Remember the text that says of Jesus, "A bruised reed will He not break, and smoking flax shall He not quench." (Matt. xii. 20.) Take comfort in the thought that this text is for you. What though your faith be feeble? It is better than no faith at all. The least grain of life is better than death. Perhaps you are expecting too much in this world. Earth is not heaven.

You are yet in the body. Expect little from self, but much from Christ. Look more to Jesus, and less to self.

(e) Finally, is any reader of this paper *sometimes downcast* by the trials he meets with in the way to heaven, bodily trials, family trials, trials of circumstances, trials from neighbours, and trials from the world? Look up to a sympathizing Saviour at God's right hand, and pour out your heart before Him. He can be touched with the feeling of your infirmities, for He suffered Himself being tempted.—Are you alone? So was He. Are you misrepresented and calumniated? So was He. Are you forsaken by friends? So was He. Are you persecuted? So was He. Are you wearied in body and grieved in spirit? So was He.—Yes! He can feel for you, and He can help as well as feel. Then learn to draw nearer to Christ. The time is short. Yet a little time, and all will be over: we shall soon be "with the Lord." "There is an end; and thine expectation shall not be cut off." (Prov. xxiii. 18.) "Ye have need of patience, that, after ye have done the will of God, ye might receive the promise. For yet a little while, and He that shall come will come, and will not tarry." (Heb. x. 36, 37.)

II

SELF-EXERTION

"Strive to enter in at the strait gate: for many, I say unto you, will seek to enter in, and shall not be able."—LUKE xiii. 24.

THERE was once a man who asked our Lord Jesus Christ a very deep question. He said to Him, "Lord, are there few that be saved?"

Who this man was we do not know. What his motive was for asking this question we are not told. Perhaps he wished to gratify an idle curiosity: perhaps he wanted an excuse for not seeking salvation himself. The Holy Ghost has kept back all this from us: the name and motive of the inquirer are both hidden.

But one thing is very clear, and that is the vast importance of the saying of our Lord to which the question gave rise. Jesus seized the opportunity to direct the minds of all around Him to their own plain duty. He knew the train of thought which the man's inquiry had set moving in their hearts: He saw what was going on within them. "Strive," He cries, "to enter in at the strait gate." Whether there be few saved or many, your course is clear;—strive to enter in. Now is the accepted time. Now is the day of salvation. A day shall come when many will seek to enter in and shall not be able. "Strive to enter in now."

I desire to call the serious attention of all who read this paper to the solemn lessons which this saying of the Lord

Jesus is meant to teach. It is one which deserves special remembrance in the present day. It teaches unmistakeably that mighty truth, our own personal responsibility for the salvation of our souls. It shows the immense danger of putting off the great business of religion, as so many unhappily do. On both these points the witness of our Lord Jesus Christ in the text is clear. He, who is the eternal God, and who spoke the words of perfect wisdom, says to the sons of men,—" Strive to enter in at the strait gate : for many, I say unto you, will seek to enter in, and shall not be able."

I. Here is a *description* of the way of salvation. Jesus calls it " the strait gate."

II. Here is a plain *command*. Jesus says, " Strive to enter in."

III. Here is an awful *prophecy*. Jesus says, " Many will seek to enter in, and shall not be able."

May the Holy Ghost apply the subject to the hearts of all into whose hands this paper may fall ! May all who read it know the way of salvation experimentally, obey the command of the Lord practically, and be found safe in the great day of His second coming !

I. Here is a *description* of the way of salvation Jesus calls it "*the strait gate*."

There is a gate which leads to pardon, peace with God, and heaven. Whosoever goes in by that gate shall be saved. Never, surely, was a gate more needed. Sin is a vast mountain between man and God. How shall a man climb over it ?—Sin is a high wall between man and God. How shall man get through it ?—Sin is a deep gulf between man and God. How shall man cross over it ?— God is in heaven, holy, pure, spiritual, undefiled, light without any darkness at all, a Being who cannot bear that which is evil, or look upon iniquity. Man is a poor fallen worm, crawling on earth for a few years,—sinful, corrupt, erring, defective,—a being whose imagination is only evil, and whose heart is deceitful above all things, and desperately wicked. How shall man and God be brought together? How shall man ever draw near to his Maker without fear and shame? Blessed be God, there is a way! There is a road. There is a path. There is a door. It is the gate spoken of in the words of Christ,—"the strait gate."

This gate was *made for sinners by the Lord Jesus Christ.* From all eternity He covenanted and engaged that He would make it. In the fulness of time He came into the world and made it, by His own atoning death on the cross. By that death He made satisfaction for man's sin, paid man's debt to God, and bore man's punishment. He built a great gate at the cost of His own body and blood. He reared a ladder on earth whose top reached to heaven. He made a door by which the chief of sinners may enter into the holy presence of God, and not be afraid. He opened a road by which the vilest of men, believing in Him, may draw near to God and have peace. He cries to us, "I am the door: by Me if any man enter in, he shall be saved." (John x. 9.) "I am the way: no man cometh unto the Father but by Me." (John xiv. 6.) "By Him," says Paul, "we have boldness and access with confidence." (Eph. iii. 12.) Thus was the gate of salvation formed.

This gate is called *the strait gate,* and it is not called so without cause. It is always strait, narrow, and difficult to pass through to some persons, and it will be so as long as the world stands. It is narrow to all who love sin, and are determined not to part with it. It is narrow to all who set their affection on this world, and seek first its pleasures and rewards. It is narrow to all who dislike trouble, and are unwilling to take pains and make sacrifices for their souls. It is narrow to all who like company, and want to keep in with the crowd. It is narrow to all who are self-righteous, and think they are good people, and deserve to be saved. To all such the great gate, which Christ made, is narrow and strait. In vain they seek to pass through. The gate will not admit them. God is not unwilling to receive them; their sins are not too many to be forgiven: but they are not willing to be saved in God's way. Thousands, for the last eighteen centuries, have tried to make the gate-way wider: thousands have worked and toiled to get to heaven on lower terms. But the gate never alters. It is not elastic : it will not stretch to accommodate one man more than another. It is still the strait gate.

Strait as this gate is, it is *the only one by which men can get to heaven*. There is no side door; there is no bye-path; there is no gap or low-place in the wall. All that are ever saved will be saved only by Christ, and only by simple faith in Him.—Not one will be saved by repentance. To-day's sorrow does not wipe off yesterday's score.—Not one will be saved by his own works. The best works that any man can do are little better than splendid sins.—Not one will be saved by his formal regularity in the use of the outward means of grace. When we have done all, we are poor "unprofitable servants." Oh, no! it is mere waste of time to seek any other road to eternal life. Men may look right and left, and weary themselves with their own devices, but they will never find another door. Proud men may dislike the gate if they will. Profligate men may scoff at it, and make a jest of those who use it. Lazy men may complain that the way is hard. But men will discover no other salvation than that of faith in the blood and righteousness of a crucified Redeemer. There stands between us and heaven one great gate: it may be strait; but it is the only one. We must either enter heaven by the strait gate, or not at all.

Strait as this gate is, it is *a gate ever ready to open.*
No sinners of any kind are forbidden to draw near:
whosoever will may enter in and be saved. There is but
one condition of admission: that condition is that you
really feel your sins and desire to be saved by Christ in
His own way. Art thou really sensible of thy guilt and
vileness? Hast thou a truly broken and contrite heart?
Behold the gate of salvation, and come in. He that made
it declares,—"Him that cometh unto Me I will in no wise
cast out." (John vi. 37.) The question to be considered is not
whether you are a great sinner or a little sinner—whether
you are elect or not,—whether you are converted or not.
The question is simply this, "Do you feel your sins? Do you
feel labouring and heavy-laden? Are you willing to put
your soul into Christ's hand?" Then if that be the case,
the gate will open to you at once. Come in this very
day. "Wherefore standest thou without?" (Gen. xxiv. 31.)

Strait as this gate is, it is *one through which thousands
have gone in and been saved.* No sinner was ever turned
back, and told he was too bad to be admitted, if he came
really sick of his sins. Thousands of all sorts have been
received, cleansed, washed, pardoned, clothed, and made
heirs of eternal life. Some of them seemed very unlikely
to be admitted: you and I might have thought they were
too bad to be saved. But He that built the gate did not
refuse them. As soon as they knocked, He gave orders
that they should be let in.

Manasseh, King of Judah, went up to this gate. None
could have been worse than he. He had despised his
good father Hezekiah's example and advice. He had
bowed down to idols. He had filled Jerusalem with
bloodshed and cruelty. He had slain his own children.
But as soon as his eyes were opened to his sins, and he
fled to the gate for pardon, the gate flew wide open, and
he was saved.

Saul the Pharisee went up to this gate. He had been

a great offender. He had been a blasphemer of Christ, and a persecutor of Christ's people. He had laboured hard to stop the progress of the Gospel. But as soon as his heart was touched, and he found out his own guilt and fled to the gate for pardon, at once the gate flew wide open, and he was saved.

Many of the Jews who crucified our Lord went up to this gate. They had been grievous sinners indeed. They had refused and rejected their own Messiah. They had delivered Him to Pilate, and entreated that He might be slain. They had desired Barabbas to be let go, and the Son of God to be crucified. But in the day when they were pricked to the heart by Peter's preaching, they fled to the gate for pardon, and at once the gate flew open, and they were saved.

The jailer at Philippi went up to this gate. He had been a cruel, hard, godless man. He had done all in his power to ill-treat Paul and his companion. He had thrust them into the inner prison, and made their feet fast in the stocks. But when his conscience was aroused by the earthquake, and his mind enlightened by Paul's teaching, he fled to the gate for pardon, and at once the gate flew open, and he was saved.

But why need I stop short in Bible examples? Why should I not say that multitudes have gone to "the strait gate" since the days of the Apostles, and have entered in by it and been saved? Thousands of all ranks, classes, and ages,—learned and unlearned, rich and poor, old and young,—have tried the gate and found it ready to open,— have gone through it and found peace to their souls. Yes: thousands of persons yet living have made proof of the gate, and found it the way to real happiness. Noblemen and commoners, merchants and bankers, soldiers and sailors, farmers and tradesmen, labourers and workmen, are still upon earth, who have found the strait gate to be "a way of pleasantness and a path of peace." They have not brought up an evil report of the country inside. They have found Christ's yoke to be easy, and His burden to be light. Their only regret has been that so few enter in, and that they themselves did not enter in before.

This is the gate which I want every one to enter, into whose hand this paper may fall. I want you not merely to go to church or chapel, but to go with heart and soul to the gate of life. I want you not merely to believe there is such a gate, and to think it a good thing, but to enter by faith and be saved.

Think *what a privilege* it is to have a gate at all. The angels who kept not their first estate, fell, never to rise again. To them there was no door of escape opened.— The heathen never heard of any way to eternal life. What would not many a black man and many a red man give, if he only heard one plain sermon about Christ?—The Jews in Old Testament times only saw the gate dimly and far away. "The way into the holiest was not made manifest, while the first tabernacle was standing." (Heb. ix. 8.) You have the gate set plainly before you: you have Christ and full salvation offered to you, without money and without price. You never need be at a loss which way to turn. Oh, consider what a mercy this is! Beware that you do not despise the gate and perish in unbelief. Better a thousand times not to know of the gate than to know of it and yet tarry outside. How indeed will you escape if you neglect so great salvation?

Think *what a thankful man* you ought to be if you have really gone in at the strait gate. To be a pardoned, forgiven, justified soul,—to be ready for sickness, death, judgment and eternity,—to be ever provided for in both worlds,—surely this is matter for daily praise. True Christians ought to be more full of thanksgivings than they are. I fear that few sufficiently remember what they were by nature, and what debtors they are to grace. A heathen remarked that singing hymns of praise was one

special mark of the early Christians. Well would it be for
Christians in the present day, if they knew more of this
frame of mind. It is no mark of a healthy state of soul
when there is much complaining and little praise. It is
an amazing mercy that there is any gate of salvation at
all; but it is a still greater mercy when we are taught to
enter in by it and be saved.

II. In the second place, here is a plain *command.*—
Jesus says to us, "*Strive to enter in at the strait gate.*"
There is often much to be learned in a single word of
Scripture. The words of our Lord Jesus in particular, are
always full of matter for thought. Here is a word which
is a striking example of what I mean. Let us see what
the great Teacher would have us gather out of the word
"*Strive.*"

"STRIVE" teaches that a man must use means
diligently, if he would have his soul saved. There are
means which God has appointed to help man in his
endeavours to approach Him. There are ways in which
a man must walk, if he desires to be found of Christ.
Public Worship, reading the Bible, hearing the Gospel
preached,—these are the kind of things to which I refer.
They lie, as it were, in the middle, between man and God.
Doubtless no one can change his own heart, or wipe away
one of his sins, or make himself in the least degree
acceptable to God; but I do say that if man could do
nothing but sit still, Christ would never have said
"Strive."

"STRIVE" teaches that man is a free agent, and will
be dealt with by God as a responsible being. The Lord
Jesus does not bid us to wait, and wish, and feel, and
hope, and desire. He says, "Strive." I call that miserable
religion which teaches people to be content with saying,
"We can do nothing of ourselves," and makes them
continue in sin. It is as bad as teaching people that it is

not their fault if they are not converted, and that God only is to blame if they are not saved. I find no such theology in the New Testament. I hear Jesus saying to sinners, "Come—repent—believe—labour—ask—seek—knock." I see plainly that our salvation, from first to last, is entirely *of God;* but I see with no less plainness that our ruin, if lost, is wholly and entirely *of ourselves.* I maintain that sinners are always addressed as accountable and responsible; and I want no better proof of this than is contained in the word "Strive."

"STRIVE" teaches that a man must expect many adversaries and a hard battle, if he would have his soul saved. And this, as a matter of experience, is strictly true. There are no "gains without pains" in spiritual things any more than in temporal. That roaring lion, the devil, will never let a soul escape from him without a struggle. The heart which is naturally sensual and earthly will never be turned to spiritual things without a daily fight. The world, with all its opposition and temptations, will never be overcome without a conflict. But why should all this surprise us? What great and good thing was ever done without trouble? Wheat does not grow without ploughing and sowing; riches are not obtained without care and attention; success in life is not won without hardships and toil; and heaven, above all, is not to be reached without the cross and the battle. The "violent take the kingdom by force." (Matt xi. 12.) A man must "strive."

"STRIVE" teaches that it is worth while for a man to seek salvation. That may well be said. If there be anything that deserves a struggle in this world, it is the prosperity of the soul. The objects for which the great majority of men strive are comparatively poor and trifling things. Riches, and greatness, and rank, and learning, are "a corruptible crown." The incorruptible things are all within the strait gate. The peace of God which passeth all understanding,—the bright hope of good things to come,—the sense of the Spirit dwelling in us,—the consciousness that we are pardoned, safe, ready, insured, provided for in time and eternity, whatever may happen,— these are true gold, and durable riches. Well may the Lord Jesus call on us to "strive."

"STRIVE" teaches that laziness in religion is a great sin. It is not merely a misfortune, as some fancy,—a thing for which people are to be pitied, and a matter for regret. It is something far more than this. It is a breach of a plain commandment. What shall be said of the man who transgresses God's law, and does something which God says, Thou shalt not do? There can be but one answer. He is a sinner. "Sin is the transgression of the law." (1 John iii. 4.) And what shall be said of the man who neglects his soul, and makes no effort to enter the strait gate? There can be only one reply. He is omitting a positive duty. Christ says to him, "Strive," and behold, he sits still!

"STRIVE" teaches that all outside the strait gate are in great danger. They are in danger of being lost for ever. There is but a step between them and death. If death finds them in their present condition, they will perish without hope. The Lord Jesus saw that clearly. He knew the uncertainty of life and the shortness of time: He would fain have sinners make haste and delay not, lest they put off soul business too late. He speaks as one who saw the devil drawing near to them daily, and the days of their life gradually ebbing away. He would have them take heed they be not too late: therefore He cries, "Strive."

That word "Strive," raises solemn thoughts in my mind. It is brimful of condemnation for thousands of baptized persons. It condemns the ways and practices of multitudes who profess and call themselves Christians. Many there are who neither swear, nor murder, nor commit adultery, nor steal, nor lie; but one thing unhappily cannot be said of them: they cannot be said to "strive" to be saved. The "spirit of slumber" possesses their hearts in everything that concerns religion. About the things of the world they are active enough: they rise early, and late take rest; they labour; they toil; they are busy; they are careful: but about the one thing needful they never "strive" at all.

What shall I say of those who are irregular about public worship on Sundays? There are thousands all over Great Britain who answer this description. Sometimes, if they feel disposed, they go to some church or chapel, and attend a religious service; at other times they stay at home and read the paper, or idle about, or look over their accounts, or seek some amusement. *Is this "striving"?* I speak to men of common sense. Let them judge what I say.

What shall I say of those who come regularly to a place of worship, but come entirely as a matter of form? There are many in every parish of Great Britain in this condition. Their fathers taught them to come; their custom has always been to come: it would not be respectable to stay away. But they care nothing for the worship of God when they do come. Whether they hear law or Gospel, truth or error, it is all the same to them. They remember nothing afterwards. They put off their form of religion with their Sunday clothes, and return to the world. And *is this "striving"?* I speak to men of common sense. Let them judge what I say.

What shall I say of those who seldom or never read the Bible? There are thousands of persons, I fear, who answer this description. They know the Book by name; they know it is commonly regarded as the only Book which teaches us how to live and how to die: but they can never find time for reading it. Newspapers, reviews, novels, romances, they can read, but not the Bible. And *is this "striving"* to enter in? I speak to men of common sense. Let them judge what I say.

What shall I say of those who never pray? There are multitudes, I firmly believe, in this condition. Without God they rise in the morning, and without God they lie down at night. They ask nothing; they confess nothing; they return thanks for nothing; they seek nothing. They are all dying creatures, and yet they are not even on speaking terms with their Maker and their Judge! And *is this striving"?* I speak to men of common sense. Let them judge what I say.

It is a solemn thing to be a minister of the Gospel. It is a painful thing to look on, and notice the ways of mankind in spiritual matters. We hold in our hands that great statute Book of God, which declares that without repentance, and conversion, and faith in Christ, and holiness, no man living can be saved. In discharge of our office we urge on men to repent, believe, and be saved; but, alas, how frequently we have to lament that our labour seems all in vain. Men attend our churches, and listen, and approve, but do not "strive" to be saved. We show the sinfulness of sin; we unfold the loveliness of Christ; we expose the vanity of the world; we set forth the happiness of Christ's service; we offer the living water, to the wearied and heavy laden sons of toil: but, alas, how often we seem to speak to the winds. Our words are patiently heard on Sundays; our arguments are not refuted: but we see plainly in the week that men are not "striving" to be saved. There comes the devil on Monday morning, and offers his countless snares; there comes the world, and holds out its seeming prizes: our hearers follow them greedily. They work hard for this world's goods; they toil at Satan's bidding: but for the one thing needful they will not "strive" at all.

I am not writing from hear-say. I speak what I have seen. I write down the result of thirty-seven years' experience in the ministry. I have learned lessons about human nature during that period which I never knew before. I have seen how true are our Lord's words about the narrow way. I have discovered how few there are that "strive" to be saved.

Earnestness about temporal matters is common enough. Striving to be rich and prosperous in this world is not rare at all. Pains about money, and business, and politics, —pains about trade, and science, and fine arts, and amusements,—pains about rent, and wages, and labour, and land, —pains about such matters I see in abundance both in town and country. But I see few who take pains about their souls. I see few any where who "strive" to enter in at the strait gate.

I am not surprised at all this. I read in the Bible that it is only what I am to expect. The parable of the great supper is an exact picture of things that I have seen with my own eyes ever since I became a minister. (Luke xiv. 16.) I find, as my Lord and Saviour tells me, that "men make excuse." One has his piece of land to see; another has his oxen to prove; a third has his family hindrances. But all this does not prevent my feeling deeply grieved for the souls of men. I grieve to think that they should have eternal life so close to them, and yet be lost because they will not "strive" to enter in and be saved.

I know not in what state of soul many readers of this paper may be. But I warn you to take heed that you do not perish for ever for want of "striving." Do not suppose that it needs some great scarlet sin to bring you to the pit of destruction. You have only to sit still and do nothing, and you will find yourself there at last. Yes! Satan does not ask you to walk in the steps of Cain, and Pharaoh, and Ahab, and Belshazzar, and Judas Iscariot. There is another road to hell quite as sure,—the road of spiritual indolence, spiritual laziness, and spiritual sloth. Satan has no objection to your being a respectable member of the Christian Church. He will let you pay your tithes, and rates, and pew rents; he will allow you to sit comfortably in church every Sunday you live. He knows full well, that so long as you do not "strive," you must come at last to the worm that never dies, and the fire that is not quenched. Take heed that you do not come to this end. I repeat it, *you have only to do nothing, and you will be lost.*

If you have been taught to "strive" for your soul's prosperity, I entreat you never to suppose you can go too far. Never give way to the idea that you are taking too much trouble about your spiritual condition, and that there is no need for so much carefulness. Settle it rather in your mind that "in all labour there is profit," and that no labour is so profitable as that bestowed on the soul. It is a maxim among good farmers that the more they do for the land the more the land does for them. I am sure it should be a maxim among Christians that the more they do for their religion the more their religion will do for them. Watch against the slightest inclination to be careless about any means of grace. Beware of shortening your prayers, your Bible reading, your private communion with God. Take heed that you do not give way to a thoughtless, lazy manner of using the public services of God's house. Fight against any rising disposition to be sleepy, critical, and fault-finding, while you listen to the preaching of the Gospel. Whatever you do for God, do it with all your heart and mind and strength. In other things be moderate, and dread running into extremes. In soul matters fear moderation just as you would fear the plague. Care not what men think of you. Let it be enough for you that your Master says, "STRIVE."

III. The last thing I wish to consider in this paper is the *awful prophecy which the Lord Jesus delivers.* He says, "Many will seek to enter in, and shall not be able."

When shall this be? At what period shall the gate of salvation be shut for ever? When shall "striving" to enter be of no use ? These are serious questions. The gate is now ready to open to the chief of sinners; but a day comes when it shall open no more.

The time foretold by our Lord is the time of His own second coming to judge the world. The long-suffering of God will at last have an end. The throne of grace will at length be taken down; and the throne of judgment shall be set up in its place. The fountain of living waters shall at length be closed. The strait gate shall at last be barred and bolted. The day of grace will be passed and over. The day of reckoning with a sin-laden world shall at length begin. And then shall be brought to pass the solemn prophecy of the Lord Jesus,—" Many will seek to enter in, and shall not be able."

All prophecies of Scripture that have been fulfilled hitherto, have been fulfilled to the very letter. They have seemed to many unlikely, improbable, impossible, up to the very time of their accomplishment; but not one word of them has ever failed.

The promises of *good things* have come to pass, in spite of difficulties that seemed insuperable. Sarah had a son when she was past bearing; the children of Israel were brought out of Egypt and planted in the promised land; the Jews were redeemed from the captivity of Babylon, after seventy years, and enabled once more to build the temple; the Lord Jesus was born of a pure virgin, lived, ministered, was betrayed, and cut off, precisely as Scripture foretold. The Word of God was pledged in all these cases, that it should be. *And so it was.*

The predictions of *judgments* on cities and nations have come to pass, though at the time they were first spoken they seemed incredible. Egypt is the basest of kingdoms; Edom is a wilderness; Tyre is a rock for drying nets; Nineveh, that "exceeding great city," is laid waste, and become a desolation; Babylon is a dry land and a wilderness,—her broad walls are utterly broken down; the Jews are scattered over the whole earth as a separate people. In all these cases the Word of God foretold that it should be so. *And so it was.*

The prophecy of the Lord Jesus Christ which I press on your attention this day, shall be fulfilled in like manner. Not one word of it shall fail when the time of its accomplishment is due. "Many will seek to enter in, and shall not be able."

There is a time coming when seeking God shall be useless. Oh, that men would remember that! Too many seem to fancy that the hour will never arrive when they shall seek and not find: but they are sadly mistaken. They will discover their mistake one day to their own confusion, except they repent. When Christ comes "many shall seek to enter in, and *not be able.*"

There is a time coming when many shall be shut out from heaven for ever. It shall not be the lot of a few, but of a great multitude; it shall not happen to one or two in this parish, and one or two in that: it shall be the miserable end of a vast crowd. "*Many* will seek to enter in, and shall not be able."

Knowledge shall come to many too late. They shall see at last the value of an immortal soul, and the happiness of having it saved. They shall understand at last their own sinfulness and God's holiness, and the glorious fitness of the Gospel of Christ. They shall comprehend at last why ministers seemed so anxious, and preached so long, and entreated them so earnestly to be converted. But, alas, they shall know all this *too late!*

Repentance shall come to many too late. They shall discover their own exceeding wickedness and be thoroughly ashamed of their past folly. They shall be full of bitter regret and unavailing lamentations, of keen convictions and of piercing sorrows. They shall weep, and wail, and mourn, when they reflect on their sins. The remembrance of their lives will be grievous to them; the burden o their guilt will seem intolerable. But, alas, like Judas Iscariot, they will repent *too late!*

Faith shall come to many too late. They will no longer be able to deny that there is a God, and a devil, a heaven, and a hell. Deism, and scepticism, and infidelity shall be laid aside for ever; scoffing, and jesting, and free-thinking shall cease. They will see with their own eyes, and feel in their own bodies, that the things of which ministers spoke were not cunningly devised fables, but great real truths. They will find out to their cost that evangelical religion was not cant, extravagance, fanaticism, and enthusiasm: they will discover that it was the one thing needful, and that for want of it they are lost for ever. Like the devil, they will at length believe and tremble, but *too late!*

A desire of salvation shall come to many too late. They shall long after pardon, and peace, and the favour of God, when they can no more be had. They will wish they might have one more Sunday over again, have one more offer of forgiveness, have one more call to prayer. But it will matter nothing what they think, or feel, or desire then: the day of grace will be over; the gate of salvation will be bolted and barred. It will be *too late!*

I often think what a change there will be one day in the price and estimation at which things are valued. I look round this world in which my lot is cast; I mark the current price of everything this world contains; I look forward to the coming of Christ, and the great day of God. I think of the new order of things, which that day will bring in; I read the words of the Lord Jesus, when He describes the master of the house rising up and shutting the door; and as I read, I say to myself, "There will be a great change soon."

What are the *dear things* now? Gold, silver, precious stones, bank notes, mines, ships, lands, houses, horses, carriages, furniture, meat, drink, clothes, and the like.

These are the things that are thought valuable; these are the things that command a ready market; these are the things which you can never get below a certain price. He that has much of these things is counted a wealthy man. Such is the world!

And what are the *cheap things* now? The knowledge of God, the free salvation of the Gospel, the favour of Christ, the grace of the Holy Ghost, the privilege of being God's son, the title to eternal life, the right to the tree of life, the reversion of a mansion in heaven, the promises of an incorruptible inheritance, the offer of a crown of glory that fadeth not away. These are the things that no man hardly cares for. They are offered to the sons of men without money and without price: they may be had for nothing,—freely and gratuitously. Whosoever will may take his portion. But, alas, there is no demand for these things! They go a begging. They are scarcely looked at. They are offered in vain. Such is the world!

But a day is coming upon us all when the value of everything shall be altered. A day is coming when banknotes shall be as useless as rags, and gold shall be as worthless as the dust of the earth. A day is coming when thousands shall care nothing for the things for which they once lived, and shall desire nothing so much as the things which they once despised. The halls and palaces will be forgotten in the desire of a "house not made with hands." The favour of the rich and great will be no more remembered, in the longing for the favour of the King of kings. The silks, and satins, and velvets, and laces, will be lost sight of in the anxious want of the robe of Christ's righteousness. All shall be altered, all shall be changed in the great day of the Lord's return. "Many will seek to enter in, and shall not be able."

It was a weighty saying of some wise man, that "hell is truth known too late." I fear that thousands of professing Christians in this day will find this out by experience. They will discover the value of their souls when it is too late to obtain mercy, and see the beauty of the Gospel when they can derive no benefit from it. Oh, that men would be wise betimes! I often think there are few passages of Scripture more awful than that in the first chapter of Proverbs,—" Because I have called, and ye refused; I have stretched out my hand, and no man regarded; but ye have set at nought all my counsel, and would none of my reproof: I also will laugh at your calamity; I will mock when your fear cometh; when your fear cometh as desolation, and your destruction cometh as a whirlwind; when distress and anguish cometh upon you. Then shall they call upon Me, but I will not answer; they shall seek Me early, but they shall not find Me: for that they hated knowledge, and did not choose the fear of the Lord: they would none of my counsel; they despised all my reproof. Therefore shall they eat of the fruit of their own way, and be filled with their own devices." (Prov. i. 24—31.)

Some reader of this paper may be one of those who neither like the faith nor practice which the Gospel of Christ requires. You think us extreme when we beseech you to repent and be converted. You think we ask too much when we urge you to come out from the world, and take up the cross, and follow Christ. But take notice that you will one day confess *that we were right*. Sooner or later, in this world or the next, you will acknowledge that you were wrong. Yes! it is a melancholy consideration for the faithful minister of the Gospel, that all who hear him will one day allow that his counsel was good. Mocked, despised, scorned, neglected as his testimony may be on earth, a day is coming which shall prove effectually that truth was on his side. The rich man who hears us and yet makes a god of this world,—the trades-man who hears us and yet makes his ledger his Bible,—the farmer who hears us and yet remains cold as the clay on his land,—the labourer who hears us and feels no more for his soul than a stone,—all, all will at length acknowledge before the world that they were wrong. All will at length desire earnestly that very mercy which we now set before them in vain. "They will seek to enter in, and shall not be able."

Some reader of this paper may be one of those who love the Lord Jesus Christ in sincerity. Such an one may well take comfort when he looks forward. You often suffer persecution now for your religion's sake. You have to bear hard words and unkind insinuations. Your motives are often misrepresented, and your conduct slandered. The reproach of the cross has not ceased. But you may well take courage when you look forward and think of the Lord's second coming. That day shall make amends for all. You will see those who now laugh at you because you read the Bible, and pray, and love Christ, in a very different state of mind. They will come to you as the foolish virgins came to the wise, saying, "Give us of your oil, because our lamps are gone out." (Matt. xxv. 8.) You will see those who now hate you and call you fools because, like Caleb and Joshua, you bring up a good report of Christ's service, altered, changed, and no longer like the same men. They will say, "Oh, that we had taken part with you! You have been the truly wise, and we the foolish." Then fear not the reproach of men. Confess Christ boldly before the world. Show your colours, and be not ashamed of your Master. Time is short: eternity hastens on. The cross is only for a little season: the crown is for ever. Make sure work about that crown: leave nothing uncertain. "Many will seek to enter in, and shall not be able."

And now let me offer to every one who reads this paper a few parting words, in order to apply the whole subject to his soul. You have heard the words of the Lord Jesus unfolded and expounded. You have seen the picture of the way of salvation: it is a strait gate.—You have heard the command of the King: "Strive to enter in."—You have been told of His solemn warning: "Many shall seek to enter in, and shall not be able."—Bear with me a little longer while I try to impress the whole matter on your conscience. I have yet something to say on God's behalf.

(1) For one thing, I will ask you a plain question. *Have you entered in at the strait gate or not?* Old or young, rich or poor, churchman or dissenter, I repeat my question, Have you entered in at the strait gate?

I ask not whether you have heard of it, and believe there is a gate. I ask not whether you have looked at it, and admired it, and hope one day to go in. I ask whether you have gone up to it, knocked at it, been admitted, and *are now inside?*

If you are not inside, what good have you got from your religion? You are not pardoned and forgiven. You are not reconciled to God. You are not born again, sanctified, and meet for heaven. If you die as you are, the devil will have you for ever, and your soul will be eternally miserable.

Oh, think, think what a state this is to live in! Think, think above all things, what a state this is to die in! Your life is but a vapour. A few more years at most and you are gone: your place in the world will soon be filled up; your house will be occupied by another. The sun will go on shining; the grass and daises will soon grow thick over your grave; your body will be food for worms, and your soul will be lost to all eternity.

And all this time there stands open before you a gate of salvation. God invites you. Jesus Christ offers to save you. All things are ready for your deliverance. One thing only is wanting, and that is that you should be willing to be saved.

Oh think of these things, and be wise!

(2) For another thing, I will give plain advice to all

who are not yet inside the strait gate. That advice is simply this: *to enter in without a day's delay.*

Tell me, if you can, of any one who ever reached heaven excepting through "the strait gate." I know of none. From Abel, the first who died, down to the end of the list of Bible names, I see none saved by any way but that of faith in Christ.

Tell me, if you can, of any one who ever entered in at the strait gate without " striving." I know of none excepting those who die in infancy. He that would win heaven must be content to fight for it.

Tell me, if you can, of any one who ever strove earnestly to enter, and failed to succeed. I know of none. I believe that however weak and ignorant men may be, they never seek life heartily and conscientiously, at the right door, and are left without an answer of peace.

Tell me, if you can, of any one who ever entered in at the strait gate, and was afterwards sorry. I know of none. I believe the footsteps on the threshold of that gate are all one way. All have found it a good thing to serve Christ, and have never regretted taking up His cross.

If these things are so, seek Christ without delay, and enter in at the gate of life while you can! Make a beginning this very day. Go to that merciful and mighty Saviour in prayer, and pour out your heart before Him. Confess to Him your guilt and wickedness and sin. Unbosom yourself freely to Him: keep nothing back. Tell Him that you cast yourself and all your soul's affairs wholly on His hands, and ask Him to save you according to His promise, and put His Holy Spirit within you.

There is everything *to encourage you to do this.* Thousands as bad as you have applied to Christ in this way, and not one of them has been sent away and refused. They have found a peace of conscience they never knew before, and have gone on their way rejoicing. They have found strength for all the trials of life, and none of them have been allowed to perish in the wilderness. Why should not you also seek Christ?

There is everything to encourage you to do what I tell you *at once*. I know no reason why your repentance and conversion should not be as immediate as that of others before you. The Samaritan woman came to the well an ignorant sinner, and returned to her home a new creature. The Philippian jailor turned from darkness to light, and became a professed disciple of Christ in a single day. And why should not others do the same? Why should not you give up your sins, and lay hold on Christ this very day?

I know that the advice I have given you is good. The grand question is, Will you take it?

(3) The last thing I have to say shall be a request to all who have really entered in at the strait gate. That request is, that you will *tell others* of the blessings which you have found.

I want all converted people to be missionaries. I do not want them all to go out to foreign lands, and preach to the heathen; but I do want all to be of a missionary spirit, and to strive to do good at home. I want them to testify to all around them that the strait gate is the way to happiness, and to persuade them to enter in by it.

When Andrew was converted he found his brother Peter, and said to him, "We have found the Messias, which is, being interpreted, the Christ. And he brought him to Jesus." (John i. 41, 42.) When Philip was converted he found Nathaniel, and said to him, "We have found Him, of whom Moses in the law, and the prophets did write, Jesus of Nazareth, the son of Joseph. And Nathaniel said unto him, Can there any good thing come out of Nazareth? Philip said unto him, Come and see." (John i. 45, 46.) When the Samaritan woman was converted, she "left her waterpot, and went into the city, and said to the men, Come, see a man which told me all things that ever I did: is not this the Christ?" (John iv. 28, 29.) When Saul the Pharisee was converted, "Straightway he preached Christ in the synagogues, that He is the son of God." (Acts ix. 20.)

I long to see this kind of spirit among Christians in the present day. I long to see more zeal to commend the strait gate to all who are yet outside, and more desire to persuade them to enter in and be saved. Happy indeed is that Church whose members not only desire to reach heaven themselves, but desire also to take others with them!

The great gate of salvation is yet ready to open, but the hour draws near when it will be closed for ever. Let us work while it is called to-day, for "the night cometh when no man can work." (John ix. 4.) Let us tell our relatives and friends, that we have proved the way of life and found it pleasant, that we have tasted the bread of life and found it good.

I have heard it calculated that if every believer in the world were to bring one soul to Christ each year, the whole human race would be converted in less than twenty years. I make no comment on such a calculation. Whether such a thing might be or not, one thing is sure: that thing is, that many more *souls might probably be converted to God, if Christians were more zealous to do good.*

This, at least, we may remember, that God is "not willing that any should perish, but that all should come to repentance." (2 Pet. iii. 9.) He that endeavours to show his neighbour the strait gate is doing a work which God approves. He is doing a work which angels regard with interest, and with which the building of a pyramid will not compare in importance. What saith the Scripture? "He which converteth a sinner from the error of his way, shall save a soul from death, and shall hide a multitude of sins." (James v. 20.)

Let us all awaken to a deeper sense of our responsibility in this matter. Let us look round the circle of those among whom we live, and consider their state before God. Are there not many of them yet outside the gate, unforgiven, unsanctified, and unfit to die? Let us watch for opportunities of speaking to them. Let us tell them of the strait gate, and entreat them to "strive to enter in."

Who can tell what "a word spoken in due season" may do? Who can tell what it may do when spoken in faith and prayer? It may be the turning-point in some man's history. It may be the beginning of thought, prayer, and eternal life. Oh, for more love and boldness among believers! Think what a blessing to be allowed to speak one converting word!

I know not what the feelings of my readers may be on this subject. My heart's desire and prayer is that you may daily remember Christ's solemn words,—" Many will seek to enter in, and shall not be able." Keep these words in mind, and then be careless about the souls of others, if you can.

III

REALITY

"*Reprobate silver.*"—JER. vi. 30.

"*Nothing but leaves.*"—MARK xi. 13.

"*Let us not love in word, neither in tongue, but in deed and in truth.*"
—1 JOHN iii. 18.

"*Thou hast a name that thou livest, and art dead.*"—REV. iii. 1.

IF we profess to have any religion at all, let us take care that it is real. I say it emphatically, and I repeat the saying: Let us mind that our religion is real.

What do I mean when I use the word "real." I mean that which is genuine, and sincere, and honest, and thorough. I mean that which is not base, and hollow, and formal, and false, and counterfeit, and sham, and nominal. "Real" religion is not mere show, and pretence, and skin-deep feeling, and temporary profession, and outside work. It is something inward, solid, substantial, intrinsic, living, lasting. We know the difference between base coin and good money,—between solid gold and tinsel, —between plated metal and silver,—between real stone and plaster imitation. Let us think of these things as we consider the subject of this paper. What is the character of our religion? Is it real? It may be weak, and feeble, and mingled with many infirmities. That is not the point before us to-day. Is our religion real? Is it true?

The times in which we live demand attention to this

subject. A want of reality is a striking feature of a vast amount of religion in the present day. Poets have sometimes told us that the world has passed through four different states or conditions. We have had a golden age, and a silver age, a brazen age, and an iron age. How far this is true, I do not stop to inquire. But I fear there is little doubt as to the character of the age in which we live. It is universally an age of base metal and alloy. If we measure the religion of the age by its apparent quantity, there is much of it. But if we measure it by its quality, there is very little indeed. On every side we want MORE REALITY.

I ask attention, while I try to bring home to men's consciences the question of this paper. There are two things which I propose to do:—

I. In the first place, I will show the *importance of reality in religion.*

II. In the second place, I will supply *some tests by which we may prove whether our own religion is real.*

Has any reader of this paper the least desire to go to heaven when he dies? Do you wish to have a religion which will comfort you in life, give you good hope in death, and abide the judgment of God at the last day? Then, do not turn away from the subject before you. Sit down, and consider calmly, whether your Christianity is real and true, or base and hollow.

I. I have to show *the importance of reality in religion.* The point is one which, at first sight, may seem to require very few remarks to establish it. All men, I shall be told, are fully convinced of the importance of reality.

But is this true? Can it be said indeed that reality is rightly esteemed among Christians? I deny it entirely. The greater part of people who profess to admire reality, seem to think that every one possesses it!—They tell us

" that all have got good hearts at bottom,"—that all are sincere and true in the main, though they may make mistakes. They call us uncharitable, and harsh, and censorious, if we doubt anybody's goodness of heart. In short, they destroy the value of reality, by regarding it as a thing which almost every one has.

This wide-spread delusion is precisely one of the causes why I take up this subject. I want men to understand that *reality* is a far more rare and uncommon thing than is commonly supposed. I want men to see that *unreality* is one of the great dangers of which Christians ought to beware.

What saith the Scripture ? This is the only judge that can try the subject. Let us turn to our Bibles, and examine them fairly, and then deny, if we can, the importance of reality in religion, and the danger of not being real.

(1) Let us look then, for one thing, at the parables spoken by our Lord Jesus Christ. Observe how many of them are intended to put in strong contrast the true believer and the mere nominal disciple. The parables of the sower, of the wheat and tares, of the draw-net, of the two sons, of the wedding garment, of the ten virgins, of the talents, of the great supper, of the pounds, of the two builders, have all one great point in common. They all bring out in striking colours the difference between reality and unreality in religion. They all show the uselessness and danger of any Christianity which is not real, thorough, and true.

(2) Let us look, for another thing, at the language of our Lord Jesus Christ about the scribes and the Pharisees. Eight times over in one chapter we find Him denouncing them as " hypocrites," in words of almost fearful severity.— "Ye serpents, ye generation of vipers," He says, "How can ye escape the damnation of hell ? " (Matt. xxiii. 33.) What may we learn from these tremendously strong expressions ? How is it that our gracious and merciful Saviour used

such cutting words about people who at any rate were more moral and decent than the publicans and harlots? It is meant to teach us the exceeding abominableness of false profession and mere outward religion in God's sight. Open profligacy and wilful obedience to fleshly lusts are no doubt ruinous sins, if not given up. But there seems nothing which is so displeasing to Christ as hypocrisy and unreality.

(3) Let us look, for another thing, at the startling fact, that there is hardly a grace in the character of a true Christian of which you will not find a counterfeit described in the Word of God. There is not a feature in a believer's countenance of which there is not an imitation. Give me your attention, and I will show you this in a few particulars.

Is there not an unreal *repentance?* Beyond doubt there is. Saul and Ahab, and Herod, and Judas Iscariot had many feelings of sorrow about sin. But they never really repented unto salvation.

Is there not an unreal *faith?* Beyond doubt there is. It is written of Simon Magus, at Samaria, that he "believed," and yet his heart was not right in the sight of God. It is even written of the devils that they "believe and tremble." (Acts viii. 13; James ii. 19.)

Is there not an unreal *holiness?* Beyond doubt there is. Joash, king of Judah, became to all appearance very holy and good, so long as Jehoiada the priest lived. But as soon as he died the religion of Joash died at the same time. (2 Chron. xxiv. 2.)—Judas Iscariot's outward life was as correct as that of any of the apostles up to the time that he betrayed his Master. There was nothing suspicious about him. Yet in reality he was "a thief" and a traitor. (John xii. 6.)

Is there not an unreal *love and charity?* Beyond doubt there is. There is a love which consists in words and tender expressions, and a great show of affection, and calling other people "dear brethren," while the heart does

not love at all. It is not for nothing that St. John says,
" Let us not love in word, neither in tongue, but in deed
and in truth." It was not without cause that St. Paul
said: " Let love be without dissimulation." (1 John iii.
18; Rom. xii. 19.)

Is there not an unreal *humility*? Beyond doubt there
is. There is a pretended lowliness of demeanour, which
often covers over a very proud heart. St. Paul warns us
against a "voluntary humility," and speaks of "things
which had a show of wisdom in will-worship and
humility." (Col. ii. 18, 23.)

Is there not unreal *praying*? Beyond doubt there is.
Our Lord denounces it as one of the special sins of the
Pharisees—that for a " pretence they made long prayers."
(Matt. xxiii. 14.) He does not charge them with not
praying, or with praying too shortly. Their sin lay in
this, that their prayers were not real.

Is there not unreal *worship*? Beyond doubt there is.
Our Lord says of the Jews: " This people draw nigh to
Me with their mouths, and honour Me with their lips, but
their heart is far from Me." (Matt. xv. 8.) They had
plenty of formal services in their temples and their
synagogues. But the fatal defect about them was want of
reality and want of heart.

Is there not unreal *talking* about religion? Beyond
doubt there is. Ezekiel describes some professing Jews
who talked and spoke like God's people "while their
hearts went after their covetousness." (Ezek. xxxiii. 31.)
St. Paul tells us that we may "speak with the tongue of
men and angels," and yet be no better than sounding brass
and a tinkling cymbal. (1 Cor. xiii. 1.)

What shall we say to these things? To say the least
they ought to set us thinking. To my own mind they
seem to lead to only one conclusion. They show clearly
the immense importance which Scripture attaches to
reality in religion. They show clearly what need we have

to take heed lest our Christianity turn out to be merely
nominal, formal, unreal, and base.

The subject is of deep importance in every age. There
has never been a time, since the Church of Christ was
founded, when there has not been a vast amount of
unreality and mere nominal religion among professing
Christians. I am sure it is the case in the present day.
Wherever I turn my eyes I see abundant cause for the
warning,—"Beware of base metal in religion. Be genuine.
Be thorough. Be real. Be true."

How much religion among some members of the Church
of England consists of *nothing but churchmanship*!
They belong to the Established Church. They are
baptized at her fonts, married at her communion rails,
buried in her churchyards, preached to on Sundays by her
ministers. But the great doctrines laid down in her
Articles and Liturgy have no place in their hearts, and no
influence on their lives. They neither think, nor feel, nor
care, nor know anything about them. And is the religion
of these people real Christianity? It is nothing of the
kind. It is mere base metal. It is not the Christianity
of Peter, and James, and John, and Paul. It is
Churchianity, and no more.

How much religion among some Dissenters from the
Church of England consists of *nothing but dissent*!
They pride themselves on having nothing to do with the
Establishment. They rejoice in having no liturgy, no
forms, no bishops. They glory in the exercise of their
private judgment, and the absence of everything like
ceremonial in their public worship. But all this time
they have neither grace, nor faith, nor repentance, nor
holiness, nor spirituality of conduct or conversation. The
experimental and practical piety of the old Nonconformists
is a thing of which they are utterly destitute. Their
Christianity is as sapless and fruitless as a dead tree, and
as dry and marrowless as an old bone. And is the

Christianity of these people real? It is nothing of the kind. It is base metal. It is not the Christianity of Owen, and Manton, and Goodwin, and Baxter, and Traill. It is *Dissentianity*, and nothing more.

How much Ritualistic religion is utterly unreal! You will sometimes see men boiling over with zeal about vestments, and gestures, and postures, and church decorations, and daily services, and frequent communions, while their hearts are manifestly in the world. Of the inward work of the Holy Ghost,—of living faith in the Lord Jesus,—of delight in the Bible and religious conversation, —of separation from worldly follies and amusements,—of zeal for the conversion of souls to God,—of all these things they are profoundly ignorant. And is such Christianity as this real? It is nothing of the kind. It is a mere name.

How much Evangelical religion is completely unreal? You will sometimes see men professing great affection for the pure "Gospel," while they are practically inflicting on it the greatest injury. They will talk loudly of soundness in the faith, and have a keen nose for heresy. They will run eagerly after popular preachers, and applaud Protestant speakers at public meetings to the very echo. They are familiar with all the phrases of evangelical religion, and can converse fluently about its leading doctrines. To see their faces at public meetings, or in church, you would think them eminently godly. To hear them talk you would suppose their lives were bound up in religious Societies, the "Record" or "Rock" newspapers, and Exeter Hall. And yet these people in private will sometimes do things of which even some heathens would be ashamed. They are neither truthful, nor straightforward, nor honest, nor manly, nor just, nor good-tempered, nor unselfish, nor merciful, nor humble, nor kind! And is such Christianity as this real? It is not. It is a miserable imposture, a base cheat and caricature.

How much Revivalist religion in the present day is utterly unreal! You will find a crowd of false professors bringing discredit on the work of God wherever the Holy Spirit is poured out. You will see a mixed multitude of Egyptians accompanying the Israel of God, and doing it harm, whenever Israel goes out of Egypt. How many now-a-days will profess to be suddenly convinced of sin,—to find peace in Jesus,—to be overwhelmed with joys and ecstacies of soul,—while in reality they have no grace at all. Like the stony-ground hearers, they endure but for a season. "In the time of temptation they fall away." (Luke viii. 13) As soon as the first excitement is passed off, they return to their old ways, and resume their former sins. Their religion is like Jonah's gourd, which came up in a night and perished in a night. They have neither root nor vitality. They only injure God's cause and give occasion to God's enemies to blaspheme. And is Christianity like this real? It is nothing of the kind. It is base metal from the devil's mint, **and** is worthless in God's sight.

I write these things with sorrow. I have no desire to bring any section of the Church of Christ into contempt. I have no wish to cast any slur on any movement which begins with the Spirit of God. But the times demand very plain speaking about some points in the prevailing Christianity of our day. And one point, I am quite persuaded, that demands attention, is the abounding want of reality which is to be seen on every side.

No reader, at any rate, can well deny that the subject of the paper before him is of vast importance.

II. I pass on now to the second thing which I propose to do. *I will supply some tests by which we may try the reality of our religion.*

In approaching this part of my subject, I ask every reader of this paper to deal fairly, honestly, and reasonably

with his soul. Dismiss from your mind the common idea,
—that of course all is right if you go to church or to
chapel. Cast away such vain notions for ever. You must
look further, higher, deeper than this, if you would find
out the truth. Listen to me, and I will give you a few
hints. Believe me, it is no light matter. It is your life.

(1) For one thing, if you would know whether your
religion is real, try it by *the place which it occupies* in
your inner man. It is not enough that it is in your *head*.
You may know the truth, and assent to the truth, and
believe the truth, and yet be wrong in God's sight.—It is
not enough that it is on your *lips*. You may repeat the
creed daily. You may say "Amen" to public prayer in
church, and yet have nothing more than an outward
religion.—It is not enough that it is in your *feelings*.
You may weep under preaching one day, and be lifted to
the third heaven by joyous excitement another day, and
yet be dead to God.—Your religion, if it is real, and given
by the Holy Ghost, must be in your *heart*. It must
occupy the citadel. It must hold the reins. It must
sway the affections. It must lead the will. It must
direct the tastes. It must influence the choices and de-
cisions. It must fill the deepest, lowest, inmost seat in
your soul. Is this your religion? If not, you may well
doubt whether it is "*real*" and **true**. (Acts viii. 21; Rom.
x. 10.)

(2) In the next place, if you would know whether your
religion is real, try it by the *feelings towards sin* which
it produces. The Christianity which is from the Holy
Ghost will always have a very deep view of the sinfulness
of sin. It will not merely regard sin as a blemish and
misfortune, which makes men and women objects of pity
and compassion. It will see in sin the abominable thing
which God hates, the thing which makes man guilty and
lost in his Maker's sight, the thing which deserves God's
wrath and condemnation. It will look on sin as the cause

of all sorrow and unhappiness, of strife and wars, of quarrels and contentions, of sickness and death,—the blight which has blighted God's fair creation, the cursed thing which makes the whole earth groan and travail in pain. Above all, it will see in sin the thing which will ruin us eternally, except we can find a ransom,—lead us captive, except we can get its chains broken,—and destroy our happiness, both here and hereafter, except we fight against it, even unto death. Is this your religion? Are these your feelings about sin? If not, you may well doubt whether your religion is "*real*."

(3) For another thing, if you would know whether your religion is real, try it by the *feelings toward Christ* which it produces. Nominal religion may believe that such a person as Christ existed, and was a great benefactor to mankind. It may show Him some external respect, attend His outward ordinances, and bow the head at His name. But it will go no further. Real religion will make a man glory in Christ, as the Redeemer, the Deliverer, the Priest, the Friend, without whom he would have no hope at all. It will produce confidence in Him, love towards Him, delight in Him, comfort in Him, as the mediator, the food, the light, the life, the peace of the soul. Is this your religion? Do you know anything of feelings like these toward Jesus Christ? If not, you may well doubt whether your religion is "*real*."

(4) For another thing, if you would know whether your religion is real, try it by the *fruit it bears in your heart and life*. The Christianity which is from above will always be known by its fruits. It will produce in the man who has it repentance, faith, hope, charity, humility, spirituality, kind temper, self-denial, unselfishness, forgivingness, temperance, truthfulness, brotherly-kindness, patience, forbearance. The degree in which these various graces appear may vary in different believers. The germ and seeds of them will be found in all who are the

children of God. By their fruits they may be known. Is this your religion? If not, you may well doubt whether it is "*real.*"

(5) In the last place, if you would know whether your religion is real, try it by *your feelings and habits about means of grace.* Prove it by the Sunday. Is that day a season of weariness and constraint, or a delight and a refreshment, and a sweet foretaste of the rest to come in heaven?—Prove it by the public means of grace. What are your feelings about public prayer and public praise, about the public preaching of God's Word, and the administration of the Lord's Supper? Are they things to which you give a cold assent, and tolerate them as proper and correct? Or, are they things in which you take pleasure, and without which you could not live happy?— Prove it, finally, by your feelings about private means of grace. Do you find it essential to your comfort to read the Bible regularly in private, and to speak to God in prayer? Or, do you find these practices irksome, and either slur them over, or neglect them altogether? These questions deserve your attention. If means of grace, whether public or private, are not as necessary to your soul as meat and drink are to your body, you may well doubt whether your religion is "*real.*"

I press on the attention of all my readers the five points which I have just named. There is nothing like coming to particulars about these matters. If you would know whether your religion is "real," genuine, and true, measure it by the five particulars which I have now named. Measure it fairly: test it honestly. If your heart is right in the sight of God, you have no cause to flinch from examination. If it is wrong, the sooner you find it out the better.

And now I have done what I proposed to do. I have shown from Scripture the unspeakable importance of reality in religion, and the danger in which many stand of being lost for ever, for want of it. I have given five plain tests, by which a man may find out whether his Christianity is real. I will conclude all by a direct application of the whole subject to the souls of all who read this paper. I will draw my bow at a venture, and trust that God will bring an arrow home to the hearts and consciences of many.

(1) My first word of application shall be *an inquiry.* Is your own religion real or unreal? genuine or base? I do not ask what you think about others. Perhaps you may see many hypocrites around you. You may be able to point to many who have no "reality" at all. This is not the question. You may be right in your opinion about others. But I want to know about yourself. Is your own Christianity real and true? or nominal and base?

If you love life, do not turn away from the question which is now before you. The time must come when the whole truth will be known. The judgment day will reveal every man's religion, of what sort it is. The parable of the wedding-garment will receive an awful fulfilment. Surely it is a thousand times better to find out *now* your condition, and to repent, than to find it out too late in the next world, when there will be no space for repentance. If you have common prudence, sense, and judgment, consider what I say. Sit down quietly this day, and examine yourself. Find out the real character of your religion. With the Bible in your hand, and honesty in your heart, the thing may be known. Then resolve to find out.

(2) My second word of application shall be a *warning.* I address it to all who know, in their own consciences, that their religion is not real. I ask them to remember the greatness of their danger, and their exceeding guilt in the sight of God.

An unreal Christianity is specially offensive to that Great God with whom we have to do. He is continually spoken of in Scripture as the God of Truth. Truth is peculiarly one of His attributes. Can you doubt for a moment that He abhors everything that is not genuine and true ? Better, I firmly believe, to be found an ignorant heathen at the last day, than to be found with nothing better than a nominal religion. If your religion is of this sort, beware !

An unreal Christianity is sure to fail a man at last. It will wear out; it will break down; it will leave its possessor like a wreck on a sandbank, high and dry and forsaken by the tide; it will supply no comfort in the hour when comfort is most needed,—in the time of affliction, and on the bed of death. If you want a religion to be of any use to your soul, beware of unreality ! If you would not be comfortless in death, and hopeless in the judgment day, be genuine, be real, be true.

(3) My third word of application shall be *advice.* I offer it to all who feel pricked in conscience by the subject of this paper. I advise them to cease from all trifling and playing with religion, and to become honest, thorough-going, whole-hearted followers of the Lord Jesus Christ.

Apply without delay to the Lord Jesus, and ask Him to become your Saviour, your Physician, your Priest, and your Friend. Let not the thought of your unworthiness keep you away : let not the recollection of your sins prevent your application. Never, never forget that Christ can cleanse you from any quantity of sins, if you only commit your soul to Him. But one thing He does ask of those who come to Him : He asks them to be real, honest, and true.

Let reality be one great mark of your approach to Christ, and there is everything to give you hope. Your repentance may be feeble, but let it be real; your faith may be weak, but let it be real; your desires after holiness may be mingled with much infirmity, but let them be real. Let there be nothing of reserve, of double-dealing, of part-acting of dishonesty, of sham, of counterfeit, in your Christianity. Never be content to wear a cloak of religion. Be all that you profess. Though you may err, be real. Though you may stumble, be true. Keep this principle continually before your eyes, and it will be well with your soul throughout your journey from grace to glory.

(4) My last word of application shall be *encouragement*. I address it to all who have manfully taken up the cross, and are honestly following Christ. I exhort them to persevere, and not to be moved by difficulties and opposition.

You may often find few with you, and many against you. You may often hear hard things said of you. You may often be told that you go too far, and that you are extreme. Heed it not. Turn a deaf ear to remarks of this kind. Press on.

If there is anything which a man ought to do thoroughly, really, truly, honestly, and with all his heart, it is the business of his soul. If there is any work which he ought never to slur over, and do in a slovenly fashion, it is the great work of "working out his own salvation." (Phil. ii. 12.) Believer in Christ, remember this! Whatever you do in religion, do it well. Be real. Be thorough. Be honest. Be true.

If there is anything in the world of which a man need not be ashamed, it is the service of Jesus Christ. Of sin, of worldliness, of levity, of trifling, of time-wasting, of pleasure-seeking, of bad temper, of pride, of making an idol of money, dress, dancing, hunting, shooting, card-playing, novel-reading, and the like,—of all this a man may well be ashamed. Living after this fashion he makes the angels sorrow, and the devils rejoice. But of living for his soul,—caring for his soul,—thinking of his soul,—providing for his soul,—making his soul's salvation the principal and chief thing in his daily life,—of all this a man has no cause to be ashamed at all. Believer in Christ, remember this! Remember it in your Bible-reading and your private praying. Remember it on your Sabbaths. Remember it in your worship of God. In all these things never be ashamed of being whole-hearted, real, thorough, and true.

The years of our life are fast passing away. Who knows but this year may be the last in his life? Who can tell but that he may be called this very year to meet his God? As ever you would be found ready, be a real and true Christian. Do not be base metal.

The time is fast coming when nothing but reality will stand the fire. Real repentance towards God,—real faith towards our Lord Jesus Christ,—real holiness of heart and life,—these, these are the things which will alone pass current at the last day. It is a solemn saying of our Lord Jesus Christ, "Many shall say in that day, Lord, Lord, have we not prophesied in Thy name, and in Thy name have cast out devils, and in Thy name done many wonderful works? And then will I profess to them, I never knew you. Depart from Me, ye that work iniquity." (Matt. vii. 22, 23.)

IV

PRAYER

" Men ought always to pray."—LUKE xviii. 1.
" I will that men pray everywhere."—1 TIM. ii. 8.

PRAYER is the most important subject in practical religion. All other subjects are second to it. Reading the Bible, keeping the Sabbath, hearing sermons, attending public worship, going to the Lord's Table,—all these are very weighty matters. But none of them are so important as private prayer.

I propose in this paper to offer seven plain reasons why I use such strong language about prayer. I invite to these reasons the attention of every thinking man into whose hands this paper may fall. I venture to assert with confidence that they deserve serious consideration.

I. In the first place, *Prayer is absolutely needful to a man's salvation.*

I say absolutely needful, and I say so advisedly. I am not speaking now of infants and idiots. I am not settling the state of the heathen. I remember that where little is given, there little will be required. I speak especially of those who call themselves Christians, in a land like our own. And of such I say no man or woman can expect to be saved who does not pray.

I hold salvation by grace as strongly as any one. I would gladly offer a free and full pardon to the greatest sinner that ever lived. I would not hesitate to stand by his dying bed, and say, "Believe on the Lord Jesus Christ even now, and you shall be saved." But that a man can have salvation without *asking* for it, I cannot see in the Bible. That a man will receive pardon of his sins, who will not so much as lift up his heart inwardly, and say, "Lord Jesus, give it to me," this I cannot find. I can find that nobody will be saved by his prayers, but I cannot find that without prayer anybody will be saved.

It is not absolutely needful to salvation that a man should *read* the Bible. A man may have no learning, or be blind, and yet have Christ in his heart. It is not absolutely needful that a man should *hear* the public preaching of the Gospel. He may live where the Gospel is not preached, or he may be bedridden, or deaf. But the same thing cannot be said about prayer. It is absolutely needful to salvation that a man should *pray*.

There is no royal road either to health or learning. Princes and kings, poor men and peasants, all alike must attend to the wants of their own bodies and their own minds. No man can eat, drink, or sleep by proxy. No man can get the alphabet learned for him by another. All these are things which everybody must do for himself, or they will not be done at all.

Just as it is with the mind and body, so it is with the soul. There are certain things absolutely needful to the soul's health and well-being. Each one must attend to these things for himself. Each must repent for himself. Each must apply to Christ for himself. And for himself each one must speak to God and pray. You must do it for yourself, for by nobody else can it be done.

How can we expect to be saved by an "unknown" God? And how can we know God without prayer? We know nothing of men and women in this world,

unless we speak with them. We cannot know God in
Christ, unless we speak to Him in prayer. If we wish
to be with Him in heaven, we must be His friends on
earth. If we wish to be His friends on earth, *we must
pray.*

There will be many at Christ's right hand in the last
day. The saints gathered from North and South, and East
and West, will be "a multitude that no man can number."
(Rev. vii. 9.) The song of victory that will burst from their
mouths, when their redemption is at length complete, will
be a glorious song indeed. It will be far above the noise
of many waters, and of mighty thunders. But there will
be no discord in that song. They that sing will sing with
one heart as well as one voice. Their experience will be
one and the same. All will have believed. All will have
been washed in the blood of Christ. All will have been
born again. All will have prayed. Yes, we must pray
on earth, or we shall never praise in heaven. We must
go through the school of prayer, or we shall never be fit
for the holiday of praise. In short, to be prayerless is to
be without God,—without Christ,—without grace,—without hope,—and without heaven. It is to be in the road
to hell.

II. In the second place, *a habit of prayer is one of
the surest marks of a true Christian.*

All the children of God on earth are alike in this
respect. From the moment there is any life and reality
about their religion, they pray. Just as the first sign of
life in an infant when born into the world, is the act of
breathing, so the first act of men and women when they
are born again, is *praying.*

This is one of the common marks of all the elect of
God: "They cry unto Him day and night." (Luke
xviii. 1.) The Holy Spirit, who makes them new
creatures, works in them the feeling of adoption, and

makes them cry, "Abba, Father." (Rom. viii. 15.) The Lord Jesus, when He quickens them, gives them a voice and a tongue, and says to them, "Be dumb no more." God has no dumb children. It is as much a part of their new nature to pray, as it is of a child to cry. They see their need of mercy and grace. They feel their emptiness and weakness. They cannot do otherwise than they do. They *must* pray.

I have looked carefully over the lives of God's saints in the Bible. I cannot find one of whose history much is told us, from Genesis to Revelation, who was not a man of prayer. I find it mentioned as a characteristic of the godly, that "they call on the Father," that "they call on the name of the Lord Jesus Christ." I find it recorded as a characteristic of the wicked, that "they call not upon the Lord." (1 Peter i. 17; 1 Cor. i. 2; Psalm xiv. 4.)

I have read the lives of many eminent Christians who have been on earth since the Bible days. Some of them, I see, were rich, and some poor. Some were learned, and some unlearned. Some of them were Episcopalians, some Presbyterians, some Baptists, some Independents. Some were Calvinists, and some Arminians. Some have loved to use a liturgy, and some to use none. But one thing, I see, they all had in common. They have all been *men of prayer*.

I study the reports of Missionary Societies in our own times. I see with joy that heathen men and women are receiving the Gospel in various parts of the globe. There are conversions in Africa, in New Zealand, in Hindostan, in America. The people converted are naturally unlike one another in every respect. But one striking thing I observe at all the Missionary stations. The converted people *always pray*.

I do not deny that a man may pray without heart, and without sincerity. I do not for a moment pretend to say that the mere fact of a person praying proves everything about his soul. As in every other part of religion, so also in this, there is plenty of deception and hypocrisy.

But this I do say,—that not praying is a clear proof that a man is not yet a true Christian. He cannot really feel his sins. He cannot love God. He cannot feel himself a debtor to Christ. He cannot long after holiness. He cannot desire heaven. He has yet to be born again. He has yet to be made a new creature. He may boast confidently of election, grace, faith, hope, and knowledge, and deceive ignorant people. But you may rest assured it is all vain talk *if he does not pray.*

And I say furthermore, that of all the evidences of real work of the Spirit, a habit of hearty private prayer is one of the most satisfactory that can be named. A man may preach from false motives. A man may write books, and make fine speeches, and seem diligent in good works, and yet be a Judas Iscariot. But a man seldom goes into his closet, and pours out his soul before God in secret, unless he is in earnest. The Lord Himself has set His stamp on prayer as the best proof of a true conversion. When He sent Ananias to Saul in Damascus, He gave him no other evidence of his change of heart than this,—"*Behold, he prayeth.*" (Acts ix. 11.)

I know that much may go on in a man's mind before he is brought to pray. He may have many convictions, desires, wishes, feelings, intentions, resolutions, hopes, and fears. But all these things are very uncertain evidences. They are to be found in ungodly people, and often come to nothing. In many a case they are not more lasting than "the morning cloud, and the dew that goeth away." (Hos. vi. 4.) A real hearty prayer, flowing from a broken and contrite spirit, is worth all these things put together.

I know that the elect of God are chosen to salvation from all eternity. I do not forget that the Holy Spirit, who calls them in due time, in many instances leads them by very slow degrees to acquaintance with Christ. But the eye of man can only judge by what it sees. I cannot call any one justified until he believes. I dare not say that any one believes until he prays. I cannot understand a dumb faith. The first act of faith will be to speak to God. Faith is to the soul what life is to the body. Prayer is to faith what breath is to life. How a man can live and not breathe is past my comprehension, and how a man can believe and not pray is past my comprehension too.

Let no one be surprised if he hears ministers of the Gospel dwelling much on the importance of prayer. This is the point we want to bring you to,—we want to know that you pray. Your views of doctrine may be correct. Your love of Protestantism may be warm and unmistakeable. But still this may be nothing more than head knowledge and party spirit. The great point is this,— whether you can speak *to* God as well as speak *about* God.

III. In the third place, *there is no duty in religion so neglected as private prayer.*

We live in days of abounding religious profession. There are more places of public worship now than there ever were before. There are more persons attending them than there ever have been since England was a nation. And yet in spite of all this public religion, I believe there is a vast neglect of private prayer.

I should not have said so a few years ago. I once thought, in my ignorance, that most people said their prayers, and many people prayed. I have lived to think differently. I have come to the conclusion that the great majority of professing Christians do not pray at all.

I know this sounds very shocking, and will startle many. But I am satisfied that prayer is just one of those things which is thought a "matter of course," and, like many matters of course, is shamefully neglected. It is "every-body's business;" and, as it often happens in such cases, it is a business carried on by very few. It is one of those private transactions between God and our souls which no eye sees, and therefore one which there is every temptation to pass over and leave undone.

I believe that thousands *never say a word of prayer at all.* They eat; they drink; they sleep; they rise; they go forth to their labour; they return to their homes; they breathe God's air; they see God's sun; they walk on God's earth; they enjoy God's mercies; they have dying bodies; they have judgment and eternity before them. But they *never speak to God!* They live like the beasts that perish; they behave like creatures without souls; they have not a word to say to Him in whose hand are their life, and breath, and all things, and from whose mouth they must one day receive their everlasting sentence. How dreadful this seems! But if the secrets of men were only known, how common!

I believe there are tens of thousands *whose prayers are nothing but a mere form,*—a set of words repeated by rote, without a thought about their meaning. Some say over a few hasty sentences picked up in the nursery when they were children. Some content themselves with repeating the Belief, forgetting that there is not a request in it. Some add the Lord's Prayer, but without the slightest desire that its solemn petitions may be granted. Some among the poor, even at this day, repeat the old popish lines:—

> "Matthew, Mark, Luke, and John,
> Bless the bed that I lie on."

Many, even of those who use good forms, mutter their prayers over after they have got into bed, or scramble over them while they wash or dress in the morning. Men may think what they please, but they may depend that in the sight of God *this is not praying.* Words said without heart are as utterly useless to our souls as the drum-beating of the poor heathen before their idols. Where there is *no heart,* there may be lip-work and tongue-work, but there is nothing that God listens to,—there is *no prayer.* Saul, I have no doubt, said many a long prayer before the Lord met him on the way to Damascus. But it was not till his heart was broken that the Lord said, "He prayeth."

Does this surprise any reader? Listen to me and I will show you that I am not speaking as I do without reason. Do you think that my assertions are extravagant and unwarrantable? Give me your attention, and I will soon show you that I am only telling you the truth.

Have you forgotten that it is *not natural* to any one to pray? The carnal mind is enmity against God. The desire of man's heart is to get far away from God, and to have nothing to do with Him. His feeling toward Him is not love but fear. Why then should a man pray when he has no real sense of sin, no real feeling of spiritual wants,—no thorough belief in unseen things,—no desire after holiness and heaven? Of all these things the vast majority of men know and feel nothing. The multitude walk in the broad way. I cannot forget this. Therefore I say boldly, I believe that few pray.

Have you forgotten that it is *not fashionable* to pray? It is just one of the things that many would be rather ashamed to own. There are hundreds who would sooner storm a breach, or lead a forlorn hope, than confess publicly that they make a habit of prayer. There are thousands who, if obliged by chance to sleep in the same room with a stranger, would lie down in bed without a prayer. To ride well, to shoot well, to dress well, to go to balls, and concerts, and theatres, to be thought clever and agreeable,—all this is fashionable, but not to pray. I cannot forget this. I cannot think a habit is common which so many seem ashamed to own. I believe that few pray.

Have you forgotten *the lives that many live?* Can we

really suppose that people are praying against sin night and day, when we see them plunging right into it ? Can we suppose they pray against the world, when they are entirely absorbed and taken up with its pursuits ? Can we think they really ask God for grace to serve Him, when they do not show the slightest desire to serve Him at all ? Oh, no ! It is plain as daylight that the great majority of men either ask nothing of God, or *do not mean what they say* when they do ask,—which is just the same thing. Praying and sinning will never live together in the same heart. Prayer will consume sin, or sin will choke prayer. I cannot forget this. I look at men's lives. I believe that few pray.

Have you forgotten *the deaths that many die ?* How many, when they draw near death, seem entirely strangers to God. Not only are they sadly ignorant of His Gospel, but sadly wanting in the power of speaking to Him. There is a terrible awkwardness, and shyness, and newness, and rawness, in their endeavours to approach Him. They seem to be taking up a fresh thing. They appear as if they wanted an introduction to God, and as if they had never talked with Him before. I remember having heard of a lady who was anxious to have a minister to visit her in her last illness. She desired that he would pray with her. He asked her what he should pray for. She did not know and could not tell. She was utterly unable to name any one thing which she wished him to ask God for her soul. All she seemed to want was the form of a minister's prayers. I can quite understand this. Death-beds are great revealers of secrets. I cannot forget what I have seen of sick and dying people. This also leads me to believe that few pray.

IV. In the fourth place, *prayer is that act in religion to which there is the greatest encouragement.*

There is everything on God's part to make prayer easy,

if men will only attempt it. "All things are ready" on
His side. (Luke xiv. 17.) Every objection is anticipated.
Every difficulty is provided for. The crooked places are
made straight, and the rough places are made smooth.
There is no excuse left for the prayerless man.

There is *a way* by which any man, however sinful and
unworthy, may draw near to God the Father. Jesus
Christ has opened that way by the sacrifice He made for
us upon the cross. The holiness and justice of God need
not frighten sinners and keep them back. Only let them
cry to God in the name of Jesus,—only let them plead
the atoning blood of Jesus,—and they shall find God
upon a throne of grace, willing and ready to hear. The
name of Jesus is a never-failing passport to our prayers.
In that name a man may draw near to God with boldness,
and ask with confidence. God has engaged to hear him.
Think of this. Is not this encouragement ?

There is *an advocate* and intercessor always waiting to
present the prayers of those who will employ Him. That
advocate is Jesus Christ. He mingles our prayers with
the incense of His own almighty intercession. So mingled
they go up as a sweet savour before the throne of God.
Poor as they are in themselves, they are mighty and
powerful in the hand of our High Priest and elder
brother. The bank-note without a signature at the
bottom is nothing but a worthless piece of paper. A few
strokes of a pen confer on it all its value. The prayer of
a poor child of Adam is a feeble thing in itself, but once
endorsed by the hand of the Lord Jesus it availeth much.
There was an officer in the city of Rome who was
appointed to have his doors always open, in order to
receive any Roman citizen who applied to him for help.
Just so the ear of the Lord Jesus is ever open to the cry
of all who want mercy and grace. It is His office to help
them. Their prayer is His delight. Think of this. Is
not this encouragement ?

There is *the Holy Spirit* ever ready to help our infirmities in prayer. It is one part of His special office to assist us in our endeavours to speak to God. We need not be cast down and distressed by the fear of not knowing what to say. The Spirit will give us words if we will only seek His aid. He will supply us with "thoughts that breathe and words that burn." The prayers of the Lord's people are the inspiration of the Lord's Spirit,—the work of the Holy Ghost who dwells within them as the Spirit of grace and supplications. Surely the Lord's people may well hope to be heard. It is not they merely that pray, but the Holy Ghost pleading in them. (Rom. viii. 26.) Think of this. Is not this encouragement?

There are exceeding great and precious *promises* to those who pray. What did the Lord Jesus mean when He spoke such words as these, "Ask, and it shall be given you; seek, and ye shall find; knock, and it shall be opened unto you: for every one that asketh receiveth; and he that seeketh findeth; and to him that knocketh it shall be opened." (Matt. vii. 7, 8.) "All things, whatsoever ye shall ask in prayer believing, ye shall receive." (Matt. xxi. 22.) "Whatsoever ye shall ask in my name, that will I do, that the Father may be glorified in the Son. If ye shall ask any thing in my name, I will do it." (John xiv. 13, 14.) What did the Lord mean when He spoke the parables of the friend at midnight and the importunate widow? (Luke xi. 5, and xviii. 1.) Think over these passages. If this is not encouragement to pray, words have no meaning at all.

There are wonderful *examples* in Scripture of the power of prayer. Nothing seems to be too great, too hard, or too difficult for prayer to do. It has obtained things that seemed impossible and out of reach. It has won victories over fire, air, earth, and water. Prayer opened the Red Sea. Prayer brought water from the rock and bread from heaven. Prayer made the sun stand still. Prayer brought fire from the sky on Elijah's sacrifice. Prayer turned the counsel of Ahithophel into foolishness. Prayer overthrew the army of Sennacherib. Well might Mary, Queen of Scots, say, "I fear John Knox's prayers more than an army of ten thousand men." Prayer has healed the sick. Prayer has raised the dead. Prayer has procured the conversion of souls. "The child of many prayers," said an old Christian to Augustine's mother, "shall never perish." Prayer, pains, and faith can do anything. Nothing seems impossible when a man has the Spirit of adoption. "Let me alone," is the remarkable saying of God to Moses, when Moses was about to intercede for the children of Israel. (Exod. xxxii. 10.) The Chaldee version has it "Leave off praying." So long as Abraham asked mercy for Sodom, the Lord went on giving. He never ceased to give till Abraham ceased to pray. Think of this. Is not this encouragement?

What more can a man want to lead him to take any step in religion than the things I have just told him about prayer? What more could be done to make the path to the mercy-seat easy, and to remove all occasions of stumbling from the sinner's way? Surely if the devils in hell had such a door set open before them they would leap for gladness, and make the very pit ring with joy.

But where will the man hide his head at last who neglects such glorious encouragements? What can be possibly said for the man who after all dies without prayer? God forbid that any reader of this paper should be that man.

V. In the fifth place, *diligence in prayer is the secret of eminent holiness.*

Without controversy there is a vast difference among true Christians. There is an immense interval between the foremost and the hindermost in the army of God.

They are all fighting the same good fight;—but how much more valiantly some fight than others! They are all doing the Lord's work;—but how much more some do than others! They are all light in the Lord;—but how much more brightly some shine than others! They are all running the same race;—but how much faster some get on than others! They all love the same Lord and Saviour;—but how much more some love Him than others! I ask any true Christian whether this is not the case. Are not these things so?

There are some of the Lord's people who seem *never able to get on* from the time of their conversion. They are born again, but they remain babies all their lives. They are learners in Christ's school, but they never seem to get beyond A B C, and the lowest form. They have got inside the fold, but there they lie down and get no further. Year after year you see in them the same old besetting sins. You hear from them the same old experience. You remark in them the same want of spiritual appetite,—the same squeamishness about anything but the milk of the Word, and the same dislike to strong meat,—the same childishness,—the same feebleness,—the same littleness of mind,—the same narrowness of heart,— the same want of interest in anything beyond their own little circle, which you remarked ten years ago. They are pilgrims indeed, but pilgrims like the Gibeonites of old;— their bread is always dry and mouldy,—their shoes always old and clouted, and their garments always rent and torn. (Josh. ix. 4, 5.) I say this with sorrow and grief. But I ask any real Christian, Is it not true?

There are others of the Lord's people who seem to be *always getting on*. They grow like the grass after rain. They increase like Israel in Egypt. They press on like Gideon,—though sometimes "faint, yet always pursuing." (Judges viii. 4.) They are ever adding grace to grace, and faith to faith, and strength to strength. Every time you meet them their hearts seem larger, and their spiritual stature bigger, taller, and stronger. Every year they appear to see more, and know more, and believe more, and feel more in their religion. They not only have good works to prove the reality of their faith, but they are *zealous* of them. They not only do well, but they are *unwearied* in well-doing. (Titus ii. 14 ; Gal. vi. 9.) They attempt great things, and they do great things. When they fail they try again, and when they fall they are soon up again. And all this time they think themselves poor unprofitable servants, and fancy they do nothing at all !—These are those who make religion lovely and beautiful in the eyes of all. They wrest praise even from the unconverted, and win golden opinions even from the selfish men of the world. These are those whom it does one good to see, to be with, and to hear. When you meet them, you could believe that, like Moses, they had just come out from the presence of God. When you part with them you feel warmed by their company, as if your soul had been near a fire. I know such people are rare. I only ask, Is it not so ?

Now, how can we account for the difference which I have just described ? What is the reason that some believers are so much brighter and holier than others ? I believe the difference, in nineteen cases out of twenty, arises from different habits about private prayer. I believe that those who are not eminently holy pray *little*, and those who are eminently holy pray *much*.

I daresay this opinion will startle some readers. I have little doubt that many look on eminent holiness as a kind of special gift, which none but a few must pretend to aim at. They admire it at a distance, in books : they think it beautiful when they see an example near themselves. But as to its being a thing within the reach of any but a very few, such a notion never seems to enter their minds. In short, they consider it a kind of monopoly granted to a few favoured believers, but certainly not to all.

Now I believe that this is a most dangerous mistake. I believe that spiritual, as well as natural, greatness, depends far more on the use of means within everybody's reach, than on anything else. Of course I do not say we have a right to expect a miraculous grant of intellectual gifts. But this I do say, that when a man is once converted to God, whether he shall be eminently holy or not depends chiefly on his own diligence in the use of God's appointed means. And I assert confidently, that the principal means by which most believers have beecome great in the Church of Christ is the habit of *diligent private prayer*.

Look through the lives of the brightest and best of God's servants, whether in the Bible or not. See what is written of Moses, and David, and Daniel, and Paul. Mark what is recorded of Luther and Bradford, the Reformers. Observe what is related of the private devotions of Whitfield, and Cecil, and Venn, and Bickersteth, and M'Cheyne. Tell me of one of all the goodly fellowship of saints and martyrs, who has not had this mark most prominently,—he was *a man of prayer*. Oh, depend upon it, prayer is power !

Prayer obtains fresh and continued outpourings of the Spirit. He alone begins the work of grace in a man's heart: He alone can carry it forward and make it prosper. But the good Spirit loves to be entreated. And those who ask most, will always have most of His influence.

Prayer is the surest remedy against the devil and besetting sins. That sin will never stand firm which is heartily prayed against: that devil will never long keep dominion over us which we beseech the Lord to cast forth. But, then, we must spread out all our case before our Heavenly Physician, if He is to give us daily relief: we

must drag our indwelling devils to the feet of Christ, and
cry to Him to send them back to the pit.

Do we wish to grow in grace and be very holy Christians?
Then let us never forget the value of prayer.

VI. In the sixth place, *neglect of prayer is one great
cause of backsliding.*

There is such a thing as going back in religion, after
making a good profession. Men may run well for a
season, like the Galatians, and then turn aside after false
teachers. Men may profess loudly, while their feelings
are warm, as Peter did; and then, in the hour of trial,
deny their Lord. Men may lose their first love, as the
Ephesians did. Men may cool down in their zeal to do
good, like Mark, the companion of Paul. Men may follow
an apostle for a season, and then, like Demas, go back to
the world.—All these things men may do.

It is a miserable thing to be a backslider. Of all
unhappy things that can befall a man, I suppose it is the
worst. A stranded ship, a broken-winged eagle, a garden
overrun with weeds, a harp without strings, a church in
ruins,—all these are sad sights; but a backslider is a
sadder sight still. That true grace shall never be extin-
guished, and true union with Christ never be broken off,
I feel no doubt. But I do believe that a man may fall
away so far that he shall lose sight of his own grace, and
despair of his own salvation. And if this is not hell, it is
certainly the next thing to it! A wounded conscience, a
mind sick of itself, a memory full of self-reproach, a heart
pierced through with the Lord's arrows, a spirit broken
with a load of inward accusation,—all this is *a taste of
hell.* It is a hell on earth. Truly that saying of the
wise man is solemn and weighty,—" The backslider in
heart shall be filled with his own ways." (Prov. xiv. 14.)

Now, what is the cause of most backsliding? I believe,
as a general rule, one of the chief causes is neglect of

private prayer. Of course the secret history of falls will not be known till the last day. I can only give my opinion as a minister of Christ and a student of the heart. That opinion is, I repeat distinctly, that backsliding generally first begins with *neglect of private prayer*.

Bibles read without prayer, sermons heard without prayer, marriages contracted without prayer, journeys undertaken without prayer, residences chosen without prayer, friendships formed without prayer, the daily act of private prayer itself hurried over or gone through without heart,—these are the kind of downward steps by which many a Christian descends to a condition of spiritual palsy, or reaches the point where God allows him to have a tremendous fall.

This is the process which forms the lingering Lots, the unstable Samsons, the wife-idolizing Solomons, the inconsistent Asas, the pliable Jehoshaphats, the over-careful Marthas, of whom so many are to be found in the Church of Christ. Often the simple history of such cases is this, —they became *careless about private prayer*.

We may be very sure that men fall in private long before they fall in public. They are backsliders on their knees long before they backslide openly in the eyes of the world. Like Peter, they first disregard the Lord's warning to watch and pray; and then, like Peter, their strength is gone, and in the hour of temptation they deny their Lord.

The world takes notice of their fall, and scoffs loudly. But the world knows nothing of the real reason. The heathen succeeded in making Origen, the old Christian Father, offer incense to an idol, by threatening him with a punishment worse than death. They then triumphed greatly at the sight of his cowardice and apostacy. But the heathen did not know the fact, which Origen himself tells us, that on that very morning he had left his bedchamber hastily, and without finishing his usual prayers.

If any reader of this paper is a Christian indeed I

trust he will never be a backslider. But if you do not wish to be a backsliding Christian, remember the hint I give you,—Mind your prayers.

VII. In the seventh place, *prayer is one of the best receipts for happiness and contentment.*

We live in a world where sorrow abounds. This has always been its state since sin came in. There cannot be sin without sorrow. And till sin is driven out from the world it is vain for any one to suppose he can escape sorrow.

Some, without doubt, have a larger cup of sorrow to drink than others. But few are to be found who live long without sorrows or cares of one sort or another. Our bodies, our property, our families, our children, our relations, our servants, our friends, our neighbours, our worldly callings, —each and all of these are fountains of care. Sicknesses, deaths, losses, disappointments, partings, separations, in-gratitude, slander,—all these are common things. We cannot get through life without them. Some day or other they find us out. The greater are our affections, the deeper are our afflictions; and the more we love, the more we have to weep.

And what is the best receipt for cheerfulness in such a world as this? How shall we get through this valley of tears with least pain? I know no better receipt than the habit of *taking everything to God in prayer.*

This is the plain advice that the Bible gives, both in the Old Testament and the New. What says the Psalmist? "Call upon Me in the day of trouble: I will deliver thee, and thou shalt glorify Me." (Psalm l. 15.) "Cast thy burden upon the Lord, and He shall sustain thee: He shall never suffer the righteous to be moved." (Psalm lv. 22.) What says the Apostle Paul? "Be careful for nothing; but in everything by prayer and supplication with thanksgiving let your requests be made known unto

God. And the peace of God, which passeth all under-standing, shall keep your hearts and minds through Christ Jesus." (Phil. iv. 6, 7.) What says the Apostle James? "Is any afflicted among you? let him pray." (James v. 13.)

This was the practice of all the saints whose history we have recorded in the Scriptures. This is what Jacob did, when he feared his brother Esau. This is what Moses did, when the people were ready to stone him in the wilderness. This is what Joshua did, when Israel was defeated before Ai. This is what David did, when he was in danger at Keliah. This is what Hezekiah did, when he received the letter from Sennacherib. This is what the Church did, when Peter was put in prison. This is what Paul did, when he was cast into the dungeon at Philippi.

The only way to be really happy, in such a world as this is to be ever casting all our cares on God. It is the trying to carry their own burdens which so often makes believers sad. If they will only tell their troubles to God He will enable them to bear them as easily as Samson did the gates of Gaza. If they are resolved to keep them to themselves they will find one day that the very grass-hopper is a burden. (Eccles. xii. 5.)

There is a friend ever waiting to help us, if we will only unbosom to Him our sorrow,—a friend who pitied the poor, and sick, and sorrowful, when He was upon earth,—a friend who knows the heart of a man, for He lived thirty-three years as a man amongst us,—a friend who can weep with the weepers, for He was a man of sorrows and acquainted with grief,—a friend who is able to help us, for there never was earthly pain He could not cure. That friend is Jesus Christ. The way to be happy is to be always opening our hearts to Him. Oh, that we were all like that poor Christian negro, who only answered, when threatened and punished, "*I must tell the Lord.*"

Jesus can make those happy who trust Him and call on Him, whatever be their outward condition. He can give them peace of heart in a prison,—contentment in the midst of poverty,—comfort in the midst of bereavements, —joy on the brink of the grave. There is a mighty fulness in Him for all His believing members,—a fulness that is ready to be poured out on every one who will ask in prayer. Oh, that men would understand that happiness does not depend on outward circumstances, but on the state of the heart!

Prayer can lighten crosses for us however heavy. It can bring down to our side One who will help us to bear them.—Prayer can open a door for us when our way seems hedged up. It can bring down One who will say, "This is the way, walk in it."—Prayer can let in a ray of hope, when all our earthly prospects seem darkened. It can bring down One who will say, "I will never leave thee nor forsake thee."—Prayer can obtain relief for us when those we love most are taken away, and the world feels empty. It can bring down One who can fill the gap in our hearts with Himself, and say to the waves within, "Peace: be still!" Oh, that men were not so like Hagar in the wilderness, blind to the well of living waters close beside them! (Gen. xxi. 19.)

I want the readers of this paper to be really happy Christians. I am certain I cannot urge on them a more important duty than prayer.

And now it is high time for me to bring this paper to an end. I trust I have brought before my readers things that will be seriously considered. I heartily pray God that this consideration may be blessed to their souls.

(1) Let me speak a parting word *to those who do not pray*. I dare not suppose that all who read these pages will be praying people. If you are a prayerless person, suffer me to speak to you this day on God's behalf.

Prayerless friend, I can only warn you; but I do warn you most solemnly. I warn you that you are in a position of fearful danger. If you die in your present state you are a lost soul. You will only rise again to be eternally miserable. I warn you that of all professing Christians you are most utterly without excuse. There is not a single good reason that you can show for living without prayer.

It is useless to say you *know not how* to pray. Prayer is the simplest act in all religion. It is simply speaking to God. It needs neither learning, nor wisdom, nor book-knowledge to begin it. It needs nothing but heart and will. The weakest infant can cry when he is hungry. The poorest beggar can hold out his hand for an alms, and does not wait to find fine words. The most ignorant man will find something to say to God, if he has only a mind.

It is useless to say you have *no convenient place* to pray in. Any man can find a place private enough, if he is disposed. Our Lord prayed on a mountain; Peter on the house-top; Isaac in the field; Nathanael under the fig-tree; Jonah in the whale's belly. Any place may become a closet, an oratory, and a Bethel, and be to us the presence of God.

It is useless to say *you have no time.* There is plenty of time, if men will only employ it. Time may be short, but time is always long enough for prayer. Daniel had all the affairs of a kingdom on his hands, and yet he prayed three times a day. David was ruler over a mighty nation, and yet he says, "Evening and morning and at noon will I pray." (Psalm lv. 17.) When time is really wanted, time can always be found.

It is useless to say you *cannot pray till you have faith and a new heart,* and that you must sit still and wait for them. This is to add sin to sin. It is bad enough to be unconverted and going to hell. It is even worse to say, "I know it, but I will not cry for mercy." This is a kind of argument for which there is no warrant in Scripture. "Call ye upon the Lord," saith Isaiah, "while He is near." (Isaiah lv. 6.) "Take with you words, and come unto the

Lord," says Hosea. (Hosea xiv. 1.) "Repent and pray," says Peter to Simon Magus. (Acts viii. 22.) If you want faith and a new heart, go and cry to the Lord for them. The very attempt to pray has often been the quickening of a dead soul. Alas, there is no devil so dangerous as a dumb devil.

Oh, prayerless man, who and what are you that you will not ask anything of God? Have you made a covenant with death and hell? Are you at peace with the worm and the fire? Have you no sins to be pardoned? Have you no fear of eternal torment? Have you no desire after heaven? Oh, that you would awake from your present folly! Oh, that you would consider your latter end! Oh, that you would arise and call upon God! Alas, there is a day coming when men shall pray loudly, "Lord, Lord, open to us," but all too late;—when many shall cry to the rocks to fall on them, and the hills to cover them, who would never cry to God. In all affection I warn you. Beware lest this be the end of your soul. Salvation is very near you. Do not lose heaven for want of asking.

(2) Let me speak in the next place *to those who have real desires for salvation*, but know not what steps to take or where to begin. I cannot but hope that some readers may be in this state of mind, and if there be but one such I must offer him encouragement and advice.

In every journey there must be a first step. There must be a change from sitting still to moving forward. The journeyings of Israel from Egypt to Canaan were long and wearisome. Forty years passed away before they crossed Jordan. Yet there was someone who moved first when they marched from Rameses to Succoth. When does a man really take his first step in coming out from sin and the world? He does it in the day when he first prays with his heart.

In every building the first stone must be laid, and the first blow must be struck. The ark was 120 years in building. Yet there was a day when Noah laid his axe to the first tree he cut down to form it. The temple of Solomon was a glorious building. But there was a day when the first huge stone was laid at the foot of Mount Moriah. When does the building of the Spirit really begin to appear in a man's heart? It begins, so far as we can judge, when he first pours out his heart to God in prayer.

If any reader of this paper desires salvation, and wants to know what to do, I advise him to go this very day to the Lord Jesus Christ, in the first private place he can find, and entreat Him in prayer to save his soul.

Tell Him that you have heard that He receives sinners, and has said, "Him that cometh unto Me I will in nowise cast out." (John vi. 37.) Tell Him that you are a poor vile sinner, and that you come to Him on the faith of His own invitation. Tell Him you put yourself wholly and entirely in His hands,—that you feel vile and helpless, and hopeless in yourself,—and that except He saves you, you have no hope to be saved at all. Beseech Him to deliver you from the guilt, the power, and the consequences of sin. Beseech Him to pardon you and wash you in His own blood. Beseech Him to give you a new heart, and plant the Holy Spirit in your soul. Beseech Him to give you grace, and faith, and will, and power to be His disciple and servant from this day for ever. Yes: go this very day, and tell these things to the Lord Jesus Christ, if you really are in earnest about your soul.

Tell Him in your own way and your own words. If a doctor came to see you when sick you could tell him where you felt pain. If your soul really feels its disease you can surely find something to tell Christ.

Doubt not His willingness to save you, because you are a sinner. It is Christ's office to save sinners. He says Himself, "I came not to call the righteous, but sinners to repentance." (Luke v. 32.)

Wait not, because you feel unworthy. Wait for nothing:

wait for nobody. Waiting comes from the devil. Just as you are, go to Christ. The worse you are, the more need you have to apply to Him. You will never mend yourself by staying away.

Fear not because your prayer is stammering, your words feeble, and your language poor. Jesus can understand you. Just as a mother understands the first babblings of her infant, so does the blessed Saviour understand sinners. He can read a sigh, and see a meaning in a groan.

Despair not, because you do not get an answer immediately. While you are speaking, Jesus is listening. If He delays an answer, it is only for wise reasons, and to try if you are in earnest. Pray on, and the answer will surely come. Though it tarry, wait for it: it will surely come at last.

If you have any desire to be saved, remember the advice I have given you this day. Act upon it honestly and heartily, and you shall be saved.

(3) Let me speak, lastly, *to those who do pray.* I trust that some who read this paper know well what prayer is, and have the Spirit of adoption. To all such I offer a few words of brotherly counsel and exhortation. The incense offered in the tabernacle was ordered to be made in a particular way. Not every kind of incense would do. Let us remember this, and be careful about the matter and manner of our prayers.

If I know anything of a Christian's heart, you to whom I now speak are often sick of your own prayers. You never enter into the Apostle's words, "When I would do good, evil is present with me" (Rom. vii. 21), so thoroughly as you sometimes do upon your knees. You can understand David's words, "I hate vain thoughts." You can sympathize with that poor converted Hottentot, who was overheard praying, "Lord, deliver me from all my enemies; and, above all, from that bad man myself!"—There are few children of God who do not often find the season of prayer a season of conflict. The devil has special wrath against us when he sees us on our knees. Yet I believe that prayers which cost us no trouble should be regarded with great suspicion. I believe we are very poor judges of the goodness of our prayers, and that the prayer which pleases us *least* often pleases God *most*. Suffer me then, as a companion in the Christian warfare, to offer you a few words of exhortation. One thing, at least, we all feel,—we must pray. We cannot give it up: we must go on.

(*a*) I commend, then, to your attention the importance of *reverence and humility* in prayer. Let us never forget what we are, and what a solemn thing it is to speak with God. Let us beware of rushing into His presence with carelessness and levity. Let us say to ourselves, " I am on holy ground. This is no other than the gate of heaven. If I do not mean what I say, I am trifling with God. If I regard iniquity in my heart, the Lord will not hear me." Let us keep in mind the words of Solomon : " Be not rash with thy mouth, and let not thine heart be hasty to utter anything before God ; for God is in heaven. and thou on earth." (Eccles. v. 2.) When Abraham spoke to God, he said, " I am dust and ashes." When Job spoke, he said, " I am vile." (Gen. xviii. 27 ; Job xl. 4.) Let us do likewise.

(*b*) I commend to you, in the next place, the importance of praying *spiritually*. I mean by this that we should labour always to have the direct help of the Spirit in our prayers, and beware above all things of formality. There is nothing so spiritual but that it may become a form, and this is specially true of private prayer. We may insensibly get into the habit of using the fittest possible words, and offering the most Scriptural petitions ; and yet we may do it all by rote, without feeling it, and walk daily round an old beaten path, like a horse in a mill. I desire to touch this point with caution and delicacy. I know that there are certain great things we daily want, and that there is nothing necessarily formal in asking for these things in the same words. The world, the devil, and our hearts, are daily the same. Of necessity we must daily go over old ground. But this I say,—we must be very careful on this point. If the skeleton and outline of our prayers be by habit almost a form, let us strive that the clothing and filling up of our prayers be as far as possible of the Spirit. As to praying out of a book, it is a habit I cannot praise. If we can tell our doctors the state of our bodies without a book, we ought to be able to tell the state of our souls to God. I have no objection to a man using crutches, when he is first recovering from a broken limb. It is better to use crutches than not to walk at all. But if I saw him all his life on crutches, I should not think it matter for congratulation. I should like to see him strong enough to throw his crutches away.

(c) I commend to you, in the next place, the importance of making prayer *a regular business of life*. I might say something of the value of regular times in the day for prayer. God is a God of order. The hours for morning and evening sacrifice in the Jewish temple were not fixed as they were without a meaning. Disorder is eminently one of the fruits of sin. But I would not bring any under bondage. This only I say, that it is essential to your soul's health to make praying a part of the business of every twenty-four hours in your life. Just as you allot time to eating, sleeping, and business, so also allot time to prayer. Choose your own hours and seasons. At the very least, speak with God in the morning, before you speak with the world; and speak with God at night, after you have done with the world. But settle it down in your minds that prayer is one of the great things of every day. Do not drive it into a corner. Do not give it the scraps, and leavings, and parings of your day. Whatever else you make a business of, make a business of prayer.

(*d*) I commend to you, in the next place, the importance of *perseverance* in prayer. Once having begun the habit, never give it up. Your heart will sometimes say, " We have had family prayers; what mighty harm if we leave private prayer undone ? "—Your body will sometimes say. " You are unwell, or sleepy, or weary ; you need not pray." —Your mind will sometimes say, " You have important business to attend to to-day; cut short your prayers." Look on all such suggestions as coming direct from the devil. They are all as good as saying, " Neglect your soul." I do not maintain that prayers should always be of the same length ;—but I do say, let no excuse make you give up prayer. It is not for nothing that Paul said, " Continue in prayer," and " Pray without ceasing." (Colos. iv. 2 ; 1 Thess. v. 7.) He did not mean that men should be always on their knees, as an old sect, called the Euchitæ, supposed. But he did mean that our prayers should be like the continual burnt offering,—a thing steadily persevered in every day ;—that it should be like seed-time and harvest, and summer and winter,— a thing that should unceasingly come round at regular seasons ;—that it should be like the fire on the altar, not always consuming sacrifices, but never completely going out. Never forget that you may tie together morning and evening devotions by an endless chain of short ejaculatory prayers throughout the day. Even in company, or business, or in the very streets, you may be silently sending up little winged messengers to God, as Nehemiah did in the very presence of Artaxerxes. (Neh. ii. 4.) And never think that time is wasted which is given to God. A nation does not become poorer because it loses one year of working days in seven by keeping the Sabbath. A Christian never finds he is a loser in the long run by persevering in prayer.

(*e*) I commend to you, in the next place, the importance of *earnestness* in prayer. It is not necessary that a man

should shout, or scream, or be very loud, in order to prove
that he is in earnest. But it is desirable that we should
be hearty, and fervent, and warm, and ask as if we were
really interested in what we were doing. It is the
"effectual fervent" prayer that "availeth much," and not
the cold, sleepy, lazy, listless one. This is the lesson that
is taught us by the expressions used in Scripture about
prayer. It is called, "crying, knocking, wrestling, labouring,
striving." This is the lesson taught us by Scripture
examples. Jacob is one. He said to the angel at Penuel,
"I will not let thee go, except thou bless me." (Gen.
xxxii. 26.) Daniel is another. Hear how he pleaded
with God: "O Lord, hear; O Lord, forgive; O Lord,
hearken and do; defer not, for thine own sake, O my
God." (Dan. ix. 19.) Our Lord Jesus Christ is another.
It is written of Him, "In the days of His flesh He offered
up prayer and supplication, with strong crying and tears."
(Heb. v. 7.) Alas, how unlike is this to many of our
supplications! How tame and lukewarm they seem by
comparison! How truly might God say to many of us,
"You do not really want what you pray for!" Let us try
to amend this fault. Let us knock loudly at the door of
grace, like Mercy in "Pilgrim's Progress," as if we must
perish unless heard. Let us settle it down in our minds,
that cold prayers are a sacrifice without fire. Let us
remember the story of Demosthenes, the great orator,
when one came to him, and wanted him to plead his
cause. He heard him without attention, while he told
his story without earnestness. The man saw this, and
cried out with anxiety that it was all true. "Ah!" said
Demosthenes, "I believe you *now*."

(*f*) I commend to you, in the next place, the importance
of *praying with faith*. We should endeavour to believe that
our prayers are always heard, and that if we ask things
according to God's will, we shall always be answered. This is
the plain command of our Lord Jesus Christ: "Whatsoever

things ye desire, when ye pray, believe that ye receive them, and ye shall have them." (Mark xi. 24). Faith is to prayer what the feather is to the arrow: without it prayer will not hit the mark. We should cultivate the habit of pleading promises in our prayers. We should take with us some promise, and say, " Lord, here is Thine own word pledged. Do for us as Thou hast said." (2 Sam. vii. 25.) This was the habit of Jacob, and Moses, and David. The 119th Psalm is full of things asked, "according to Thy word." Above all, we should cultivate the habit of expecting answers to our prayers. We should do like the merchant who sends his ships to sea. We should not be satisfied unless we see some return. Alas, there are few points on which Christians come short so much as this. The Church at Jerusalem made prayer without ceasing for Peter in prison ; but when the prayer was answered, they would hardly believe it. (Acts xii. 15.) It is a solemn saying of old Traill's, " There is no surer mark of trifling in prayer, than when men are careless what they get by prayer."

(g) I commend to you, in the next place, the importance of *boldness* in prayer. There is an unseemly familiarity in some men's prayers, which I cannot praise. But there is such a thing as a holy boldness, which is exceedingly to be desired. I mean such boldness as that of Moses, when he pleads with God not to destroy Israel: " Wherefore," says he, " should the Egyptians speak and say, For mischief did He bring them out, to slay them in the mountains ? Turn from Thy fierce anger." (Exod. xxxii. 12.) I mean such boldness as that of Joshua, when the children of Israel were defeated before Ai: " What," says he, " wilt Thou do unto Thy great name ?" (Josh. vii. 9.) This is the boldness for which Luther was remarkable. One who heard him praying said, " What a spirit,—what a confidence was in his very expressions ! With such a reverence he sued, as one begging of God, and yet with such hope and assurance,

as if he spake with a loving father or friend." This is the
boldness which distinguished Bruce, a great Scotch divine
of the 17th century. His prayers were said to be "like
bolts shot up into heaven." Here also I fear we sadly
come short. We do not sufficiently realize the believer's
privileges. We do not plead as often as we might, "Lord,
are we not Thine own people? Is it not for Thy glory that
we should be sanctified? Is it not for Thine honour that
thy Gospel should increase?"

(*h*) I commend to you, in the next place, the importance
of *fulness* in prayer. I do not forget that our Lord warns
us against the example of the Pharisees, who for pretence
made long prayers, and commands us, when we pray, not
to use vain repetitions. But I cannot forget, on the other
hand, that He has given His own sanction to large and
long devotions, by continuing all night in prayer to God.
At all events we are not likely in this day to err on the
side of praying *too much*. Might it not rather be feared
that many believers in this generation pray *too little*? Is
not the actual amount of time that many Christians give
to prayer in the aggregate very small? I am afraid these
questions cannot be answered satisfactorily. I am afraid
the private devotions of many are most painfully scanty
and limited,—just enough to prove they are alive, and no
more. They really seem to want little from God. They
seem to have little to confess, little to ask for, and little to
thank Him for. Alas, this is altogether wrong! Nothing
is more common than to hear believers complaining that
they do not get on. They tell us that they do not grow
in grace, as they could desire. Is it not rather to be
suspected that many have quite as much grace as they ask
for? Is it not the true account of many, that they have
little, because they ask little? The cause of their weakness
is to be found in their own stunted, dwarfish, clipped,
contracted, hurried, little, narrow, diminutive prayers.
They have not because they ask not. Oh, reader, we are

not straitened in Christ, but in ourselves. The Lord says, "Open thy mouth wide, and I will fill it." But we are like the king of Israel who smote on the ground thrice and stayed, when he ought to have smitten five or six times. (Psalm lxxxi. 10; 2 Kings xiii. 18, 19.)

(*i*) I commend to you, in the next place, the importance of *particularity* in prayer. We ought not to be content with great general petitions. We ought to specify our wants before the throne of grace. It should not be enough to confess we are sinners. We should name the sins of which our conscience tells us we are most guilty. It should not be enough to ask for holiness. We should name the graces in which we feel most deficient. It should not be enough to tell the Lord we are in trouble. We should describe our trouble and all its peculiarities. This is what Jacob did, when he feared his brother Esau. He tells God exactly what it is that he fears. (Gen. xxxii. 11.) This is what Eliezer did, when he sought a wife for his master's son. He spreads before God precisely what he wants. (Gen. xxiv. 12.) This is what Paul did, when he had a thorn in the flesh. He besought the Lord. (2 Cor. xii. 8.) This is true faith and confidence. We should believe that nothing is too small to be named before God. What should we think of the patient who told his doctor he was ill, but never went into particulars? What should we think of the wife who told her husband she was unhappy, but did not specify the cause? What should we think of the child who told his father he was in trouble, but nothing more? Let us never forget that Christ is the true bridegroom of the soul,—the true physician of the heart,—the real father of all His people. Let us show that we feel this, by being unreserved in our communications with Him. Let us hide no secrets from Him. Let us tell Him all our hearts.

(*j*) I commend to you, in the next place, the importance of *intercession* in our prayers. We are all selfish by nature, and our selfishness is very apt to stick to us, even when we are converted. There is a tendency in us to think only of our own souls,—our own spiritual conflict,—our own progress in religion, and to forget others. Against this tendency we have all need to watch and strive, and not least in our prayers. We should study to be of a public spirit. We should stir ourselves up to name other names beside our own before the throne of grace. We should try to bear in our hearts the whole world,—the heathen,—the Jews,—the Roman Catholics,—the body of true believers,—the professing Protestant Churches,—the country in which we live,—the congregation to which we belong,—the household in which we sojourn,—the friends and relations we are connected with. For each and all of these we should plead. This is the highest charity. He loves me best who loves me in his prayers. This is for our soul's health. It enlarges our sympathies and expands our hearts. This is for the benefit of the Church. The wheels of all machinery for extending the Gospel are oiled by prayer. They do as much for the Lord's cause who intercede like Moses on the mount, as they do who fight like Joshua in the thick of the battle. This is to be like Christ. He bears the names of His people on His breast and shoulders as their High Priest before the Father. Oh, the privilege of being like Jesus! This is to be a true helper to ministers. If I must needs choose a congregation, give me a people that prays.

(*k*) I commend to you, in the next place, the importance of *thankfulness* in prayer. I know well that asking God is one thing, and praising God is another. But I see so close a connection between prayer and praise in the Bible, that I dare not call that true prayer in which thankfulness has no part. It is not for nothing that Paul says, "By prayer and supplication, with thanksgiving, let your request be made known unto God." (Phil. iv. 6.) "Continue in prayer, and watch in the same with thanksgiving."

(Coloss. iv. 2.) It is of mercy that we are not in hell. It is of mercy that we have the hope of heaven. It is of mercy that we live in a land of spiritual light. It is of mercy that we have been called by the Spirit, and not left to reap the fruit of our own ways. It is of mercy that we still live, and have opportunities of glorifying God actively or passively. Surely, these thoughts should crowd on our minds whenever we speak with God. Surely, we should never open our lips in prayer without blessing God for that free grace by which we live, and for that loving-kindness which endureth for ever. Never was there an eminent saint who was not full of thankfulness. St. Paul hardly ever writes an Epistle without beginning with thankfulness. Men like Whitfield in the last century, and Bickersteth, and Marsh, and Haldane Stewart, in our own time, were ever running over with thankfulness. Oh, if we would be bright and shining lights in our day, we must cherish a spirit of praise! And above all, let our prayers be thankful prayers.

(*l*) I commend to you, in the last place, the importance of *watchfulness over your prayers.* Prayer is that point of all others in religion at which you must be on your guard. Here it is that true religion begins: here it flourishes, and here it decays. Tell me what a man's prayers are, and I will soon tell you the state of his soul. Prayer is the spiritual pulse: by this the spiritual health may always be tested. Prayer is the spiritual weather-glass: by this we may always know whether it is fair or foul with our hearts. Oh, let us keep an eye continually upon our private devotions! Here is the pith, and marrow, and backbone of our practical Christianity. Sermons, and books, and tracts, and committee meetings, and the company of good men, are all good in their way; but they will never make up for the neglect of private prayer. Mark well the places, and society, and companions, that unhinge your hearts for communion with God, and make your prayers drive heavily. *There be on your guard.* Observe narrowly what friends and what employments leave your soul in the most spiritual frame, and most ready to speak with God. *To these cleave and stick fast.* If you will only take care of your prayers, I will engage that nothing shall go very wrong with your soul.

I offer these points for private consideration. I do it in all humility. I know no one who needs to be reminded of them more than I do myself. But I believe them to be God's own truth, and I should like myself and all I love to feel them more.

I want the times we live in to be praying times. I want the Christians of our day to be praying Christians. I want the Church of our age to be a praying Church. My heart's desire and prayer in sending forth this paper is to promote a spirit of prayerfulness. I want those who never prayed yet, to arise and call upon God; and I want those who do pray, to improve their prayers every year, and to see that they are not getting slack, and praying amiss.

V

BIBLE-READING

"Search the Scriptures."—John v. 39.
"How readest thou?"—Luke x. 26.

Next to praying there is nothing so important in practical religion as Bible-reading. God has mercifully given us a book which is "able to make us wise unto salvation through faith which is in Christ Jesus." (2 Tim. iii. 15.) By reading that book we may learn what to believe, what to be, and what to do; how to live with comfort, and how to die in peace. Happy is that man who possesses a Bible! Happier still is he who reads it! Happiest of all is he who not only reads it, but obeys it, and makes it the rule of his faith and practice!

Nevertheless it is a sorrowful fact that man has an unhappy skill in abusing God's gifts. His privileges, and power, and faculties, are all ingeniously perverted to other ends than those for which they were bestowed. His speech, his imagination, his intellect, his strength, his time, his influence, his money,—instead of being used as instruments for glorifying his Maker,—are generally wasted, or employed for his own selfish ends. And just as man naturally makes a bad use of his other mercies, so he does of the written Word. One sweeping charge may be brought against the whole of Christendom, and that charge is neglect and abuse of the Bible.

To prove this charge we have no need to look abroad:

the proof lies at our own doors. I have no doubt that
there are more Bibles in Great Britain at this moment
than there ever were since the world began. There is
more Bible buying and Bible selling,—more Bible printing
and Bible distributing,—than ever was since England was
a nation. We see Bibles in every bookseller's shop,—
Bibles of every size, price, and style,—Bibles great, and
Bibles small,—Bibles for the rich, and Bibles for the poor.
There are Bibles in almost every house in the land. But
all this time I fear we are in danger of forgetting, that to
have the Bible is one thing, and to *read* it quite another.

This neglected Book is the subject about which I
address the readers of this paper to-day. Surely it is no
light matter *what you are doing with the Bible*. Surely,
when the plague is abroad, you should search and see
whether the plague-spot is on you. Give me your attention
while I supply you with a few plain reasons why every one
who cares for his soul ought to value the Bible highly, to
study it regularly, and to make himself thoroughly
acquainted with its contents.

I. In the first place, *there is no book in existence
written in such a manner as the Bible.*

The Bible was "given by inspiration of God." (2 Tim.
iii. 16.) In this respect it is utterly unlike all other
writings. God taught the writers of it what to say. God
put into their minds thoughts and ideas. God guided
their pens in setting down those thoughts and ideas.
When you read it, you are not reading the self-taught
compositions of poor imperfect men like yourself, but the
words of the eternal God. When you hear it, you are not
listening to the erring opinions of short-lived mortals, but
to the unchanging mind of the King of kings. The men
who were employed to indite the Bible, spoke not of
themselves. They "spake as they were moved by the
Holy Ghost." (2 Peter i. 21.) All other books in the

world, however good and useful in their way, are more or less defective. The more you look at them the more you see their defects and blemishes. The Bible alone is absolutely perfect. From beginning to end it is " the Word of God."

I shall not waste time by attempting any long and laboured proof of this. I say boldly, that the Book itself is the best witness of its own inspiration. It is utterly inexplicable and unaccountable in any other point of view. It is the greatest standing miracle in the world. He that dares to say the Bible is not inspired, let him give a reasonable account of it, if he can. Let him explain the peculiar nature and character of the Book in a way that will satisfy any man of common sense. The burden of proof seems to my mind to lie on him.

It proves nothing against inspiration, as some have asserted, that the writers of the Bible have each a different style. Isaiah does not write like Jeremiah, and Paul does not write like John. This is perfectly true,— and yet the works of these men are not a whit less equally inspired. The waters of the sea have many different shades. In one place they look blue, and in another green. And yet the difference is owing to the depth or shallowness of the part we see, or to the nature of the bottom. The water in every case is the same salt sea.— The breath of a man may produce different sounds, according to the character of the instrument on which he plays. The flute, the pipe, and the trumpet, have each their peculiar note. And yet the breath that calls forth the notes, is in each case one and the same.—The light of the planets we see in heaven is very various. Mars, and Saturn, and Jupiter, have each a peculiar colour. And yet we know that the light of the sun, which each planet reflects, is in each case one and the same. Just in the same way the books of the Old and New Testaments are all inspired truth, and yet the aspect of that truth varies according to the mind through which the Holy Ghost makes it flow. The handwriting and style of the writers differ enough to prove that each had a distinct individual being; but the Divine Guide who dictates and directs the whole is always one. All is alike inspired. Every chapter, and verse, and word, is from God.

Oh, that men who are troubled with doubts, and questionings, and sceptical thoughts about inspiration, would calmly examine the Bible for themselves! Oh, that they would act on the advice which was the first step to Augustine's conversion,—"Take it up and read it!—take it up and read it!" How many Gordian knots this course of action would cut! How many difficulties and objections would vanish away at once like mist before the rising sun! How many would soon confess, "The finger of God is here! God is in this Book, and I knew it not."

This is the Book about which I address the readers of this paper. Surely it is no light matter *what you are doing with this Book*. It is no light thing that God should have caused this Book to be "written for your learning," and that you should have before you "the oracles of God." (Rom. iii. 2; xv. 4.) I charge you, I summon you to give an honest answer to my question. What art thou doing with the Bible?—Dost thou read it at all?—HOW READEST THOU?

II. In the second place, *there is no knowledge absolutely needful to a man's salvation, except a knowledge of the things which are to be found in the Bible.*

We live in days when the words of Daniel are fulfilled before our eyes:—"Many run to and fro, and knowledge is increased." (Dan. xii. 4.) Schools are multiplying on every side. New colleges are set up. Old Universities are reformed and improved. New books are continually coming forth. More is being taught,—more is being learned,—more is being read,—than there ever was since the world began.

It is all well. I rejoice at it. An ignorant population is a perilous and expensive burden to any nation. It is a ready prey to the first Absalom, or Catiline, or Wat Tyler, or Jack Cade, who may arise to entice it to do evil. But this I say,—we must never forget that all the education a man's head can receive, will not save his soul from hell, unless he knows the truths of the Bible.

A man *may have prodigious learning, and yet never be saved.* He may be master of half the languages spoken round the globe. He may be acquainted with the highest and deepest things in heaven and earth. He may have read books till he is like a walking cyclopædia. He may be familiar with the stars of heaven,—the birds of the air,—the beasts of the earth, and the fishes of the sea. He may be able, like Solomon, to "speak of trees, from the cedar of Lebanon to the hyssop that grows on the wall, of beasts also, and fowls, and creeping things, and fishes." (1 King iv. 33.) He may be able to discourse of all the secrets of fire, air, earth, and water. And yet, if he dies ignorant of Bible truths, he dies a miserable man! Chemistry never silenced a guilty conscience. Mathematics never healed a broken heart. All the sciences in the world never smoothed down a dying pillow. No earthly philosophy ever supplied hope in death. No natural theology ever gave peace in the prospect of meeting a holy God. All these things are of the earth, earthy, and can never raise a man above the earth's level. They may enable a man to strut and fret his little season here below with a more dignified gait than his fellow-mortals, but they can never give him wings, and enable him to soar towards heaven. He that has the largest share of them, will find at length that without Bible knowledge he has got no lasting possession. Death will make an end of all his attainments, and after death they will do him no good at all.

A man *may be a very ignorant man, and yet be saved.*

He may be unable to read a word, or write a letter. He may know nothing of geography beyond the bounds of his own parish, and be utterly unable to say which is nearest to England, Paris or New York. He may know nothing of arithmetic, and not see any difference between a million and a thousand. He may know nothing of history, not even of his own land, and be quite ignorant whether his country owes most to Semiramis, Boadicea, or Queen Elizabeth. He may know nothing of the affairs of his own times, and be incapable of telling you whether the Chancellor of the Exchequer, or the Commander-in-Chief, or the Archbishop of Canterbury is managing the national finances. He may know nothing of science, and its discoveries,—and whether Julius Cæsar won his victories with gunpowder, or the apostles had a printing press, or the sun goes round the earth, may be matters about which he has not an idea. And yet if that very man has heard Bible truth with his ears, and believed it with his heart, he knows enough to save his soul. He will be found at last with Lazarus in Abraham's bosom, while his scientific fellow-creature, who has died unconverted, is lost for ever.

There is much talk in these days about science and "useful knowledge." But after all a knowledge of the Bible is the one knowledge that is needful and eternally useful. A man may get to heaven without money, learning, health, or friends,—but without Bible knowledge he will never get there at all. A man may have the mightiest of minds, and a memory stored with all that mighty mind can grasp,—and yet, if he does not know the things of the Bible, he will make shipwreck of his soul for ever. Woe! woe! woe to the man who dies in ignorance of the Bible!

This is the Book about which I am addressing the readers of these pages to-day. It is no light matter *what you do with such a book.* It concerns the life of your soul. I summon you,—I charge you to give an honest answer to my question. What are you doing with the Bible? Do you read it? HOW READEST THOU?

III. In the third place, *no book in existence contains such important matter as the Bible.*

The time would fail me if I were to enter fully into all the great things which are to be found in the Bible, and only in the Bible. It is not by any sketch or outline that the treasures of the Bible can be displayed. It would be easy to fill this volume with a list of the peculiar truths it reveals, and yet the half of its riches would be left untold.

How glorious and soul-satisfying is the description it gives us of God's plan of salvation, and the way by which our sins can be forgiven! The coming into the world of Jesus Christ, the God-man, to save sinners,—the atonement He has made by suffering in our stead, the just for the unjust,—the complete payment He has made for our sins by His own blood,—the justification of every sinner who simply believes on Jesus,—the readiness of Father, Son, and Holy Ghost, to receive, pardon, and save to the uttermost,—how unspeakably grand and cheering are all these truths! We should know nothing of them without the Bible.

How comforting is the account it gives us of the great Mediator of the New Testament,—the man Christ Jesus! Four times over His picture is graciously drawn before our eyes. Four separate witnesses tell us of His miracles and His ministry,—His sayings and His doings,—His life and His death,—His power and His love,—His kindness and His patience,—His ways, His words, His works, His thoughts, His heart. Blessed be God, there is one thing in the Bible which the most prejudiced reader can hardly fail to understand, and that is the character of Jesus Christ!

How encouraging are the examples the Bible gives us of good people! It tells us of many who were of like passions with ourselves,—men and women who had cares,

crosses, families, temptations, afflictions, diseases, like
ourselves,—and yet " by faith and patience inherited the
promises," and got safe home. (Heb. vi. 12.) It keeps
back nothing in the history of these people. Their mistakes, their infirmities, their conflicts, their experience,
their prayers, their praises, their useful lives, their happy
deaths,—all are fully recorded. And it tells us the God
and Saviour of these men and women still waits to be
gracious, and is altogether unchanged.

How instructive are the examples the Bible gives us of
bad people! It tells us of men and women who had light,
and knowledge, and opportunities, like ourselves, and yet
hardened their hearts, loved the world, clung to their sins,
would have their own way, despised reproof, and ruined
their own souls for ever. And it warns us that the God
who punished Pharaoh, and Saul, and Ahab, and Jezebel,
and Judas, and Ananias and Sapphira, is a God who never
alters, and that there is a hell.

How precious are the promises which the Bible contains
for the use of those who love God! There is hardly any
possible emergency or condition for which it has not some
" word in season." And it tells men that God loves to be
put in remembrance of these promises, and that if He has
said He will do a thing, His promise shall certainly be
performed.

How blessed are the hopes which the Bible holds out to
the believer in Christ Jesus! Peace in the hour of death,
—rest and happiness on the other side of the grave,—a
glorious body in the morning of the resurrection,—a full
and triumphant acquittal in the day of judgment,—an
everlasting reward in the kingdom of Christ,—a joyful
meeting with the Lord's people in the day of gathering
together;—these, these are the future prospects of every
true Christian. They are all written in the book,—in the
book which is all true.

How striking is the light which the Bible throws on the

character of man! It teaches us what men may be expected to be and do in every position and station of life. It gives us the deepest insight into the secret springs and motives of human actions, and the ordinary course of events under the control of human agents. It is the true "discerner of the thoughts and intents of the heart." (Heb. iv. 12.) How deep is the wisdom contained in the books of Proverbs and Ecclesiastes! I can well understand an old divine saying, "Give me a candle and a Bible, and shut me up in a dark dungeon, and I will tell you all that the whole world is doing."

All these are things which men could find nowhere except in the Bible. We have probably not the least idea how little we should know about these things if we had not the Bible. We hardly know the value of the air we breathe, and the sun which shines on us, because we have never known what it is to be without them. We do not value the truths on which I have been just now dwelling, because we do not realize the darkness of men to whom these truths have not been revealed. Surely no tongue can fully tell the value of the treasures this one volume contains. Well might old John Newton say that some books were *copper* books in his estimation, some were *silver*, and some few were *gold* ;—but the Bible alone was like a book all made up of *bank notes*.

This is the Book about which I address the reader of this paper this day. Surely it is no light matter *what you are doing with the Bible*. It is no light matter in what way you are using this treasure. I charge you, I summon you to give an honest answer to my question,—What art thou doing with the Bible ?—Dost thou read it ?—HOW READEST THOU ?

IV. In the fourth place, *no book in existence has produced such wonderful effects on mankind at large as the Bible.*

(a) This is the Book whose doctrines turned the world upside down in the days of the Apostles.

Eighteen centuries have now passed away since God sent forth a few Jews from a remote corner of the earth, to do a work which according to man's judgment must have seemed impossible. He sent them forth at a time when the whole world was full of superstition, cruelty, lust, and sin. He sent them forth to proclaim that the established religions of the earth were false and useless, and must be forsaken. He sent them forth to persuade men to give up old habits and customs, and to live different lives. He sent them forth to do battle with the most grovelling idolatry, with the vilest and most disgusting immorality, with vested interests, with old associations, with a bigoted priesthood, with sneering philosophers, with an ignorant population, with bloody-minded emperors, with the whole influence of Rome. Never was there an enterprise to all appearance more Quixotic, and less likely to succeed!

And how did He arm them for this battle? He gave them no carnal weapons. He gave them no worldly power to compel assent, and no worldly riches to bribe belief. He simply put the Holy Ghost into their hearts, and the Scriptures into their hands. He simply bade them to expound and explain, to enforce and to publish the doctrines of the Bible. The preacher of Christianity in the first century was not a man with a sword and an army, to frighten people, like Mahomet,—or a man with a license to be sensual, to allure people, like the priests of the shameful idols of Hindostan. No! he was nothing more than one holy man with one holy book.

And how did these men of one book prosper? In a few generations they entirely changed the face of society by the doctrines of the Bible. They emptied the temples of the heathen gods. They famished idolatry, or left it high and dry like a stranded ship. They brought into the world a higher tone of morality between man and man. They raised the character and position of woman. They altered the standard of purity and decency. They put an end to many cruel and bloody customs, such as the gladiatorial fights.—There was no stopping the change. Persecution and opposition were useless. One victory after another was won. One bad thing after another melted away. Whether men liked it or not, they were insensibly affected by the movement of the new religion, and drawn within the whirlpool of its power. The earth shook, and their rotten refuges fell to the ground. The flood rose, and they found themselves obliged to rise with it. The tree of Christianity swelled and grew, and the chains they had cast round it to arrest its growth, snapped like tow. And all this was done by the doctrines of the Bible! Talk of victories indeed! What are the victories of Alexander, and Cæsar, and Marlborough, and Napoleon, and Wellington, compared with those I have just mentioned? For extent, for completeness, for results, for permanence, there are no victories like the victories of the Bible.

(b) This is the Book which turned Europe upside down in the days of the glorious Protestant Reformation.

No man can read the history of Christendom as it was five hundred years ago, and not see that darkness covered the whole professing Church of Christ, even a darkness that might be felt. So great was the change which had come over Christianity, that if an apostle had risen from the dead he would not have recognised it, and would have thought that heathenism had revived again. The doctrines of the Gospel lay buried under a dense mass of human traditions. Penances, and pilgrimages, and indulgences, relic-worship, and image-worship, and saint-worship, and worship of the Virgin Mary, formed the sum and substance of most people's religion. The Church was made an idol. The priests and ministers of the Church usurped the place of Christ. And by what means was all this miserable darkness cleared away ? By none so much as by bringing forth once more the Bible.

It was not merely the preaching of Luther and his friends, which established Protestantism in Germany. The grand lever which overthrew the Pope's power in that country, was Luther's translation of the Bible into the German tongue.—It was not merely the writings of Cranmer and the English Reformers which cast down popery in England. The seeds of the work thus carried forward were first sown by Wycliffe's translation of the Bible many years before.—It was not merely the quarrel of Henry VIII. and the Pope of Rome, which loosened the Pope's hold on English minds. It was the royal permission to have the Bible translated and set up in churches, so that every one who liked might read it. Yes ! it was the reading and circulation of Scripture which mainly established the cause of Protestantism in England, in Germany, and Switzerland. Without it the people would probably have returned to their former bondage when the first reformers died. But by the reading of the Bible the public mind became gradually leavened with the principles of true religion. Men's eyes became thoroughly open. Their spiritual understandings became thoroughly enlarged. The abominations of popery became distinctly visible. The excellence of the pure Gospel became a rooted idea in their hearts. It was then in vain for Popes to thunder forth excommunications. It was useless for Kings and Queens to attempt to stop the course of Protestantism by fire and sword. It was all too late. The people knew too much. They had seen the light. They had heard the joyful sound. They had tasted the truth. The sun had risen on their minds. The scales had fallen from their eyes. The Bible had done its appointed work within them, and that work was not to be overthrown. The people would not return to Egypt. The clock could not be put back again. A mental and moral revolution had been effected, and mainly effected by God's Word. Those are the true revolutions which the Bible effects. What are all the revolutions recorded by Vertot,—what are all the revolutions which France and England have gone through, compared to these? No revolutions are so bloodless, none so satisfactory, none so rich in lasting results, as the revolutions accomplished by the Bible!

This is the book on which the well-being of nations has always hinged, and with which the best interests of every nation in Christendom at this moment are inseparably bound up. Just in proportion as the Bible is honoured or not, light or darkness, morality or immorality, true religion or superstition, liberty or despotism, good laws or bad, will be found in a land. Come with me and open the pages of history, and you will read the proofs in time past. Read it in the history of Israel under the Kings. How great was the wickedness that then prevailed! But who can wonder? The law of the Lord had been completely lost sight of, and was found in the days of Josiah thrown aside in a corner of the temple. (2 Kings xxii. 8.)—Read it in the history of the Jews in our Lord Jesus Christ's time. How awful the picture of Scribes and Pharisees, and their religion! But who can wonder? The Scripture was "made of none effect by man's traditions." (Matt. xv. 6.)—Read it in the history of the Church of Christ in the middle ages. What can be worse than the accounts we have of its ignorance and superstition? But who can wonder? The times might well be dark, when men had not the light of the Bible.

This is the Book to which the civilized world is indebted for many of its best and most praise-worthy institutions. Few probably are aware how many are the good things that men have adopted for the public benefit, of which the origin may be clearly traced up to the Bible. It has left lasting marks wherever it has been received. From

the Bible are drawn many of the best laws by which
society is kept in order. From the Bible has been obtained the standard of morality about truth, honesty, and
the relations of man and wife, which prevails among
Christian nations, and which,—however feebly respected
in many cases,—makes so great a difference between
Christians and heathen. To the Bible we are indebted
for that most merciful provision for the poor man, the
Sabbath day. To the influence of the Bible we owe nearly
every humane and charitable institution in existence.
The sick, the poor, the aged, the orphan, the lunatic, the
idiot, the blind, were seldom or never thought of before
the Bible leavened the world. You may search in vain
for any record of institutions for their aid in the histories of
Athens or of Rome. Alas! there are many who sneer at the
Bible, and say the world would get on well enough without
it, who little think how great are their own obligations to
the Bible. Little does the infidel workman think, as he lies
sick in some of our great hospitals, that he owes all his
present comforts to the very book he affects to despise.
Had it not been for the Bible, he might have died in
misery, uncared for, unnoticed and alone. Verily the
world we live in is fearfully unconscious of its debts. The
last day alone, I believe, will tell the full amount of
benefit conferred upon it by the Bible.

This wonderful book is the subject about which I
address the reader of this paper this day. Surely it is no
light matter *what you are doing with the Bible*. The
swords of conquering Generals,—the ship in which Nelson
led the fleets of England to victory,—the hydraulic press
which raised the tubular bridge at the Menai;—each and
all of these are objects of interest as instruments of
mighty power. The Book I speak of this day is an
instrument a thousand-fold mightier still. Surely it is no
light matter whether you are paying it the attention it
deserves. I charge you, I summon you to give me an

honest answer this day,—What art thou doing with the Bible? Dost thou read it? HOW READEST THOU?

V. In the fifth place, *no book in existence can do so much for every one who reads it rightly as the Bible.*

The Bible does not profess to teach the wisdom of this world. It was not written to explain geology or astronomy. It will neither instruct you in mathematics, nor in natural philosophy. It will not make you a doctor, or a lawyer, or an engineer.

But there is another world to be thought of, beside that world in which man now lives. There are other ends for which man was created, beside making money and working. There are other interests which he is meant to attend to, beside those of his body, and those interests are the interests of his soul. It is the interests of the immortal soul which the Bible is especially able to promote. If you would know law, you may study Blackstone or Sugden. If you would know astronomy or geology, you may study Herschel and Lyell. But if you would know how to have your soul saved, you must study the written Word of God.

The Bible is "*able to make a man wise unto salvation, through faith which is in Christ Jesus.*" (2 Tim. iii. 15.) It can show you the way which leads to heaven. It can teach you everything you need to know, point out everything you need to believe, and explain everything you need to do. It can show you what you are,—*a sinner*. It can show you what God is,—perfectly *holy*. It can show you the great giver of pardon, peace, and grace,—*Jesus Christ.* I have read of an Englishman who visited Scotland in the days of Blair, Rutherford, and Dickson, three famous preachers,—and heard all three in succession. He said that the first showed him the majesty of God,—the second showed him the beauty of Christ,—and the third showed him all his heart. It is the glory and beauty of the Bible that it is always teaching these three things more or less, from the first chapter of it to the last.

The Bible applied to the heart by the Holy Ghost, is *the grand instrument by which souls are first converted to God.* That mighty change is **generally** begun by some text or doctrine of the Word, brought home to a man's conscience. In this way the Bible has worked moral miracles by thousands. It has made drunkards become sober,—unchaste people become pure,—thieves become honest,—and violent-tempered people become meek. It has wholly altered the course of men's lives. It has caused their old things to pass away, and made all their ways new. It has taught worldly people to seek first the kingdom of God. It has taught lovers of pleasure to become lovers of God. It has taught the stream of men's affections to run upwards instead of running downwards. It has made men think of heaven, instead of always thinking of earth, and live by faith, instead of living by sight. All this it has done in every part of the world. All this it is doing still. What are the Romish miracles which weak men believe, compared to all this, even if they were true? Those are the truly great miracles which are yearly worked by the Word.

The Bible applied to the heart by the Holy Ghost, is *the chief means by which men are built up and stablished in the faith,* after their conversion. It is able to cleanse them, to sanctify them, to instruct them in righteousness, and to furnish them thoroughly for all good works. (Psalm cxix. 9; John xvii. 17; 2 Tim. iii. 16, 17.) The Spirit ordinarily does these things by the written Word; sometimes by the Word read, and sometimes by the Word preached, but seldom, if ever, without the Word. The Bible can show a believer how to walk in this world so as to please God. It can teach him how to glorify Christ in all the relations of life, and can make him a good master, servant, subject, husband, father, or son. It can enable him to bear afflictions and privations without murmuring, and say, "It is well." It can enable him to look down into the grave, and say, "I fear no evil." (Psalm xxiii. 4.) It can enable him to think on judgment and eternity, and not feel afraid. It can enable him to bear persecution without flinching, and to give up liberty and life rather than deny Christ's truth. Is he drowsy in soul? It can awaken him.—Is he mourning? It can comfort him.— Is he erring? It can restore him.—Is he weak? It can make him strong.—Is he in company? It can keep him from evil.—Is he alone? It can talk with him.—(Prov. vi. 22.) All this the Bible can do for all believers,—for the least as well as the greatest,—for the richest as well as the poorest. It has done it for thousands already, and is doing it for thousands every day.

The man who has the Bible, and the Holy Spirit in his heart, has everything which is absolutely needful to make him spiritually wise. He needs no priest to break the bread of life for him. He needs no ancient traditions, no writings of the Fathers, no voice of the Church, to guide him into all truth. He has the well of truth open before him, and what can he want more? Yes! though he be shut up alone in a prison, or cast on a desert island,— though he never see a church, or minister, or sacrament again,—if he has but the Bible, he has got the infallible guide, and wants no other. If he has but the will to read that Bible rightly, it will certainly teach him the road that leads to heaven. It is here alone that infallibility resides. It is not in the Church. It is not in the Councils. It is not in ministers. It is only in the written Word.

(a) I know well that many say they have found no saving power in the Bible. They tell us they have tried to read it, and have learned nothing from it. They can see in it nothing but hard and deep things. They ask us what we mean by talking of its power.

I answer, that the Bible no doubt contains hard things, or else it would not be the book of God. It contains things hard to comprehend, but only hard because we have not grasp of mind to comprehend them. It contains things above our reasoning powers, but nothing that might not be explained if the eyes of our understanding were not feeble and dim. But is not an acknowledgment of our own ignorance the very corner-stone and foundation of all knowledge? Must not many things be taken for granted in the beginning of every science, before we can proceed one step towards acquaintance with it? Do we not require our children to learn many things of which they cannot see the meaning at first? And ought we not then to expect to find "deep things" when we begin studying the Word of God, and yet to believe that if we persevere in reading it the meaning of many of them will one day be made clear? No doubt we ought so to expect, and so to believe. We must read with humility. We must take much on trust. We must believe that what we know not now, we shall know hereafter,—some part in this world, and all in the world to come.

But I ask that man who has given up reading the Bible because it contains hard things, whether he did not find many things in it easy and plain? I put it to his conscience whether he did not see great landmarks and principles in it all the way through? I ask him whether the things needful to salvation did not stand out boldly before his eyes, like the light-houses on English headlands from the Land's-end to the mouth of the Thames. What should we think of the captain of a steamer who brought up at night in the entrance of the Channel, on the plea that he did not know every parish, and village, and creek, along the British coast? Should we not think him a lazy coward, when the lights on the Lizard, and Eddystone, and the Start, and Portland, and St. Catherine's, and Beachy Head, and Dungeness, and the Forelands, were shining forth like so many lamps, to guide him up to the river? Should we not say, Why did you not steer by the great leading lights? And what ought we to say to the man who gives up reading the Bible because it contains hard things, when his own state, and the path to heaven, and the way to serve God, are all written down clearly and unmistakably, as with a sunbeam? Surely we ought to tell that man that his objections are no better than lazy excuses, and do not deserve to be heard.

(b) I know well that many raise the objection, that thousands read the Bible and are not a whit the better for their reading. And they ask us, when this is the case, what becomes of the Bible's boasted power?

I answer, that the reason why so many read the Bible without benefit is plain and simple;—they do not read it in the right way. There is generally a right way and a wrong way of doing everything in the world; and just as it is with other things, so it is in the matter of reading the Bible. The Bible is not so entirely different from all other books as to make it of no importance in what spirit and manner you read it. It does not do good, as a matter of course, by merely running our eyes over the print, any more than the sacraments do good by mere virtue of our receiving them. It does not ordinarily do good, unless it is read with humility and earnest prayer. The best steam-engine that was ever built is useless if a man does not know how to work it. The best sun-dial that was ever constructed will not tell its owner the time of day if he is so ignorant as to put it up in the shade. Just as it is with that steam-engine, and that sun-dial, so it is with the Bible. When men read it without profit, *the fault is not in the Book, but in themselves.*

I tell the man who doubts the power of the Bible, because many read it, and are no better for the reading, that the abuse of a thing is no argument against the use of it. I tell him boldly, that never did man or woman

read that book in a childlike persevering spirit,—like the
Ethiopian eunuch, and the Bereans (Acts viii. 28; xvii. 11),
—and miss the way to heaven. Yes, many a broken
cistern will be exposed to shame in the day of judgment;
but there will not rise up one soul who will be able to
say, that he went thirsting to the Bible, and found in it no
living water,—he searched for truth in the Scriptures, and
searching, did not find it. The words which are spoken of
Wisdom in the Proverbs are strictly true of the Bible: "If
thou criest after knowledge, and liftest up thy voice for
understanding; if thou seekest her as silver, and searchest
for her as for hid treasures; then shalt thou understand
the fear of the Lord, and find the knowledge of God."
(Prov. ii. 3, 4, 5.)

This wonderful Book is the subject about which I
address the readers of this paper this day. Surely it is no
light matter *what you are doing with the Bible.* What
should you think of the man who in time of cholera
despised a sure receipt for preserving the health of his
body? What must be thought of you if you despise the
only sure receipt for the everlasting health of your soul?
I charge you, I entreat you, to give an honest answer to
my question. What dost thou do with the Bible?—Dost
thou read it?—HOW READEST THOU?

VI. In the sixth place, *the Bible is the only rule
by which all questions of doctrine or of duty can be
tried.*

The Lord God knows the weakness and infirmity of our
poor fallen understandings. He knows that, even after
conversion, our perceptions of right and wrong are
exceedingly indistinct. He knows how artfully Satan can
gild error with an appearance of truth, and can dress up
wrong with plausible arguments, till it looks like right.
Knowing all this, He has mercifully provided us with an
unerring standard of truth and error, right and wrong,

and has taken care to make that standard a written book, —even the Scripture.

No one can look round the world, and not see the wisdom of such a provision. No one can live long, and not find out that he is constantly in need of a counsellor and adviser,—of a rule of faith and practice, on which he can depend. Unless he lives like a beast, without a soul and conscience, he will find himself constantly assailed by difficult and puzzling questions. He will be often asking himself, What must I believe? and what must I do?

(a) The world is full of difficulties about points of *doctrine*. The house of error lies close alongside the house of truth. The door of one is so like the door of the other that there is continual risk of mistakes.

Does a man read or travel much? He will soon find the most opposite opinions prevailing among those who are called Christians. He will discover that different persons give the most different answers to the important question, What shall I do to be saved? The Roman Catholic and the Protestant,—the Neologian and the Tractarian,—the Mormonite and the Swedenborgian,—each and all will assert that he alone has the truth. Each and all will tell him that safety is only to be found in his party. Each and all say, "Come with us." All this is puzzling. What shall a man do?

Does he settle down quietly in some English or Scotch parish? He will soon find that even in our own land the most conflicting views are held. He will soon discover that there are serious differences among Christians as to the comparative importance of the various parts and articles of the faith. One man thinks of nothing but Church government,—another of nothing but sacraments, services, and forms,—a third of nothing but preaching the Gospel. Does he apply to ministers for a solution? He will perhaps find one minister teaching one doctrine, and another another. All this is puzzling. What shall a man do?

There is only one answer to this question. A man must make the Bible alone his rule. He must receive nothing and believe nothing, which is not according to the Word. He must try all religious teaching by one simple test,— Does it square with the Bible? What saith the Scripture?

I would to God the eyes of the laity of this country were more open on this subject. I would to God they would learn to weigh sermons, books, opinions, and ministers, in the scales of the Bible, and to value all according to their conformity to the Word. I would to God they would see that it matters little who says a thing,— whether he be Father or Reformer,—Bishop or Archbishop, —Priest or Deacon,—Archdeacon or Dean. The only question is,—Is the thing said Scriptural? If it is, it ought to be received and believed. If it is not, it ought to be refused and cast aside. I fear the consequences of that servile acceptance of everything which " the parson " says, which is so common among many English laymen. I fear lest they be led they know not whither, like the blinded Syrians, and awake some day to find themselves in the power of Rome. (2 Kings vi. 20.) Oh, that men in England would only remember for what purpose the Bible was given them!

I tell English laymen that it is nonsense to say, as some do, that it is presumptuous to judge a minister's teaching by the Word. When one doctrine is proclaimed in one parish, and another in another, people must read and judge for themselves. Both doctrines cannot be right, and both ought to be tried by the Word. I charge them, above all things, never to suppose that any true minister of the Gospel will dislike his people measuring all he teaches by the Bible. On the contrary, the more they read the Bible, and prove all he says by the Bible, the better he will be pleased. A false minister may say, " You have no right to use your private judgment : leave the Bible to us who are ordained." A true minister will say, "Search the Scriptures, and if I do not teach you what is Scriptural, do not believe me." A false minister may cry, "Hear the Church," and "Hear me." A true minister will say, "Hear the Word of God."

(b) But the world is not only full of difficulties about points of doctrine; it is equally full of difficulties about points of *practice*. Every professing Christian, who wishes to act conscientiously, must know that it is so. The most puzzling questions are continually arising. He is tried on every side by doubts as to the line of duty, and can often hardly see what is the right thing to do.

He is tried by questions connected with the management of his *worldly calling*, if he is in business or in trade. He sometimes sees things going on of a very doubtful character,—things that can hardly be called fair, straightforward, truthful, and doing as you would be done by. But then everybody in the trade does these things. They have always been done in the most respectable houses. There would be no carrying on a profitable business if they were not done. They are not things distinctly named and prohibited by God. All this is very puzzling. What is a man to do?

He is tried by questions about *worldly amusements*. Races, and balls, and operas, and theatres, and card parties, are all very doubtful methods of spending time. But then he sees numbers of great people taking part in them. Are all these people wrong? Can there really be such mighty harm in these things? All this is very puzzling. What is a man to do?

He is tried by questions about the *education of his children*. He wishes to train them up morally and religiously, and to remember their souls. But he is told by many sensible people, that young persons will be young, —that it does not do to check and restrain them too much, and that he ought to attend pantomimes and children's parties, and give children's balls himself. He is informed that this nobleman, or that lady of rank, always does so, and yet they are reckoned religious people. Surely it cannot be wrong. All this is very puzzling. What is he to do?

There is only one answer to all these questions. A man must make the Bible his rule of conduct. He must make its leading principles the compass by which he steers his course through life. By the letter or spirit of the Bible he must test every difficult point and question. *"To the law and to the testimony! What saith the Scripture?"* He ought to care nothing for what other people may think right. He ought not to set his watch by the clock of his neighbour, but by the sun-dial of the Word.

I charge my readers solemnly to act on the maxim I have just laid down, and to adhere to it rigidly all the days of their lives. You will never repent of it. Make it a leading principle never to act contrary to the Word. Care not for the charge of over-strictness, and needless precision. Remember you serve a strict and holy God. Listen not to the common objection, that the rule you have laid down is impossible, and cannot be observed in such a world as this. Let those who make such an objection speak out plainly, and tell us for what purpose the Bible was given to man. Let them remember that by the Bible we shall all be judged at the last day, and let them learn to judge themselves by it here, lest they be judged and condemned by it hereafter.

This mighty rule of faith and practice is the book about which I am addressing the readers of this paper this day. Surely it is no light matter *what you are doing with the Bible.* Surely when danger is abroad on the right hand and on the left, you should consider what you are doing with the safe-guard which God has provided. I charge you, I beseech you, to give an honest answer to my question. What art thou doing with the Bible?—Dost thou read it? HOW READEST THOU?

VII. In the seventh place, *the Bible is the book which all true servants of God have always lived on and loved.*

Every living thing which God creates requires food. The life that God imparts needs sustaining and nourishing. It is so with animal and vegetable life,—with birds, beasts, fishes, reptiles, insects, and plants. It is equally so with spiritual life. When the Holy Ghost raises a man from the death of sin and makes him a new creature in Christ Jesus, the new principle in that man's heart requires food, and the only food which will sustain it is the Word of God.

There never was a man or woman truly converted, from one end of the world to the other, who did not love the revealed will of God. Just as a child born into the world desires naturally the milk provided for its nourishment, so does a soul "born again" desire the sincere milk of the Word. This is a common mark of all the children of God —they "delight in the law of the Lord." (Psalm. i. 2.)

Show me a person who despises Bible reading, or thinks little of Bible preaching, and I hold it to be a certain fact that he is not yet "born again." He may be zealous about forms and ceremonies. He may be diligent in attending sacraments and daily services. But if these things are more precious to him than the Bible, I cannot think he is a converted man. Tell me what the Bible is to a man, and I will generally tell you what he is. This is the pulse to try,—this is the barometer to look at,—if we would know the state of the heart. I have no notion of the Spirit dwelling in a man and not giving clear evidence of His presence. And I believe it to be a signal evidence of the Spirit's presence when the Word is really precious to a man's soul.

Love to the Word is one of the characteristics we see in Job. Little as we know of this Patriarch and his age, this at least stands out clearly. He says, "I have esteemed the words of His mouth more than my necessary food." (Job xxiii. 12.)

Love to the Word is a shining feature in the character of David. Mark how it appears all through that wonderful part of Scripture, the cxixth Psalm. He might well say, "Oh, how I love thy law!" (Psalm cxix. 97.)

Love to the Word is a striking point in the character of St. Paul. What were he and his companions but men "mighty in the Scriptures?" What were his sermons but expositions and applications of the Word?

Love to the Word appears pre-eminently in our Lord and Saviour Jesus Christ. He read it publicly. He quoted it continually. He expounded it frequently. He advised the Jews to "search" it. He used it as His weapon to resist the devil. He said repeatedly, "The Scripture must be fulfilled."—Almost the last thing He did was to "open the understanding of His disciples, that they might understand the Scriptures." (Luke xxiv. 45.) I am afraid that man can be no true servant of Christ, who has not something of his Master's mind and feeling towards the Bible.

Love to the Word has been a prominent feature in the history of all the saints, of whom we know anything, since the days of the Apostles. This is the lamp which Athanasius and Chrysostom and Augustine followed. This is the compass which kept the Vallenses and Albigenses from making shipwreck of the faith. This is the well which was re-opened by Wycliffe and Luther, after it had been long stopped up. This is the sword with which Latimer, and Jewell, and Knox won their victories. This is the manna which fed Baxter and Owen, and the noble host of the Puritans, and made them strong to battle. This is the armoury from which Whitefield and Wesley drew their powerful weapons. This is the mine from which Bickersteth and M'Cheyne brought forth rich gold. Differing as these holy men did in some matters, on one point they were all agreed,—they all delighted in the Word.

Love to the Word is one of the first things that appears in the converted heathen, at the various Missionary stations throughout the world. In hot climates and in cold,—among savage people and among civilized,—in New Zealand, in the South Sea Islands, in Africa, in Hindostan,—it is always the same. They enjoy hearing it read. They long to be able to read it themselves. They wonder why Christians did not send it to them before. How striking is the picture which Moffat draws of Africaner, the fierce South African chieftain, when first brought under the power of the Gospel! "Often have I seen him," he says, "under the shadow of a great rock nearly the live-long day, eagerly perusing the pages of the Bible."—How touching is the expression of a poor converted Negro, speaking of the Bible! He said, "It is never old and never cold."—How affecting was the language of another old negro, when some would have dissuaded him from learning to read, because of his great age. "No!" he said, "I will never give it up till I die. It is worth all the labour to be able to read that one verse, 'God so loved the world, that he gave his only begotten Son, that whosoever believeth in him should not perish, but have eternal life.'"

Love to the Bible is one of the grand points of agreement among all converted men and women in our own land. Episcopalians and Presbyterians, Baptists and Independents, Methodists and Plymouth Brethren,—all unite in honouring the Bible, as soon as they are real Christians. This is the manna which all the tribes of our Israel feed upon, and find satisfying food. This is the fountain round which all the various portions of Christ's flock meet together, and from which no sheep goes thirsty away. Oh, that believers in this country would learn to cleave more closely to the written Word! Oh, that they would see that the more the Bible, and the Bible only, is the substance of men's religion, the more they agree! It is probable there never was an uninspired book more universally admired than Bunyan's Pilgrim's Progress. It is a book which all denominations of Christians delight to honour. It has won praise from all parties. Now what a striking fact it is, that the author was pre-eminently a man of one book! He had read hardly anything but the Bible.

It is a blessed thought that there will be "much people" in heaven at last. Few as the Lord's people undoubtedly are at any one given time or place, yet all gathered together at last, they will be "a multitude that no man can number." (Rev. vii. 9; xix. 1.) They will be of one heart and mind. They will have passed through like experience. They will all have repented, believed, lived holy, prayerful, and humble. They will all have washed their robes and made them white in the blood of the Lamb. But one thing beside all this they will have in common: they will all love the texts and doctrines of the Bible. The Bible will have been their food and delight in the days of their pilgrimage on earth. And the Bible will be a common subject of joyful meditation and retrospect, when they are gathered together in heaven.

This Book, which all true Christians live upon and love, is the subject about which I am addressing the readers of this paper this day. Surely it is no light matter *what you are doing with the Bible*. Surely it is matter for serious inquiry, whether you know anything of this love to the Word, and have this mark of walking "in the footsteps of the flock." (Cant. i. 8.) I charge you, I entreat you to give me an honest answer. What art thou doing with the Bible?—Dost thou read it?—HOW READEST THOU?

VIII. In the last place, *the Bible is the only book which can comfort a man in the last hours of his life.*

Death is an event which in all probability is before us all. There is no avoiding it. It is the river which each of us must cross. I who write, and you who read, have each one day to die. It is good to remember this. We are all sadly apt to put away the subject from us. "Each man thinks each man mortal but himself." I want every one to do his duty in life, but I also want every one to think of death. I want every one to know how to live, but I also want every one to know how to die.

Death is a solemn event to all. It is the winding up of all earthly plans and expectations. It is a separation from all we have loved and lived with. It is often accompanied by much bodily pain and distress. It brings us to the grave, the worm, and corruption. It opens the door to judgment and eternity,—to heaven or to hell. It is an event after which there is no change, or space for repentance. Other mistakes may be corrected or retrieved, but not a mistake on our death-beds. As the tree falls, there it must lie. No conversion in the coffin! No new birth after we have ceased to breathe! And death is before us all. It may be close at hand. The time of our departure is quite uncertain. But sooner or later we must each lie down alone and die. All these are serious considerations.

Death is a solemn event even to the believer in Christ. For him no doubt the "sting of death" is taken away. (1 Cor. xv. 55.) Death has become one of his privileges, for he is Christ's. Living or dying, he is the Lord's. If he lives, Christ lives in him; and if he dies, he goes to live with Christ. To him "to live is Christ, and to die is gain." (Phil. i. 21.) Death frees him from many trials,—from a weak body, a corrupt heart, a tempting devil, and an ensnaring or persecuting world. Death admits him to the enjoyment of many blessings. He rests from his labours:—the hope of a joyful resurrection is changed into a certainty:—he has the company of holy redeemed spirits:—he is "with Christ." All this is true,—and yet, even to a believer, death is a solemn thing. Flesh and blood naturally shrink from it. To part from all we love, is a wrench and trial to the feelings. The world we go to is a world unknown, even though it is our home. Friendly and harmless as death is to a believer, it is not an event to be treated lightly. It always must be a very solemn thing.

It becomes every thoughtful and sensible man to consider calmly how he is going to meet death. Gird up your loins, like a man, and look the subject in the face. Listen to me, while I tell you a few things about the end to which we are coming.

The good things of the world cannot comfort a man when he draws near death. All the gold of California and Australia will not provide light for the dark valley. Money can buy the best medical advice and attendance for a man's body; but money cannot buy peace for his conscience, heart, and soul.

Relatives, loved friends, and servants, cannot comfort a man when he draws near death. They may minister affectionately to his bodily wants. They may watch by his bed-side tenderly, and anticipate his every wish. They may smooth down his dying pillow, and support his sinking frame in their arms. But they cannot "minister to a mind diseased." They cannot stop the achings of a troubled heart. They cannot screen an uneasy conscience from the eye of God.

The pleasures of the world cannot comfort a man when he draws near death. The brilliant ball-room,—the merry dance,—the midnight revel,—the party to Epsom races,— the card table,—the box at the opera,—the voices of singing men and singing women,—all these are at length distasteful things. To hear of hunting and shooting engagements gives him no pleasure. To be invited to feasts, and regattas, and fancy-fairs, gives him no ease. He cannot hide from himself that these are hollow, empty, powerless things. They jar upon the ear of his conscience. They are out of harmony with his condition. They cannot stop one gap in his heart, when the last enemy is coming in like a flood. They cannot make him calm in the prospect of meeting a holy God.

Books and newspapers cannot comfort a man when he draws near death. The most brilliant writings of Macaulay or Dickens will pall on his ear. The most able article in the Times will fail to interest him. The Edinburgh and Quarterly Reviews will give him no pleasure. Punch and the Illustrated News, and the last new novel, will lie unopened and unheeded. Their time will be past. Their vocation will be gone. Whatever they may be in health, they are useless in the hour of death.

There is but one fountain of comfort for a man drawing near to his end, and that is the Bible. Chapters out of the Bible,—texts out of the Bible,—statements of truth taken out of the Bible,—books containing matter drawn from the Bible,—these are a man's only chance of comfort when he comes to die. I do not at all say that the Bible will do good, as a matter of course, to a dying man, if he has not valued it before. I know, unhappily, too much of death-beds to say that. I do not say whether it is probable that he who has been unbelieving and neglectful of the Bible in life, will at once believe and get comfort from it in death. But I do say positively, that no dying man will ever get real comfort, except from the contents of the Word of God. All comfort from any other source is a house built upon sand.

I lay this down as a rule of universal application. I make no exception in favour of any class on earth. Kings and poor men, learned and unlearned,—all are on a level in this matter. There is not a jot of real consolation for any dying man, unless he gets it from the Bible. Chapters, passages, texts, promises, and doctrines of Scripture,— heard, received, believed, and rested on,—these are the only comforters I dare promise to any one, when he leaves the world. Taking the sacrament will do a man no more good than the Popish extreme unction, so long as the

Word is not received and believed. Priestly absolution will no more ease the conscience than the incantations of a heathen magician, if the poor dying sinner does not receive and believe Bible truth. I tell every one who reads this paper, that although men may seem to get on comfortably without the Bible while they live, they may be sure that without the Bible they cannot comfortably die. It was a true confession of the learned Selden,— "There is no book upon which we can rest in a dying moment but the Bible."

I might easily confirm all I have just said, by examples and illustrations. I might show you the death-beds of men who have affected to despise the Bible. I might tell you how Voltaire and Paine, the famous infidels, died in misery, bitterness, rage, fear, and despair. I might show you the happy death-beds of those who have loved the Bible and believed it, and the blessed effect the sight of their death-beds had on others. Cecil,—a minister whose praise ought to be in all churches,—says, "I shall never forget standing by the bed-side of my dying mother. 'Are you afraid to die?' I asked.—'No!' she replied.—'But why does the uncertainty of another state give you no concern?'—'Because God has said, Fear not; when thou passest through the waters I will be with thee, and through the rivers, they shall not overflow thee.'" (Isa. xliii. 2.) I might easily multiply illustrations of this kind. But I think it better to conclude this part of my subject by giving the result of my own observations as a minister.

I have seen not a few dying persons in my time. I have seen great varieties of manner and deportment among them. I have seen some die sullen, silent, and comfortless. I have seen others die ignorant, unconcerned, and apparently without much fear. I have seen some die so wearied out with long illness that they were quite willing to depart, and yet they did not seem to me at all in a fit state to go before God. I have seen others die with professions of hope and trust in God, without leaving satisfactory evidences that they were on the rock. I have seen others die who, I believe, were "in Christ," and safe, and yet they never seemed to enjoy much sensible comfort. I have seen some few dying in the full assurance of hope, and like Bunyan's "Standfast," giving glorious testimony to Christ's faithfulness, even in the river. But one thing I have never seen. I never saw any one enjoy what I should call real, solid, calm, reasonable peace on his death-bed, who did not draw his peace from the Bible. And this I am bold to say, that the man who thinks to go to his death-bed without having the Bible for his comforter, his companion, and his friend, is one of the greatest mad-men in the world. There are no comforts for the soul but Bible comforts, and he who has not got hold of these, has got hold of nothing at all, unless it be a broken reed.

The only comforter for a death-bed is the book about which I address the readers of this paper this day. Surely it is no light matter whether you read that book or not. Surely a dying man, in a dying world, should seriously consider whether he has got anything to comfort him when his turn comes to die. I charge you, I entreat you, for the last time, to give an honest answer to my question. What art thou doing with the Bible?—Dost thou read it? —HOW READEST THOU?

I have now given the reasons why I press on every reader the duty and importance of reading the Bible. I have shown that no book is written in such a manner as the Bible,—that knowledge of the Bible is absolutely necessary to salvation,—that no book contains such matter, —that no book has done so much for the world generally, —that no book can do so much for every one who reads it aright,—that this book is the only rule of faith and practice,—that it is, and always has been, the food of all true servants of God,—and that it is the only book which can comfort men when they die. All these are ancient things. I do not pretend to tell anything new. I have only gathered together old truths, and tried to mould them into a new shape. Let me finish all by addressing a few plain words to the conscience of every class of readers.

(1) This paper may fall into the hands of some who *can read, but never do read the Bible at all.* Are you one of them? If you are, I have something to say to you.

I cannot comfort you in your present state of mind. It would be mockery and deceit to do so. I cannot speak to you of peace and heaven, while you treat the Bible as you do. You are in danger of losing your soul.

You are in danger, because *your neglected Bible is a plain evidence that you do not love God.* The health of a man's body may generally be known by his appetite. The health of a man's soul may be known by his treatment of the Bible. Now you are manifestly labouring under a sore disease. Will you not repent?

I know I cannot reach your heart. I cannot make you see and feel these things. I can only enter my solemn protest against your present treatment of the Bible, and lay that protest before your conscience. I do so with all my soul. Oh, beware lest you repent too late! Beware lest you put off reading the Bible till you send for the doctor in your last illness, and then find the Bible a sealed book, and dark, as the cloud between the hosts of Israel and Egypt, to your anxious soul! Beware lest you go on saying all your life, "Men do very well without all this Bible-reading," and find at length, to your cost, that men do very ill, and end in hell! Beware lest the day come when you will feel, "Had I but honoured the Bible as much as I have honoured the newspaper, I should not have been left without comfort in my last hours!" Bible-neglecting reader, I give you a plain warning. The plague-cross is at present on your door. The Lord have mercy upon your soul!

(2) This paper may fall into the hands of some one who is *willing to begin reading the Bible, but wants advice* on the subject. Are you that man ? Listen to me, and I will give a few short hints.

(*a*) For one thing, *begin reading your Bible this very day.* The way to do a thing is to do it, and the way to read the Bible is actually to read it. It is not meaning, or wishing, or resolving, or intending, or thinking about it, which will advance you one step. You must positively read. There is no royal road in this matter, any more than in the matter of prayer. If you cannot read yourself, you must persuade somebody else to read to you. But one way or another, through eyes or ears, the words of Scripture must actually pass before your mind.

(*b*) For another thing, *read the Bible with an earnest desire to understand it.* Think not for a moment that the great object is to turn over a certain quantity of printed paper, and that it matters nothing whether you understand it or not. Some ignorant people seem to fancy that all is done if they clear off so many chapters every day, though they may not have a notion what they are all about, and only know that they have pushed on their mark so many leaves. This is turning Bible reading into a mere form. It is almost as bad as the Popish habit of buying indulgences, by saying an almost fabulous number of ave-marias and paternosters. It reminds one of the poor Hottentot who ate up a Dutch hymn-book because he saw it comforted his neighbours' hearts. Settle it down in your mind as a general principle, that a Bible not understood is a Bible that does no good. Say to yourself often as you read, "What is all this about ?" Dig for the meaning like a man digging for Australian gold. Work hard, and do not give up the work in a hurry.

(*c*) For another thing, *read the Bible with child-like faith and humility.* Open your heart as you open your book, and say, "Speak, Lord, for thy servant heareth." Resolve to believe implicitly whatever you find there, however much it may run counter to your own prejudices. Resolve to receive heartily every statement of truth, whether you like it or not. Beware of that miserable habit of mind into which some readers of the Bible fall. They receive some doctrines because they like them : they reject others because they are condemning to themselves, or to some lover, or relation, or friend. At this rate the Bible is useless. Are we to be judges of what ought to be in the Word? Do we know better than God? Settle it down in your mind that you will receive all and believe all, and that what you cannot understand you will take on trust. Remember, when you pray, you are speaking to God, and God hears you. But, remember, when you read, God is speaking to you, and you are not to "answer again," but to listen.

(d) For another thing, *read the Bible in a spirit of obedience and self-application.* Sit down to the study of it with a daily determination that *you* will live by its rules, rest on its statements, and act on its commands. Consider, as you travel through every chapter, "How does this affect *my* position and course of conduct? What does this teach *me?*" It is poor work to read the Bible from mere curiosity, and for speculative purposes, in order to fill your head and store your mind with opinions, while you do not allow the book to influence your heart and life. That Bible is read best which is practised most.

(e) For another thing, *read the Bible daily.* Make it a part of every day's business to read and meditate on some portion of God's Word. Private means of grace are just as needful every day for our souls as food and clothing are for our bodies. Yesterday's bread will not feed the labourer to-day, and to-day's bread will not feed the labourer to-morrow. Do as the Israelites did in the wilderness. Gather your manna fresh every morning. Choose your own seasons and hours. Do not scramble over and hurry your reading. Give your Bible the best, and not the worst part of your time. But whatever plan you pursue, let it be a rule of your life to visit the throne of grace and the Bible every day.

(*f*) For another thing, *read all the Bible, and read it in an orderly way.* I fear there are many parts of the Word which some people never read at all. This is to say the least, a very presumptuous habit. "All Scripture is profitable." (2 Tim. iii. 16.) To this habit may be traced that want of broad, well-proportioned views of truth, which is so common in this day. Some people's Bible-reading is a system of perpetual dipping and picking. They do not seem to have an idea of regularly going through the whole book. This also is a great mistake. No doubt in times of sickness and affliction, it is allowable to search out seasonable portions. But with this exception, I believe it is by far the best plan to begin the Old and New Testaments at the same time,—to read each straight through to the end, and then begin again. This is a matter in which every one must be persuaded in his own mind. I can only say it has been my own plan for nearly forty years, and I have never seen cause to alter it.

(*g*) For another thing, *read the Bible fairly and honestly.* Determine to take everything in its plain, obvious meaning, and regard all forced interpretations with great suspicion. As a general rule, whatever a verse of the Bible seems to mean, it does mean. Cecil's rule is a very valuable one,— "The right way of interpreting Scripture is to take it as we find it, without any attempt to force it into any particular system." Well said Hooker, "I hold it for a most infallible rule in the exposition of Scripture, that when a literal construction will stand, the furthest from the literal is commonly the worst."

(*h*) In the last place, *read the Bible with Christ continually in view.* The grand primary object of all Scripture is to testify of Jesus. Old Testament ceremonies are shadows of Christ. Old Testament judges and deliverers are types of Christ. Old Testament history shows the world's need of Christ. Old Testament prophecies are full of Christ's sufferings, and of Christ's glory yet to come. The first advent and the second,—the Lord's humiliation and the Lord's kingdom,—the cross and the crown, shine forth everywhere in the Bible. Keep fast hold on this clue, if you would read the Bible aright.

I might easily add to these hints, if space permitted. Few and short as they are, you will find them worth attention. Act upon them, and I firmly believe you will never be allowed to miss the way to heaven. Act upon them, and you will find light continually increasing in your mind. No book of evidence can be compared with that internal evidence which he obtains who daily uses the Word in the right way. Such a man does not need the books of learned men, like Paley, and Wilson, and M'Ilvaine. He has the witness in himself. The book satisfies and feeds his soul. A poor Christian woman once said to an infidel, "I am no scholar. I cannot argue like you. But I know that honey is honey, because it leaves a sweet taste in my mouth. And I know the Bible to be God's book, because of the taste it leaves in my heart."

(3) This paper may fall into the hands of some one who *loves and believes the Bible, and yet reads it but little.* I fear there are many such in this day. It is a day of bustle and hurry. It is a day of talking, and committee-meetings, and public work. These things are all very well in their way, but I fear that they sometimes clip and cut short the private reading of the Bible. Does your conscience tell you that you are one of the persons I speak of? Listen to me, and I will say a few things which deserve your serious attention.

You are the man that is likely to *get little comfort from the Bible in time of need.* Trial is a sifting season.

Affliction is a searching wind, which strips the leaves off the trees, and brings to light the birds' nests. Now I fear that your stores of Bible consolations may one day run very low. I fear lest you should find yourself at last on very short allowance, and come into harbour weak, worn and thin.

You are the man that is likely *never to be established in the truth.* I shall not be surprised to hear that you are troubled with doubts and questionings about assurance, grace, faith, perseverance, and the like. The devil is an old and cunning enemy. Like the Benjamites, he can "throw stones at a hair-breadth, and not miss." (Judges xx. 16.) He can quote Scripture readily enough when he pleases. Now you are not sufficiently ready with your weapons to be able to fight a good fight with him. Your armour does not fit you well. Your sword sits loosely in your hand.

You are the man that is likely to *make mistakes in life.* I shall not wonder if I am told that you have erred about your own marriage,—erred about your children's education,—erred about the conduct of your household,—erred about the company you keep. The world you steer through is full of rocks, and shoals, and sandbanks. You are not sufficiently familiar either with the lights or charts.

You are the man that is likely to *be carried away by some specious false teacher for a season.* It will not surprise me if I hear that some one of those clever, eloquent men, who can "make the worse appear the better cause," is leading you into many follies. You are wanting in ballast. No wonder if you are tossed to and fro, like a cork on the waves.

All these are uncomfortable things. I want every reader of this paper to escape them all. Take the advice I offer you this day. Do not merely read your Bible "a little," but read it a great deal. "Let the Word of Christ dwell in you richly." (Coloss. iii. 16.) Do not be a mere babe in spiritual knowledge. Seek to become "well instructed in the kingdom of heaven," and to be continually adding new things to old. A religion of feeling is an uncertain thing. It is like the tide, sometimes high, and sometimes low. It is like the moon, sometimes bright, and sometimes dim. A religion of deep Bible knowledge, is a firm and lasting possession. It enables a man not merely to say, "I feel hope in Christ,"—but "I know whom I have believed." (2 Tim. i. 12.)

(4) This paper may fall into the hands of some one who *reads the Bible much, and yet fancies he is no better for his reading.* This is a crafty temptation of the devil. At one stage he says, "Do not read the Bible at all." At another he says, "Your reading does you no good: give it up." Are you that man? I feel for you from the bottom of my soul. Let me try to do you good.

Do not think you are getting no good from the Bible, merely because you do not see that good day by day. The greatest effects are by no means those which make the most noise, and are most easily observed. The greatest effects are often silent, quiet, and hard to detect at the time they are being produced. Think of the influence of the moon upon the earth, and of the air upon the human lungs. Remember how silently the dew falls, and how imperceptibly the grass grows. There may be far more doing than you think in your soul by your Bible-reading.

The Word may be gradually producing deep *impressions* on your heart, of which you are not at present aware. Often when the memory is retaining no facts, the character of a man is receiving some everlasting impression. Is sin becoming every year more hateful to you? Is Christ becoming every year more precious? Is holiness becoming every year more lovely and desirable in your eyes? If these things are so, take courage. The Bible is doing you good, though you may not be able to trace it out day by day.

The Bible may be restraining you from some sin or delusion into which you would otherwise run. It may be daily keeping you back, and hedging you up, and preventing many a false step. Ah, you might soon find this out to your cost, if you were to cease reading the Word! The very familiarity of blessings sometimes makes us insensible to their value. Resist the devil. Settle it down in your mind as an established rule, that, whether you feel it at the moment or not, you are inhaling spiritual health by reading the Bible, and insensibly becoming more strong.

(5) This paper may fall into the hands of some who *really love the Bible, live upon the Bible, and read it much.* Are you one of these? Give me your attention, and I will mention a few things which we shall do well to lay to heart for time to come.

Let us resolve to *read the Bible more and more* every year we live. Let us try to get it rooted in our memories, and engrafted into our hearts. Let us be thoroughly well provisioned with it against the voyage of death. Who knows but we may have a very stormy passage? Sight and hearing may fail us, and we may be in deep waters. Oh, to have the Word "hid in our hearts" in such an hour as that! (Ps. cxix. 11.)

Let us resolve to be *more watchful over our Bible-reading* every year that we live. Let us be jealously careful about the time we give to it, and the manner that time is spent. Let us beware of omitting our daily reading without sufficient cause. Let us not be gaping, and yawning, and dozing over our book, while we read. Let us read like a London merchant studying the city article in the Times,—or like a wife reading a husband's letter from a distant land. Let us be very careful that we never exalt any minister, or sermon, or book, or tract, or friend above the Word. Cursed be that book, or tract, or human counsel, which creeps in between us and the Bible, and hides the Bible from our eyes! Once more I say, let us be very watchful. The moment we open the Bible the devil sits down by our side. Oh, to read with a hungry spirit, and a simple desire for edification!

Let us resolve to *honour the Bible more in our families.* Let us read it morning and evening to our children and households, and not be ashamed to let men see that we do so. Let us not be discouraged by seeing no good arise from it. The Bible-reading in a family has kept many a one from the gaol, the workhouse, and the Gazette, if it has not kept him from hell.

Let us resolve to *meditate more on the Bible.* It is good to take with us two or three texts when we go out into the world, and to turn them over and over in our minds whenever we have a little leisure. It keeps out many vain thoughts. It clenches the nail of daily reading. It preserves our souls from stagnating and breeding corrupt things. It sanctifies and quickens our memories, and prevents them becoming like those ponds where the frogs live but the fish die.

Let us resolve to *talk more to believers about the Bible* when we meet them. Alas, the conversation of Christians, when they do meet, is often sadly unprofitable! How many frivolous, and trifling, and uncharitable things are said! Let us bring out the Bible more, and it will help to drive the devil away, and keep our hearts in tune. Oh, that we may all strive so to walk together in this evil world, that Jesus may often draw near, and go with us, as He went with the two disciples journeying to Emmaus!

Last of all, let us resolve to *live by the Bible more and more* every year we live. Let us frequently take account of all our opinions and practices,—of our habits and tempers,—of our behaviour in public and in private,—in the world, and by our own firesides. Let us measure all by the Bible, and resolve, by God's help, to conform to it. Oh that we may learn increasingly to "cleanse our ways" by the Word! (Ps. cxix. 9.)

I commend all these things to the serious and prayerful attention of every one into whose hands this paper may fall. I want the ministers of my beloved country to be Bible-reading ministers,—the congregations, Bible-reading congregations,—and the nation, a Bible-reading nation. To bring about this desirable end I cast in my mite into God's treasury. The Lord grant that it may prove not to have been in vain!

VI

GOING TO THE TABLE

" Let a man examine himself, and so let him eat of that bread, and drink of that cup."—1 COR. xi. 28.

THE words which form the title of this paper refer to a subject of vast importance. That subject is the Sacrament of the Lord's Supper.

Perhaps no part of the Christian religion is so thoroughly misunderstood as the Lord's Supper. On no point have there been so many disputes, strifes, and controversies for almost 1800 years. On no point have mistakes done so much harm. Even at this very day the battle is still raging, and Christians seem hopelessly divided. The very ordinance which was meant for our peace and profit has become the cause of discord and the occasion of sin. These things ought not so to be!

I make no excuse for including the Lord's Supper among the leading points of *practical* Christianity. I believe firmly that ignorant views or false doctrine about this sacrament lie at the root of half the present divisions of professing Christians. Some neglect it altogether; some completely misunderstand it; some exalt it to a position it was never meant to occupy, and turn it into an idol. If I can throw a little light on it, and clear up the doubts of some minds, I shall feel very thankful. It is hopeless, I fear, to expect that the controversy about the

Lord's Supper will ever be finally closed until the Lord comes. But it is not too much to hope that the fog and mystery and obscurity with which it is surrounded in some minds, may be cleared away by plain Bible truth.

In examining the Sacrament of the Lord's Supper I shall content myself with asking four practical questions, and offering answers to them.

I. Why was the Lord's supper ordained?

II. Who ought to go to the Table and be communicants?

III. What may communicants expect from the Lord's Supper?

IV. Why do many so-called Christians never go to the Lord's Table?

I think it will be impossible to handle these four questions fairly, honestly, and impartially, without seeing the subject of this paper more clearly, and getting some distinct and practical ideas about some leading errors of our day. I say " practical " emphatically. My chief aim in this volume is to promote practical Christianity.

I. In the first place, *why was the Lord's Supper ordained?*

I answer that question in the words of the Church Catechism. I am sure I cannot mend them. It was ordained "for the continual remembrance of the sacrifice of the death of Christ, and of the benefits which we receive thereby."—The bread which in the Lord's Supper is broken, given, and eaten, is meant to remind us of Christ's body given on the cross for our sins. The wine which is poured out and received, is meant to remind us of Christ's blood shed on the cross for our sins. He that eats that bread and drinks that wine is reminded, in the most striking and forcible manner, of the benefits Christ has obtained for his soul, and of the death of Christ as the hinge and turning point on which all those benefits depend.

Now is the view here stated the doctrine of the New Testament? If it is not, for ever let it be rejected, cast aside, and refused by men. If it is, let us never be ashamed to hold it fast, profess our belief in it, pin our faith on it, and steadfastly refuse to hold any other view, no matter by whom it is taught. In subjects like this we must call no man master. It signifies little what great Bishops and learned divines have thought fit to put forth about the Lord's Supper. If they teach more than the Word of God contains they are not to be believed.

I take down my Bible and turn to the New Testament. There I find no less than four separate accounts of the first appointment of the Lord's Supper. St. Matthew, St. Mark, St. Luke, and St. Paul, all four describe it: all four agree in telling us what our Lord did on this memorable occasion.—Two only tell us the reason which our Lord assigned why His disciples were to eat the bread and drink the cup. St. Paul and St. Luke both record the remarkable words, "*Do this in remembrance of Me.*"—St. Paul adds his own inspired comment: "As often as ye eat this bread and drink this cup, ye do shew (or declare or proclaim) the Lord's death till He come." (Luke xxii. 19; 1 Cor. xi. 25, 26.) When Scripture speaks so plainly, why cannot men be content with it? Why should we mystify and confuse a subject which in the New Testament is so simple? The "continual remembrance of Christ's death" was the one grand object for which the Lord's Supper was ordained. He that goes further than this is adding to God's Word, and does so to the great peril of his soul.

Now is it reasonable to suppose that our Lord would appoint an ordinance for so simple a purpose as the "*keeping His death in remembrance*"? Most certainly it is. Of all the facts in His earthly ministry none are equal in importance to that of His death. It was the great satisfaction for man's sin, which had been appointed in God's covenant from the foundation of the world. It was the great atonement of almighty power, to which every sacrifice of animals, from the fall of man, continually pointed. It was the grand end and purpose for which Messiah came into the world. It was the corner-stone and foundation of all man's hopes of pardon and peace with God. In short, Christ would have lived, and taught, and preached, and prophesied, and wrought miracles in vain, if He had not *crowned all by dying for our sins as our Substitute!* His death was our life. His death was the payment of our debt to God. Without His death we should have been of all creatures most miserable. No wonder that an ordinance was specially appointed to remind us of our Saviour's death. It is the very one thing of which poor, weak, sinful man needs to be continually reminded.

Does the New Testament warrant men in saying that the Lord's Supper was ordained to be a sacrifice, and that in it Christ's body and blood are present under the forms of bread and wine? *Most certainly not!* When the Lord Jesus said to the disciples, "This is my Body," and "this is my Blood," He evidently meant, "This bread in my hand is an emblem of my Body, and this cup of wine in my hand contains an emblem of my Blood." The disciples were accustomed to hear Him use such language. They remembered His saying, "The field *is* the world," "The good seed *are* the children of the kingdom." (Matt. xiii. 38.) It never entered into their minds that He meant to say He was holding His own body and His own blood in His hands, and literally giving them His literal body and blood to eat and drink. Not one of the writers of the New Testament ever speaks of the sacrament as a sacrifice, or calls the Lord's Table an altar, or even hints that a Christian minister is a sacrificing priest. The universal doctrine of the New Testament is that after the one offering of Christ there remains no more need of sacrifice.*

Does the English Prayer-book warrant any Churchman in saying that the Lord's Supper was meant to be a sacrifice, and that Christ's body and blood are present under the forms of bread and wine? Once more I reply, *Most certainly not!* Not once is the word *altar* to be found in the Prayer-book: not once is the Lord's Supper called a *sacrifice*. Throughout the Communion Service the one idea of the ordinance continually pressed on our attention is that of a "remembrance" of Christ's death. As to any presence of Christ's natural body and blood under the forms of bread and wine, the rubric at the end of the Service gives the most flat and distinct contradiction to the idea. That rubric expressly asserts that "the natural body and blood of Christ are in heaven, and not here." Those many Churchmen, so-called, who delight in talking of the "altar," the "sacrifice," the "priest," and the "real presence" in the Lord's Supper, would do well to remember that they are using language which is entirely unused by the Church of England.

The point before us is one of vast importance. Let us lay hold upon it firmly, and never let it go. It is the very point on which our Reformers had their sharpest controversy with the Romanists, and went to the stake, rather than give way. Sooner than admit that the Lord's Supper was a sacrifice, they cheerfully laid down their lives. To bring back the doctrine of the "real presence," and to turn the good old English communion into the

* If any one fancies that St. Paul's words to the Hebrews, "We have an altar," are a proof that the Lord's table is an altar, I advise him to read what Waterland, no mean theologian, says on the subject:— "Christians have an altar whereof they partake. That altar is Christ our Lord, who is Altar, Priest, and Sacrifice, all in One."— *Waterland's Works*, Vol. V., 268. Oxford edition.

Romish "mass," is to pour contempt on our Martyrs, and to upset the first principles of the Protestant Reformation. Nay, rather, it is to ignore the plain teaching of God's Word, and do dishonour to the priestly office of our Lord Jesus Christ. The Bible teaches expressly that the Lord's Supper was ordained to be "a remembrance of Christ's body and blood," and not an offering. The Bible teaches that Christ's vicarious death on the cross was the one perfect sacrifice for sin, which never needs to be repeated. Let us stand fast in these two great principles of the Christian faith. A clear view of the intention of the Lord's Supper is one of the soul's best safeguards against the delusions of modern days.

II. In the second place, let me try to show *who ought to be communicants? What kind of persons were meant to go to the Table and receive the Lord's Supper?*

It will clear the ground if I first show who ought not to be partakers of this ordinance. The ignorance which prevails on this, as well as on every part of the subject, is vast, lamentable, and appalling. If I can contribute anything that may throw light upon it, I shall feel very thankful. The principal giants whom John Bunyan describes, in "Pilgrim's Progress," as dangerous to Christian pilgrims, were two, Pope and Pagan. If the good old Puritan had foreseen the times we live in, he would have said something about the giant Ignorance.

(*a*) It is not right to urge all baptized persons to become communicants. There is such a thing as fitness and preparedness for the ordinance. It does not work like a medicine, independently of the state of mind of those who receive it. The teaching of those who press all their congregation to come to the Lord's Table, as if the coming *must* necessarily do every one good, is entirely without warrant of Scripture. Nay, rather, it is teaching which is calculated to do immense harm to men's souls, and to

turn the reception of the sacrament into a mere form.
Ignorance can never be the mother of acceptable worship,
and an ignorant communicant who comes to the Lord's
Table without knowing why he comes, is altogether in the
wrong place.—"Let a man examine himself, and so let
him eat of that bread and drink of that cup."—"To
discern the Lord's body,"—that is to understand what the
elements of bread and wine represent, and why they are
appointed, and what is the particular use of remembering
Christ's death,—is an essential qualification of a true
communicant. God "commands all men everywhere to
repent" and believe the Gospel (Acts xvii. 30 ; but He does
not in the same way, or in the same manner, command every
body to come to the Lord's Table. No : this thing is not
to be taken in hand unadvisedly, lightly, or carelessly! It
is a solemn ordinance, and solemnly it ought to be used.

(*b*) But this is not all. Sinners living in open sin, and determined not to give it up, ought on no account to come to
the Lord's Table. To do so is a positive insult to Christ,
and to pour contempt on His Gospel. It is nonsense to
profess we desire to remember Christ's death, while we
cling to the accursed thing which made it needful for
Christ to die. The mere fact that a man is continuing in
sin, is plain evidence that he does not care for Christ, and
feels no gratitude for redemption. The ignorant Papist
who goes to the priest's confessional and receives absolution,
may think he is fit to go to the Popish mass, and after
mass may return to his sins. He never reads the Bible,
and knows no better! But the Englishman who habitually
breaks any of God's commandments, and yet goes to the
Sacrament, as if it would do him good and wipe away his
sins, is very guilty indeed. So long as he chooses to continue his wicked habits he cannot receive the slightest
benefit from Christ's ordinances, and is only adding sin to
sin. To carry unrepented sin up to the Communion Rail,
and there receive the bread and wine, knowing in our own

hearts that we and wickedness are yet friends, is one of the worst things a man can do, and one of the most hardening to conscience. If a man must have his sins, and cannot give them up, let him by all means stay away from the Lord's Supper. There is such a thing as "eating and drinking unworthily," and to our own "condemnation." To no one do these words apply so thoroughly as to an open sinner.

(c) But I have not done yet. Self-righteous people, who think that they are to be saved by their own works, have no business to come to the Lord's Table. Strange as it may sound at first, these persons are the least qualified of all to receive the Sacrament. They may be outwardly correct, moral and respectable in their lives, but so long as they trust in their own goodness for salvation, they are entirely in the wrong place at the Lord's Supper. For what do we declare at the Lord's Supper? We publicly profess that we have no goodness, righteousness, or worthiness of our own, and that all our hope is in Christ. We publicly profess that we are guilty, sinful, and corrupt, and naturally deserve God's wrath and condemnation. We publicly profess that Christ's merit and not our's, Christ's righteousness and not our's, is the alone cause why we look for acceptance with God. Now what has a self-righteous man to do with an ordinance like this? Clearly nothing at all. One thing, at any rate, is very plain: a self-righteous man has no business to receive the sacrament in the Church of England. The Communion Service of the Church bids all communicants declare that "they do not presume to come to the Table trusting in their own righteousness, but in God's manifold and great mercies."—It tells them to say,—"We are not worthy so much as to gather up the crumbs under Thy table,"—"the remembrance of our sins is grievous unto us; the burden of them is intolerable."—How any self-righteous Churchman can ever go to the Lord's Table, and take these words

into his mouth, passes my understanding! It only shows
that many professing Christians use excellent "forms" of
worship without taking the trouble to consider what they
mean.

The plain truth is that the Lord's Supper was not meant
for dead souls, but for living ones. The careless, the
ignorant, the wilfully wicked, the self-righteous, are no
more fit to come to the Communion rail than a dead corpse
is fit to sit down at a king's feast. To enjoy a spiritual
feast we must have a spiritual heart, and taste, and appetite. To suppose that Christ's ordinances can do good to
an unspiritual man, is as foolish as to put bread and wine
into the mouth of a dead person. The careless, the
ignorant, and the wilfully wicked, so long as they continue
in that state, are utterly unfit to be communicants. To
urge them to attend is not to do them good but harm.
The Lord's Supper is not a converting or justifying ordinance. If a man goes to the Table unconverted or
unforgiven, he will come away no better at all.

But, after all, the ground having been cleared of error,
the question still remain to be answered,—Who are the sort
of persons who ought to be communicants? I answer that
question in the words of the Church Catechism. I there
find the inquiry made, "What is required of them who
come to the Lord's Supper?" In reply I find it taught
that people should "examine themselves whether they
repent them truly of their former sins, steadfastly purposing to lead a new life;"—whether they "have a lively
faith in God's mercy through Christ, with a thankful
remembrance of His death;"—and whether they "are in
charity with all men."—In a word, I find that a worthy
communicant is one who possesses three simple marks and
qualifications,—repentance, faith, and charity. Does a man
truly repent of sin and hate it? Does a man put
his trust in Jesus Christ as his only hope of salvation?
Does a man live in charity towards others? He that can

truly say to each of these questions, "I do," he is a man that is Scripturally qualified for the Lord's Supper. Let him come boldly. Let no barrier be put in his way. He comes up to the Bible standard of communicants. He may draw near with confidence, and feel assured that the great Master of the banquet is not displeased.

Such a man's repentance may be very imperfect. Never mind! Is it real? Does he truly repent at all?—His faith in Christ may be very weak. Never mind! Is it real? A penny is as truly the current coin of the realm, and as really stamped with the Queen's image as a sovereign. His charity may be very defective in quantity and degree. Never mind! Is it genuine? The grand test of a man's Christianity is not the quantity of grace he has got, but whether he has any grace at all. The first twelve communicants, when Christ Himself gave the bread and wine, were weak indeed,—weak in knowledge, weak in faith, weak in courage, weak in patience, weak in love! But eleven of them had that about them which outweighed all defects: they were real, genuine, sincere, and true.

For ever let this great principle be rooted in our minds, —the only worthy communicant is the man who is experimentally acquainted with repentance toward God, faith toward our Lord Jesus Christ, and practical love toward others. Are you that man? Then you may draw near to the table, and take the sacrament to your comfort. Lower than this I dare not pitch my standard of a communicant. I will never help to crowd a communion rail with careless, ignorant, self-righteous attendants.—Higher than this I will not pitch my standard. I will never tell any one to keep away till he is perfect, and to wait till his heart is as unruffled as an angel's. I will not do so, because I believe that neither my Master nor His Apostles would have done so. Show me a man that really feels his sins, really leans on Christ, really struggles to be holy, and I will bid him welcome in my Master's name. He may feel weak, erring, empty, feeble, doubting, wretched, and poor. What matter? St. Paul, I believe, would have received him as a right communicant, and I will do likewise.

III. In the third place, let us consider *what benefit communicants may expect to get by going to the Table and attending the Lord's Supper.* This is a point of grave importance, and one on which vast mistakes abound. On no point, perhaps, connected with this ordinance, are the views of Christians so vague and misty and undefined.

One common idea among men is that "taking the sacrament must do them good." Why, they cannot explain. What good, they cannot exactly say. But they have a loose general notion that it is the right thing to be a communicant, and that somehow or other it is of service to their souls! This is of course nothing better than ignorance. It is unreasonable to suppose that such communicants can please Christ, or receive any real benefit from what they do. If there is any principle clearly laid down in the Bible about any act of religious worship, it is this,—that it must be *intelligent.* The worshipper must at least understand something about what he is doing. Mere bodily worship, unaccompanied by mind or heart, is utterly worthless. The man who walks up to a communion rail, and eats the bread and drinks the wine, as a mere matter of form, because his minister tells him, without any clear idea of what it all means, derives no benefit. He might just as well stay at home!

Another common idea among men is that, "taking the sacrament will help them to heaven, and take away their sins." To this delusive idea you may trace up the habit in some parishes of going to the sacrament once a year, in order, as an old farmer once said, "to wipe off the year's sins." To this idea again, you may trace the too common practice of sending for a minister in time of sickness, in order to receive the sacrament before death. Alas, how many take comfort about their relatives, after they have lived a most ungodly life, for no better reason than this,— that *they took the sacrament* when they were dying! Whether they repented and believed and had new hearts, they neither seem to know or care. All they know is that "they took the sacrament before they died." My heart sinks within me when I hear people resting on such evidence as this.

Ideas like these are mournful proofs of the ignorance that fills the minds of men about the Lord's Supper. They are ideas for which there is not the slightest warrant either in Scripture or the Prayer-book. The sooner they are cast aside and given up, the better for the Church and the world.

Let us settle it firmly in our minds that the Lord's Supper was not given to be a means either of justification or of conversion. It was never meant to give grace where there is no grace already, or to provide pardon when pardon is not already enjoyed. It cannot possibly supply the absence of repentance to God, and faith toward the Lord Jesus Christ. It is an ordinance for the penitent, not for the impenitent,—for the believing, not for the unbelieving,—for the converted, not for the unconverted. The unconverted man, who fancies that he can find a short-cut road to heaven by taking the sacrament, without treading the well-worn steps of repentance and faith, will find to his cost one day, that he is totally deceived. The Lord's Supper was meant to increase and help the grace that a man has, but not to impart the grace that he has not. It was certainly never intended to make our peace with God, to justify, or to convert.

The simplest statement of the benefit which a true-hearted communicant may expect to receive from the Lord's Supper, is that which is supplied by the Church Catechism,—"The strengthening and refreshing of our souls."—Clearer views of Christ and His atonement, clearer views of all the offices which Christ fills as our Mediator and Advocate, clearer views of the complete redemption Christ has obtained for us by His vicarious death on the cross, clearer views of our full and perfect acceptance in Christ before God, fresh reasons for deep repentance for sin, fresh reasons for lively faith,—these are among the leading returns which a believer may confidently expect to get from his attendance at the Lord's Table. He that eats the bread and drinks the wine in a right spirit, will find himself drawn into closer communion with Christ, and will feel to know Him more, and understand Him better.

(*a*) Right reception of the Lord's Supper has a *humbling* effect on the soul. The sight of these emblems of Christ's body and blood, reminds us how sinful sin must be, if nothing less than the death of God's own Son could make satisfaction for it, or redeem us from its guilt. Never surely ought we to be so "clothed with humility," as when we kneel at the Communion rail.

(*b*) Right reception of the Lord's Supper has a *cheering* effect on the soul. The sight of the bread broken, and the wine poured out, reminds us how full, perfect, and complete is our salvation. Those lively emblems remind us what an enormous price has been paid for our redemption. They press on us the mighty truth, that believing on Christ, we have nothing to fear, because a sufficient payment has been made for our debt. The "precious blood of Christ" answers every charge that can be brought against us. God can be a "just God, and yet the justifier of every one that believeth on Jesus." (Rom. iii. 26.)

(*c*) Right reception of the Lord's Supper has a *sanctifying* effect on the soul. The bread and wine remind us how great is our debt of gratitude to our Lord, and how thoroughly we are bound to live for Him who died for our sins. They seem to say to us, "Remember what Christ has done for you, and ask yourself whether there is anything too great to do for Him."

(d) Right reception of the Lord's Supper into hearts, has a *restraining* effect on the soul. Every time a believer goes up to the Communion rail he is reminded what a serious thing it is to be a Christian, and what an obligation is laid on him to lead a consistent life. Bought with such a price as that bread and wine call to his recollection, ought he not to glorify Christ in body and spirit, which are His? The man that goes regularly and intelligently to the Lord's Table finds it increasingly hard to yield to sin and conform to the world.

Such is a brief account of the benefits which a right-hearted communicant may expect to receive from the Lord's Supper. In eating that bread and drinking that cup, such a man will have his repentance deepened, his faith increased, his knowledge enlarged, his habit of holy living strengthened. He will realize more of the "real presence" of Christ in his heart. Eating that bread by faith, he will feel closer communion with the body of Christ. Drinking that wine by faith, he will feel closer communion with the blood of Christ. He will see more clearly what Christ is to him, and what he is to Christ. He will understand more thoroughly what it is to be "one with Christ, and Christ one with him." He will feel the roots of his soul's spiritual life watered, and the work of grace in his heart stablished, built up, and carried forward. All these things may seem and sound foolishness to a natural man, but to a true Christian these things are light, and health, and life, and peace. No wonder that a true Christian finds the Lord's Supper a source of blessing!

Remember, I do not pretend to say that all Christians experience the full blessing of the Lord's Supper, which I have just attempted to describe. Nor yet do I say that the same believer will always find his soul in the same spiritual frame, and always receive the same amount of benefit from the sacrament. But this I will boldly say: you will rarely find a true believer who will not say that he reckons the Lord's Supper one of his best helps and highest privileges. He will tell you that if he were deprived of the Lord's Supper he should find the loss of it a great drawback to his soul. There are some things of which we never know the value till they are taken from us. So I believe it is with the Lord's Supper. The weakest and humblest of God's children gets a blessing from this sacrament, to an extent of which he is not aware.

IV. In the last place, I have to consider *why it is that many so-called Christians never come to the Lord's Supper.*

It is a simple matter of fact, that myriads of baptized persons never come to the Table of the Lord. They would not endure to be told that they deny the faith, and are practically not in communion with Christ. When they worship, they attend a place of Christian worship; when they hear religious teaching, it is the teaching of Christianity; when they are married, they use a Cristian service; when their children are baptized, they ask for the Sacrament of Baptism. Yet all this time they never come to the Lord's Supper! They often live on in this state of mind for many years, and to all appearance are not ashamed. They often die in this condition without ever having received the sacrament, and yet profess to feel hope at the last, and their friends express a hope about them. And yet they live and die in open disobedience to a plain command of Christ! These are simple facts. Let any one look around him, and deny them if he can. I challenge any one to deny that the non-communicants in all English congregations form the majority, and the communicants the minority of the worshippers.

Now how is this? What account can we give of it? Our Lord Jesus Christ's last injunctions to His disciples are clear, plain, and unmistakable. He says to all, "Eat, drink: do this in remembrance of Me." Did He leave it to our discretion whether we would attend to His injunction or not? Did He mean that it did not signify whether His disciples did or did not keep up the ordinance He had just established? Certainly not. The very idea is absurd, and one certainly never dreamed of in apostolic times.—St. Paul evidently takes it for granted that every Christian is a communicant. A class of Christian worshippers who never came to the Table, was a class whose existence was unknown to him. What, then, are we to say of that large multitude of non-communicants which walks out of our churches every sacrament Sunday, unabashed, unhumbled, not afraid, not the least ashamed? Why is it? How is it? What does it all mean? Let us look these questions fairly in the face, and endeavour to give an answer to them.

(1) For one thing, many are not communicants because they are utterly careless and thoughtless about religion, and ignorant of the very first principles of Christianity. They go to church, as a matter of form, because other people go; but they neither know, nor care anything about what is done at church! The faith of Christ has no place either in their hearts, or heads, or consciences, or wills, or understandings. It is a mere affair of "words and names," about which they know no more than Festus or Gallio. There were very few such Christians in St. Paul's times, if indeed there were any. There are far too many in these last days of the world, when everything seems to be wearing out and running to seed. They are the dead-weight of the Churches, and the scandal of Christianity. What such people need is light, knowledge, grace, a renewed conscience, a changed heart. In their present state they have no part or lot in Christ; and dying in this state they are unfit for heaven. Do I wish them to come to the Lord's Supper? Certainly not, till they are converted. Except a man be converted he will never enter the kingdom of God.

(2) For another thing, many are not communicants because they know they are living in the habitual practice of some sin, or in the habitual neglect of some Christian duty. Their conscience tells them that so long as they live in this state, and do not break off from their sins, they are unfit to come to the Table of the Lord. Well: they are so far quite right! I wish no man to be a communicant if he cannot give up his sins. But I warn these people not to forget that if they are unfit for the Lord's Supper they are unfit to die, and that if they die in their present condition they will be lost eternally. The same sins which disqualify them for the sacrament, most certainly disqualify them for heaven. Do I want them to come to the Lord's Supper as they are? Certainly not! But I do want them to repent and be converted, to cease to do evil, and to break off from their sins. For ever let it be remembered that the man unfit for the Lord's Supper is unfit to die.

(3) For another thing, some are not communicants because they fancy it will add to their responsibility. They are not, as many, ignorant and careless about religion. They even attend regularly on the means of grace, and like the preaching of the Gospel. But they say they dread coming forward and making a profession. They fear that they might afterwards fall away, and bring scandal on the cause of Christianity. They think it wisest to be on the safe side, and not commit themselves at all. Such people would do well to remember that if they avoid responsibility of one kind by not coming to the Lord's Table, they incur responsibility of another kind, quite as grave, and quite as injurious to the soul. They are responsible for open disobedience to a command of Christ. They are shrinking from doing that which their Master continually enjoins on His disciples,—from confessing Him before men. No doubt it is a serious step to come forward and receive the sacrament. It is a step that none should take lightly and without self-examination. But it is *no less a serious step*

to walk away and refuse the ordinance, when we remember Who invites us to receive it, and for what purpose it was appointed! I warn the people I am now dealing with to take heed what they are doing. Let them not flatter themselves that it can ever be a wise, a prudent, a safe line of conduct to neglect a plain command of Christ. They may find at length, to their cost, that they have only increased their guilt and forsaken their mercies.

(4) For another thing, some are not communicants because they fancy they are not yet worthy. They wait and stand still, under the mistaken notion that no one is qualified for the Lord's Supper unless he feels within him something like perfection. They pitch their idea of a communicant so high that they despair of attaining to it. Waiting for inward perfection they live, and waiting for it too often they die. Now such persons would do well to understand that they are completely mistaken in their estimate of what "worthiness" really is. They are forgetting that the Lord's Supper was not intended for unsinning angels, but for men and women compassed with infirmity, dwelling in a world full of temptations, and needing mercy and grace every day they live. A sense of our own utter unworthiness is the best worthiness we can bring to the Communion rail. A deep feeling of our own entire indebtedness to Christ for all we have and hope for, is the best feeling we can bring with us. The people I now have in view ought to consider seriously whether the ground they have taken up is tenable, and whether they are not standing in their own light. If they are waiting till they feel in themselves perfect hearts, perfect motives, perfect feelings, perfect repentance, perfect love, perfect faith, they will wait for ever. There never were such communicants in any age,—certainly not in the days of our Lord and of the Apostles,—there never will be as long as the world stands. Nay, rather, the very thought that we feel literally worthy, is a symptom of secret

self-righteousness, and proves us unfit for communion in God's sight. Sinners we are when we first come to the throne of grace,—sinners we shall be till we die; converted changed, renewed, sanctified, but sinners still. In short, no man is a really worthy communicant who does not deeply feel that he is a "miserable sinner."

(5) In the last place, some object to be communicants because they see others coming to the Lord's Table who are not worthy, and not in a right state of mind. Because others eat and drink unworthily, they refuse to eat and drink at all. Of all the grounds taken up by non-communicants to justify their own neglect of Christ's ordinance, I must plainly say, I know none which seems to me so foolish, so weak, so unreasonable, and so unscriptural as this. It is as good as saying that we will never receive the Lord's Supper at all! When shall we ever find a body of communicants on earth of which all the members are converted?—It is setting up ourselves in the most un-healthy attitude of judging others. "Who art thou that judgest another?" "What is that to thee? Follow thou Me."—It is depriving ourselves of a great privilege merely because others profane it and make a bad use of it.—It is pretending to be wiser than our Master Himself. If the words of St. Luke mean anything, Judas Iscariot was present at the first Communion, and received the bread and wine among others.—It is taking up ground for which there is no warrant in Scripture. St. Paul rebukes the Corinthians sharply for the irreverent behaviour of some of the communicants; but I cannot find him giving a single hint that when some came to the Table unworthily, others ought to draw back or stay away. Let me advise the non-communicants I have now in view to beware of being wise above that which was written. Let them study the parable of the Wheat and Tares, and mark how both were to "grow together till the harvest." (Matt. xiii. 30.) Perfect Churches, perfect congregations, perfect bodies of

communicants, are all unattainable in this world of confusion and sin. Let us covet the best gifts, and do all we can to check sin in others; but let us not starve our own selves because others are ignorant sinners, and turn their meat into poison. If others are foolish enough to eat and drink unworthily, let us not turn our backs on Christ's ordinance, and refuse to eat and drink at all.

Such are the five common excuses why myriads in the present day, though professing themselves Christians, never come to the Lord's Supper. One common remark may be made about them: there is not a single reason among the five which deserves to be called "good," and which does not condemn the man who gives it. I challenge any one to deny this. I have said repeatedly that I want no one to be a communicant who is not properly qualified. But I ask those who stay away never to forget that the very reasons they assign for their conduct are their condemnation. I tell them that they stand convicted before God of either being very ignorant of what a communicant is, and what the Lord's Supper is; or else of being persons who are not living rightly, and are unfit to die. In short, to say, I am a non-communicant, is as good as saying one of three things:—" I am living in sin, and cannot come;— I know Christ commands me, but I will not obey Him;— I am an ignorant man, and do not understand what the Lord's Supper means."

I know not in what state of mind this book may find the reader of this paper, or what his opinions may be about the Lord's Supper. But I will conclude the whole subject by offering to all some warnings, which I venture to think are peculiarly required by the times.

(1) In the first place, *do not neglect* the Lord's Supper. The man who coolly and deliberately refuses to use an ordinance which the Lord Jesus Christ appointed for his profit, may be very sure that his soul is in a very wrong

state. There is a judgment yet to come; there is an account to be rendered of all our conduct on earth. How any one can look forward to that day, and expect to meet Christ with comfort and in peace, if he has refused all his life to meet Christ in His own ordinance, is a thing that I cannot understand. Does this come home to you? Mind what you are doing.

(2) In the second place, *do not receive the Lord's Supper carelessly*, irreverently, and as a matter of form. The man who walks up to the Communion rail, and eats the bread and drinks the wine, while his heart is far away, is committing a great sin, and robbing himself of a great blessing. In this, as in every other means of grace, everything depends on the state of mind in which the ordinance is used. He that draws near without repentance, faith, and love, and with a heart full of sin and the world, will certainly be nothing better, but rather worse. Does this come home to you? Mind what you are about.

(3) In the third place, *do not make an idol* of the Lord's Supper. The man who tells you that it is the first, foremost, chief, and principal ordinance in Christianity, is telling you that which he will find it hard to prove. In the great majority of the books of the New Testament the Lord's Supper is not even named. In the letter to Timothy and Titus, about a minister's duties, the subject is not even mentioned. To repent and be converted, to believe and be holy, to be born again and have grace in our hearts,—all these things are of far more importance than to be a communicant. Without them we cannot be saved. Without the Lord's Supper we can. The penitent thief was not a communicant, and Judas Iscariot was! Are you tempted to make the Lord's Supper override and overshadow everything in Christianity, and place it above prayer and preaching? Take care. Mind what you are about.

(4) In the fourth place, *do not use the Lord's Supper*

irregularly. Never be absent when this ordinance is administered. Make every sacrifice to be in your place. Regular habits are essential to the maintenance of the health of our bodies. Regular use of every means of grace is essential to the prosperity of our souls. The man who finds it a weariness to attend on every occasion when the Lord's Table is spread, may well doubt whether all is right within him, and whether he is ready for the Marriage Supper of the Lamb. If Thomas had not been absent when the Lord appeared the first time to the assembled disciples, he would not have said the foolish things he did. Absence made him miss a blessing. Does this come home to you? Mind what you are about.

(5) In the fifth place, *do not do anything to bring discredit* on your profession as a communicant. The man who after attending the Lord's Table runs into sin, does more harm perhaps than any sinner. He is a walking sermon on behalf of the devil. He gives occasion to the enemies of the Lord to blaspheme. He helps to keep people away from Christ. Lying, drinking, adulterous, dishonest, passionate communicants are the helpers of the devil, and the worst enemies of the Gospel. Does this come home to you? Mind what you are about.

(6) In the last place, *do not despond* and be cast down, if with all your desires you do not feel to get great good from the Lord's Supper. Very likely you are expecting too· much. Very likely you are a poor judge of your own state. Your soul's roots may be strengthening and growing, while you think you are not getting on. Very likely you are forgetting that earth is not heaven, and that here we walk by sight and not by faith, and must expect nothing perfect. Lay these things to heart. Do not write bitter things against yourself without cause.

To every reader into whose hands this paper may fall, I commend the whole subject of it as deserving of serious and solemn consideration. I am nothing better than a

poor fallible man myself. But if I have made up my
mind on any point it is this,—that there is no truth which
demands such plain speaking as truth about the Lord's
Supper.

NOTE

I ask the special attention of my readers to the following extracts
from the last Charge of the late Dr. Longley, Archbishop of Canterbury.

The office held by the Archbishop, the remarkable gentleness and
mildness of his character, the fact that this Charge contains his last
sentiments, and that it was not made public till after his death,—all
this appears to me to invest these extracts about the Lord's Supper with
peculiar interest.

"It is far from my intention to impute to all those who have taken
the ill-advised step of adopting the Sacrificial Vestments (in administer-
ing the Lord's Supper) any sympathy with Roman error ; but I am
constrained to avow that there are plain indications in some of the
publications which have been issued as manifestoes of the opinions of
that section of our Church, that some of its professed members, yea,
even of her ministers, think themselves at liberty to hold the doctrines
of the Church of Rome in relation to the Sacrifice of the Mass, and yet
retain their position within the pale of the Anglican Church with the
avowed purpose of eliminating from its formularies every trace of the
Reformation, as regards its protest against Romish error.   The language
they hold with respect to it is entirely incompatible with loyalty to the
Church to which they profess to belong.   They call it 'a Communion
deeply tainted with Protestant heresy:' 'Our duty,' they say, 'is the
expulsion of the evil, not flight from it.' It is no want of charity,
therefore, to declare that they remain with us in order that they may
substitute the Mass for the Communion ; the obvious aim of our Reformers having been to substitute the Communion for the Mass.   Doubtless the Church of England admits of considerable latitude in the views
that may be taken of that most mysterious of all mysteries, the Sacrament of the Lord's Supper.   And so long as those solemn words of its
original institution, 'This is my Body,' 'This is my Blood,' shall remain
in the sentence of consecration (and they never can be erased from it),
so long will there be varieties of interpretation of these words, all of
which may be consistent with a true allegiance to our Church, provided
these three conditions be observed :—

"1.   That they be not construed to signify that the Natural Body
of Christ is present in the Sacrament :

"2. Nor to admit of any adoration either of the Sacramental bread and wine there bodily received, or of any corporal presence of Christ's Natural Body and Blood :

"3. Nor to justify the belief that the Body and Blood are again offered as a satisfaction for sin ; seeing that the offering of Christ once made was a perfect redemption, propitiation, and satisfaction for the sins of the whole world, original and actual.

"These are the limits which our Church imposes upon the liberty of interpretation of the words of our blessed Lord.

"The use of these sacrificial vestments is in the minds of many intimately connected with the idea that an essential element in the Holy Communion is the offering to God a Sacrifice of the Body and Blood of Christ, which abide with the elements in a mysterious manner after the act of Consecration. The minister wears the vestments at that time as a sacrificing priest. According to this view it would seem that the most important part of this Holy Sacrament is what we offer to God, not what we receive from Him.

"This view is not recognised by the Church of England in her formularies. The general definition in the XXVth Article states that Sacraments are ‘ certain sure witnesses and effectual signs of grace, by the which [God] doth work invisibly in us ;’ and it is said specifically of the Lord's Supper (Art. XXVIII.), that it ‘is a Sacrament of our Redemption by Christ's death : insomuch that to such as rightly, worthily, and with faith, receive the same, the Bread which we break is a partaking of the Body of Christ ; and likewise the Cup of Blessing is a partaking of the Blood of Christ.’ The idea of the Sacrifice of that Body and Blood finds no place in either of these strict definitions. The Catechism speaks the same language when it defines a Sacrament to be ‘ an outward and visible sign of an inward and spiritual grace given unto us.’ Nor will an examination of the Office of the Holy Communion itself give any countenance to the idea in question. The only distinct oblation or offering mentioned in that Office is previous to the Consecration of the elements, in the Prayer for the Church Militant, and therefore cannot be an offering or sacrifice of the Body and Blood of Christ ; and the only sacrifice which we are spoken of as making, is the offering of ‘ourselves, our souls and bodies, to be a reasonable, holy, and lively sacrifice.’ * Our Church seems most studiously to have avoided any expression which could countenance the notion of a perpetual Sacrifice of Christ, while on the other hand it speaks of Christ's death upon the cross as ‘His own oblation of Himself once offered as a full, perfect, and sufficient sacrifice for the sins of the whole world.’ No room is left for the repetition of that sacrifice, or for the admission of any other sacrifice for sin.

---

* See Proctor on the Common Prayer, p. 320.

"'The Romish notion of a true, real, and substantial Sacrifice of the Body and Blood of Christ, as it is called in the Council of Trent, entailed the use of the term *altar*. But this term appears nowhere in the Book of Common Prayer, and was no doubt omitted lest any countenance should be given to the sacrificial view. The notion, therefore, of making in the material elements a perpetual offering of the Body and Blood of Christ, is as foreign to the spirit and the letter of our Service as I hold it to be to the doctrine of the early Fathers, as well as of the leading divines of our Church. This latter point also I shall endeavour to establish hereafter.

"Meanwhile it cannot be denied, on the other hand, that the doctrine of the Real Presence is, in one sense, the doctrine of the Church of England. She asserts that the Body and Blood of Christ are 'verily and indeed taken and received by the faithful in the Lord's Supper.' And she asserts equally that such presence is not material or corporal; but that Christ's Body 'is given, taken, and eaten, in the Supper, only after a heavenly and spiritual manner.' (Art. XXVIII.) Christ's presence is effectual for all those intents and purposes for which His Body was broken, and His Blood shed. As to a presence elsewhere than in the heart of the believer, the Church of England is silent, and the words of Hooker therefore represent her views: 'The real presence of Christ's most blessed Body and Blood is not to be sought in the Sacrament, but in the worthy receiver of the Sacrament.'"

VII

CHARITY

"Now abideth faith, hope, charity, these three; but the greatest of these is charity."—1 Cor. xiii. 13.

CHARITY is rightly called "the Queen of Christian graces." "The end of the commandment," says St. Paul, "is charity." (1 Tim. i. 5.) It is a grace which all people profess to admire. It seems a plain practical thing which everybody can understand. It is none of "those troublesome doctrinal points" about which Christians are disagreed. Thousands, I suspect, would not be ashamed to tell you that they knew nothing about justification or regeneration, about the work of Christ or the Holy Spirit. But nobody, I believe, would like to say that he knew nothing about "charity!" If men possess nothing else in religion, they always flatter themselves that they possess "charity."

A few plain thoughts about charity may not be without use. There are false notions abroad about it which require to be dispelled. There are mistakes about it which require to be rectified. In my admiration of charity I yield to none. But I am bold to say that in many minds the whole subject seems completely misunderstood.

I. Let me show, firstly, *the place the Bible gives to charity.*

II. Let me show, secondly, *what the charity of the Bible really is.*

III. Let me show, thirdly, *whence true charity comes.*

IV. Let me show, lastly, *why charity is "the greatest" of the graces.*

I ask the best attention of my readers to the subject. My heart's desire and prayer to God is, that the growth of charity may be promoted in this sin-burdened world. In nothing does the fallen condition of man show itself so strongly as in the scarcity of Christian charity. There is little faith on earth, little hope, little knowledge of Divine things. But nothing, after all, is so scarce as real charity.

I. Let me show *the place which the Bible gives to charity.*

I begin with this point in order to establish the immense practical importance of my subject. I do not forget that there are many high-flying Christians in this present day, who almost refuse to look at anything *practical* in Christianity. They can talk of nothing but two or three favourite doctrines. Now I want to remind my readers that the Bible contains much about practice as well as about doctrine, and that one thing to which it attaches great weight is "charity."

I turn to the New Testament, and ask men to observe what it says about charity. In all religious inquiries there is nothing like letting the Scripture speak for itself. There is no surer way of finding out truth than the old way of turning to plain texts. Texts were our Lord's weapons, both in answering Satan, and in arguing with the Jews. Texts are the guides we must never be ashamed to refer to in the present day.—" What saith the Scripture? What is written? How readest thou?"

Let us hear what St. Paul says to the Corinthians: "Though I speak with the tongues of men and of angels, and have not charity, I am become as sounding brass, or a tinkling cymbal. And though I have the gift of prophecy, and understand all mysteries, and all knowledge; and though I have all faith, so that I could remove mountains, and have not charity, I am nothing. And though I bestow all my goods to feed the poor, and though I give my body to be burned, and have not charity, it profiteth me nothing." (1 Cor. xiii. 1—3.)

Let us hear what St. Paul says to the Colossians: "Above all these things put on charity, which is the bond of perfectness." (Col. iii. 14.)

Let us hear what St. Paul says to Timothy: "The end of the commandment is charity out of a pure heart, and of a good conscience, and of faith unfeigned." (1 Tim. i. 5.)

Let us hear what St. Peter says: "Above all things have fervent charity among yourselves: for charity shall cover the multitude of sins." (1 Peter iv. 8.)

Let us hear what our Lord Jesus Christ Himself says about that love, which is only another name for charity.* "A new commandment give I unto you, That ye love one another; as I have loved you, that ye also love one another. By this shall all men know that ye are my disciples, if ye have love one to another." (John xiii. 34, 35.) Above all, let us read our Lord's account of the last judgment, and mark that want of love will condemn millions. (Matt. xxv. 41, 42.)

Let us hear what St. Paul says to the Romans: "Owe no man anything, but to love one another: for he that loveth another hath fulfilled the law." (Rom. xiii. 8.)

Let us hear what St. Paul says to the Ephesians: "Walk in love, as Christ also hath loved us." (Eph. v. 2.)

Let us hear what St. John says: "Beloved, let us love one another: for love is of God; and every one that loveth is born of God, and knoweth God. He that loveth not knoweth not God; for God is love." (1 John iv. 7, 8.)

---

* In the Greek language one and the same word only is used for "love" and "charity." In our English version our translators have sometimes rendered this word one way and sometimes another.

I shall make no comment upon these texts. I think it better to place them before my readers in their naked simplicity, and to let them speak for themselves. If any one is disposed to think the subject of this paper a matter of light importance, I will only ask him to look at these texts, and to think again. He that would take down "charity" from the high and holy place which it occupies in the Bible, and treat it as a matter of secondary moment, must settle his account with God's Word. I certainly shall not waste time in arguing with him.

To my own mind the evidence of these texts appears clear, plain, and incontrovertible. They show the immense importance of charity, as one of the "things that accompany salvation." They prove that it has a right to demand the serious attention of all who call themselves Christians, and that those who despise the subject are only exposing their own ignorance of Scripture.

II. Let me show, secondly, *what the charity of the Bible really is.*

I think it of great importance to have clear views on this point. It is precisely here that mistakes about charity begin. Thousands delude themselves with the idea that they have "charity," when they have not, from downright ignorance of Scripture. Their charity is not the charity described in the Bible.

(a) The charity of the Bible does not consist in giving to the poor. It is a common delusion to suppose that it does. Yet St. Paul tells us plainly, that a man may "bestow all his goods to feed the poor" (1 Cor. xiii. 3), and not have charity. That a charitable man will "remember the poor," there can be no question. (Gal. ii. 10.) That he will do all he can to assist them, relieve them, and lighten their burdens, I do not for a moment deny. All I say is, that this does not make up "charity." It is easy to spend a fortune in giving away money, and soup, and wine, and bread, and coals, and blankets, and clothing, and yet to be utterly destitute of Bible charity.

(b) The charity of the Bible does not consist in never disapproving anybody's conduct. Here is another very common delusion! Thousands pride themselves on never condemning others, or calling them wrong, whatever they may do. They convert the precept of our Lord, "judge not," into an excuse for having no unfavourable opinion at all of anybody. They pervert His prohibition of rash and censorious judgments, into a prohibition of all judgment whatsoever. Your neighbour may be a drunkard, a liar, a Sabbath-breaker, a passionate man. Never mind! 'It is not charity," they tell you, "to pronounce him, wrong." You are to believe that he has a good heart at bottom! This idea of charity is, unhappily, a very common one. It is full of mischief. To throw a veil over sin, and to refuse to call things by their right names,—to talk of "hearts" being good, when "lives" are flatly wrong,—to shut our eyes against wickedness, and say smooth things of immorality,—this is not Scriptural charity.

(c) The charity of the Bible does not consist in never disapproving anybody's religious opinions. Here is another most serious and growing delusion. There are many who pride themselves on never pronouncing others mistaken, whatever views they may hold. Your neighbour, forsooth, may be an Arian, or a Socinian, a Roman Catholic, or a Mormonite, a Deist, or a Sceptic, a mere Formalist, or a thorough Antinomian. But the "charity" of many says that you have no right to think Him wrong! If he is sincere, it is "uncharitable" to think unfavourably of his spiritual condition!—From such charity may I ever be delivered! At this rate the Apostles were wrong in going out to preach to the Gentiles! At this rate there is no use in missions! At this rate we had better close our Bibles, and shut up our churches! Everybody is right, and nobody is wrong! Everybody is going to heaven, and nobody is going to hell! Such charity is a monstrous caricature. To say that all are equally right in their opinions, though their opinions flatly contradict one another,—to say that all are equally in the way to heaven, though their doctrinal sentiments are as opposite as black and white,—this is not Scriptural charity. Charity like this pours contempt on the Bible, and talks as if God had not given us a written test of truth. Charity like this confuses all our notions of heaven, and would fill it with a discordant inharmonious rabble. True charity does not think everybody right in doctrine. True charity cries,— " Believe not every spirit, but try the spirits whether they be of God : because many false prophets are gone out into the world."—" If there come any unto you, and bring not this doctrine, receive him not." (1 John iv. 1; 2 John 10.)

I leave the negative side of the question here. I have dwelt upon it at some length because of the days in which we live and the strange notions which abound. Let me now turn to the positive side. Having shown what charity is not, let me now show what it is.

Charity is that " love," which St. Paul places first among those fruits which the Spirit causes to be brought forth in the heart of a believer. " The fruit of the Spirit is love." (Gal. v. 2.) Love to God, such as Adam had before the fall, is its first feature. He that has charity, desires to love God with heart, and soul and mind, and strength. Love to man is its second feature. He that has charity,. desires to love his neighbour as himself. This is indeed that view in which the word " charity " in Scripture · is more especially regarded. When I speak of a believer having " love " in his heart, I mean that he has love to both God and man. When I speak of a believer having " charity," I mean more particularly that he has love to man.

The charity of the Bible will show itself in a *believer's doings*. It will make him ready to do kind acts to every one within his reach,—both to their bodies and souls. It will not let him be content with soft words and kind wishes. It will make him diligent in doing all that lies in his power to lessen the sorrow and increase the happiness of others. Like his Master, he will care more for ministering than for being ministered to, and will look for nothing in return. Like his Master's great apostle, he will very willingly "spend and be spent" for others, even though they repay him with hatred, and not with love. True charity does not want wages. Its work is its reward.

The charity of the Bible will show itself in a believer's *readiness to bear* evil as well as to do good. It will make him patient under provocation, forgiving when injured, meek when unjustly attacked, quiet when slandered. It will make him bear much and forbear much, put up with much and look over much, submit often and deny himself often, all for the sake of peace. It will make him put a strong bit on his temper, and a strong bridle on his tongue. True charity is not always asking,—" What are my rights ? Am I treated as I deserve ? " but, " How can I best promote peace ? How can I do that which is most edifying to others ? "

The charity of the Bible will show itself in the *general spirit and demeanour* of a believer. It will make him kind, unselfish, good-natured, good-tempered, and considerate for others. It will make him gentle, affable, and courteous, in all the daily relations of private life, thoughtful for others' comfort, tender for others' feelings, and more anxious to give pleasure than to receive. True charity never envies others when they prosper, nor rejoices in the calamities of others when they are in trouble. At all times it will believe, and hope, and try to put a good construction on others' doings. And even at the worst, it will be full of pity, mercy, and compassion.

Would we like to know where the true Pattern of charity like this can be found ? We have only to look at the life

of our Lord Jesus Christ, as described in the Gospels, and
we shall see it perfectly exemplified. Charity shone forth
in all His doings. His daily life was an incessant "going
about" doing good.—Charity shone forth in all His
bearing. He was continually hated, persecuted, slandered,
misrepresented. But He patiently endured it all. No
angry word ever fell from His lips. No ill-temper ever
appeared in His demeanour. "When He was reviled, He
reviled not again: when He suffered, He threatened not."
(1 Pet. ii. 23.)—Charity shone forth in all His spirit and
deportment. The law of kindness was ever on His lips.
Among weak and ignorant disciples, among sick and
sorrowful petitioners for help and relief, among publicans
and sinners, among Pharisees and Sadducees, He was
always one and the same.—kind and patient to all.

And yet, be it remembered, our blessed Master never
flattered sinners, or connived at sin. He never shrunk
from exposing wickedness in its true colours, or from
rebuking those who would cleave to it. He never
hesitated to denounce false doctrine, by whomsoever it
might be held, or to exhibit false practice in its true
colours, and the certain end to which it tends. He called
things by their right names. He spoke as freely of hell
and the fire that is not quenched, as of heaven and the
kingdom of glory. He has left on record an everlasting
proof that perfect charity does not require us to approve
everybody's life or opinions, and that it is quite possible
to condemn false doctrine and wicked practice, and yet to
be full of love at the same time.

I have now set before my readers the true nature of
Scriptural charity. I have given a slight and very brief
account of what it is not, and what it is. I cannot pass
on without suggesting two practical thoughts, which press
home on my mind with weighty force, and I hope may
press home on others.

You have heard of charity. Think, for a moment, how

deplorably little charity there is upon earth! How conspicuous is the absence of true love among Christians! I speak not of heathen now, I speak of Christians. What angry tempers, what passions, what selfishness, what bitter tongues, are to be found in private families! What strifes, what quarrels, what spitefulness, what malice, what revenge, what envy between neighbours and fellow-parishioners! What jealousies and contentions between Churchmen and Dissenters, Calvinists and Arminians, High Churchmen and Low Churchmen! "Where is charity?" we may well ask,—"Where is love? where is the mind of Christ?" when we look at the spirit which reigns in the world. No wonder that Christ's cause stands still, and infidelity abounds, when men's hearts know so little of charity! Surely, we may well say,—"When the Son of man cometh, shall He find charity upon earth?"

Think, for another thing, what a happy world this would be if there was more charity. It is the want of love which causes half the misery there is upon earth. Sickness, and death, and poverty, will not account for more than half the sorrows. The rest come from ill-temper, ill-nature, strifes, quarrels, lawsuits, malice, envy, revenge, frauds, violence, wars, and the like. It would be one great step towards doubling the happiness of mankind, and halving their sorrows, if all men and women were full of Scriptural charity.

III. Let me show, thirdly, *whence the charity of the Bible comes.*

Charity, such as I have described, is certainly not natural to man. Naturally, we are all more or less selfish, envious, ill-tempered, spiteful, ill-natured, and unkind. We have only to observe children, when left to themselves, to see the proof of this. Let boys and girls grow up without proper training and education, and you will not see one of them possessing Christian charity. Mark how some of them think first of themselves, and their own comfort and advantage! Mark how others are full of pride, passion, and evil tempers! How can we account for it? There is but one reply. The natural heart knows nothing of true charity.

The charity of the Bible will never be found except in a heart prepared by the Holy Ghost. It is a tender plant, and will never grow except in one soil. You may as well expect grapes on thorns, or figs on thistles, as look for charity when the heart is not right.

The heart in which charity grows is a heart changed, renewed, and transformed by the Holy Ghost. The image and likeness of God, which Adam lost at the fall, has been restored to it, however feeble and imperfect the restoration may appear. It is a "partaker of the Divine nature," by union with Christ and sonship to God; and one of the first features of that nature is love. (2 Pet. i. 4.)

Such a heart is deeply convinced of sin, hates it, flees from it, and fights with it from day to day. And one of the prime motions of sin which it daily labours to overcome, is selfishness and want of charity.

Such a heart is deeply sensible of its mighty debt to our Lord Jesus Christ. It feels continually that it owes to Him who died for us on the cross, all its present comfort, hope, and peace. How can it show forth its gratitude? What can it render to its Redeemer? If it can do nothing else, it strives to be like Him, to drink into His spirit, to walk in His footsteps, and, like Him, to be full of love. "The love of Christ shed abroad in the heart by the Holy Ghost" is the surest fountain of Christian charity. Love will produce love.

I ask my reader's special attention to this point. It is one of great importance in the present day. There are many who profess to admire charity, while they care nothing about vital Christianity. They like some of the fruits and results of the Gospel, but not the root from which these fruits alone can grow, or the doctrines with which they are inseparably connected.

Hundreds will praise love and charity, who hate to be told of man's corruption, of the blood of Christ, and of the inward work of the Holy Ghost. Many a parent would like his children to grow up unselfish and good tempered, who would not be much pleased if conversion, and repentance, and faith, were pressed home on their attention.

Now I desire to protest against this notion, that you can have the fruits of Christianity without the roots,— that you can produce Christian tempers without teaching Christian doctrines,—that you can have charity that will wear and endure without grace in the heart.

I grant, most freely, that every now and then one sees a person who seems very charitable and amiable, without any distinctive doctrinal religion. But such cases are so rare and remarkable, that, like exceptions, they only prove the truth of the general rule. And often, too often, it may be feared in such cases the apparent charity is only seeming, and in private completely fails. I firmly believe, as a general rule, you will not find such charity as the Bible describes, except in the soil of a heart thoroughly imbued with Bible religion. Holy practice will not flourish without sound doctrine. What God has joined together, it is useless to expect to have separate and asunder.

The delusion which I am trying to combat is helped forward to a most mischievous degree by the vast majority of novels, romances, and tales of fiction. Who does not know that the heroes and heroines of these works are constantly described as patterns of perfection? They are always doing the right thing, saying the right thing, and showing the right temper! They are always kind, and amiable, and unselfish, and forgiving! And yet you never hear a word about their religion! In short, to judge by the generality of works of fiction, it is possible to have excellent practical religion without doctrine, the fruits of the Spirit without the grace of the Spirit, and the mind of Christ without union with Christ!

Here, in short, is the great danger of reading most novels, romances, and works of fiction. The greater part of them give a false or incorrect view of human nature. They paint their model men and women as they ought to be, and not as they really are. The readers of such writings get their minds filled with wrong conceptions of what the world is. Their notions of mankind become visionary and unreal. They are constantly looking for men and women such as they never meet, and expecting what they never find.

Let me entreat my readers, once for all, to draw their ideas of human nature from the Bible, and not from novels. Settle it down in your mind, that there cannot be true charity without a heart renewed by grace. A certain degree of kindness, courtesy, amiability, good nature, may undoubtedly be seen in many who have no vital religion. But the glorious plant of Bible charity, in all its fulness and perfection, will never be found without union with Christ, and the work of the Holy Ghost. Teach this to your children, if you have any. Hold it up in schools, if you are connected with any. Lift up charity. Make much of charity. Give place to none in exalting the grace of kindness, love, good nature, unselfishness, good temper. But never, never forget, that there is but one school in which these things can be thoroughly learned, and that is the school of Christ. Real charity comes down from above. True love is the fruit of the Spirit. He that would have it must sit at Christ's feet, and learn of Him.

IV. Let me show, lastly, *why charity is called the "greatest" of the graces.*

The words of St. Paul, on this subject, are distinct and unmistakable. He winds up his wonderful chapter on charity in the following manner: "Now abideth faith, hope, charity, these three: but the greatest of these is charity." (1 Cor. xiii. 13.)

This expression is very remarkable. Of all the writers in the New Testament, none, certainly, exalts "faith" so highly as St. Paul. The Epistles to the Romans and Galatians abound in sentences showing its vast importance. By it the sinner lays hold on Christ and is saved. Through it we are justified, and have peace with God. Yet here the same St. Paul speaks of something which is even greater than faith. He puts before us the three leading Christian graces, and pronounces the following judgment on them,—"The greatest is charity." Such a sentence from such a writer demands special attention. What are we to understand when we hear of charity being greater than faith and hope?

We are not to suppose, for a moment, that charity can atone for our sins, or make our peace with God. Nothing can do that for us but the blood of Christ, and nothing can give us an interest in Christ's blood but faith. It is unscriptural ignorance not to know this. The office of justifying and joining the soul to Christ belongs to faith alone. Our charity, and all our other graces, are all more or less imperfect, and could not stand the severity of God's judgment. When we have done all, we are "unprofitable servants." (Luke xvii. 10.)

We are not to suppose that charity can exist independently of faith. St. Paul did not intend to set up one grace in rivalry to the other. He did not mean that one man might have faith, another hope, and another charity, and that the best of these was the man who had charity. The three graces are inseparably joined together. Where there is faith, there will always be love; and where there is love, there will be faith. Sun and light, fire and heat, ice and cold, are not more intimately united than faith and charity.

The reasons why charity is called the greatest of the three graces, appear to me plain and simple. Let me show what they are.

(a) Charity is called the greatest of graces, because it is the one in which there is *some likeness between the believer and his God*. God has no need of faith. He is dependent on no one. There is none superior to Him in whom He must trust.—God has no need of hope. To Him all things are certain, whether past, present, or to come.—But "God is love:" and the more love His people have, the more like they are to their Father in heaven.

(b) Charity, for another thing, is called the greatest of the graces, because *it is most useful to others*. Faith and hope, beyond doubt, however precious, have special reference to a believer's own private individual benefit. Faith unites the soul to Christ, brings peace with God, and opens the way to heaven. Hope fills the soul with cheerful expectation of things to come, and, amid the many discouragements of things seen, comforts with visions of the things unseen. But charity is pre-eminently the grace which makes a man useful. It is the spring of good works and kindnesses. It is the root of missions, schools, and hospitals. Charity made apostles spend and be spent for souls. Charity raises up workers for Christ, and keeps them working. Charity smooths quarrels, and stops strife, and in this sense "covers a multitude of sins." (1 Pet. iv. 8.) Charity adorns Christianity, and recommends it to the world. A man may have real faith, and feel it, and yet his faith may be invisible to others. But a man's charity cannot be hid.

(c) Charity, in the last place, is the greatest of the graces, because it is the one which *endures the longest*. In fact, it will never die. Faith will one day be swallowed up in sight, and hope in certainty. Their office will be useless in the morning of the resurrection, and, like old almanacs, they will be laid aside. But love will live on through the endless ages of eternity. Heaven will be the abode of love. The inhabitants of heaven will be full of love. One common feeling will be in all their hearts, and that will be charity.

I leave this part of my subject here, and pass on to a conclusion. On each of the three points of comparison I have just named, between charity and the other graces, it would be easy to enlarge. But time and space both forbid me to do so. If I have said enough to guard men against mistakes about the right meaning of the "greatness" of charity, I am content. Charity, be it ever remembered, cannot justify and put away our sins. It is neither Christ, nor faith. But charity makes us somewhat like God. Charity is of mighty use to the world. Charity will live and flourish when faith's work is done. Surely, in these points of view, charity well deserves the crown.

(1) And now let me ask every one into whose hands this paper may come a simple question. Let me press home on your conscience the whole subject of this paper. Do you know anything of the grace of which I have been speaking? *Have you charity?*

The strong language of the Apostle St. Paul must surely convince you that the inquiry is not one that ought to be lightly put aside. The grace, without which that holy man could say, "I am nothing," the grace which the Lord Jesus says expressly is the great mark of being His disciple,—such a grace as this demands the serious consideration of every one who is in earnest about the salvation of his soul. It should set him thinking,—"How does this affect me? Have I charity?"

You have some knowledge, it may be, of religion. You know the difference between true and false doctrine. You can, perhaps, even quote texts, and defend the opinions you hold. But, remember the knowledge which is barren of practical results in life and temper is a useless pos-

session. The words of the Apostle are very plain:
"Though I understand all knowledge, and have not
charity, I am nothing." (1 Cor. xiii. 3.)

You think you have faith, perhaps. You trust you are
one of God's elect, and rest in that. But surely you
should remember that there is a faith of devils, which is
utterly unprofitable, and that the faith of God's elect is a
"faith that worketh by love." It was when St. Paul
remembered the "love" of the Thessalonians, as well as
their faith and hope, that he said,—"I know your election
of God." (1 Thess. i. 4.)

Look at your own daily life, both at home and abroad,
and consider what place the charity of Scripture has in it.
What is your temper? What are your ways of behaving
toward all around you in your own family? What is
your manner of speaking, especially in seasons of vexation and provocation? Where is your good-nature, your
courtesy, your patience, your meekness, your gentleness,
your forbearance? Where are your practical actions of
love in your dealing with others? What do you know
of the mind of Him who "went about doing good,"—
who loved all, though specially His disciples,—who returned good for evil, and kindness for hatred, and had a
heart wide enough to feel for all?

What would you do in heaven, I wonder, if you got
there without charity? What comfort could you have in
an abode where love was the law, and selfishness and ill-
nature completely shut out? Alas! I fear that heaven
would be no place for an uncharitable and ill-tempered
man!—What said a little boy one day? "If grandfather
goes to heaven, I hope I and brother will not go there."
"Why do you say that?" he was asked. He replied,—
"If he sees us there, I am sure he will say, as he does
now,—'What are these boys doing here? Let them get
out of the way.' He does not like to see us on earth, and
I suppose he would not like to see us in heaven."

Give yourself no rest till you know something by experience of real Christian charity. Go and learn of Him who is meek and lowly of heart, and ask Him to teach you how to love. Ask the Lord Jesus to put His Spirit within you, to take away the old heart, to give you a new nature, to make you know something of His mind. Cry to Him night and day for grace, and give Him no rest until you feel something of what I have been describing in this paper. Happy indeed will your life be when you really understand " walking in love."

(2) But I do not forget that I am writing to some who are not ignorant of the charity of Scripture, and who long to feel more of it every year. I will give you two simple words of exhortation. They are these,—" Practice and teach the grace of charity."

Practice charity diligently. It is one of those graces, above all, which grow by constant exercise. Strive more and more to carry it into every little detail of daily life. Watch over your own tongue and temper throughout every hour of the day,—and especially in your dealings with servants, children, and near relatives. Remember the character of the excellent woman:—" In her tongue is the law of kindness." (Prov. xxxi. 26.)—Remember the words of St. Paul: " Let ALL your things be done with charity." (1 Cor. xvi. 14.) Charity should be seen in little things as well as in great ones.—Remember, not least, the words of St. Peter: " Have fervent charity among yourselves;" not a charity which just keeps alight, but a burning shining fire, which all around can see. (1 Pet. iv. 8.) It may cost pains and trouble to keep these things in mind. There may be little encouragement from the example of others. But persevere. Charity like this brings its own reward.

Finally, teach charity to others. Press it continually on servants, if you have any. Tell them the great duty of kindness, helpfulness, and considerateness, one for another.

Press it, above all, on children, if you have any. Remind
them constantly that kindness, good nature, and good
temper, are among the first evidences which Christ requires in children. If they cannot know much, or explain
doctrines, they can understand love. A child's religion
is worth very little if it only consists in repeating texts
and hymns. Useful as they are, they are often learned
without thought, remembered without feeling, said over
without consideration of their meaning, and forgotten
when childhood is gone. By all means let children be
taught texts and hymns; but let not such teaching be
made everything in their religion. Teach them to keep
their tempers, to be kind one to another, to be unselfish,
good-natured, obliging, patient, gentle, forgiving. Tell
them never to forget to their dying day, if they live as
long as Methuselah, that without charity, the Holy Ghost
says, "we are nothing." Tell them "*above all things* to
put on charity, which is the bond of perfectness." (Colos.
iii. 14.)

VIII

ZEAL

"It is good to be zealously affected always in a good thing."—
GAL. iv. 18.

ZEAL is a subject, like many others in religion, most sadly misunderstood. Many would be ashamed to be thought "zealous" Christians. Many are ready to say of zealous people what Festus said of Paul: "They are beside themselves,—they are mad." (Acts xxvi. 24.)

But zeal is a subject which no reader of the Bible has any right to pass over. If we make the Bible our rule of faith and practice, we cannot turn away from it. We must look it in the face. What says the Apostle Paul to Titus? "Christ gave Himself for us that He might redeem us from all iniquity, and purify unto Himself a peculiar people, *zealous* of good works." (Titus ii. 14.) What says the Lord Jesus to the Laodicean Church? "Be *zealous* and repent." (Rev. iii. 19.)

My object in this paper is to plead the cause of zeal in religion. I believe we ought not to be afraid of it, but rather to love and admire it. I believe it to be a mighty blessing to the world, and the origin of countless benefits to mankind. I want to strike a blow at the lazy, easy, sleepy Christianity of these latter days, which can see no beauty in zeal, and only uses the word "zealot" as a word of reproach. I want to remind Christians that

"Zealot" was a name given to one of our Lord Jesus Christ's Apostles, and to persuade them to be zealous men.

I ask every reader of this paper to give me his attention while I tell him something about zeal. Listen to me for your own sake,—for the sake of the world,—for the sake of the Church of Christ. Listen to me, and by God's help I will show you that to be "zealous" is to be wise.

I. Let me show, in the first place, *what is zeal in religion.*

II. Let me show, in the second place, *when a man can be called rightly zealous in religion?*

III. Let me show, in the third place, *why it is a good thing for a man to be zealous in religion?*

I. First of all, I propose to consider this question. "What is *zeal* in religion?"

Zeal in religion is a burning desire to please God, to do His will, and to advance His glory in the world in every possible way. It is a desire which no man feels by nature, —which the Spirit puts in the heart of every believer when he is converted,—but which some believers feel so much more strongly than others that they alone deserve to be called "zealous" men.

This desire is so strong, when it really reigns in a man, that it impels him to make any sacrifice,—to go through any trouble,—to deny himself to any amount,—to suffer, to work, to labour, to toil,—to spend himself and be spent, and even to die,—if only he can please God and honour Christ.

A zealous man in religion is pre-eminently *a man of one thing.* It is not enough to say that he is earnest, hearty, uncompromising, thorough-going, whole-hearted, fervent in spirit. He only sees one thing, he cares for one thing, he lives for one thing, he is swallowed up in one thing; and that one thing is to please God. Whether he lives, or whether he dies,—whether he has health, or whether he has sickness,—whether he is rich, or whether he is poor,—whether he pleases man, or whether he gives offence,—whether he is thought wise, or whether he is thought foolish,—whether he gets blame, or whether he gets praise,—whether he gets honour, or whether he gets shame,—for all this the zealous man cares nothing at all. He burns for one thing; and that one thing is to please God, and to advance God's glory. If he is consumed in the very burning, he cares not for it,—he is content. He feels that, like a lamp, he is made to burn; and if consumed in burning, he has but done the work for which God appointed him. Such an one will always find a sphere for his zeal. If he cannot preach, and work, and give money, he will cry, and sigh, and pray. Yes: if he is only a pauper, on a perpetual bed of sickness, he will make the wheels of sin around him drive heavily, by continually interceding against it. If he cannot fight in the valley with Joshua, he will do the work of Moses, Aaron, and Hur, on the hill. (Exod. xvii. 9—13.) If he is cut off from working himself, he will give the Lord no rest till help is raised up from another quarter, and the work is done. This is what I mean when I speak of "zeal" in religion.

We all know the habit of mind that makes men great in this world,—that makes such men as Alexander the Great, or Julius Cæsar, or Oliver Cromwell, or Peter the Great, or Charles XII., or Marlborough, or Napoleon, or Pitt. We know that, with all their faults, they were all men of one thing. They threw themselves into one grand pursuit. They cared for nothing else. They put every thing else aside. They counted every thing else as second-rate, and of subordinate importance, compared to the one thing that they put before their eyes every day they lived. I say that the same habit of mind applied to the service of the Lord Jesus Christ becomes religious *zeal*.

We know the habit of mind that makes men great in the sciences of this world,—that makes such men as Archimedes, or Sir Isaac Newton, or Galileo, or Ferguson the astronomer, or James Watt. All these were men of one thing. They brought the powers of their minds into one single focus. They cared for nothing else beside. And this was the secret of their success. I say that this same habit consecrated to the service of God becomes religious *zeal*.

We know the habit of mind that makes men rich,— that makes men amass mighty fortunes, and leave millions behind them. What kind of people were the bankers, and merchants, and tradesmen, who have left a name behind them, as men who acquired immense wealth and became rich from being poor? They were all men that threw themselves entirely into their business, and neglected every thing else for the sake of that business. They gave their first attention, their first thoughts, the best of their time, and the best part of their mind, to pushing forward the transactions in which they were engaged. They were men of one thing. Their hearts were not divided. They devoted themselves, body, soul, and mind to their business. They seemed to live for nothing else. I say that if you turn that habit of mind to the service of God and His Christ it makes religious *zeal*.

(*a*) Now this habit of mind,—this zeal was *the character-istic of all the Apostles*. See for example the Apostle Paul. Hear him when he speaks to the Ephesian elders for the last time: "None of these things move me, neither count I my life dear unto myself, so that I might finish my course with joy, and the ministry that I have received of the Lord Jesus, to testify the Gospel of the grace of God." (Acts xx. 24.) Hear him again, when he writes to the Philippians: "This one thing I do; I press towards the

mark for the prize of the high calling of God in Christ
Jesus." (Phil. iii. 13, 14.) See him from the day of his
conversion, giving up his brilliant prospects,—forsaking
all for Christ's sake,—and going forth to preach that very
Jesus whom he had once despised. See him going to and
fro throughout the world from that time,—through
persecution,—through oppression,—through opposition,—
through prisons,—through bonds,—through afflictions,—
through things next to death itself, up to the very day
when he sealed his faith with his blood, and died at Rome,
a martyr for that Gospel which he had so long proclaimed.
This was true religious *zeal*.

(*b*) This again was *the characteristic of the early
Christians*. They were men "every where spoken against."
(Acts xxviii. 22.) They were driven to worship God in
dens and caves of the earth. They often lost every thing
in the world for their religion's sake. They generally
gained nothing but the cross, persecution, shame, and
reproach. But they seldom, very seldom, went back. If
they could not dispute, at least they could suffer. If they
could not convince their adversaries by argument, at any
rate they could die, and prove that they themselves were
in earnest. Look at Ignatius cheerfully travelling to the
place where he was to be devoured by lions, and saying as
he went, "Now do I begin to be a disciple of my Master,
Christ." Hear old Polycarp before the Roman Governor,
saying boldly, when called upon to deny Christ, "Four
score and six years have I served Christ, neither hath He
ever offended me in any thing, and how then can I revile
my King?" This was true *zeal*.

(*c*) This again was *the characteristic of Martin Luther*.
He boldly defied the most powerful hierarchy that the
world has ever seen. He unveiled its corruptions with
an unflinching hand. He preached the long-neglected
truth of justification by faith, in spite of anathemas and
excommunications, fast and thickly poured upon him.

See him going to the Diet at Worms, and pleading his cause before the Emperor and the Legate, and a host of the children of this world. Hear him saying,—when men were dissuading him from going, and reminding him of the fate of John Huss, "Though there were a devil under every tile on the roofs of Worms, in the name of the Lord I shall go forward." This was true *zeal*.

(*d*) This again was *the characteristic of our own English Reformers.* You have it in our first Reformer, Wickliffe, when he rose up on his sick bed, and said to the Friars, who wanted him to retract all he had said against the Pope, "I shall not die, but live to declare the villanies of the Friars." You have it in Cranmer, dying at the stake, rather than deny Christ's Gospel, holding forth that hand to be first burned which, in a moment of weakness, had signed a recantation, and saying, as he held it in the flames, "This unworthy hand!" You have it in old father Latimer, standing boldly on his faggot, at the age of seventy years, and saying to Ridley, "Courage, brother Ridley! we shall light such a candle this day as, by God's grace, shall never be put out." This was *zeal*.

(*e*) This again has been *the characteristic of all the greatest Missionaries.* You see it in Dr. Judson, in Carey, in Morrison, in Schwartz, in Williams, in Brainerd, in Elliott. You see it in none more brightly than in Henry Martyn. Here was a man who had reached the highest academical honours that Cambridge could bestow. Whatever profession he chose to follow, he had the most dazzling prospects of success. He turned his back upon it all. He chose to preach the Gospel to poor benighted heathen. He went forth to an early grave, in a foreign land. He said when he got there and saw the condition of the people, "I could bear to be torn in pieces, if I could but hear the sobs of penitence,—if I could but see the eyes of faith directed to the Redeemer!" This was *zeal*.

(*f*) But let us look away from all earthly examples,—and

remember that zeal was pre-eminently the characteristic of our Lord and Saviour Jesus Christ Himself. Of Him it was written hundreds of years before He came upon earth, that He was "clad with *zeal* as with a cloak," and "the *zeal* of thine house hath even eaten me." And His own words were "My meat is to do my Father's will, and to finish His work." (Psalm lxix. 9; Isaiah lix. 17; John iv. 34.)

Where shall we begin, if we try to give examples of His zeal? Where should we end, if we once began? Trace all the narratives of His life in the four Gospels. Read all the history of what He was from the beginning of His ministry to the end. Surely if there ever was one who was *all zeal*, it was our great Example,—our Head,—our High Priest,—the great Shepherd of our profession, the Lord Jesus Christ.

If these things are so, we should not only beware of running down zeal, but we should also beware of allowing zeal to be run down in our presence. It may be badly directed, and then it becomes a curse;—but it may be turned to the highest and best ends, and then it is a mighty blessing. Like fire, it is one of the best of servants;—but, like fire also, if not well directed, it may be the worst of masters. Listen not to those people who talk of zeal as weakness and enthusiasm. Listen not to those who see no beauty in missions, who laugh at all attempts at the conversion of souls,—who call Societies for sending the Gospel to the world useless,—and who look upon City Missions, and District Visiting, and Ragged Schools and Open Air Preaching, as nothing but foolishness and fanaticism. Beware, lest in joining a cry of that kind you condemn the Lord Jesus Christ Himself. Beware lest you speak against Him who has "left us an example that we should follow His steps." (1 Pet. ii. 21.)

Alas! I fear there are many professing Christians who if they had lived in the days when our Lord and His Apostles walked upon earth would have called Him and

all His followers enthusiasts and fanatics.   There are many,
I fear, who have more in common with Annas and Caiaphas,
—with Pilate and Herod,—with Festus and Agrippa,—
with Felix and Gallio,—than with St. Paul and the Lord
Jesus Christ.

II.   I pass on now to the second thing I proposed to
speak of.   *When is a man truly zealous in religion?*

There never was a grace of which Satan has not made
a counterfeit.   There never was a good coin issued from
the mint but forgers at once have coined something
very like it.   It was one of Nero's cruel practices first to
sew up Christians in the skins of wild beasts, and then
bait them with dogs.   It is one of Satan's devices to place
distorted copies of the believer's graces before the eyes of
men, and so to bring the true graces into contempt.   No
grace has suffered so much in this way as zeal.   Of none
perhaps are there so many shams and counterfeits abroad.
We must therefore clear the ground of all rubbish on this
question.   We must find out when zeal in religion is
really good, and true, and of God.

(1) If zeal be true, it will be a *zeal according to knowledge.*   It must not be a blind, ignorant zeal.   It must be
a calm, reasonable, intelligent principle, which can show
the warrant of Scripture for every step it takes.   The
unconverted Jews had zeal.   Paul says, "I bear them
record that they have a zeal of God, *but not according to
knowledge.*" (Rom. x. 2.)   Saul had zeal when he was
a persecuting Pharisee.   He says himself, in one of his
addresses to the Jews, "I was *zealous* toward God as ye
all are this day." (Acts xxii. 3.)—Manasseh had zeal in
the days when he was an idolater.   The man who made
his own children pass through the fire,—who gave up the
fruit of his body to Moloch, to atone for the sin of his soul,
—that man had zeal.—James and John had zeal when
they would have called down fire on a Samaritan village,

But our Lord rebuked them.—Peter had zeal when he drew his sword and cut off the ear of Malchus. But he was quite wrong.—Bonner and Gardiner had zeal when they burned Latimer and Cranmer. Were they not in earnest? Let us do them justice. They were zealous, though it was for an unscriptural religion.—The members of the Inquisition in Spain had zeal when they tortured men, and put them to horrible deaths, because they would not forsake the Gospel. Yes! they marched men and women to the stake in solemn procession, and called it "An Act of Faith," and believed they were doing God service.—The Hindoos, who used to lie down before the car of Juggernaut and allow their bodies to be crushed under its wheels:—had not they zeal?—The Indian widows, who used to burn themselves on the funeral pile of their deceased husbands,—the Roman Catholics, who persecuted to death the Vaudois and Albigenses, and cast down men and women from rocks and precipices, because they were heretics;—had not they zeal?—The Saracens, —the Crusaders,—the Jesuits,—the Anabaptists of Munster—the followers of Joanna Southcote,—had they not all zeal? Yes! Yes! I do not deny it. All these had zeal beyond question. They were all zealous. They were all in earnest. But their zeal was not such zeal as God approves,—it was not a "zeal according to knowledge."

(2) Furthermore, if zeal be true, it will be a zeal *from true motives*. Such is the subtlety of the heart that men will often do right things from wrong motives. Amaziah and Joash, kings of Judah, are striking proofs of this. Just so a man may have zeal about things that are good and right, but from second-rate motives, and not from a desire to please God. And such zeal is worth nothing. It is reprobate silver. It is utterly wanting when placed in the balance of God. Man looks only at the action: God looks at the motive. Man only thinks of the quantity of work done: God considers the doer's heart.

There is such a thing as zeal from *party spirit*. It is quite possible for a man to be unwearied in promoting the interests of his own Church or denomination, and yet to have no grace in his own heart,—to be ready to die for the peculiar opinions of his own section of Christians, and yet to have no real love to Christ. Such was the zeal of the Pharisees. They "compassed sea and land to make one proselyte, and when he was made, they made him two-fold more the child of hell than themselves." (Matt. xxiii. 15.) This zeal is not true.

There is such a thing as zeal from mere *selfishness*. There are times when it is men's interest to be zealous in religion. Power and patronage are sometimes given to godly men. The good things of the world are sometimes to be attained by wearing a cloak of religion. And whenever this is the case there is no lack of false zeal. Such was the zeal of Joab, when he served David. Such was the zeal of only too many Englishmen in the days of the Commonwealth, when the Puritans were in power.

There is such a thing as zeal from the *love of praise*. Such was the zeal of Jehu, when he was putting down the worship of Baal. Remember how he met Jonadab the son of Rechab, and said, "Come with me, and see my zeal for the Lord." (2 Kings x. 16.) Such is the zeal that Bunyan refers to in "Pilgrim's Progress," when he speaks of some who went "for praise " to mount Zion. Some people feed on the praise of their fellow-creatures. They would rather have it from Christians than have none at all.

It is a sad and humbling proof of man's corruption that there is no degree of self-denial and self-sacrifice to which men may not go from false motives. It does not follow that a man's religion is true because he " gives his body to be burned," or because he "gives his goods to feed the poor." The Apostle Paul tells us that a man may do this, and yet not have true charity. (1 Cor. xiii. 1, etc.) It does not follow because men go into a wilderness, and become hermits, that therefore they know what true self-denial is. It does not follow because people immure themselves in monasteries and nunneries, or become "sisters of charity," and "sisters of mercy," that therefore they know what true crucifixion of the flesh and self-sacrifice is in the sight of God. All these things people may do on wrong principles. They may do them from wrong motives,—to satisfy a secret pride and love of notoriety,—but not from the true motive of zeal for the glory of God. All such zeal, let us understand, is false. It is of earth, and not of heaven.

(3) Furthermore, if zeal be true, it will be a zeal *about things according to God's mind, and sanctioned by plain examples in God's Word.* Take, for one instance, that highest and best kind of zeal,—I mean zeal for our own growth in personal holiness. Such zeal will make a man feel incessantly that sin is the mightiest of all evils, and conformity to Christ the greatest of all blessings. It will make him feel that there is nothing which ought not to be done, in order to keep up a close walk with God. It will make him willing to cut off the right hand, or pluck out the right eye, or make any sacrifice, if only he can attain a closer communion with Jesus. Is not this just what you see in the Apostle Paul? He says, "I keep under my body and bring it into subjection, lest that by any means, when I have preached to others, I myself should be a castaway."—"I count not myself to have apprehended: but this one thing I do, forgetting those things which are behind, and reaching forth unto those things which are before, I press toward the mark." (1 Cor. ix. 27; Phil. iii. 13, 14.)

Take, for another instance, zeal for the salvation of souls. Such zeal will make a man burn with desire to enlighten the darkness which covers the souls of multitudes, and to bring every man, woman, and child he sees to the knowledge of the Gospel. Is not this what you see in the Lord Jesus? It is said that He neither gave

Himself nor His disciples leisure so much as to eat.
(Mark vi. 31.) Is not this what you see in the Apostle
Paul ? He says, " I am made all things to all men, that
I might by all means save some." (1 Cor. ix. 22.)

Take, for another instance, zeal against evil practices.
Such zeal will make a man hate everything which God
hates, such as drunkenness, slavery, or infanticide, and
long to sweep it from the face of the earth. It will make
him jealous of God's honour and glory, and look on everything which robs him of it as an offence. Is not this what
you see in Phinehas, the son of Eleazar ?—or in Hezekiah
and Josiah, when they put down idolatry ?

Take, for another instance, zeal for maintaining the
doctrines of the Gospel. Such zeal will make a man hate
unscriptural teaching, just as he hates sin. It will make
him regard religious error as a pestilence which must be
checked, whatever may be the cost. It will make him
scrupulously careful about every jot and tittle of the
counsel of God, lest by some omission the whole Gospel
should be spoiled. Is not this what you see in Paul at
Antioch, when he withstood Peter to the face. and said he
was to be blamed ? (Gal. ii. 11.) These are the kind of
things about which true zeal is employed. Such zeal, let
us understand, is honourable before God.

(4) Furthermore, if zeal be true, it will be a zeal *tempered with charity and love.* It will not be a bitter zeal.
It will not be a fierce enmity against persons. It will not
be a zeal ready to take the sword, and to smite with
carnal weapons. The weapons of true zeal are not carnal,
but spiritual. True zeal will hate sin, and yet love the
sinner. True zeal will hate heresy, and yet love the heretic.
True zeal will long to break the idol, but deeply pity the
idolater. True zeal will abhor every kind of wickedness,
but labour to do good even to the vilest of transgressors.

True zeal will warn as St. Paul warned the Galatians,
and yet feel tenderly, as a nurse or a mother over erring

children. It will expose false teachers, as Jesus did the Scribes and Pharisees, and yet weep tenderly, as Jesus did over Jerusalem when He came near to it for the last time. True zeal will be decided, as a surgeon dealing with a diseased limb; but true zeal will be gentle, as one that is dressing the wounds of a brother. True zeal will speak truth boldly, like Athanasius, against the world, and not care who is offended; but true zeal will endeavour, in all its speaking, to "speak the truth in love."

(5) Furthermore, if zeal be true, *it will be joined to a deep humility.* A truly zealous man will be the last to discover the greatness of his own attainments. All that he is and does will come so immensely short of his own desires, that he will be filled with a sense of his own unprofitableness, and amazed to think that God should work by him at all. Like Moses, when he came down from the Mount, he will not know that his face shines. Like the righteous, in the twenty-fifth chapter of St. Matthew, he will not be aware of his own good works. Dr. Buchanan is one whose praise is in all the churches. He was one of the first to take up the cause of the perishing heathen. He literally spent himself, body and mind, in labouring to arouse sleeping Christians to see the importance of missions. Yet he says in one of his letters, "I do not know that I ever had what Christians call zeal." Whitefield was one of the most zealous preachers of the Gospel the world has ever seen. Fervent in spirit, instant in season and out of season, he was a burning and shining light, and turned thousands to God. Yet he says after preaching for thirty years, "Lord help me to begin to begin." M'Cheyne was one of the greatest blessings that God ever gave to the Church of Scotland. He was a minister insatiably desirous of the salvation of souls. Few men ever did so much good as he did, though he died at the age of twenty-nine. Yet he says in one of his letters, "None but God knows what an abyss of corruption is in

my heart. It is perfectly wonderful that ever God could bless such a ministry." We may be very sure where there is self-conceit there is little true zeal.

I ask the readers of this paper particularly to remember the description of true zeal which I have just given. Zeal according to knowledge,—zeal from true motives,—zeal warranted by Scriptural examples,—zeal tempered with charity,—zeal accompanied by deep humility,—this is true genuine zeal,—this is the kind of zeal which God approves. Of such zeal you and I never need fear having too much.

I ask you to remember the description, because of the times in which you live. Beware of supposing that sincerity alone can ever make up true zeal,—that earnestness, however ignorant, makes a man a really zealous Christian in the sight of God. There is a generation in these days which makes an idol of what it is pleased to call "*earnestness*" in religion. These men will allow no fault to be found with an "*earnest man.*" Whatever his theological opinions may be,—if he be but an earnest man, that is enough for these people, and we are to ask no more. They tell you we have nothing to do with minute points of doctrine, and with questions of "words and names," about which Christians are not agreed. Is the man an earnest man? If he is, we ought to be satisfied. "Earnestness" in their eyes covers over a multitude of sins. I warn you solemnly to beware of this specious doctrine. In the name of the Gospel, and in the name of the Bible, I enter my protest against the theory that mere earnestness can make a man a truly zealous and pious man in the sight of God.

These idolaters of earnestness would make out that God has given us no standard of truth and error, or that the true standard, the Bible, is so obscure, that no man can find out what truth is by simply going to it. They pour contempt upon the Word, the written Word, and therefore they must be wrong.

These idolaters of earnestness would make us condemn

every witness for the truth, and every opponent of false
teaching, from the time of the Lord Jesus down to this
day. The Scribes and Pharisees were "in earnest," and yet
our Lord opposed them. And shall we dare even to hint
a suspicion that they ought to have been let alone ?—Queen
Mary, and Bonner, and Gardiner were "in earnest" in
restoring Popery, and trying to put down Protestantism,
and yet Ridley and Latimer opposed them to the death.
And shall we dare to say that as both parties were "in
earnest," both were in the right ?—Devil-worshippers and
idolaters at this day are in earnest, and yet our missionaries
labour to expose their errors. And shall we dare to say
that "earnestness" would take them to heaven, and that
missionaries to heathen and Roman Catholics had better
stay at home ?—Are we really going to admit that the
Bible does not show us what is truth ? Are we really
going to put a mere vague thing called "earnestness," in
the place of Christ, and to maintain that no "earnest" man
can be wrong ? God forbid that we should give place to
such doctrine ! I shrink with horror from such theology.
I warn men solemnly to beware of being carried away by
it, for it is common and most seductive in this day.
Beware of it, for it is only a new form of an old error,—
that old error which says that a man "Can't be wrong
whose life is in the right." Admire zeal. Seek after zeal.
Encourage zeal. But see that your own zeal be true. See
that the zeal which you admire in others is a zeal
"according to knowledge,"—a zeal from right motives,—a
zeal that can bring chapter and verse out of the Bible for
its foundation. Any zeal but this is but a false fire. It
is not lighted by the Holy Ghost.

III. I pass on now to the third thing I proposed to
speak of. Let me show *why it is good for a man to be
zealous.*

It is certain that God never gave man a commandment

which it was not man's interest as well as duty to obey.
He never set a grace before His believing people which
His people will not find it their highest happiness to follow
after. This is true of all the graces of the Christian
character. Perhaps it is preeminently true in the case of
zeal.

(a) Zeal is *good for a Christian's own soul.* We all
know that exercise is good for the health, and that regular
employment of our muscles and limbs promotes our bodily
comfort, and increases our bodily vigour. Now that which
exercise does for our bodies, zeal will do for our souls.
It will help mightily to promote inward feelings of joy,
peace, comfort, and happiness. None have so much enjoyment of Christ as those who are ever zealous for His glory,
—jealous over their own walk,—tender over their own
consciences,—full of anxiety about the souls of others,—
and ever watching, working, labouring, striving, and toiling
to extend the knowledge of Jesus Christ upon earth.
Such men live in the full light of the sun, and therefore their hearts are always warm. Such men water others,
and therefore they are watered themselves. Their hearts
are like a garden daily refreshed by the dew of the Holy
Ghost. They honour God, and so God honours them.

I would not be mistaken in saying this. I would not
appear to speak slightingly of any believer. I know that
"the Lord takes pleasure in all His people." (Ps. cxlix. 4.)
There is not one, from the least to the greatest,—from the
smallest child in the kingdom of God, to the oldest warrior
in the battle against Satan,—there is not one in whom the
Lord Jesus Christ does not take great pleasure. We are all
His children,—and however weak and feeble some of us
may be, "as a father pitieth his children, so does the Lord
pity them that love and fear Him." (Ps. ciii. 13.) We are all
the plants of His own planting;—and though many of us
are poor, weakly exotics, scarcely keeping life together in
a foreign soil,—yet as the gardener loves that which his

hands have reared, so does the Lord Jesus love the poor sinners that trust in Him. But while I say this, I do also believe that the Lord takes special pleasure in those who are *zealous* for Him,—in those who give themselves body, soul, and spirit, to extend His glory in this world. To them He reveals Himself, as he does not to others. To them He shows things that other men never see. He blesses the work of their hands. He cheers them with spiritual consolations, which others only know by the hearing of the ear. They are men after His own heart, for they are men more like Himself than others. None have such joy and peace in believing,—none have such sensible comfort in their religion.—none have so much of "heaven upon earth" (Deut. xi. 21),—none see and feel so much of the consolations of the Gospel as those who are zealous, earnest, thorough-going, devoted Christians. For the sake of our own souls, if there were no other reason, it is good to be zealous,—to be very zealous in our religion.

(*b*) As zeal is good for ourselves individually, so it is also *good for the professing Church of Christ generally.* Nothing so much keeps alive true religion as a leaven of zealous Christians scattered to and fro throughout a Church. Like salt, they prevent the whole body falling into a state of corruption. None but men of this kind can revive Churches when ready to die. It is impossible to over-estimate the debt that all Christians owe to zeal. The greatest mistake the rulers of a Church can make is to drive zealous men out of its pale. By so doing they drain out the life-blood of the system, and hasten on ecclesiastical decline and death.

Zeal is in truth that grace which God seems to delight to honour. Look through the list of Christians who have been eminent for usefulness. Who are the men that have left the deepest and most indelible marks on the Church of their day? Who are the men that God has generally honoured to build up the walls of His Zion, and turn the battle from the gate? Not so much men of learning and literary talents, as men of zeal.

Bishop Latimer was not such a deeply-read scholar as Cranmer or Ridley. He could not quote Fathers from memory, as they did. He refused to be drawn into arguments about antiquity. He stuck to his Bible. Yet it is not too much to say that no English reformer made such a lasting impression on the nation as old Latimer did. And what was the reason? His simple zeal.

Baxter, the Puritan, was not equal to some of his contemporaries in intellectual gifts. It is no disparagement to say that he does not stand on a level with Manton or Owen. Yet few men probably exercised so wide an influence on the generation in which he lived. And what was the reason? His burning zeal.

Whitefield, and Wesley, and Berridge, and Venn were inferior in mental attainments to Bishops Butler and Watson. But they produced effects on the people of this country which fifty Butlers and Watsons would probably never have produced. They saved the Church of England from ruin. And what was one secret of their power? Their zeal.

These men stood forward at turning points in the history of the Church. They bore unmoved storms of opposition and persecution.—They were not afraid to stand alone. They cared not though their motives were misinterpreted.—They counted all things but loss for the truth's sake.—They were each and all and every one eminently *men of one thing :*—and that one thing was to advance the glory of God, and to maintain His truth in the world. They were all fire, and so they lighted others. —They were wide awake, and so they awakened others.— They were all alive, and so they quickened others.—They were always working, and so they shamed others into working too.—They came down upon men like Moses from the mount.—They shone as if they had been in the presence of God.—They carried to and fro with them, as they walked their course through the world, something of the atmosphere and savour of heaven itself.

There is a sense in which it may be said that zeal is contagious. Nothing is more useful to the professors of Christianity than to see a real live Christian, a thoroughly zealous man of God. They may rail at him,—they may carp at him,—they may pick holes in his conduct,—they may look shy upon him,—they may not understand him any more than men understand a new comet when a new comet appears;—but insensibly a zealous man does them good. He opens their eyes. He makes them feel their own sleepiness. He makes their own great darkness visible. He obliges them to see their own barrenness. He compels them to think, whether they like it or not— "What are we doing? Are we not no better than mere cumberers of the ground?" It may be sadly true that "one sinner *destroyeth* much good;" but it is also a blessed truth that one zealous Christian can *do* much good. Yes: one single zealous man in a town,—one zealous man in a congregation,—one zealous man in a society,—one zealous man in a family, may be a great, a most extensive blessing. How many machines of usefulness such a man sets a going! How much Christian activity he often calls into being which would otherwise have slept! How many fountains he opens which would otherwise have been sealed! Verily there is a deep mine of truth in those words of the Apostle Paul to the Corinthians: "Your zeal hath provoked very many." (2 Cor. ix, 2.)

(c) But, as zeal is good for the Church and for individuals, so zeal is *good for the world.* Where would the Missionary work be if it were not for zeal? Where would our City Missions and Ragged Schools be if it were not for zeal? Where would our District-Visiting and Pastoral Aid Societies be if it were not for zeal? Where would be our

Societies for rooting out sin and ignorance, for finding out the dark places of the earth, and recovering poor lost souls? Where would be all these glorious instruments for good if it were not for Christian zeal? Zeal called these institutions into being, and zeal keeps them at work when they have begun. Zeal gathers a few despised men, and makes them the nucleus of many a powerful Society. Zeal keeps up the collections of a Society when it is formed. Zeal prevents men from becoming lazy and sleepy when the machine is large and begins to get favour from the world. Zeal raises up men to go forth, putting their lives in their hands, like Moffatt and Williams in our own day. Zeal supplies their place when they are gathered into the garner, and taken home.

What would become of the ignorant masses who crowd the lanes and alleys of our overgrown cities, if it were not for Christian zeal? Governments can do nothing with them: they cannot make laws that will meet the evil. The vast majority of professing Christians have no eyes to see it: like the priest and Levite, they pass by on the other side. But zeal has eyes to see, and a heart to feel, and a head to devise, and a tongue to plead, and hands to work, and feet to travel, in order to rescue poor souls, and raise them from their low estate. Zeal does not stand poring over difficulties, but simply says, "Here are souls perishing, and something *shall* be done." Zeal does not shrink back because there are Anakims in the way: it looks over their heads, like Moses on Pisgah, and says, "The land *shall* be possessed." Zeal does not wait for company, and tarry till good works are fashionable: it goes forward like a forlorn hope, and trusts that others will follow by and bye. Ah! the world little knows what a debt it owes to Christian zeal. How much crime it has checked! How much sedition it has prevented! How much public discontent it has calmed! How much obedience to law and love of order it has produced! How many souls it has saved!

Yes! and I believe we little know what might be done if every Christian was a zealous man! How much if ministers were more like Bickersteth, and Whitefield, and M'Cheyne! How much if laymen were more like Howard, and Wilberforce, and Thornton, and Nasmith, and George Moore! Oh, for the world's sake, as well as your own, resolve, labour, strive to be a zealous Christian!

Let every one who professes to be a Christian beware of checking zeal. Seek it. Cultivate it. Try to blow up the fire in your own heart, and the hearts of others, but never, never check it. Beware of throwing cold water on zealous souls, whenever you meet with them. Beware of nipping in the bud this precious grace when first it shoots. If you are a parent, beware of checking it in your children; —if you are a husband, beware of checking it in your wife;—if you are a brother, beware of checking it in your sisters,—and if you are a minister, beware of checking it in the members of your congregation. It is a shoot of heaven's own planting. Beware of crushing it, for Christ's sake. Zeal may make mistakes.—Zeal may need directing. —Zeal may want guiding, controlling, and advising. Like the elephants on ancient fields of battle, it may sometimes do injury to its own side. But zeal does not need damping in a wretched, cold, corrupt, miserable world like this. Zeal, like John Knox pulling down the Scotch monasteries, may hurt the feelings of narrow-minded and sleepy Christians. It may offend the prejudices of those old-fashioned religionists who hate everything new, and (like those who wanted soldiers and sailors to go on wearing pigtails) abhor all change. But zeal in the end will be justified by its results. Zeal, like John Knox, in the long run of life will do infinitely more good than harm. There is little danger of there ever being too much zeal for the glory of God. God forgive those who think there is! You know little of human nature. You forget that sickness is far more contagious than health, and that it is much easier to catch a chill than impart a glow. Depend upon it, the Church seldom needs a bridle, but often needs a spur. It seldom needs to be checked, it often needs to be urged on.

And now, in conclusion, let me try to apply this subject to the conscience of every person who reads this paper. It is a warning subject, an arousing subject, an encouraging subject, according to the state of our several hearts. I wish, by God's help, to give every reader his portion.

(1) First of all, let me offer a warning to all *who make no decided profession of religion.* There are thousands and tens of thousands, I fear, in this condition. If you are one, the subject before you is full of solemn warning. Oh, that the Lord in mercy may incline your heart to receive it!

I ask you, then, in all affection, Where is your zeal in religion? With the Bible before me, I may well be bold in asking. But with your life before me, I may well tremble as to the answer. I ask again, Where is your zeal for the glory of God? Where is your zeal for extending Christ's Gospel through an evil world? Zeal, which was the characteristic of the Lord Jesus; zeal, which is the characteristic of the angels; zeal, which shines forth in all the brightest Christians: where is your zeal, unconverted reader?—where is your zeal indeed! You know well it is nowhere at all; you know well you see no beauty in it; you know well it is scorned and cast out as evil by you and your companions; you know well it has no place, no portion, no standing ground, in the religion of your soul. It is not perhaps that you know not what it is to be zealous in a certain way. You have zeal, but it is all misapplied. It is all earthly: it is all about the things of time. It is not zeal for the glory of God: it is not zeal for the salvation of souls. Yes: many a man has zeal for the newspaper, but not for the Bible,—zeal for the daily reading of the *Times*, but no zeal for the daily reading of God's blessed Word. Many a man has zeal for the account book and the business book, but no zeal about the Book of Life and the last great account,—zeal about Australian and Californian gold, but no zeal about the unsearchable riches of Christ. Many a man has zeal about his earthly concerns,—his family, his pleasures, his daily pursuits; but no zeal about God, and heaven, and eternity.

If this is the state of any one who is reading this paper, awake, I do beseech you, to see your gross *folly*. You cannot live for ever. You are not ready to die. You are utterly unfit for the company of saints and angels. Awake: be zealous and repent!—Awake to see the *harm* you are doing! You are putting arguments in the hands of infidels by your shameful coldness. You are pulling down as fast as ministers build. You are helping the devil. Awake: be zealous, and repent!—Awake to see your childish *inconsistency!* What can be more worthy of zeal than eternal things, than the glory of God, than the salvation of souls? Surely if it is good to labour for rewards that are temporal, it is a thousand times better to labour for those that are eternal. Awake: be zealous and repent! Go and read that long-neglected Bible. Take up that blessed Book which you have, and perhaps never use. Read that New Testament through. Do you find nothing there to make you zealous,—to make you earnest about your soul? Go and look at the cross of Christ. Go and see how the Son of God there shed His precious blood for you,—how He suffered and groaned, and died for you,—how He poured out His soul as an offering for sin, in order that you, sinful brother or sister, might not perish, but have eternal life. Go and look at the cross of Christ, and never rest till you feel some zeal for your own soul,—some zeal for the glory of God,—some zeal for extension of the Gospel throughout the world. Once more I say, awake: be zealous, and repent!

(2) Let me, in the next place, say something to arouse those *who make a profession of being decided Christians, and are yet lukewarm in their practice.* There are only too many, I regret to say, in this state of soul. If you are one, there is much in this subject which ought to lead you to searchings of heart.

Let me speak to your conscience. To you also I desire to put the question in all brotherly affection, Where is your zeal?—Where is your zeal for the glory of God, and for extending the gospel throughout the world? You know well it is very low. You know well that your zeal is a little feeble glimmering spark, that just lives, and no more;—it is like a thing "ready to die." (Rev. iii. 2.) Surely, there is a fault somewhere, if this is the case. This state of things ought not to be. You, the child of God,—you, redeemed at so glorious a price,—you, ransomed with such precious blood, you, who are an heir of glory such as no tongue ever yet told, or eye saw;—surely you ought to be a man of another kind. Surely your zeal ought not to be so small.

I deeply feel that this is a painful subject to touch upon. I do it with reluctance, and with a constant remembrance of my own unprofitableness. Nevertheless, truth ought to be spoken. The plain truth is that many believers in the present day seem so dreadfully afraid of doing harm that they hardly ever dare to do good. There are many who are fruitful in objections, but barren in actions;—rich in wet blankets, but poor in anything like Christian fire. They are like the Dutch deputies, recorded in the history of last century, who would never allow Marlborough to venture anything, and by their excessive caution prevented many a victory being won. Truly, in looking round the Church of Christ, a man might sometimes think that God's kingdom had come, and God's will was being done upon earth, so small is the zeal that some believers show. It is vain to deny it. I need not go far for evidence. I point to Societies for doing good to the heathen, the colonies, and the dark places of our own land, languishing and standing still for want of active support. I ask, *Is this zeal?* I point to thousands of miserable guinea subscriptions which are never missed by the givers, and yet make up the sum of their Christian liberality. I ask, *Is this zeal?* I point to false doctrine allowed to grow up in parishes and families without an effort being made to check it, while so-called believers look on, and content themselves with wishing it was not so. I ask, *Is this zeal?* Would the apostles have been satisfied with such a state of things? We know they would not.

If the conscience of any one who read this paper pleads guilty to any participation in the short-comings I have spoken of, I call upon him, in the name of the Lord, to awake, be zealous, and repent. Let not zeal be confined to Lincoln's Inn, the Temple, and Westminster;—to banks, and shops, and counting houses. Let us see the same zeal in the Church of Christ. Let not zeal be abundant to lead forlorn hopes, or get gold from Australia, or travel over thick ribbed ice in voyages of discovery, but defective to send the Gospel to the heathen, or to pluck Roman Catholics like brands from the fire, or to enlighten the dark places of the colonies of this great land. Never were there such doors of usefulness opened,— never were there so many opportunities for doing good. I loathe that squeamishness which refuses to help religious works if there is a blemish about the instrument by which the work is carried on. At this rate we might never do anything at all. Let us resist the feeling, if we are tempted by it. It is one of Satan's devices. It is better to work with feeble instruments than not to work at all. At all events, try to do something for God and Christ,—something against ignorance and sin. Give, collect, teach, exhort, visit, pray, according as God enables you. Only make up your mind that all can do something, and resolve that by you, at any rate, something shall be done. If you have only one talent, do not bury it in the ground. Try to live so as to be missed. There is far more to be done in twelve hours than most of us have ever yet done on any day in our lives.

Think of the *precious souls* which are perishing while you are sleeping. Be taken up with your inward conflicts if you will. Go on anatomizing your own feelings, and poring over your own corruptions, if you are so determined. But remember all this time souls are going to hell, and you might do something to save them by working, by giving, by writing, by begging, and by prayer. Oh, awake! be zealous, and repent!

Think of the *shortness of time.* You will soon be gone. You will have no opportunity for works of mercy in another world. In heaven there will be no ignorant people to instruct, and no unconverted to reclaim. Whatever you do must be done now. Oh, when are you going to begin? Awake! be zealous, and repent.

Think of *the devil,* and his zeal to do harm. It was a solemn saying of old Bernard when he said that "Satan would rise up in judgment against some people at the last day, because he had shown more zeal to ruin souls than they had to save them." Awake! be zealous, and repent.

Think of *your Saviour,* and all His zeal for you. Think of Him in Gethsemane and on Calvary, shedding His blood for sinners. Think of His life and death,—His sufferings and His doings. This He has done for you. What are you doing for Him? Oh, resolve that for the time to come you will spend and be spent for Christ! Awake! be zealous and repent.

(3) Last of all, let me encourage *all readers of this paper who are truly zealous Christians.*

I have but one request to make, and that is *that you will persevere.* I do beseech you to hold fast your zeal, and never let it go. I do beseech you never to go back from your first works, never to leave your first love, never to let it be said of you that your first things were better than your last.—Beware of cooling down. You have only to be lazy, and to sit still, and you will soon lose all your warmth. You will soon become another man from what you are now. Oh, do not think this a needless exhortation!

It may be very true that wise young believers are very rare. But it is no less true that zealous old believers are very rare also. Never allow yourself to think that you can do too much,—that you can spend and be spent too much for Christ's cause. For one man that does too much I will show you a thousand who do not do enough. Rather think that "the night cometh, when no man can work" (John ix. 4),—and give, collect, teach, visit, work, pray, as if you were doing it for the last time. Lay to heart the words of that noble-minded Jansenist, who said, when told that he ought to rest a little, "What should we rest for? have we not all eternity to rest in?"

Fear not the reproach of men. Faint not because you are sometimes abused. Heed it not if you are sometimes called bigot, enthusiast, fanatic, madman, and fool. There is nothing disgraceful in these titles. They have often been given to the best and wisest of men. If you are only to be zealous when you are praised for it,—if the wheels of your zeal must be oiled by the world's commendation, your zeal will be but short-lived. Care not for the praise or frown of man. There is but one thing worth caring for, and that is the praise of God. There is but one question worth asking about our actions: "How will they look in the day of judgment?"

IX

FREEDOM

" If the Son shall make you free, ye shall be free indeed."—
JOHN viii. 36.

THE subject before our eyes deserves a thousand thoughts. It should ring in the ears of Englishmen and Scotchmen like the voice of a trumpet. We live in a land which is the very cradle of freedom. But are we ourselves free?

The question is one which demands special attention at the present state of public opinion in Great Britain. The minds of many are wholly absorbed in politics. Yet there is a freedom, within the reach of all, which few, I am afraid, ever think of,—a freedom independent of all political changes,—a freedom which neither Queen, Lords and Commons, nor the cleverest popular leaders can bestow. This is the freedom about which I write this day. Do we know anything of it? Are we free?

In opening this subject, there are three points which I wish to bring forward.

I. I will show, in the first place, *the general excellence of freedom.*

II. I will show, in the second place, *the best and truest kind of freedom.*

III. I will show, in the last place, *the way in which the best kind of freedom may become your own.*

Let no reader think for a moment that this is going to be a political paper. I am no politician: I have no politics but those of the Bible. The only party I care for is the Lord's side: show me where that is, and it shall have my support. The only election I am very anxious about is the election of grace. My one desire is, that sinners should make their own calling and election sure.— The liberty I desire above all things to make known, and further, is the glorious liberty of the children of God.— The Government I care to support is the government which is on the shoulder of my Lord and Saviour Jesus Christ. Before Christ I want every knee to bow, and every tongue to confess that He is Lord. I ask attention while I canvass these subjects. If you are not free, I want to guide you into true liberty. If you are free, I want you to know the full value of your freedom.

I. The first thing I have to show is *the general excellence of freedom.*

On this point some readers may think it needless to say anything: they imagine that all men know the value of freedom, and that to dwell on it is mere waste of time. I do not agree with such people at all. I believe that myriads of Englishmen know nothing of the blessings which they enjoy in their own land: they have grown up from infancy to manhood in the midst of free institutions. They have not the least idea of the state of things in other countries: they are ignorant alike of those two worst forms of tyranny,—the crushing tyranny of a cruel military despot, and the intolerant tyranny of an un-reasoning mob. In short, many Englishmen know nothing of the value of liberty, just because they have been born in the middle of it, and have never been for a moment without it.

I call then on every one who reads this paper to re-member that liberty is one of the greatest temporal blessings that man can have on this side the grave. We live in a land where our *bodies* are free. So long as we hurt nobody's person, or property, or character, no one can touch us: the poorest man's house is his castle.—We live in a land where our *actions* are free. So long as we support ourselves, we are free to choose what we will do, where we will go, and how we will spend our time.—We live in a land where our *consciences* are free. So long as we hold quietly on our own way, and do not interfere with others, we are free to worship God as we please, and no man can compel us to take his way to heaven. We live in a land where no foreigner rules over us. Our laws are made and altered by Englishmen like ourselves, and our Governors dwell by our side, bone of our bone and flesh of our flesh.

In short, we have every kind of freedom to an extent which no other nation on earth can equal. We have personal freedom, civil freedom, religious freedom, and national freedom. We have free bodies, free consciences, free speech, free thought, free action, free Bibles, a free press, and free homes. How vast is this list of privileges! How endless the comforts which it contains! The full value of them can never perhaps be known. Well said the Jewish Rabbins in ancient days: "If the sea were ink and the world parchment, it would never serve to describe the praises of liberty."

The want of this freedom has been the most fertile cause of misery to nations in every age of the world. What reader of the Bible can fail to remember the sorrows of the children of Israel, when they were bondmen under Pharaoh in Egypt, or under Philistines in Canaan? What student of history needs to be reminded of the woes inflicted on the Netherlands, Poland, Spain, and Italy by the hand of foreign oppressors, or the Inquisition? Who, even in our own time, has not heard of that enormous fountain of wretchedness, the slavery of the Negro race? No misery certainly is so great as the misery of slavery.

To win and preserve freedom has been the aim of many national struggles which have deluged the earth with blood. Liberty has been the cause in which myriads of Greeks, and Romans, and Germans, and Poles, and Swiss, and Englishmen, and Americans have willingly laid down their lives. No price has been thought too great to pay in order that nations might be free.

The champions of freedom in every age have been justly esteemed among the greatest benefactors of mankind. Such names as Moses and Gideon in Jewish history, such names as the Spartan Leonidas, the Roman Horatius, the German Martin Luther, the Swedish Gustavus Vasa, the Swiss William Tell, the Scotch Robert Bruce and John Knox, the English Alfred and Hampden and the Puritans, the American George Washington, are deservedly embalmed in history, and will never be forgotten. To be the mother of many patriots is the highest praise of a nation.

The enemies of freedom in every age have been rightly regarded as the pests and nuisances of their times. Such names as Pharaoh in Egypt, Dionysius at Syracuse, Nero at Rome, Charles IX. in France, bloody Mary in England, are names which will never be rescued from disgrace. The public opinion of mankind will never cease to condemn them, on the one ground that they would not let people be free.

But why should I dwell on these things? Time and space would fail me if I were to attempt to say a tenth part of what might be said in praise of freedom. What are the annals of history but a long record of conflicts between the friends and foes of liberty? Where is the nation upon earth that has ever attained greatness, and left its mark on the world, without freedom? Which are the countries on the face of the globe at this very moment which are making the most progress in trade, in arts, in sciences, in civilization, in philosophy, in morals, in social happiness? Precisely those countries in which there is

the greatest amount of true freedom. Which are the
countries at this very day where is the greatest amount
of internal misery, where we hear continually of secret
plots, and murmuring, and discontent, and attempts on
life and property? Precisely those countries where
freedom does not exist, or exists only in name,—where
men are treated as serfs and slaves, and are not allowed
to think and act for themselves. No wonder that a
mighty Transatlantic Statesman declared on a great
occasion to his assembled countrymen : "Is life so dear, or
peace so sweet, as to be purchased at the price of chains
and slavery? Forbid it, almighty God! I know not
what course others may take; but as for me, give me
liberty or give me death!" *

Let us beware of *undervaluing* the liberty we enjoy in
this country of ours, as Englishmen. I am sure there is
need of this warning. There is, perhaps, no country on
earth where there is so much grumbling and fault-finding
as there is in England. Men look at the fancied evils
which they see around them, and exaggerate both their
number and their intensity. They refuse to look at the
countless blessings and privileges which surround us, or
underrate the advantages of them. They forget that
comparison should be applied to everything. With all our
faults and defects there is at this hour no country on earth
where there is so much liberty and happiness for all
classes, as there is in England. They forget that as long
as human nature is corrupt, it is vain to expect perfection
here below. No laws or government whatever can possibly
prevent a certain quantity of abuses and corruptions.
Once more then, I say, let us beware of undervaluing
English liberty, and running eagerly after every one who

---

* To prevent mistakes, I think it well to say that the man I refer to is
Patrick Henry, an American Statesman of the last century.

proposes sweeping changes. Changes are not always improvements. The old shoes may have some holes and defects, but the new shoes may pinch so much that we cannot walk at all. No doubt we might have better laws and government than we have: but I am quite sure we might easily have worse. At this very day there is no country on the face of the globe where there is so much care taken of the life, and health, and property, and character, and personal liberty of the meanest inhabitant, as there is in England. Those who want to have more liberty, would soon find, if they crossed the seas, that there is no country on earth where there is so much real liberty as our own.*

But while I bid men not undervalue English liberty, so also on the other hand I charge them not to *overvalue* it. Never forget that temporal slavery is not the only slavery, and temporal freedom not the only freedom. What shall

---

* The following weighty passage, from the pen of the judicious Hooker, is commended to the attention of all in the present day. It is the opening passage of the first book of his "Ecclesiastical Polity."

"He that goeth about to persuade a multitude that they are not so well governed as they ought to be, shall never want attentive and favourable hearers, because they know the manifold defects whereunto every kind of regiment or government is subject; but the secret lets and difficulties, which in public proceedings are innumerable and inevitable, they have not ordinarily the judgment to consider. And because such as openly reprove disorders of States are taken for principal friends to the common benefit of all, and for men that carry singular freedom of mind, under this fair and plausible colour whatsoever they utter passeth for good and current. That which is wanting in the weight of their speech is supplied by the aptness of men's minds to accept and believe it. Whereas, on the other side, if we maintain things that are established, we have not only to strive with a number of heavy prejudices, deeply rooted in the breasts of men, who think that herein we serve the times, and speak in favour of the present state, because we either hold or seek preferment; but also to bear such reception as minds so averted before-hand usually take against that which they are loth should be poured into them."

it profit you to be a citizen of a free country, so long as
your soul is not free? What is the use of living in a free
land like England, with free thought, free speech, free
action, free conscience, so long as you are a slave to sin,
and a captive to the devil? Yes: there are tyrants whom
no eye can see, as real and destructive as Pharaoh or Nero!
There are chains which no hands can touch, as true and
heavy and soul-withering as ever crushed the limbs of an
African! It is these tyrants whom I want you this day
to remember. It is these chains from which I want you
to be free. Value by all means your English liberty, but
do not overvalue it. Look higher, further than any
temporal freedom. In the highest sense let us take care
that " we are free."

II. The second thing I have to show is *the truest and
best kind of freedom.*

The freedom I speak of is a freedom that is within the
reach of every child of Adam who is willing to have it.
No power on earth can prevent a man or woman having
it, if they have but the will to receive it. Tyrants may
threaten and cast in prison, but nothing they can do can
stop a person having this liberty. And, once our own,
nothing can take it away. Men may torture us, banish
us, hang us, behead us, burn us, but they can never tear
from us true freedom. The poorest may have it no less
than the richest: the most unlearned may have it as well
as the most learned, and the weakest as well as the
strongest. Laws cannot deprive us of it: Pope's bulls
cannot rob us of it. Once our own, it is an everlasting
possession.

Now, what is this glorious freedom? Where is it to be
found? What is it like? Who has obtained it for man?
Who has got it at this moment to bestow? I ask my
readers to give me their attention, and I will supply a
plain answer to these questions.

The true freedom I speak of is spiritual freedom,—freedom of soul. It is the freedom which Christ bestows, without money and without price, on all true Christians. Those whom the Son makes free are free indeed: "Where the Spirit of the Lord is, there is liberty." (2 Cor. iii. 17.) Let men talk what they please of the comparative freedom of monarchies and republics; let them struggle, if they will, for universal liberty, fraternity, and equality: we never know the highest style of liberty till we are enrolled citizens of the kingdom of God. We are ignorant of the best kind of freedom if we are not Christ's freemen.

Christ's freemen are free from the *guilt of sin*. That heavy burden of unforgiven transgressions, which lies so heavy on many consciences, no longer presses them down. Christ's blood has cleansed it all away. They feel pardoned, reconciled, justified, and accepted in God's sight. They can look back to their old sins, however black and many, and say,—"Ye cannot condemn me." They can look back on long years of carelessness and worldliness and say,—"Who shall lay anything to my charge?" This is true liberty. This is to be free.

Christ's freemen are free from the *power of sin*. It no longer rules and reigns in their hearts, and carries them before it like a flood. Through the power of Christ's Spirit they mortify the deeds of their bodies, and crucify their flesh with its affections and lusts. Through His grace working in them they get the victory over their evil inclinations. The flesh may fight, but it does not conquer them; the devil may tempt and vex, but does not overcome them: they are no longer the bondslaves of lusts and appetites, and passions, and tempers. Over all these things they are more than conquerors, through Him that loved them. This is true liberty. This is to be free.

Christ's freemen are free from the *slavish fear of God*. They no longer look at Him with dread and alarm, as an offended Maker; they no longer hate Him, and get away from Him, like Adam among the trees of the garden; they no longer tremble at the thought of His judgment. Through the Spirit of adoption which Christ has given them, they look on God as a reconciled Father, and rejoice in the thought of His love. They feel that anger is passed away. They feel that when God the Father looks down upon them, He sees them in Christ, and unworthy as they are in themselves, is well-pleased. This is true liberty. This is to be free.

Christ's freemen are free from the *fear of man*. They are no longer afraid of man's opinions, or care much what man thinks of them; they are alike indifferent to his favour or his enmity, his smile or his frown. They look away from man who can be seen, to Christ who is not seen, and having the favour of Christ, they care little for the blame of man. "The fear of man" was once a snare to them. They trembled at the thought of what man would say, or think, or do: they dared not run counter to the fashions and customs of those around them; they shrank from the idea of standing alone. But the snare is now broken and they are delivered. This is true liberty. This is to be free.

Christ's freemen are free from the *fear of death*. They no longer look forward to it with silent dismay, as a horrible thing which they do not care to think of. Through Christ they can look this last enemy calmly in the face, and say,—"Thou canst not harm me." They can look forward to all that comes after death,—decay, resurrection, judgment, and eternity,—and yet not feel cast down. They can stand by the side of an open grave, and say, "O death, where is thy sting? O grave, where is thy victory?" They can lay them down on their death-beds, and say, "Though I walk through the valley of the shadow of death, I will fear no evil." (Ps. xxiii. 4.) "Not a hair of my head shall perish." This is true liberty. This is to be free.

Best of all, Christ's freemen are *free for ever*. Once

enrolled in the list of heavenly citizens, their names shall never be struck off. Once presented with the freedom of Christ's kingdom, they shall possess it for evermore. The highest privileges of this world's freedom can only endure for a life-time; the freest citizen on earth must submit at length to die, and lose his franchise for ever: but the franchise of Christ's people is eternal. They carry it down to the grave, and it lives still; they will rise again with it at the last day, and enjoy the privileges of it for evermore. This is true liberty. This is to be free.

Does anyone ask how and in what way Christ has obtained these mighty privileges for His people? You have a right to ask the question, and it is one that can never be answered too clearly. Give me your attention, and I will show you by what means Christ has made His people free.

The freedom of Christ's people has been procured, like all other freedom, at a mighty cost and by a mighty sacrifice. Great was the bondage in which they were naturally held, and great was the price necessary to be paid to set them free: mighty was the enemy who claimed them as his captives, and it needed mighty power to release them out of his hands. But, blessed be God, there was grace enough, and power enough ready in Jesus Christ. He provided to the uttermost everything that was required to set His people free. The price that Christ paid for His people was nothing less than His own life-blood. He became their Substitute, and suffered for their sins on the cross: He redeemed them from the curse of the law, by being made a curse for them. (Gal. iii. 13.) He paid all their debt in His own person, by allowing the chastisement of their peace to be laid on Him. (Isaiah liii. 5.) He satisfied every possible demand of the law against them, by fulfilling its righteousness to the uttermost. He cleared them from every imputation of sin, by becoming sin for them. (2 Cor. v. 21.) He fought

their battle with the devil, and triumphed over him on
the cross. As their Champion, He spoiled principalities
and powers, and made a show of them openly on Calvary.
In a word, Christ having given Himself for us, has
purchased the full right of redemption for us. Nothing
can touch those to whom He gives freedom: their debts
are paid, and paid a thousand times over; their sins are
atoned for by a full, perfect, and sufficient atonement. A
Divine Substitute's death meets completely the justice of
God, and provides completely redemption for man.

Let us look well at this glorious plan of redemption,
and take heed that we understand it. Ignorance on this
point is one great secret of faint hopes, little comfort, and
ceaseless doubts in the minds of Christians. Too many
are content with a vague idea that Christ will somehow
save sinners: but how or why they cannot tell. I protest
against this ignorance. Let us set fully before our eyes
the doctrine of Christ's vicarious death and substitution,
and rest our souls upon it. Let us grasp firmly the mighty
truth, that Christ on the cross, stood in the place of His
people, died for His people, suffered for His people, was
counted a curse and sin for His people, paid the debts of
His people, made satisfaction for His people, became the
surety and representative of His people, and in this way
procured His people's freedom. Let us understand this
clearly, and then we shall see what a mighty privilege it
is to be made free by Christ.

This is the freedom which, above all other, is worth
having. We can never value it too highly: there is no
danger of overvaluing it. All other freedom is an unsatisfying thing at the best, and a poor uncertain possession
at any time. Christ's freedom alone can never be overthrown. It is secured by a covenant ordered in all things
and sure: its foundations are laid in the eternal councils
of God, and no foreign enemy can overthrow them. They
are cemented and secured by the blood of the Son of God

Himself, and can never be cast down. The freedom of nations often lasts no longer than a few centuries: the freedom which Christ gives to any one of His people is a freedom that shall outlive the solid world.

This is the truest, highest kind of freedom. This is the freedom which in a changing, dying world, I want men to possess.

III. I have now to show, in the last place, *the way in which the best kind of freedom is made our own.*

This is a point of vast importance, on account of the many mistakes which prevail about it. Thousands, perhaps, will allow that there is such a thing as spiritual freedom, and that Christ alone has purchased it for us: but when they come to the application of redemption, they go astray. They cannot answer the question, "Who are those whom Christ effectually makes free?" and for want of knowledge of the answer, they sit still in their chains. I ask every reader to give me his attention once more, and I will try to throw a little light on the subject. Useless indeed is the redemption which Christ has obtained, unless you know how the fruit of that redemption can become your own. In vain have you read of the freedom wherewith Christ makes people free, unless you understand how you yourself may have an interest in it.

We are not born Christ's freemen. The inhabitants of many a city enjoy privileges by virtue of their birth-place. St. Paul, who drew life-breath first at Tarsus in Cilicia, could say to the Roman Commander, "I was free-born." But this is not the case with Adam's children, in spiritual things. We are born slaves and servants of sin: we are by nature "children of wrath," and destitute of any title to heaven.

We are not made Christ's freemen by baptism. Myriads are every year brought to the font, and solemnly baptized in the name of the Trinity, who serve sin like slaves, and neglect Christ all their days. Wretched indeed is that man's state of soul who can give no better evidence of his citizenship of heaven than the mere naked fact of his baptism!

We are not made Christ's freemen by mere membership of Christ's Church. There are Companies and Corporations whose members are entitled to vast privileges, without any respect to their personal character, if their names are only on the list of members. The kingdom of Christ is not a corporation of this kind. The grand test of belonging to it is personal character.

Let these things sink down into our minds. Far be it from me to narrow the extent of Christ's redemption: the price He paid on the cross is sufficient for the whole world. Far be it from me to undervalue baptism or Church-membership: the ordinance which Christ appointed, and the Church which He maintains in the midst of a dark world, ought neither of them to be lightly esteemed.—All I contend for is the absolute necessity of not being content either with baptism or Church-membership. If our religion stops short here it is unprofitable and unsatisfying. It needs something more than this to give us an interest in the redemption which Christ has purchased.

There is no other way to become Christ's freemen than that of simply believing. It is by faith, simple faith in Him as our Saviour and Redeemer, that men's souls are made free. It is by receiving Christ, trusting Christ, committing ourselves to Christ, reposing our whole weight on Christ,—it is by this, and by no other plan, that spiritual liberty is made our own. Mighty as are the privileges which Christ's freemen possess, they all become a man's property in the day that he first believes. He may not yet know their full value, but they are all his own. He that believeth in Christ is not condemned,—is justified, is born again, is an heir of God, and hath everlasting life.

The truth before us is one of priceless importance. Let us cling to it firmly, and never let it go. If you desire peace of conscience, if you want inward rest and consolation, stir not an inch off the ground that faith is the grand secret of an interest in Christ's redemption.—Take the simplest view of faith: beware of confusing your mind by complicated ideas about it. Follow holiness as closely as you can: seek the fullest and clearest evidence of the inward work of the Spirit. But in the matter of an interest in Christ's redemption remember that faith stands alone. It is by believing, simply believing, that souls become free.

No doctrine like this to suit the ignorant and unlearned! Visit the poorest and humblest cottager, who knows nothing of theology, and cannot even repeat the creed. Tell him the story of the cross, and the good news about Jesus Christ, and His love to sinners; show him that there is freedom provided for him, as well as for the most learned in the land,—freedom from guilt, freedom from the devil, freedom from condemnation, freedom from hell. And then tell him plainly, boldly, broadly, unreservedly, that this freedom may be all his own, if he will but trust in Christ and believe.

No doctrine like this to suit the sick and dying! Go to the bedside of the vilest sinner, when death is coming nigh, and tell him lovingly that there is a hope even for him, if he can receive it. Tell him that Christ came into the world to save sinners, even the chief of them; tell him that Christ has done all, paid all, performed all, purchased all that the soul of man can possibly need for salvation. And then assure him that he, even he, may be freed at once from all his guilt, if he will only believe. Yes, say to him, in the words of Scripture, "If thou shalt confess with thy mouth the Lord Jesus, and believe in thine heart that God hath raised Him from the dead, thou shalt be saved." (Rom. x. 9.)

Let us never forget that this is the point to which we must turn our own eyes, if we would know whether we have a saving interest in Christ's redemption. Waste not your time in speculations whether you are elect, and converted, and a vessel of grace. Stand not poring over the unprofitable question whether Christ died for you or not. That is a point of which no one ever made any question in the Bible. Settle your thoughts on this one simple inquiry,—" Do I really trust in Christ, as a humble sinner ? Do I cast myself on Him ? Do I believe ? "—Look not to anything else. Look at this alone. Fear not to rest your soul on plain texts and promises of Scripture. If you believe, you are free.

(1) And now as I bring this paper to a conclusion, let me affectionately press upon every reader the inquiry which grows naturally out of the whole subject. Let me ask every one a plain question: " Are you free ? "

I know not who or what you are into whose hands this paper has fallen. But this I do know, there never was an age when the inquiry I press upon you was more thoroughly needed. Political liberty, civil liberty, commercial liberty, liberty of speech, liberty of the press,—all these, and a hundred other kindred subjects, are swallowing up men's attention. Few, very few, find time to think of spiritual liberty. Many, too many, forget that no man is so thoroughly a slave, whatever his position, as the man who serves sin. Yes ! there are thousands in this country who are slaves of beer and spirits, slaves of lust, slaves of ambition, slaves of political party, slaves of money, slaves of gambling, slaves of fashion, or slaves of temper ! You may not see their chains with the naked eye, and they themselves may boast of their liberty: but for all that they are thoroughly slaves. Whether men like to hear it or not, the gambler and the drunkard, the covetous and the passionate, the glutton and the sensualist, are not free, but slaves. They are bound hand and foot by the devil. " He

that committeth sin is the servant of sin." (Rom. viii. 34.)
He that boasts of liberty, while he is enslaved by lusts and
passions, is going down to hell with a lie in his right hand.

Awake to see these things, while health, and time, and
life are granted to you. Let not political struggles and
party strife make you forget your precious soul. Take any
side in politics you please, and follow honestly your conscientious convictions; but never, never forget that there
is a liberty far higher and more lasting than any that
politics can give you. Rest not till that liberty is your
own. Rest not till YOUR SOUL IS FREE.

(2) Do you feel any desire to be free? Do you find any
longing within you for a higher, better liberty than this
world can give—a liberty that will not die at your death,
but will go with you beyond the grave? Then take the
advice I give you this day. Seek Christ, repent, believe,
and be free. Christ has a glorious liberty to bestow on all
who humbly cry to Him for freedom. Christ can take
burdens off your heart, and strike chains off your inward
man. "If the Son shall make you free, you shall be free
indeed." (John viii. 36.)

Freedom like this is the secret of true happiness. None
go through the world with such ease and content as those
who are citizens of a heavenly country. Earth's burdens
press lightly upon their shoulders; earth's disappointments
do not crush them down as they do others; earth's duties
and anxieties do not drink up their spirit. In their darkest
hours they have always this sustaining thought to fall back
on,—"I have something which makes me independent of
this world: I am spiritually free."

Freedom like this is the secret of being a good politician.
In every age Christ's freemen have been the truest friends
to law and order, and to measures for the benefit of all
classes of mankind. Never, **never** let it be forgotten that
the despised Puritans, two hundred years ago, did more
for the cause of real liberty in England than all the

Governments which ever ruled this land. No man ever made this country so feared and respected as Oliver Cromwell. The root of the most genuine patriotism is to be one of those whom Christ has made free.

(3) Are you spiritually free? Then rejoice, and be thankful for your freedom. Care not for the scorn and contempt of man: you have no cause to be ashamed of your religion or your Master. He whose citizenship is in heaven (Phil. iii. 20), who has God for his Father, and Christ for his Elder Brother, angels for his daily guards, and heaven itself for his home, is one that is well provided for. No change of laws can add to his greatness: no extension of franchise can raise him higher than he stands in God's sight. "The lines are fallen to him in pleasant places, and he has a goodly heritage." (Psalm xvi. 6.) Grace now, and the hope of glory hereafter, are more lasting privileges than the power of voting for twenty boroughs or counties.

Are you free? Then stand fast in your liberty, and be not entangled again in the yoke of bondage. Listen not to those who by good words and fair speeches would draw you back to the Church of Rome. Beware of those who would fain persuade you that there is any mediator but the one Mediator, Christ Jesus,—any sacrifice but the one Sacrifice offered on Calvary,—any priest but the great High Priest Emmanuel,—any incense needed in worship but the savour of His name who was crucified,—any rule of faith and practice but God's Word,—any confessional but the throne of grace,—any effectual absolution but that which Christ bestows on the hearts of His believing people,—any purgatory but the one fountain open for all sins, the blood of Christ, to be only used while we are alive. On all these points stand fast, and be on your guard. Scores of misguided teachers are trying to rob Christians of Gospel liberty, and to bring back among us exploded superstitions. Resist them manfully, and do not give way for a moment. Remember what Romanism was in this country before the blessed Reformation. Remember at what mighty cost our martyred Reformers brought spiritual freedom to light by the Gospel. Stand fast for this freedom like a man, and labour to hand it down to your children, whole and unimpaired.

Are you free? Then think every day you live of the millions of your fellow-creatures who are yet bound hand and foot in spiritual darkness. Think of six hundred millions of heathens who never yet heard of Christ and salvation. Think of the poor homeless Jews, scattered and wandering over the face of the earth, because they have not yet received their Messiah. Think of the millions of Roman Catholics who are yet in captivity under the Pope, and know nothing of true liberty, light, and peace. Think of the myriads of your own fellow-countrymen in our great cities, who, without Sabbaths and without means of grace, are practically heathens, and whom the devil is continually leading captive at his will. Think of them all, and feel for them. Think of them all, and often say to yourself,—" What can I do for them? How can I help to set them free?"

What! Shall it be proclaimed at the last day that Pharisees and Jesuits have compassed sea and land to make proselytes,—that politicians have leagued and laboured night and day to obtain catholic emancipation and free trade,—that philanthropists have travailed in soul for years to procure the suppression of negro slavery, —and shall it appear at the same time that Christ's free-men have done little to rescue men and women from hell? Forbid it, faith! Forbid it, charity! Surely if the children of this world are zealous to promote temporal freedom, the children of God ought to be much more zealous to promote spiritual freedom. Let the time past suffice us to have been selfish and indolent in this matter. For the rest of our days let us use **every** effort to promote spiritual emancipation. If we have tasted the blessings of freedom, let us spare no pains to make others free.

Are you free ? Then look forward in faith and hope for good things yet to come. Free as we are, if we believe on Christ, from the guilt and power of sin, we must surely feel every day that we are not free from its presence and the temptations of the devil. Redeemed as we are from the eternal consequences of the fall, we must often feel that we are not yet redeemed from sickness and infirmity, from sorrow and from pain. No, indeed! Where is the freeman of Christ on earth who is not often painfully reminded that we are not yet in heaven ? We are yet in the body ; we are yet travelling through the wilderness of this world : we are not at home. We have shed many tears already, and probably we shall have to shed many more ; we have got yet within us a poor weak heart : we are yet liable to be assaulted by the devil. Our redemption is begun indeed, but it is not yet completed. We have redemption now in the root, but we have it not in the flower.

But let us take courage : there are better days yet to come. Our great Redeemer and Liberator has gone before us to prepare a place for His people, and when He comes again our redemption will be complete. The great jubilee year is yet to come. A few more returns of Christmas and New Year's Days,—a few more meetings and partings, —a few more births and deaths,—a few more weddings and funerals,—a few more tears and struggles,—a few more sicknesses and pains,—a few more Sabbaths and sacraments,—a few more preachings and prayings,—a few more, and the end will come ! Our Master will come back again. The dead saints shall be raised. The living saints shall be changed. Then, and not till then, we shall be completely free. The liberty which we enjoyed by faith shall be changed into the liberty of sight, and the freedom of hope into the freedom of certainty.

Come, then, and let us resolve to wait, and watch, and hope, and pray, and live like men who have something laid up for them in heaven. The night is far spent, and the day is at hand. Our King is not far off: our full redemption draweth nigh. Our full salvation is nearer than when we believed. The signs of the times are strange, and demand every Christian's serious attention. The kingdoms of this world are in confusion: the powers of this world, both temporal and ecclesiastical, are everywhere reeling and shaken to their foundations. Happy, thrice happy, are those who are citizens of Christ's eternal kingdom, and ready for anything that may come. Blessed indeed are those men and women who know and feel that they are free!

X

HAPPINESS

"Happy is that people whose God is the Lord."—Psalm cxliv. 15.

An infidel was once addressing a crowd of people in the open air. He was trying to persuade them that there was no God and no devil no heaven, and no hell, no resurrection, no judgment, and no life to come. He advised them to throw away their Bibles, and not to mind what parsons said. He recommended them to think as he did, and to be like him. He talked boldly. The crowd listened eagerly. It was "the blind leading the blind." Both were falling into the ditch. (Matt. xv. 14.)

In the middle of his address a poor old woman suddenly pushed her way through the crowd, to the place where he was standing. She stood before him. She looked him full in the face. "Sir," she said, in a loud voice, "Are you happy?" The infidel looked scornfully at her, and gave her no answer. "Sir," she said again, "I ask you to answer my question. Are you happy? You want us to throw away our Bibles. You tell us not to believe what parsons say about religion. You advise us to think as you do, and be like you. Now before we take your advice we have a right to know what good we shall get by it. Do your fine new notions give you much comfort? Do you yourself really feel happy?"

The infidel stopped, and attempted to answer the old woman's question. He stammered, and shuffled, and fidgetted, and endeavoured to explain his meaning. He tried hard to turn the subject. He said, he "had not come there to preach about happiness." But it was of no use. The old woman stuck to her point. She insisted on her question being answered, and the crowd took her part. She pressed him hard with her inquiry, and would take no excuse. And at last the infidel was obliged to leave the ground, and sneak off in confusion. He could not reply to the question. His conscience would not let him: he dared not say that he was happy.

The old woman showed great wisdom in asking the question that she did. The argument she used may seem very simple, but in reality it is one of the most powerful that can be employed. It is a weapon that has more effect on some minds than the most elaborate reasoning of Butler, or Paley, or Chalmers. Whenever a man begins to take up new views of religion, and pretends to despise old Bible Christianity, thrust home at his conscience the old woman's question. Ask him whether his new views make him feel comfortable within. Ask him whether he can say, with honesty and sincerity, that he is happy. The grand test of a man's faith and religion is, "Does it make him happy?"

Let me now affectionately invite every reader to consider the subject of this paper. Let me warn you to remember that the salvation of your soul, and nothing less, is closely bound up with the subject. The heart cannot be right in the sight of God which knows nothing of happiness. That man or woman cannot be in a safe state of soul who feels nothing of peace within.

There are three things which I purpose to do, in order to clear up the subject of happiness. I ask special attention to each one of them. And I pray the Spirit of God to apply all to the souls of all who read this paper.

I. Let me point out some things which are absolutely essential to all happiness.

II. Let me expose some common mistakes about the way to be happy.

III. Let me show the way to be truly happy.

I. First of all I have *to point out some things which are absolutely essential to all true happiness.*

Happiness is what all mankind want to obtain: the desire of it is deeply planted in the human heart. All men naturally dislike pain, sorrow, and discomfort. All men naturally like ease, comfort, and gladness. All men naturally hunger and thirst after happiness. Just as the sick man longs for health, and the prisoner of war for liberty,—just as the parched traveller in hot countries longs to see the cooling fountain, or the ice-bound polar voyager the sun rising above the horizon,—just in the same way does poor mortal man long to be happy. But, alas, how few consider what they really mean when they talk of happiness! How vague and indistinct and undefined the ideas of most men are upon the subject! They think some are happy who in reality are miserable : they think some are gloomy and sad who in reality are truly happy. They dream of a happiness which in reality would never satisfy their nature's wants. Let me try this day to throw a little light on the subject.

True happiness *is not perfect freedom from sorrow and discomfort.* Let that never be forgotten. If it were so there would be no such thing as happiness in the world. Such happiness is for angels who have never fallen, and not for man. The happiness I am inquiring about is such as a poor, dying, sinful creature may hope to attain. Our whole nature is defiled by sin. Evil abounds in the world. Sickness, and death, and change are daily doing their sad work on every side. In such a state of things the highest happiness man can attain to on earth must necessarily be a mixed thing. If we expect to find any literally perfect happiness on this side of the grave, we expect what we shall not find.

True happiness *does not consist in laughter and smiles.* The face is very often a poor index of the inward man. There are thousands who laugh loud and are merry as a grasshopper in company, but are wretched and miserable in private, and almost afraid to be alone. There are hundreds who are grave and serious in their demeanour, whose hearts are full of solid peace. A poet of our own has truly told us that smiles are worth but little:—

"A man may smile and smile and be a villain."

And the eternal Word of God teaches us that "even in laughter the heart is sorrowful." (Prov. xiv. 13.) Tell me not merely of smiling and laughing faces: I want to hear of something more than that when I ask whether a man is happy. A truly happy man no doubt will often show his happiness in his countenance; but a man may have a very merry face and yet not be happy at all.

Of all deceptive things on earth nothing is so deceptive as mere gaiety and merriment. It is a hollow empty show, utterly devoid of substance and reality. Listen to the brilliant talker in society, and mark the applause which he receives from an admiring company: follow him to his own private room, and you will very likely find him plunged in melancholy despondency. Colonel Gardiner confessed that even when he was thought most happy he often wished he was a dog.—Look at the smiling beauty in the ball-room, and you might suppose she knew not what it was to be unhappy; see her next day at her own home, and you may probably find her out of temper with herself and everybody else besides.—Oh, no: worldly merriment is not real happiness! There is a certain pleasure about it, I do not deny. There is an animal excitement about it, I make no question. There is a temporary elevation of spirits about it, I freely concede. But call it not by the sacred name of happiness. The most beautiful cut flowers stuck into the ground do not make a garden. When glass is called diamond, and tinsel is called gold, then, and not till then, your people who can laugh and smile will deserve to be called happy men.*

To be truly happy *the highest wants of a man's nature must be met and satisfied.* The requirements of his curiously wrought constitution must all be filled up. There must be nothing about him that cries, "Give, give," but cries in vain and gets no answer. The horse and the ox are happy as long as they are warmed and filled. And why? It is because they are satisfied. The little infant looks happy when it is clothed, and fed, and well, and in its mother's arms. And why? Because it is satisfied. And just so it is with man. His highest wants must be met and satisfied before he can be truly happy. All must be filled up. There must be no void, no empty places, no unsupplied cravings. Till then he is never truly happy.

And what are *man's principal wants?* Has he a body only? No: he has something more! He has a soul.—

---

* Cervantes, author of Don Quixote, at a time when all Spain was laughing at his humorous work, was overwhelmed with a deep cloud of melancholy.

Molière, the first of French comic writers, carried into his domestic circle a sadness which the greatest worldly prosperity could never dispel.

Samuel Foote, the noted wit of the last century, died of a broken heart.

Theodore Hooke, the facetious novel writer, who could set everybody laughing, says of himself in his diary, "I am suffering under a constant depression of spirits, which no one who sees me in society dreams of."

A wobegone stranger consulted a physician about his health. The physician advised him to keep up his spirits by going to hear the great comic actor of the day. "You should go and hear Matthews. He would make you well." "Alas, sir," was the reply, "I am Matthews himself!"—*Pictorial Pages.*

Has he sensual faculties only? Can he do nothing but hear, and see, and smell, and taste, and feel? No: he has a thinking mind and a conscience!—Has he no consciousness of any world but that in which he lives and moves? He has. There is a still small voice within him which often makes itself heard: "This life is not all! There is a world unseen: there is a life beyond the grave." Yes! it is true. We are fearfully and wonderfully made. All men know it: all men feel it, if they would only speak the truth. It is utter nonsense to pretend that food and raiment and earthly good things alone can make men happy. There are soul-wants. There are conscience-wants. There can be no true happiness until these wants are satisfied.

To be truly happy *a man must have sources of gladness which are not dependent on anything in this world.* There is nothing upon earth which is not stamped with the mark of instability and uncertainty. All the good things that money can buy are but for a moment: they either leave us or we are obliged to leave them. All the sweetest relationships in life are liable to come to an end: death may come any day and cut them off. The man whose happiness depends entirely on things here below is like him who builds his house on sand, or leans his weight on a reed.

Tell me not of your happiness if it daily hangs on the uncertainties of earth. Your home may be rich in comforts; your wife and children may be all you could desire; your means may be amply sufficient to meet all your wants. But oh, remember, if you have nothing more than this to look to, that you stand on the brink of a precipice! Your rivers of pleasure may any day be dried up. Your joy may be deep and earnest, but it is fearfully short-lived. It has no root. It is not true happiness.

To be really happy *a man must be able to look on every side without uncomfortable feelings.* He must be able to look back to the past without guilty fears; he must be able to look around him without discontent; he must be able to look forward without anxious dread. He must be able to sit down and think calmly about things past, present, and to come, and feel prepared. The man who has a weak side in his condition,—a side that he does not like looking at or considering,—that man is not really happy.

Talk not to me of your happiness, if you are unable to look steadily either before or behind you. Your present position may be easy and pleasant. You may find many sources of joy and gladness in your profession, your dwelling-place, your family, and your friends. Your health may be good, your spirits may be cheerful. But stop and think quietly over your past life. Can you reflect calmly on all the omissions and commissions of by-gone years? How will they bear God's inspection? How will you answer for them at the last day?—And then look forward, and think on the years yet to come. Think of the certain end towards which you are hastening; think of death; think of judgment; think of the hour when you will meet God face to face. Are you ready for it? Are you prepared? Can you look forward to these things without alarm?—Oh, be very sure if you cannot look comfortably at any season but the present, your boasted happiness is a poor unreal thing! It is but a whitened sepulchre,—fair and beautiful without, but bones and corruption within. It is a mere thing of a day, like Jonah's gourd. It is not real happiness.

I ask my readers to fix in their minds the account of things essential to happiness, which I have attempted to give. Dismiss from your thoughts the many mistaken notions which pass current on this subject, like counterfeit coin. To be truly happy, the wants of your soul and conscience must be satisfied; to be truly happy, your joy must be founded on something more than this world can give you;

to be truly happy, you must be able to look on every side, —above, below, behind, before,—and feel that all is right. This is real, sterling, genuine happiness: this is the happiness I have in view when I urge on your notice the subject of this paper.

II. In the next place, *let me expose some common mistakes about the way to be happy.*

There are several roads which are thought by many to lead to happiness. In each of these roads thousands and tens of thousands of men and women are continually travelling. Each fancies that if he could only attain all he wants he would be happy. Each fancies, if he does not succeed, that the fault is not in his road, but in his own want of luck and good fortune. And all alike seem ignorant that they are hunting shadows. They have started in a wrong direction: they are seeking that which can never be found in the place where they seek it.

I will mention by name some of the principal delusions about happiness. I do it in love, and charity, and compassion to men's souls. I believe it to be a public duty to warn people against cheats, quacks, and impostors. Oh, how much trouble and sorrow it might save my readers, if they would only believe what I am going to say !

It is an utter mistake to suppose that *rank and greatness alone* can give happiness. The kings and rulers of this world are not necessarily happy men. They have troubles and crosses, which none know but themselves ; they see a thousand evils, which they are unable to remedy ; they are slaves working in golden chains, and have less real liberty than any in the world ; they have burdens and responsibilities laid upon them, which are a daily weight on their hearts. The Roman Emperor Antonine often said, that " the imperial power was an ocean of miseries." Queen Elizabeth, when she heard a milk-maid singing, wished that she had been born to a lot like her's. Never did our great Poet write a truer word than when he said,

" Uneasy lies the head that wears a crown."

It is an utter mistake to suppose that *riches alone* can give happiness. They can enable a man to command and possess everything but inward peace. They cannot buy a cheerful spirit and a light heart. There is care in the getting of them, and care in the keeping of them, care in the using of them, and care in the disposing of them, care in the gathering, and care in the scattering of them. He was a wise man who said that " money " was only another name for "trouble," and that the same English letters which spelt " acres " would also spell " cares."

It is an utter mistake to suppose that *learning and science alone* can give happiness. They may occupy a man's time and attention, but they cannot really make him happy. They that increase knowledge often " increase sorrow : " the more they learn, the more they discover their own ignorance. (Eccles. i. 18.) It is not in the power of things on earth or under the earth to " minister to a mind diseased." The heart wants something as well as the head : the conscience needs food as well as the intellect. All the secular knowledge in the world will not give a man joy and gladness, when he thinks on sickness, and death, and the grave. They that have climbed the highest, have often found themselves solitary, dissatisfied, and empty of peace. The learned Selden, at the close of his life, confessed that all his learning did not give him such comfort as four verses of St. Paul. (Titus ii. 11—14.)

It is an utter mistake to suppose that *idleness alone* can give happiness. The labourer who gets up at five in the morning, and goes out to work all day in a cold clay ditch, often thinks, as he walks past the rich man's door, " What a fine thing it must be to have no work to do.' Poor fellow ! he little knows what he thinks. The most miserable creature on earth is the man who has nothing to do. Work for the hands or work for the head is absolutely essential to human happiness. Without it the mind feeds upon itself, and the whole inward man becomes diseased. The machinery within *will* work, and without something to work upon, will often wear itself to pieces. There was no idleness in Eden. Adam and Eve had to "dress the garden and keep it." There will be no idleness in heaven: God's "servants shall serve Him." Oh, be very sure the idlest man is the man most truly unhappy! (Gen. ii. 15; Rev. xxii. 3.)

It is an utter mistake to suppose that *pleasure-seeking and amusement alone* can give happiness. Of all roads that men can take in order to be happy, this is the one that is most completely wrong. Of all weary, flat, dull, and unprofitable ways of spending life, this exceeds all. To think of a dying creature, with an immortal soul, expecting happiness in feasting and revelling,—in dancing and singing,—in dressing and visiting,—in ball-going and card-playing,—in races and fairs,—in hunting and shooting, —in crowds, in laughter, in noise, in music, in wine! Surely it is a sight that is enough to make the devil laugh and the angels weep. Even a child will not play with its toys all day long. It must have food. But when grown up men and women think to find happiness in a constant round of amusement they sink far below a child.

I place before every reader of this paper these common mistakes about the way to be happy. I ask you to mark them well. I warn you plainly against these pretended short cuts to happiness, however crowded they may be. I tell you that if you fancy any one of them can lead you to true peace you are entirely deceived. Your conscience will never feel satisfied; your immortal soul will never feel easy: your whole inward man will feel uncomfortable and out of health. Take any one of these roads, or take all of them, and if you have nothing besides to look to, you will never find happiness. You may travel on and on and on, and the wished for object will seem as far away at the end of each stage of life as when you started. You are like one pouring water into a sieve, or putting money into a bag with holes. You might as well try to make an elephant happy by feeding him with a grain of sand a day, as try to satisfy that heart of your's with rank, riches, learning, idleness, or pleasure.

Do you doubt the truth of all I am saying? I dare say you do. Then let us turn to the great Book of human experience, and read over a few lines out of its solemn pages. You shall have the testimony of a few competent witnesses on the great subject I am urging on your attention.

A King shall be our first witness: I mean Solomon, King of Israel. We know that he had power, and wisdom, and wealth, far exceeding that of any ruler of his time. We know from his own confession, that he tried the great experiment how far the good things of this world can make man happy. We know, from the record of his own hand, the result of this curious experiment. He writes it by the inspiration of the Holy Ghost, for the benefit of the whole world, in the book of Ecclesiastes. Never, surely, was the experiment tried under such favourable circumstances: never was any one so likely to succeed as the Jewish King. Yet what is Solomon's testimony? You have it in his melancholy words: "All is vanity and vexation of spirit." (Eccles. i. 14.)

A famous French lady shall be our next witness: I mean Madam De Pompadour. She was the friend and favourite of Louis the Fifteenth. She had unbounded influence at the Court of France. She wanted nothing that money could procure. Yet what does she say herself? "What a situation is that of the great! They only live in the future, and are only happy in hope. There is no peace in ambition. I am always gloomy, and often so unreasonably. The kindness of the King, the regard of courtiers, the attachment of my domestics, and the fidelity of a large number of friends,—motives like these, which ought to make me happy, affect me no longer. I have no longer inclinations for all which once pleased me. I have caused my house at Paris to be magnificently furnished : well; it pleased for two days! My residence at Bellevue is charming; and I alone cannot endure it. Benevolent people relate to me all the news and adventures of Paris : they think I listen, but when they have done I ask them what they said. In a word, I do not live : I am dead before my time. I have no interest in the world. Everything conspires to embitter my life. My life is a continual death." To such testimony I need not add a single word. (*Sinclair's Anecdotes and Aphorisims, p. 33.*)

A famous German writer shall be our next witness : I mean Goethe. It is well known that he was almost idolized by many during his life. His works were read and admired by thousands. His name was known and honoured, wherever German was read, all over the world. And yet the praise of man, of which he reaped such an abundant harvest, was utterly unable to make Goethe happy. " He confessed, when about eighty years old, that he could not remember being in a really happy state of mind even for a few weeks together; and that when he wished to feel happy, he had to veil his self-consciousness." (*See Sinclair's Anecdotes and Aphorisms, p.* 280.)

An English peer and poet shall be our next witness : I mean Lord Byron. If ever there was one who ought to have been happy according to the standard of the world, Lord Byron was the man. He began life with all the advantages of English rank and position. He had splendid abilities and powers of mind, which the world soon discovered and was ready to honour. He had a sufficiency of means to gratify every lawful wish, and never knew anything of real poverty. Humanly speaking, there seemed nothing to prevent him enjoying life and being happy. Yet it is a notorious fact that Byron was a miserable man. Misery stands out in his poems: misery creeps out in his letters. Weariness, satiety, disgust, and discontent appear in all his ways. He is an awful warning that rank, and title, and literary fame, alone, are not sufficient to make a man happy.

A man of science shall be our next witness: I mean Sir Humphrey Davy. He was a man eminently successful in the line of life which he chose, and deservedly so. A distinguished philosopher,—the inventor of the famous safety-lamp which bears his name, and has preserved so many poor miners from death by fire-damp,—a Baronet of the United Kingdom and President of the Royal Society; —his whole life seemed a continual career of prosperity. If learning alone were the road to happiness, this man at least ought to have been happy. Yet what was the true record of Davy's feelings? We have it in his own melancholy journal at the latter part of his life. He describes himself in two painful words: "Very miserable!"

A man of wit and pleasure shall be our next witness: I mean Lord Chesterfield. He shall speak for himself: his own words in a letter shall be his testimony. "I have seen the silly round of business and pleasure, and have done with it all. I have enjoyed all the pleasures of the world, and consequently know their futility, and do not regret their loss. I appraise them at their real value, which in truth is very low; whereas those who have not experience always overrate them. They only see their gay outside, and are dazzled with their glare; but I have been behind the scenes. I have seen all the coarse pulleys and dirty ropes which exhibit and move the gaudy machine, and I have seen and smelt the tallow candles which illuminate the whole decoration, to the astonishment and admiration of the ignorant audience. When I reflect on what I have seen, what I have heard, and what I have done, I cannot persuade myself that all that frivolous hurry of bustle and pleasure of the world had any reality. I look on all that is past as one of those romantic dreams which opium occasions, and I do by no means wish to repeat the nauseous dose for the sake of the fugitive dream." These sentences speak for themselves. I need not add to them one single word.

The Statesmen and Politicians who have swayed the destinies of the world, ought by good right to be our last witnesses. But I forbear, in Christian charity, to bring them forward. It makes my heart ache when I run my eye over the list of names famous in English history, and think how many have worn out their lives in a breathless struggle after place and distinction. How many of our greatest men have died of broken hearts,—disappointed, disgusted, and tried with constant failure! How many have left on record some humbling confession that in the plentitude of their power they were pining for rest, as the caged eagle for liberty! How many whom the world is applauding as "masters of the situation," are in reality little better than galley-slaves, chained to the oar and unable to get free! Alas, there are many sad proofs, both among the living and the dead, that to be great and powerful is not necessarily to be happy.

I think it very likely that men do not believe what I am saying. I know something of the deceitfulness of the heart on the subject of happiness. There are few things which man is so slow to believe as the truths I am now putting forth about the way to be happy. Bear with me then while I say something more.

Come and stand with me some afternoon in the heart of the city of London. Let us watch the faces of most of the wealthy men whom we shall see leaving their houses of business at the close of the day. Some of them are worth hundreds of thousands: some of them are worth millions of pounds. But what is written in the countenances of these grave men whom we see swarming out from Lombard Street and Cornhill, from the Bank of England and the Stock Exchange? What mean those deep lines which furrow so many a cheek and so many a brow? What means that air of anxious thoughtfulness which is worn by five out of every six we meet? Ah, these things tell a serious tale. They tell us that it needs something more than gold and bank notes to make men happy.

Come next and stand with me near the Houses of Parliament, in the middle of a busy session. Let us scan the faces of Peers and Commoners, whose names are familiar and well-known all over the civilized world. There you may see on some fine May evening the mightiest Statesmen in England hurrying to a debate, like eagles to the carcase. Each has a power of good or evil in his tongue which it is fearful to contemplate. Each may say things before to-morrow's sun dawns, which may affect the peace and prosperity of nations, and convulse the world. There you may see the men who hold the reins of power and government already; there you may see the men who are daily watching for an opportunity of snatching those reins out of their hands, and governing in their stead. But what do their faces tell us as they hasten to their posts? What may be learned from their care-worn countenances? What may be read in many of their wrinkled foreheads,—so absent-looking and sunk in thought? They teach us a solemn lesson. They teach us that it needs something more than political greatness to make men happy.

Come next and stand with me in the most fashionable part of London, in the height of the season. Let us visit Regent Street or Pall Mall, Hyde Park or May Fair. How many fair faces and splendid equipages we shall see! How many we shall count up in an hour's time who seem to possess the choicest gifts of this world,—beauty, wealth, rank, fashion, and troops of friends! But, alas, how few we shall see who appear happy! In how many countenances we shall read weariness, dissatisfaction, discontent, sorrow, or unhappiness, as clearly as if it was written with a pen! Yes: it is a humbling lesson to learn, but a very wholesome one. It needs something more than rank, and fashion, and beauty, to make people happy.

Come next and walk with me through some quiet country parish in merry England. Let us visit some secluded corner in our beautiful old father-land, far away from great towns, and fashionable dissipation and political strife. There are not a few such to be found in the land. There are rural parishes where there is neither street, nor public house, nor beershop,—where there is work for all the labourers, and a church for all the population, and a school for all the children, and a minister of the Gospel to look after the people. Surely, you will say, we shall find happiness here! Surely such parishes must be the very abodes of peace and joy!—Go into those quiet-looking cottages, one by one, and you will soon be undeceived. Learn the inner history of each family, and you will soon alter your mind. You will soon discover that backbiting, and lying, and slandering, and envy, and jealousy, and pride, and laziness, and drinking, and extravagance, and lust, and petty quarrels, can murder happiness in the country quite as much as in the town. No doubt a rural village sounds pretty in poetry, and looks beautiful in pictures; but in sober reality human nature is the same evil thing everywhere. Alas, it needs something more than a residence in a quiet country parish to make any child of Adam a happy man!

I know these are ancient things. They have been said a thousand times before without effect, and I suppose they will be said without effect again. I want no greater proof of the corruption of human nature than the pertinacity with which we seek happiness where happiness cannot be

found.   Century after century wise men have left on
record their experience about the way to be happy.
Century after century the children of men will have it
that they know the way perfectly well, and need no
teaching.   They cast to the winds our warnings; they
rush, every one, on his own favourite path; they walk in
a vain shadow, and disquiet themselves in vain, and wake
up when too late to find their whole life has been a grand
mistake.   Their eyes are blinded: they will not see that
their visions are as baseless and disappointing as the
mirage of the African desert.   Like the tired traveller in
those deserts, they think they are approaching a lake of
cooling waters; like the same traveller, they find to their
dismay that this fancied lake was a splendid optical delusion, and that they are still helpless in the midst of burning
sands.

Are you a young person ?   I entreat you to accept the
affectionate warning of a minister of the Gospel, and not
to seek happiness where happiness cannot be found.   Seek
it not in riches; seek it not in power and rank; seek it
not in pleasure; seek it not in learning.   All these are
bright and splendid fountains: their waters taste sweet.
A crowd is standing round them, which will not leave
them; but, oh, remember that God has written over each
of these fountains, "He that drinketh of this water shall
thirst again." (John iv. 13.)   Remember this, and be wise.

Are you poor ?   Are you tempted to fancy that if you
had the rich man's place you would be quite happy ?
Resist the temptation, and cast it behind you.   Envy not
your wealthy neighbours : be content with such things as
you have.   Happiness does not depend on houses or land;
silks and satins cannot shut out sorrow from the heart;
castles and halls cannot prevent anxiety and care coming
in at their doors.   There is as much misery riding and
driving about in carriages as there is walking about on
foot: there is as much unhappiness in ceiled houses as in

humble cottages. Oh, remember the mistakes which are common about happiness, and be wise!

III. Let me now, in the last place, *point out the way to be really happy.*

There is a sure path which leads to happiness, if men will only take it. There never lived the person who travelled in that path, and missed the object that he sought to attain.

It is a path open to all. It needs neither wealth, nor rank, nor learning in order to walk in it. It is for the servant as well as for the master: it is for the poor as well as for the rich. None are excluded but those who exclude themselves.

It is the one only path. All that have ever been happy, since the days of Adam, have journeyed on it. There is no royal road to happiness. Kings must be content to go side by side with their humblest subjects, if they would be happy.

Where is this path? Where is this road? Listen, and you shall hear.

The way to be happy is *to be a real, thorough-going, true-hearted Christian.* Scripture declares it: experience proves it. The converted man, the believer in Christ, the child of God,—he, and he alone, is the happy man.

It sounds too simple to be true: it seems at first sight so plain a receipt that it is not believed. But the greatest truths are often the simplest. The secret which many of the wisest on earth have utterly failed to discover, is revealed to the humblest believer in Christ. I repeat it deliberately, and defy the world to disprove it: the true Christian is the only happy man.

What do I mean when I speak of a true Christian? Do I mean everybody who goes to church or chapel? Do I mean everybody who professes an orthodox creed, and bows his head at the belief? Do I mean everybody who professes to love the Gospel? No: indeed! I mean something very different. All are not Christians who are called Christians. The man I have in view is *the Christian in heart and life*. He who has been taught by the Spirit really to feel his sins,—he who really rests all his hopes on the Lord Jesus Christ, and His atonement,—he who has been born again and really lives a spiritual, holy life, —he whose religion is not a mere Sunday coat, but a mighty constraining principle governing every day of his life,—he is the man I mean, when I speak of a true Christian.

What do I mean when I say the true Christian is happy? Has he no doubts and no fears? Has he no anxieties and no troubles? Has he no sorrows and no cares? Does he never feel pain, and shed no tears? Far be it from me to say anything of the kind. He has a body weak and frail like other men; he has affections and passions like every one born of woman: he lives in a changeful world. But deep down in his heart he has a mine of solid peace and substantial joy which is never exhausted. This is true happiness.

Do I say that all true Christians are equally happy? No: not for a moment! There are babes in Christ's family as well as old men; there are weak members of the mystical body as well as strong ones; there are tender lambs as well as sheep. There are not only the cedars of Lebanon but the hyssop that grows on the wall. There are degrees of grace and degrees of faith. Those who have most faith and grace will have most happiness. But all, more or less, compared to the children of the world, are happy men.

Do I say that real true Christians are equally happy at all times? No: not for a moment! All have their ebbs and flows of comfort: some, like the Mediterranean sea, almost insensibly; some, like the tide at Chepstow, fifty or sixty feet at a time. Their bodily health is not always the same; their earthly circumstances are not always the same; the souls of those they love fill them at seasons with special anxiety: they themselves are sometimes overtaken by a fault, and walk in darkness. They sometimes give way to inconsistencies and besetting sins, and lose their sense of pardon. But, as a general rule, the true Christian has a deep pool of peace within him, which even at the lowest is never entirely dry.*

The true Christian is the only happy man, because *his conscience is at peace.* That mysterious witness for God, which is so mercifully placed within us, is fully satisfied and at rest. It sees in the blood of Christ a complete cleansing away of all its guilt. It sees in the priesthood and mediation of Christ a complete answer to all its fears. It sees that through the sacrifice and death of Christ, God can now be just, and yet be the justifier of the ungodly. It no longer bites and stings, and makes its possessor afraid of himself. The Lord Jesus Christ has amply met all its requirements. Conscience is no longer the enemy of the true Christian, but his friend and adviser. Therefore he is happy.

The true Christian is the only happy man, because he can *sit down quietly and think about his soul.* He can look behind him and before him, he can look within him and around him, and feel, "All is well."—He can think calmly on his past life, and however many and great his sins, take comfort in the thought that they are all forgiven. The righteousness of Christ covers all, as Noah's flood overtopped the highest hills.—He can think calmly about things to come, and yet not be afraid. Sickness is painful;

---

* I use the words, "as a general rule," advisedly. When a believer falls into such a horrible sin as that of David, it would be monstrous to talk of his feeling inward peace. If a man professing to be a true Christian talked to me of being happy in such a case,—before giving any evidence of the deepest, most heart-abasing repentance,—I should feel great doubts whether he ever had any grace at all.

death is solemn; the judgment day is an awful thing: but having Christ for him, he has nothing to fear.—He can think calmly about the Holy God, whose eyes are on all his ways, and feel, "He is my Father, my reconciled Father in Christ Jesus. I am weak; I am unprofitable: yet in Christ He regards me as His dear child, and is well-pleased." Oh, what a blessed privilege it is to be able to *think*, and not be afraid! I can well understand the mournful complaint of the prisoner in solitary confinement. He had warmth, and food, and clothing, and work, but he was not happy. And why? He said, "He was obliged to think."

The true Christian is the only happy man, because *he has sources of happiness entirely independent of this world.* He has something which cannot be affected by sickness and by deaths, by private losses and by public calamities, the "peace of God, which passeth all understanding." He has a hope laid up for him in heaven; he has a treasure which moth and rust cannot corrupt; he has a house which can never be taken down. His loving wife may die, and his heart feel rent in twain; his darling children may be taken from him, and he may be left alone in this cold world; his earthly plans may be crossed; his health may fail: but all this time he has a portion which nothing can hurt. He has one Friend who never dies; he has possessions beyond the grave, of which nothing can deprive him: his nether springs may fail, but his upper springs are never dry. This is real happiness.

The true Christian is happy, because he is *in his right position.* All the powers of his being are directed to right ends. His affections are not set on things below, but on things above; his will is not bent on self-indulgence, but is submissive to the will of God; his mind is not absorbed in wretched perishable trifles. He desires useful employment: he enjoys the luxury of doing good. Who does not know the misery of disorder? Who has not tasted the discomfort of a house where everything and everybody are in their wrong places,—the last things first and the first things last? The heart of an unconverted man is just such a house. Grace puts everything in that heart in its right position. The things of the soul come first, and the things of the world come second. Anarchy and confusion cease: unruly passions no longer do each one what is right in his eyes. Christ reigns over the whole man, and each part of him does his proper work. The new heart is the only really light heart, for it is the only heart that is in order.—The true Christian has found out his place. He has laid aside his pride and self-will; he sits at the feet of Jesus, and is in his right mind: he loves God and loves man, and so he is happy. In heaven all are happy because all do God's will perfectly. The nearer a man gets to this standard the happier he will be.

The plain truth is that without Christ there is no happiness in this world. He alone can give the Comforter who abideth for ever. He is the sun; without Him men never feel warm. He is the light; without Him men are always in the dark. He is the bread; without Him men are always starving. He is the living water; without Him men are always athirst. Give them what you like,—place them where you please,—surround them with all the comforts you can imagine,—it makes no difference. Separate from Christ, the Prince of Peace, a man cannot be happy.

Give a man a sensible interest in Christ, and he will be happy *in spite of poverty*. He will tell you that he wants nothing that is really good. He is provided for: he has riches in possession, and riches in reversion; he has meat to eat that the world knows not of; he has friends who never leave him nor forsake him. The Father and the Son come to him, and make their abode with him: the Lord Jesus Christ sups with him, and he with Christ. (Rev. iii. 20.)

Give a man a sensible interest in Christ, and he will be

happy *in spite of sickness*. His flesh may groan, and his body be worn out with pain, but his heart will rest and be at peace. One of the happiest people I ever saw was a young woman who had been hopelessly ill for many years with disease of the spine. She lay in a garret without a fire; the straw thatch was not two feet above her face. She had not the slightest hope of recovery. But she was always rejoicing in the Lord Jesus. The spirit triumphed mightily over the flesh. She was happy, because Christ was with her.*

Give a man a sensible interest in Christ, and he will be happy *in spite of abounding public calamities*. The government of his country may be thrown into confusion, rebellion and disorder may turn everything upside down, laws may be trampled under foot; justice and equity may be outraged; liberty may be cast down to the ground; might may prevail over right: but still his heart will not fail. He will remember that the kingdom of Christ will one day be set up. He will say, like the old Scotch minister who lived unmoved throughout the turmoil of the first French revolution: "It is all right: it shall be well with the righteous."

I know well that Satan hates the doctrine which I am endeavouring to press upon you. I have no doubt he is filling your mind with objections and reasonings, and persuading you that I am wrong. I am not afraid to meet these objections face to face. Let us bring them forward and see what they are.

You may tell me that "*you know many very religious people who are not happy at all.*" You see them diligent in attending public worship. You know that they are

---

* John Howard, the famous Christian philanthropist, in his last journey said, "I hope I have sources of enjoyment that depend not on the particular spot I inhabit. A rightly cultivated mind, under the power of religion and the exercises of beneficent dispositions, affords a ground of satisfaction little affected by *heres and theres*."

never missing at the Sacrament of the Lord's Supper. But you see in them no marks of the peace which I have been describing.

But are you sure that these people you speak of are true believers in Christ? Are you sure that, with all their appearance of religion, they are born again and converted to God? Is it not very likely that they have nothing but the name of Christianity, without the reality; and a form of godliness, without the power? Alas! you have yet to learn that people may do many religious acts, and yet possess no saving religion! It is not a mere formal, ceremonial Christianity that will ever make people happy. We want something more than going to Church, and going to sacraments, to give us peace. There must be real, vital union with Christ. It is not the formal Christian, but the true Christian, that is the happy man.

You may tell me that "*you know really spiritually-minded and converted people who do not seem happy.*" You have heard them frequently complaining of their own hearts, and groaning over their own corruption. They seem to you all doubts, and anxieties, and fears; and you want to know where is the happiness in these people of which I have been saying so much.

I do not deny that there are many saints of God such as these whom you describe, and I am sorry for it. I allow that there are many believers who live far below their privileges, and seem to know nothing of joy and peace in believing. But did you ever ask any of these people whether they would give up the position in religion they have reached, and go back to the world? Did you ever ask them, after all their groanings, and doubtings, and fearings, whether they think they would be happier if they ceased to follow hard after Christ? *Did you ever ask those questions?* I am certain if you did, that the weakest and lowest believers would all give you one answer. I am certain they would tell you that they would

rather cling to their little scrap of hope in Christ, than
possess the world. I am sure they would all answer, "Our
faith is weak, if we have any; our grace is small, if we
have any; our joy in Christ is next to nothing at all: but
we cannot give up what we have got. Though the Lord
slay us, we .must cling to Him." The root of happiness
lies deep in many a poor weak believer's heart, when
neither leaves nor blossoms are to be seen!

But you will tell me, in the last place, that "*you cannot
think most believers are happy, because they are so grave
and serious.*" You think that they do not really possess
this happiness I have been describing, because their
countenances do not show it. You doubt the reality of
their joy, because it is so little seen.

I might easily repeat what I told you at the beginning
of this paper,—that a merry face is no sure proof of a
happy heart. But I will not do so. I will rather ask you
whether you yourself may not be the cause why believers
look grave and serious when you meet them? If you are
not converted yourself, you surely cannot expect them to
look at you without sorrow. They see you on the high
road to destruction, and that alone is enough to give them
pain: they see thousands like you, hurrying on to weeping
and wailing and endless woe. Now, is it possible that
such a daily sight should not give them grief? Your
company, very likely, is one cause why they are grave
Wait till you are a converted man yourself, before you
pass judgment on the gravity of converted people. See
them in companies where all are of one heart, and all love
Christ, and so far as my own experience goes, you will find
no people so truly happy as true Christians.*

---

* When the infidel Hume asked Bishop Horne why religious people
always looked melancholy, the learned prelate replied, "The sight of
you, Mr. Hume, would make any Christian melancholy."—*Sinclair's
Aphorisms.* Page 13.

I repeat my assertion in this part of my subject. I repeat it boldly, confidently, deliberately. I say that there is no happiness among men that will at all compare with that of the true Christian. All other happiness by the side of his is moonlight compared to sunshine, and brass by the side of gold. Boast, if you will, of the laughter and merriment of irreligious men; sneer, if you will, at the gravity and seriousness, which appear in the demeanour of many Christians. I have looked the whole subject in the face, and am not moved. I say that the true Christian alone is the truly happy man, and the way to be happy is to be a true Christian.

And now I am going to close this paper by a few words of plain application. I have endeavoured to show what is essential to true happiness. I have endeavoured to expose the fallacy of many views which prevail upon the subject. I have endeavoured to point out, in plain and unmistakable words, where true happiness alone can be found. Suffer me to wind up all by an affectionate appeal to the consciences of all into whose hands this volume may fall.

(1) In the first place, *let me entreat every reader of this paper to apply to his own heart the solemn inquiry, Are you happy?*

High or low, rich or poor, master or servant, farmer or labourer, young or old, here is a question that deserves an answer,—*Are you really happy?*

Man of the world, who art caring for nothing but the things of time, neglecting the Bible, making a god of business or money, providing for everything but the day of judgment, scheming and planning about everything but eternity: are you happy? *You know you are not.*

Foolish woman, who art trifling life away in levity and frivolity, spending hours after hours on that poor frail body which must soon feed the worms, making an idol of dress and fashion, and excitement, and human praise, as if this world was all: are you happy? *You know you are not.*

Young man, who art bent on pleasure and self-indulgence, fluttering from one idle pastime to another, like
the moth about the candle,—fancying yourself clever and
knowing, and too wise to be led by parsons, and ignorant
that the devil is leading you captive, like the ox that is
led to the slaughter: are you happy? *You know you are
not.*

Yes: each and all of you, you are not happy! and in
your own consciences you know it well. You may not
allow it, but it is sadly true. There is a great empty place
in each of your hearts, and nothing will fill it. Pour
into it money, learning, rank, and pleasure, and it will be
empty still. There is a sore place in each of your consciences, and nothing will heal it. Infidelity cannot; free-
thinking cannot; Romanism cannot: they are all quack
medicines. Nothing can heal it, but that which at present
you have not used,—the simple Gospel of Christ. Yes:
you are indeed a miserable people!

Take warning this day, that you never will be happy
till you are converted. You might as well expect to feel
the sun shine on your face when you turn your back to
it, as to feel happy when you turn your back on God and
on Christ.

(2) In the next place, *let me warn all who are not true
Christians of the folly of living a life which cannot make
them happy.*

I pity you from the bottom of my heart, and would fain
persuade you to open your eyes and be wise. I stand as
a watchman on the tower of the everlasting Gospel. I see
you sowing misery for yourselves, and I call upon you to
stop and think, before it is too late. Oh, that God may
show you your folly!

You are hewing out for yourselves cisterns, broken
cisterns, which can hold no water. You are spending your
time, and strength, and affections on that which will give
you no return for your labour,—"spending your money on

that which is not bread, and your labour for that which satisfieth not." (Isa. lv. 2.) You are building up Babels of your own contriving, and ignorant that God will pour contempt on your schemes for procuring happiness, because you attempt to be happy without Him.

Awake from your dreams, I entreat you, and show yourselves men. Think of the uselessness of living a life which you will be ashamed of when you die, and of having a mere nominal religion, which will just fail you when it is most wanted.

Open your eyes and look round the world. Tell me who was ever really happy without God and Christ and the Holy Spirit. Look at the road in which you are travelling. Mark the footsteps of those who have gone before you : see how many have turned away from it, and confessed they were wrong.

I warn you plainly, that if you are not a true Christian you will miss happiness in the world that now is, as well as in the world to come. Oh, believe me, the way of happiness, and the way of salvation are one and the same ! He that will have his own way, and refuses to serve Christ, will never be really happy. But he that serves Christ has the promise of both lives. He is happy on earth, and will be happier still in heaven.

If you are neither happy in this world nor the next, it will be all your own fault. Oh, think of this ! Do not be guilty of such enormous folly. Who does not mourn over the folly of the drunkard, the opium eater, and the suicide ? But there is no folly like that of the impenitent child of the world.

(3) In the next place, *let me entreat all readers of this book, who are not yet happy,* **to** *seek happiness where alone it can be found.*

The keys of the way to happiness are in the hands of the Lord Jesus Christ. He is sealed and appointed by God the Father, to give the bread of life to them that hunger, and to give the water of life to them that thirst. The door which riches and rank and learning have so often tried to open, and tried in vain, is now ready to open to every humble, praying believer. Oh, if you want to be happy, come to Christ!

Come to Him, confessing that you are weary of your own ways, and want rest,—that you find you have no power and might to make yourself holy or happy or fit for heaven, and have no hope but in Him. Tell Him this unreservedly. This is coming to Christ.

Come to Him, imploring Him to show you His mercy, and grant you His salvation,—to wash you in His own blood, and take your sins away,—to speak peace to your conscience, and heal your troubled soul. Tell Him all this unreservedly. This is coming to Christ.

You have everything to encourage you. The Lord Jesus Himself invites you. He proclaims to you as well as to others, "Come unto Me, all ye that labour and are heavy laden, and I will give you rest. Take my yoke upon you, and learn of Me; for I am meek and lowly in heart: and ye shall find rest unto your souls. For my yoke is easy, and my burden is light." (Matt. xi. 28—30.) Wait for nothing. You may feel unworthy. You may feel as if you did not repent enough. But wait no longer. Come to Christ.

You have everything to encourage you. Thousands have walked in the way you are invited to enter, and have found it good. Once, like yourself, they served the world, and plunged deeply into folly and sin. Once, like yourself, they became weary of their wickedness, and longed for deliverance and rest. They heard of Christ, and His willingness to help and save : they came to Him by faith and prayer, after many a doubt and hesitation; they found Him a thousand times more gracious than they had expected. They rested on Him and were happy : they carried His cross and tasted peace. Oh, walk in their steps!

I beseech you, by the mercies of God, to come to Christ As ever you would be happy, I entreat you to come to Christ. Cast off delays. Awake from your past slumber: arise, and be free! This day come to Christ.

(4) In the last place, *let me offer a few hints to all true Christians for the increase and promotion of their happiness.*

I offer these hints with diffidence. I desire to apply them to my own conscience as well as to your's. You have found Christ's service happy. I have no doubt that you feel such sweetness in Christ's peace that you would fain know more of it. I am sure that these hints deserve attention.

Believers, if you would have an increase of happiness in Christ's service, *labour every year to grow in grace.* Beware of standing still. The holiest men are always the happiest. Let your aim be every year to be more holy,—to know more, to feel more, to see more of the fulness of Christ. Rest not upon old grace: do not be content with the degree of religion whereunto you have attained. Search the Scriptures more earnestly; pray more fervently; hate sin more; mortify self-will more; become more humble the nearer you draw to your end; seek more direct personal communion with the Lord Jesus; strive to be more like Enoch,—daily walking with God; keep your conscience clear of little sins; grieve not the Spirit; avoid wranglings and disputes about the lesser matters of religion: lay more firm hold upon those great truths, without which no man can be saved. Remember and practise these things, and you will be more happy.

Believers, if you would have an increase of happiness in Christ's service, *labour every year to be more thankful.* Pray that you may know more and more what it is to "rejoice in the Lord." (Phil. iii. 1.) Learn to have a deeper sense of your own wretched sinfulness and corruption, and to be more deeply grateful, that by the grace of God you are what you are. Alas, there is too much complaining and too little thanksgiving among the people of God! There is too much murmuring and poring over the things that we have not. There is too little praising and blessing for the many undeserved mercies that we have. Oh, that God would pour out upon us a great spirit of thankfulness and praise!

Believers, if you would have an increase of happiness in Christ's service, *labour every year to do more good.* Look round the circle in which your lot is cast, and lay yourself out to be useful. Strive to be of the same character with God: He is not only good, but "doeth good." (Ps. cxix. 68.) Alas, there is far too much selfishness among believers in the present day! There is far too much lazy sitting by the fire nursing our own spiritual diseases, and croaking over the state of our own hearts. Up; and be useful in your day and generation! Is there no one in all the world that you can read to? Is there no one that you can speak to? Is there no one that you can write to? Is there literally nothing that you can do for the glory of God, and the benefit of your fellow-men? Oh I cannot think it! I cannot think it. There is much that you might do, if you had only the will. For your own happiness' sake, arise and do it, without delay. The bold, outspeaking, working Christians are always the happiest. The more you do for God, the more God will do for you.

The compromising lingering Christian must never expect to taste perfect peace. THE MOST DECIDED CHRISTIAN WILL ALWAYS BE THE HAPPIEST MAN.

XI

FORMALITY

' Having a form of godliness, but denying the power thereof."—
2 TIM. iii. 5.

"He is not a Jew, which is one outwardly ; neither is that circum-
cision, which is outward in the flesh :

" But he is a Jew, which is one inwardly ; and circumcision is that
of the heart, in the spirit, and not in the letter ; whose praise is
*not of men, but of God."—*ROM. ii. 28, 29.

THE texts which head this page deserve serious attention
at any time. But they deserve especial notice in this age
of the Church and world. Never since the Lord Jesus
Christ left the earth, was there so much formality and
false profession as there is at the present day. Now, if
ever, we ought to examine ourselves, and search our
religion, that we may know of what sort it is. Let us try
to find out whether our Christianity is a thing of form or
a thing of heart.

I know no better way of unfolding the subject than by
turning to a plain passage of the Word of God. Let us
hear what St. Paul says about it. He lays down the
following great principles in his Epistle to the Romans :
" He is not a Jew, which is one outwardly ; neither is that
circumcision, which is outward in the flesh : but he is a
Jew, which is one inwardly ; and circumcision is that of
the heart, in the spirit, not in the letter ; whose praise is

not of men, but of God." (Rom. ii. 28, 29.) Three most instructive lessons appear to me to stand out on the face of that passage. Let us see what they are.

I. We learn, firstly, that formal religion is not religion, and a formal Christian is not a Christian in God's sight.

II. We learn, secondly, that the heart is the seat of true religion, and that the true Christian is the Christian in heart.

III. We learn, thirdly, that true religion must never expect to be popular. It will not have the "praise of man, but of God."

Let us thoroughly consider these great principles. Two hundred years have passed away since a mighty Puritan divine said, "Formality, formality, formality is the great sin of England at this day, under which the land groans.—There is more light than there was, but less life; more shadow, but less substance; more profession, but less sanctification." (*Thomas Hall, on 2 Tim. iii. 5, 1658.*) What would this good man have said if he had lived in our times?

I. We learn first, that *formal religion is not religion, and a formal Christian is not a Christian in God's sight.*

What do I mean when I speak of formal religion? This is a point that must be made clear. Thousands, I suspect, know nothing about it. Without a distinct understanding of this point my whole paper will be useless. My first step shall be to paint, describe, and define.

When a man is a Christian in name only, and not in reality,—in outward things only, and not in his inward feelings,—in profession only, and not in practice,—when his Christianity in short is a mere matter of form, or fashion, or custom, without any influence on his heart or life,—in such a case as this the man has what I call a "formal religion." He possesses indeed the *form*, or husk, or skin of religion, but he does not possess its substance or its *power*.

Look for example at those thousands of people whose whole religion seems to consist in keeping religious ceremonies and ordinances. They attend regularly on public worship. They go regularly to the Lord's table. But they never get any further. They know nothing of experimental Christianity. They are not familiar with the Scriptures, and take no delight in reading them. They do not separate themselves from the ways of the world. They draw no distinction between godliness and ungodliness in their friendships, or matrimonial alliances. They care little or nothing about the distinctive doctrines of the Gospel. They appear utterly indifferent as to what they hear preached. You may be in their company for weeks, and for anything you may hear or see on a week day you might suppose they were infidels or deists. What can be said about these people? They are Christians undoubtedly, by profession; and yet there is neither heart nor life in their Christianity. There is but one thing to be said about them.—They are formal Christians. Their religion is a FORM.

Look in another direction at those hundreds of people whose whole religion seems to consist in talk and high profession. They know the theory of the Gospel with their heads, and profess to delight in Evangelical doctrine. They can say much about the "soundness" of their own views, and the "darkness" of all who disagree with them. But they never get any further! When you examine their inner lives you find that they know nothing of practical godliness. They are neither truthful, nor charitable, nor humble, nor honest, nor kind-tempered, nor gentle, nor unselfish, nor honourable. What shall we say of these people? They are Christians, no doubt, in name, and yet there is neither substance nor fruit in their Christianity. There is but one thing to be said.—They are formal Christians. Their religion is an empty FORM.

Such is the formal religion against which I wish to raise a warning voice this day. Here is the rock on which myriads on every side are making miserable shipwreck of their souls. One of the wickedest things that Machiavel ever said was this: "Religion itself should not be cared for, but only the appearance of it. The credit of it is a help; the reality and use is a cumber." Such notions are of the earth, earthy. Nay, rather they are from beneath: they smell of the pit. Beware of them, and stand upon your guard. If there is anything about which the Scripture speaks expressly, it is the sin and uselessness of FORMALITY.

Hear what St. Paul tells the Romans: "He is not a Jew which is one outwardly, neither is that circumcision which is outward in the flesh." (Rom. ii. 28.) These are strong words indeed! A man might be a son of Abraham according to the flesh,—a member of one of the twelve tribes,—circumcised the eighth day,—a keeper of all the feasts,—a regular worshipper in the temple,—and yet in God's sight not be a Jew!—Just so a man may be a Christian by outward profession,—a member of a Christian Church,—baptized with Christian baptism,—an attendant on Christian ordinances,—and yet, in God's sight, not a Christian at all.

Hear what the prophet Isaiah says: "To what purpose is the multitude of your sacrifices unto Me? saith the Lord: I am full of the burnt offerings of rams, and the fat of fed beasts; and I delight not in the blood of bullocks or of lambs, or of he-goats. When ye come to appear before Me, who hath required this at your hand, to tread my courts? Bring no more vain oblations: incense is an abomination unto Me; the new moons and sabbaths, the calling of assemblies, I cannot away with; it is iniquity, even the solemn meeting. Your new moons and your appointed feasts my soul hateth: they are a trouble unto Me: I am weary to bear them. And when ye spread forth your hands I will hide mine eyes from you; yea, when ye make many prayers I will not hear: your hands are full of blood." (Isaiah i. 10—15.) These words, when duly weighed, are very extraordinary. The sacrifices which are here declared to be useless were appointed by God Himself! The feasts and ordinances which God says He "hates," had been prescribed by Himself! God Himself pronounces His own institutions to be useless when they are used formally and without heart in the worshipper! In fact they are worse than useless; they are even offensive and hurtful. Words cannot be imagined more distinct and unmistakeable. They show that formal religion is worthless in God's sight. It is not worth calling religion at all.

Hear, lastly, what our Lord Jesus Christ says. We find Him saying of the Jews of His day, "This people draweth nigh unto Me with their mouth, and honoureth Me with their lips; but their heart is far from Me. But in vain do they worship Me." (Matt. xv. 8.) We see Him repeatedly denouncing the formalism and hypocrisy of the scribes and Pharisees, and warning His disciples against it. Eight times in one chapter (Matt. xxiii. 13) He says to them, "Woe unto you, scribes and Pharisees, hypocrites!" For sinners of the worst description He always had a word of kindness, and held out to them an open door. But formalism, He would have us know, is a desperate disease, and must be exposed in the severest language. To the eye of an ignorant man a formalist may seem to have a very decent *quantity* of religion, though not perhaps of the best *quality.* In the eye of Christ, however, the case is very different. In His sight formality is no religion at all.

What shall we say to these testimonies of Scripture?

It would be easy to add to them. They do not stand alone. If words mean anything, they are a clear warning to all who profess and call themselves Christians. They teach us plainly that as we dread sin and avoid sin, so we ought to dread formality and avoid formality. Formalism may take our hand with a smile, and look like a brother, while sin comes against us with sword drawn, and strikes at us like an open enemy. But both have one end in view. Both want to ruin our souls; and of the two, formalism is far the most likely to do it. If we love life, let us beware of formality in religion.

Nothing is *so common.* It is one of the great family diseases of the whole race of mankind. It is born with us, grows with us, and is never completely cast out of us till we die. It meets us in church, and it meets us in chapel. It meets us among rich, and it meets us among poor. It meets us among learned people, and it meets us among unlearned. It meets us among Romanists, and it meets us among Protestants. It meets us among High Churchmen, and it meets us among Low Churchmen. It meets us among Evangelicals, and it meets us among Ritualists. Go where we will, and join what Church we may, we are never beyond the risk of its infection. We shall find it among Quakers and Plymouth Brethren, as well as at Rome. The man who thinks that, at any rate, there is no formal religion in his own camp, is a very blind and ignorant person. If you love life, beware of formality.

Nothing is *so dangerous* to a man's own soul. Familiarity with the form of religion, while we neglect its reality, has a fearfully deadening effect on the conscience. It brings up by degrees a thick crust of insensibility over the whole inner man. None seem to become so desperately hard as those who are continually repeating holy words and handling holy things, while their hearts are running after sin and the world. Landlords who only go to church formally, to set an example to their tenants,—masters who have family prayers formally, to keep up a good appearance in their households,—unconverted clergymen, who are every week reading prayers and lessons of Scripture, in which they feel no real interest,—unconverted clerks, who are constantly reading responses and saying "Amen," without feeling what they say,—unconverted singers, who sing the most spiritual hymns every Sunday, merely because they have good voices, while their affections are entirely on things below,—all, all, all are in awful danger. They are gradually hardening their hearts, and searing the skin of their consciences. If you love your own soul, beware of formality.

Nothing, finally, is *so foolish*, senseless, and unreasonable. Can a formal Christian really suppose that the mere outward Christianity he professes will comfort him in the day of sickness and the hour of death? The thing is impossible. A painted fire cannot warm, and a painted banquet cannot satisfy hunger, and a formal religion cannot bring peace to the soul.—Can he suppose that God does not see the heartlessness and deadness of his Christianity? Though he may deceive neighbours, acquaintances, fellow-worshippers, and ministers with a form of godliness, does he think that he can deceive God? The very idea is absurd. "He that formed the eye, shall He not see?" He knows the very secrets of the heart. He will "judge the secrets of men" at the last day. He who said to each angel of the seven Churches, "I know thy works," is not changed. He who said to the man without the wedding garment, "Friend, how camest thou in hither?" will not be deceived by a little cloak of outward religion. If you would not be put to shame at the last day, once more I say, beware of formality. (Psalm xciv. 9; Rom. ii. 16; Rev. ii. 2; Matt. xxii. 11.)

II. I pass on to the second thing which I proposed to

consider. *The heart is the seat of true religion, and the true Christian is the Christian in heart.*

The heart is the real test of a man's character. It is not what he says or what he does by which the man may be always known. He may say and do things that are right, from false and unworthy motives, while his heart is altogether wrong. The heart is the man. "As he thinketh in his heart, so is he." (Prov. xxiii. 7.)

The heart is the right test of a man's religion. It is not enough that a man holds a correct creed of doctrine, and maintains a proper outward form of godliness. What is his heart?—That is the grand question. This is what God looks at. "Man looketh at the outward appearance, but the Lord looketh at the heart." (1 Sam. xvi. 7.) This is what St. Paul lays down distinctly as the standard measure of the soul : "He is a Jew, which is one inwardly; and circumcision is that of the heart." (Rom. ii. 28.) Who can doubt that this mighty sentence was written for Christians as well as for Jews? He is a Christian, the apostle would have us know, which is one inwardly, and baptism is that of the heart.

The heart is the place where saving religion must begin. It is naturally irreligious, and must be renewed by the Holy Ghost. "A new heart will I give unto you."—It is naturally hard, and must be made tender and broken. "I will take away the heart of stone, and I will give you a heart of flesh." "The sacrifices of God are a broken spirit; a broken and contrite heart, O God, thou wilt not despise."—It is naturally closed and shut against God, and must be opened. The Lord "opened the heart" of Lydia. (Ezek. xxxvi. 26; Psalm li. 17; Acts xvi. 14.)

The heart is the seat of true saving faith. "With the heart man believeth unto righteousness." (Rom. x. 10.) A man may believe that Jesus is the Christ, as the devils do, and yet remain in his sins. He may believe that he is a sinner, and that Christ is the only Saviour, and feel occasional lazy wishes that he was a better man. But no one ever lays hold on Christ, and receives pardon and peace, until he believes with the heart. It is heart-faith that justifies.

The heart is the spring of true holiness and steady continuance in well-doing. True Christians are holy because their hearts are interested. They obey from the heart. They do the will of God from the heart. Weak, aud feeble, and imperfect as all their doings are, they please God, because they are done from a loving heart. He who commended the widow's mite more than all the offerings of the wealthy Jews, regards quality far more than quantity. What He likes to see is a thing done from "an honest and good heart." (Luke viii. 15.) There is no real holiness without a right heart.

The things I am saying may sound strange. Perhaps they run counter to all the notions of some into whose hands this paper may fall. Perhaps you have thought that if a man's religion is correct outwardly, he must be one with whom God is well pleased. You are completely mistaken. You are rejecting the whole tenor of Bible teaching. Outward correctness without a right heart is neither more nor less than Pharisaism. The outward things of Christianity,—baptism, the Lord's Supper, Church-membership, almsgiving, and the like,—will never take any man's soul to heaven, unless his heart is right. There must be inward things as well as outward,—and it is on the inward things that God's eyes are chiefly fixed.

Hear how St. Paul teaches us about this matter in three most striking texts: "In Jesus Christ neither circumcision availeth anything, nor uncircumcision; but faith that worketh by love."—"In Christ Jesus neither circumcision availeth anything, nor uncircumcision, but a new creature." —" Circumcision is nothing, and uncircumcision is nothing, but the keeping of the commandments of God." (1 Cor. vii. 19; Galat. v. 6; Galat. vi. 15.) Did the Apostle only

mean in these texts, that circumcision was no longer
needed under the Gospel? Was that all? No indeed!
I believe he meant much more. He meant that true
religion did not consist of forms, and that its essence was
something far greater than being circumcised or not
circumcised. He meant that under Christ Jesus, everything depended on being born again,—on having true
saving faith,—on being holy in life and conduct. He
meant that these are the things we ought to look at
chiefly, and not at outward forms. "Am I a new creature?
Do I really believe on Christ? Am I a holy man?"
These are the grand questions that we must seek to answer.

When the heart is wrong all is wrong in God's sight.
Many right things may be done. The forms and
ordinances which God Himself has appointed may seem
to be honoured. But so long as the heart is at fault God
is not pleased. He will have man's heart or nothing.

The ark was the most sacred thing in the Jewish
tabernacle. On it was the mercy-seat. Within it were
the tables of the law, written by God's own finger. The
High Priest alone was allowed to go into the place where
it was kept, within the veil, and that only once every year.
The presence of the ark with the camp was thought to
bring a special blessing. And yet this very ark could do
the Israelites no more good than any common wooden box,
when they trusted to it like an idol, with their hearts full
of wickedness. They brought it into the camp, on a
special occasion, saying, "Let us fetch the ark, that it may
save us out of the hand of our enemies." (1 Sam iv. 3.)
When it came in the camp they showed it all reverence
and honour. "They shouted with a great shout, so that
the earth rang again." But it was all in vain. They
were smitten before the Philistines, and the ark itself was
taken. And why was this? It was because their religion
was a mere form. They honoured the ark, but did not
give the God of the ark their hearts.

There were some kings of Judah and Israel who did many things that were right in God's sight, and yet were never written in the list of godly and righteous men. Rehoboam began well, and "for three years walked in the way of David and Solomon." (2 Chron. xi. 17.) But afterwards "he did evil, because he prepared not his *heart* to seek the Lord." (2 Chron. xii. 14.)—Abijah, according to the book of Chronicles, said many things that were right, and fought successfully against Jeroboam. Nevertheless the general verdict is against him. We read, in Kings, that "his *heart* was not perfect with the Lord his God." (1 Kings xv. 3)—Amaziah, we are expressly told, "did that which was right in the sight of the Lord, but not with a perfect *heart*." (2 Chron. xxv. 2.)—Jehu, King of Israel, was raised up, by God's command, to put down idolatry. He was a man of special zeal in doing God's work. But unhappily it is written of him: "He took no heed to walk in the law of the Lord God of Israel with all his *heart* : for he departed not from the sins of Jeroboam, which made Israel to sin." (2 Kings x. 31.) In short, one general remark applies to all these kings. They were all wrong inwardly. They were rotten at heart.

There are places of worship in England at this very day where all the outward things of religion are done to perfection. The building is beautiful. The service is beautiful. The singing is beautiful. The forms of devotion are beautiful. There is everything to gratify the senses. Eye, and ear, and natural sentimentality are all pleased. But all this time God is not pleased. One thing is lacking, and the want of that one thing spoils all. What is that one thing ? It is heart! God sees under all this fair outward show the form of religion put in the place of the substance, and when He sees that He is displeased. He sees nothing with an eye of favour in the building, the service, the minister, or the people, if He does not see converted, renewed, broken, penitent hearts. Bowed heads, bended knees, loud amens, crossed hands, faces turned to the east, all, all are nothing in God's sight without right hearts.

When the heart is right God can look over many things that are defective. There may be faults in judgment, and infirmities in practice. There may be many deviations from the best course in the outward things of religion. But if the heart is sound in the main, God is not extreme to mark that which is amiss. He is merciful and gracious, and will pardon much that is imperfect, when He sees a true heart and a single eye.

Jehoshaphat and Asa were Kings of Judah, who were defective in many things. Jehoshaphat was a timid, irresolute man, who did not know how to say "No," and joined affinity with Ahab, the wickedest king that ever reigned over Israel. Asa was an unstable man, who at one time trusted in the King of Syria more than in God, and at another time was wroth with God's prophet for rebuking him. (2 Chron. xvi. 10.) Yet both of them had one great redeeming point in their characters. With all their faults they had right *hearts*.

The passover kept by Hezekiah was one at which there were many irregularities. The proper forms were not observed by many. They ate the passover "otherwise than the commandment" ordered. But they did it with true and honest *hearts*. And we read that Hezekiah prayed for them, saying, "The good Lord pardon every one that prepareth his heart to seek God,—though he be not cleansed according to the purification of the sanctuary. And the Lord hearkened to Hezekiah, and healed the people." (2 Chron. xxx. 20.)

The passover kept by Josiah must have been far smaller and worse attended than scores of passovers in the days of David and Solomon, or even in the reign of Jehoshaphat and Hezekiah. How then can we account for the strong language used in Scripture about it? "There was no passover like to that kept in Israel from the days of

Samuel the prophet; neither did all the Kings of Israel keep such a passover as Josiah kept, and the Priests, and the Levites, and all Judah and Jerusalem that were present." (2 Chron. xxxv. 18.) There is but one explanation. There never was a passover at which the *hearts* of the worshippers were so truly in the feast. The Lord does not look at the quantity of worshippers so much as the quality. The glory of Josiah's passover was the state of people's hearts.

There are many assemblies of Christian worshippers on earth at this very day in which there is literally nothing to attract the natural man. They meet in miserable dirty chapels, so-called, or in wretched upper-rooms and cellars. They sing unmusically. They hear feeble prayers, and more feeble sermons. And yet the Holy Ghost is often in the midst of them! Sinners are often converted in them, and the kingdom of God prospers far more than in any Roman Catholic Cathedral, or than in many gorgeous Protestant Churches. How is this? How can it be explained? The cause is simply this, that in these humble assemblies heart-religion is taught and held. Heart-work is aimed at. Heart-work is honoured. And the consequence is that God is pleased and grants His blessing.

I leave this part of my subject here. I ask men to weigh well the things that I have been saying. I believe that they will bear examination, and are all true. Resolve this day, whatever Church you belong to, to be a Christian in *heart*. Whether Episcopalian or Presbyterian, Baptist or Independent, be not content with a mere form of godliness, without the power. Settle it down firmly in your mind that formal religion is not saving religion, and that heart-religion is the only religion that leads to heaven.

I only give one word of caution. Do not suppose, because formal religion will not save, that forms of religion are of no use at all. Beware of any such senseless extreme. The misuse of a thing is no argument against the right use of it. The blind idolatry of forms which prevails in some quarters is no reason why you should throw all forms aside. The ark, when made an idol of by Israel and put in the place of God, was unable to save them from the Philistines. And yet the same ark, when irreverently and profanely handled, brought death on Uzza; and when honoured and reverenced, brought a blessing on the house of Obed-edom. The words of Bishop Hall are strong, but true: "He that hath but a form is a hypocrite; but he that hath not a form is an Atheist." (*Hall's Sermons*, No. 28.) Forms cannot save us, but they are not therefore to be despised. A lantern is not a man's home, and yet it is a help to a man if he travels towards his home in a dark night. Use the forms of Christianity diligently, and you will find them a blessing. Only remember, in all your use of forms, the great principle, that the first thing in religion is the state of the heart.

III. I come now to the last thing which I proposed to consider. I said *that true religion must never expect to be popular. It will not have the praise of man, but of God.*

I dare not turn away from this part of my subject, however painful it may be. Anxious as I am to commend heart-religion to every one who reads this paper, I will not try to conceal what heart-religion entails. I will not gain a recruit for my Master's army under false pretences. I will not promise anything which the Scripture does not warrant. The words of St. Paul are clear and unmistakable. Heart-religion is a religion "whose praise is not of men, but of God." (Rom. ii. 29.)

God's truth and Scriptural Christianity are never really popular. They never have been. They never will be as long as the world stands. No one can calmly consider what human nature is, as described in the Bible, and reasonably expect anything else. As long as man is what man is, the majority of mankind will always like a religion of form far better than a religion of heart.

Formal religion just suits an unenlightened conscience. Some religion a man will have. Atheism and downright infidelity, as a general rule, are never very popular. But a man must have a religion which does not require much, —trouble his heart much,—interfere with his sins much. Formal Christianity satisfies him. It seems the very thing that he wants.

Formal religion gratifies the secret self-righteousness of man. We are all of us more or less Pharisees. We all naturally cling to the idea that the way to be saved is to do so many things, and go through so many religious observances, and that at last we shall get to heaven. Formalism meets us here. It seems to show us a way by which we can make our own peace with God.

Formal religion pleases the natural indolence of man. It attaches an excessive importance to that which is the easiest part of Christianity,—the shell and the form. Man likes this. He hates trouble in religion. He wants something which will not meddle with his conscience and inner life. Only leave conscience alone, and, like Herod, he will "do many things." Formalism seems to open a wider gate, and a more easy way to heaven. (Mark vi. 20.)

Facts speak louder than assertions. Facts are stubborn things. Look over the history of religion in every age of the world, and observe what has always been popular. Look at the history of Israel from the beginning of Exodus to the end of the Acts of the Apostles, and see what has always found favour. Formalism was one main sin against which the Old Testament prophets were continually protesting. Formalism was the great plague which had overspread the Jews, when our Lord Jesus Christ came into the world.—Look at the history of the

Church of Christ after the days of the apostles. How soon formalism ate out the life and vitality of the primitive Christians!—Look at the middle ages, as they are called. Formalism so completely covered the face of Christendom that the Gospel lay as one dead.—Look, lastly, at the history of Protestant Churches in the three last centuries. How few are the places where religion is a living thing! How many are the countries where Protestantism is nothing more than a form! There is no getting over these things. They speak with a voice of thunder. They all show that formal religion is a popular thing. It has the praise of man.

But why should we look at facts in history? Why should we not look at facts under our own eyes, and by our own doors? Can any one deny that a mere outward religion, a religion of downright formality, is the religion which is popular in England at the present day? It is not for nothing that St. John says of certain false teachers, "They are of the world: therefore speak they of the world, and the world heareth them." (1 John iv. 5.) Only say your prayers,—and go to church with tolerable regularity,—and receive the sacrament occasionally,—and the vast majority of Englishmen will set you down as an excellent Christian.—"What more would you have?" they say: "If this is not Christianity, what is?"—To require more of anyone is thought bigotry, illiberality, fanaticism, and enthusiasm! To insinuate a doubt whether such a man as this will go to heaven is called the height of uncharitableness! When these things are so it is vain to deny that formal religion is popular. It is popular. It always was popular. It always will be popular till Christ comes again. It always has had and always will have "the praise of man."

Turn now to the religion of the heart, and you will hear a very different report. As a general rule it has never had the good word of mankind. It has entailed on its professors laughter, mockery, ridicule, scorn, contempt, enmity, hatred, slander, persecution, imprisonment, and even death. Its lovers have been faithful and ardent,— but they have always been few. It has never had, comparatively, "the praise of man."

Heart-religion is too *humbling* to be popular. It leaves natural man no room to boast. It tells him that he is a guilty, lost, hell-deserving sinner, and that he must flee to Christ for salvation. It tells him that he is dead, and must be made alive again, and born of the Spirit. The pride of man rebels against such tidings as these. He hates to be told that his case is so bad.

Heart-religion is too *holy* to be popular. It will not leave natural man alone. It interferes with his worldliness and his sins. It requires of him things that he loathes and abominates,—conversion, faith, repentance, spiritual-mindedness, Bible-reading, prayer. It bids him give up many things that he loves and clings to, and cannot make up his mind to lay aside. It would be strange indeed if he liked it. It crosses his path as a kill-joy and a mar-plot, and it is absurd to expect that he will be pleased.

Was heart-religion popular in Old Testament times? We find David complaining: "They that sit in the gate speak against me; and I was the song of the drunkards." (Psalm lxix. 12.) We find the prophets persecuted and ill-treated because they preached against sin, and required men to give their hearts to God. Elijah, Micaiah, Jeremiah, Amos, are all cases in point. To formalism and ceremonialism the Jews never seem to have made objection. What they did dislike was serving God with their hearts.

Was heart-religion popular in New Testament times? The whole history of our Lord Jesus Christ's ministry and the lives of His apostles are a sufficient answer. The scribes and Pharisees would have willingly received a Messiah who encouraged formalism, and a Gospel which exalted ceremonialism. But they could not tolerate a religion of which the first principles were humiliation and sanctification of heart.

Has heart-religion even been popular in the professing Church of Christ during the last eighteen centuries? Never hardly, except in the early centuries when the primitive Church had not left her first love. Soon, very soon, the men who protested against formalism and sacramentalism were fiercely denounced as "troublers of Israel." Long before the Reformation, things came to this pass, that anyone who cried up heart-holiness and cried down formality was treated as a common enemy. He was either silenced, excommunicated, imprisoned, or put to death like John Huss.—In the time of the Reformation itself, the work of Luther and his companions was carried on under an incessant storm of calumny and slander. And what was the cause? It was because they protested against formalism, ceremonialism, monkery, and priestcraft, and taught the necessity of heart-religion.

Has heart-religion ever been popular in our own land in days gone by? Never, excepting for a little season. It was not popular in the days of Queen Mary, when Latimer and his brother-martyrs were burned.—It was not popular in the days of the Stuarts, when to be a Puritan was worse for a man than to get drunk or swear.—It was not popular in the middle of last century, when Wesley and Whitfield were shut out of the established Church. The cause of our martyred Reformers, of the early Puritans, and of the Methodists, was essentially one and the same. They were all hated because they preached the uselessness of formalism, and the impossibility of salvation without repentance, faith, regeneration, spiritual-mindedness, and holiness of heart.

Is heart-religion popular in England at this very day? I answer sorrowfully that I do not believe it is. Look at the followers of it among the laity. They are always comparatively few in number. They stand alone in their respective congregations and parishes. They have to put up with many hard things, hard words, hard imputations, hard treatment, laughter, ridicule, slander, and petty persecution. This is not popularity!—Look at the teachers of heart-religion in the pulpit. They are loved and liked, no doubt, by the few hearers who agree with them. They are sometimes admired for their talents and eloquence by the many who do not agree with them. They are even called "popular preachers," because of the crowds who listen to their preaching. But none know so well as the faithful teachers of heart-religion that few really like them. Few really help them. Few sympathize with them. Few stand by them in any time of need. They find, like their Divine Master, that they must work almost alone. I write these things with sorrow, but I believe they are true. Real heart-religion at this day, no less than in days gone by, has not "the praise of man."

But after all it signifies little what man thinks, and what man praises. He that judgeth us is the Lord. Man will not judge us at the last day. Man will not sit on the great white throne, examine our religion, and pronounce our eternal sentence. Those only whom God commends will be commended at the bar of Christ. Here lies the value and glory of heart-religion. It may not have the praise of man, but it has "the praise of God."

God approves and honours heart-religion in the life that now is. He looks down from heaven, and reads the hearts of all the children of men. Wherever He sees heart-repentance for sin,—heart-faith in Christ,—heart-holiness of life,—heart-love to His Son, His law, His will, and His Word,—wherever God sees these things He is well pleased. He writes a book of remembrance for that man, however poor and unlearned he may be. He gives His angels special charge over Him. He maintains in him the work of grace, and gives Him daily supplies of peace, hope, and strength. He regards him as a member of His own dear Son, as one who is witnessing for the truth, as His Son did. Weak as the man's heart may seem to himself, it is the living sacrifice which God loves, and the heart which He has solemnly declared He will not despise. Such praise is worth more than the praise of man!

God will proclaim His approval of heart-religion before the assembled world at the last day. He will command His angels to gather together His saints, from every part of the globe, into one glorious company. He will raise the dead and change the living, and place them at the right hand of His beloved Son's throne. Then all that have served Christ with the heart shall hear Him say, "Come, ye blessed of my Father, inherit the kingdom prepared for you from the foundation of the world :—you were faithful over few things, and I will make you rulers over many things; enter into the joy of your Lord.—Ye confessed Me before men, and I will confess you before my Father and His holy angels.—Ye are they who continued with Me in my temptations, and I appoint unto you a kingdom as my Father hath appointed unto Me." (Matt. xxv. 21—34; Luke xii. 8; xxii. 28, 29.) These words will be addressed to none but those who have given Christ their hearts! They will not be addressed to the formalist, the hypocrite, the wicked, and the ungodly. *They* will, indeed, stand by and see the fruits of heart-religion, but they will not eat of them. We shall never know the full value of heart-religion until the last day. Then, and only then, we shall fully understand how much better it is to have the praise of God than the praise of man.

If you take up heart-religion I cannot promise you the praise of man. Pardon, peace, hope, guidance, comfort, consolation, grace according to your need, strength according to your day, joy which the world can neither give nor take away,—all this I can boldly promise to the man who comes to Christ, and serves Him with his heart. But I cannot promise him that his religion will be popular with man. I would rather warn him to expect mockery and ridicule, slander and unkindness, opposition and persecution. There is a cross belonging to heart-religion, and we must be content to carry it. "Through much tribulation we must enter the kingdom."—"All that will live godly in Christ Jesus shall suffer persecution." (Acts xiv. 22; 2 Tim. iii. 12.) But if the world hates you, God will love you. If the world forsakes you, Christ has promised that He will never forsake and never fail. Whatever you may lose by heart-religion, be sure that the praise of God will make up for all.

And now I close this paper with three plain words of application. I want it to strike and stick to the conscience of every one into whose hands it falls. May God make it a blessing to many a soul both in time and eternity!

(1) In the first place, Is your religion a matter of form and not of heart? Answer this question honestly, and as in the sight of God. If it is, *consider solemnly the immense danger in which you stand.*

You have got nothing to comfort your soul in the day of trial, nothing to give you hope on your death-bed, nothing to save you at the last day. Formal religion never took any man to heaven. Like base metal, it will not stand the fire. Continuing in your present state you are in imminent peril of being lost for ever.

I earnestly beseech you this day to know your danger, to open your eyes and repent. Churchman or Dissenter, High Church or Low Church, if you have only a name to live, and a form of godliness without the power, awake and repent. Awake, above all, if you are an Evangelical formalist. "There is no devil," said the quaint old

Puritans, "like a white devil." There is no formalism so dangerous as Evangelical formalism.

I can only warn you. I do so with all affection. God alone can apply the warning to your soul. Oh, that you would see the folly as well as the danger of a heartless Christianity! It was sound advice which a dying man, in Suffolk, once gave to his son: "Son," he said, "whatever religion you have, never be content with wearing a cloak."

(2) In the second place, if your heart condemns you, and you wish to know what to do, *consider seriously the only course that you can safely take.*

Apply to the Lord Jesus Christ without delay, and spread before Him the state of your soul. Confess before Him your formality in time past, and ask Him to forgive it. Seek from Him the promised grace of the Holy Ghost, and entreat Him to quicken and renew your inward man.

The Lord Jesus is appointed and commissioned to be the Physician of man's soul. There is no case too hard for Him. There is no condition of soul that He cannot cure. There is no devil He cannot cast out. Seared and hardened as the heart of a formalist may be, there is balm in Gilead which can heal him, and a Physician who is mighty to save. Go and call on the Lord Jesus Christ this very day. "Ask, and it shall be given you; seek, and you shall find; knock, and it shall be opened to you." (Luke xi. 9.)

(3) In the last place, if your heart condemns you not, and you have real well-grounded confidence towards God, *consider seriously the many responsibilities of your position.*

Praise Him daily who hath called you out of darkness into light, and made you to differ. Praise Him daily, and ask Him never to forsake the work of His own hands.

Watch with a jealous watchfulness every part of your

inward man. Formality is ever ready to come in upon us, like the Egyptian plague of frogs, which went even into the king's chamber. Watch, and be on your guard.—Watch over your Bible-reading,—your praying,—your temper and your tongue,—your family life and your Sunday religion. There is nothing so good and spiritual that we may not fall into formal habits about it. There is none so spiritual but that he may have a heavy fall. Watch, therefore, and be on your guard.

Look forward, finally, and hope for the coming of the Lord. Your best things are yet to come. The second coming of Christ will soon be here. The time of temptation will soon be past and gone. The judgment and reward of the saints shall soon make amends for all. Rest in the hope of that day. Work, watch, and look forward.—One thing, at any rate, that day will make abundantly clear. It will show that there was never an hour in our lives in which we gave our hearts too thoroughly to Christ.

XII

THE WORLD

"Come out from among them, and be ye separate, saith the Lord."
2 COR. vi. 17.

THE text which heads this page touches a subject of vast importance in religion. That subject is the great duty of separation from the world. This is the point which St. Paul had in view when he wrote to the Corinthians, "Come out,—be separate."

The subject is one which demands the best attention of all who profess and call themselves Christians. In every age of the Church separation from the world has always been one of the grand evidences of a work of grace in the heart. He that has been really born of the Spirit, and made a new creature in Christ Jesus, has always endeavoured to "come out from the world," and live a separate life. They who have only had the name of Christian, without the reality, have always refused to "come out and be separate" from the world.

The subject perhaps was never more important than it is at the present day. There is a widely-spread desire to make things pleasant in religion,—to saw off the corners and edges of the cross, and to avoid, as far as possible, self-denial. On every side we hear professing Christians declaring loudly that we must not be "narrow and exclusive," and that there is no harm in many things which the holiest saints of old thought bad for their souls. That we may go anywhere, and do anything, and spend our time in anything, and read anything, and keep any company, and plunge into anything, and all the while may be very good Christians,—this, this is the maxim of thousands. In a day like this I think it good to raise a warning voice, and invite attention to the teaching of God's Word. It is written in that Word, " Come out, and be separate."

There are four points which I shall try to show my readers, in examining this mighty subject.

I. First, I shall try to show *that the world is a source of great danger to the soul.*

II. Secondly, I shall try to show *what is not meant by separation from the world.*

III. Thirdly, I shall try to show in *what real separation from the world consists.*

IV. Fourthly, I shall try *to show the secret of victory over the world.*

And now, before I go a single step further, let me warn every reader of this paper that he will never understand this subject unless he first understands what a true Christian is. If you are one of those unhappy people who think everybody is a Christian who goes to a place of worship, no matter how he lives, or what he believes, I fear you will care little about separation from the world. But if you read your Bible, and are in earnest about your soul, you will know that there are two classes of Christians, —converted and unconverted. You will know that what the Jews were among the nations under the Old Testament, this the true Christian is meant to be under the New. You will understand what I mean when I say that true

Christians are meant, in like manner, to be a "peculiar people" under the Gospel, and that there must be a difference between believers and unbelievers. To you, therefore, I make a special appeal this day. While many avoid the subject of separation from the world, and many positively hate it, and many are puzzled by it, give me your attention while I try to show you "the thing as it is."

I. First of all, let me show that *the world is a source of great danger to the soul.*

By " the world," be it remembered, I do not mean the material world on the face of which we are living and moving. He that pretends to say that anything which God has created in the heavens above, or the earth beneath, is in itself harmful to man's soul, says that which is unreasonable and absurd. On the contrary, the 'sun, moon, and stars,—the mountains, the valleys, and the plains,—the seas, lakes, and rivers,—the animal and vegetable creation,—all are in themselves "very good." (Gen. i. 31.) All are full of lessons of God's wisdom and power, and all proclaim daily, "The hand that made us is Divine." The idea that "matter" is in itself sinful and corrupt is a foolish heresy.

When I speak of "the world" in this paper, I mean those people who think only, or chiefly, of this world's things, and neglect the world to come,—the people who are always thinking more of earth than of heaven, more of time than of eternity, more of the body than of the soul, more of pleasing man than of pleasing God. It is of them and their ways, habits, customs, opinions, practices, tastes, aims, spirit, and tone, that I am speaking when I speak of "the world." This is the world from which St. Paul tells us to "Come out and be separate."

Now that "the world," in this sense, is an enemy to the soul, the well-known Church Catechism teaches us at its very beginning. It tells us that there are three things which a baptized Christian is bound to renounce and give up, and three enemies which he ought to fight with and resist. These three are the flesh, the devil, and "the world." All three are terrible foes, and all three must be overcome if we would be saved.

But, whatever men please to think about the Catechism, we shall do well to turn to the testimony of Holy Scripture. If the texts I am about to quote do not prove that the world is a source of danger to the soul, there is no meaning in words.

(*a*) Let us hear what St. Paul says:—

"Be not conformed to this world : but be ye transformed by the renewing of your mind." (Rom. xii. 2.)

"We have received, not the spirit of the world, but the Spirit which is of God." (1 Cor. ii. 12.)

"Christ gave Himself for us, that He might deliver us from this present evil world." (Gal. i. 4.)

"In time past ye walked according to the course of this world." (Eph. ii. 2.)

"Demas hath forsaken me, having loved this present world." (2 Tim. iv. 10.)

(*b*) Let us hear what St. James says:—

"Pure religion and undefiled before God and the Father is this, To visit the fatherless and widows in their affliction, and to keep himself unspotted from the world." (James i. 27.)

"Know ye not that the friendship of the world is enmity with God ? Whosoever therefore will be a friend of the world is the enemy of God." (James iv. 4.)

(*c*) Let us hear what St. John says:—

"Love not the world, neither the things that are in the world. If any man love the world, the love of the Father is not in him.

"For all that is in the world, the lust of the flesh, and the lust of the eyes, and the pride of life, is not of the Father, but is of the world.

"And the world passeth away, and the lust thereof; but he that doeth the will of God abideth for ever." (1 John ii. 15—17.)

"The world knoweth us not, because it knew Him not." (1 John iii. 1.)

"They are of the world: therefore speak they of the world, and the world heareth them." (1 John iv. 5.)

"Whatsoever is born of God overcometh the world." (1 John v. 4.)

"We know that we are of God and the whole world lieth in wickedness." (1 John v. 19.)

(d) Let us hear, lastly, what the Lord Jesus Christ says :—

"The cares of this world choke the Word, and it becometh unfruitful." (Matt. xiii. 22.)

"Ye are of this world: I am not of this world." (John viii. 23.)

"The Spirit of truth; whom the world cannot receive, because it seeth Him not, neither knoweth Him." (John xiv. 17.)

"If the world hate you, ye know that it hated Me before it hated you." (John xv. 18.)

"If ye were of the world, the world would love his own : but because ye are not of the world, but I have chosen you out of the world, therefore the world hateth you." (John xv. 19.)

"In the world ye shall have tribulation: but be of good cheer; I have overcome the world." (John xvi. 33.)

"They are not of the world, even as I am not of the world." (John xvii. 16.)

I make no comment on these twenty-one texts. They speak for themselves. If any one can read them carefully, and fail to see that "the world" is an enemy to the Christian's soul, and that there is an utter opposition between the friendship of the world and the friendship of Christ, he is past the reach of argument, and it is waste of time to reason with him. To my eyes they contain a lesson as clear as the sun at noon day.

I turn from Scripture to matters of fact and experience. I appeal to any old Christian who keeps his eyes open, and knows what is going on in the Churches. I ask him whether it be not true that nothing damages the cause of religion so much as "the world"? It is not open sin, or open unbelief, which robs Christ of His professing servants, so much as the love of the world, the fear of the world, the cares of the world, the business of the world, the money of the world, the pleasures of the world, and the desire to keep in with the world. This is the great rock on which thousands of young people are continually making shipwreck. They do not object to any article of the Christian faith. They do not deliberately choose evil, and openly rebel against God. They hope somehow to get to heaven at last; and they think it proper to have some religion. But they cannot give up their idol: they must have the world. And so after running well and bidding fair for heaven, while boys and girls, they turn aside when they become men and women, and go down the broad way which leads to destruction. They begin with Abraham and Moses, and end with Demas and Lot's wife.

The last day alone will prove how many souls "the world" has slain. Hundreds will be found to have been trained in religious families, and to have known the Gospel from their very childhood, and yet missed heaven. They left the harbour of home with bright prospects, and launched forth on the ocean of life with a father's blessing and a mother's prayers, and then got out of the right course through the seductions of the world, and ended their voyage in shallows and in misery. It is a sorrowful story to tell; but, alas, it is only too common! I cannot wonder that St. Paul says, "Come out and be separate."

II. Let me now try to show *what does not constitute separation from the world.*

The point is one which requires clearing up. There are many mistakes made about it. You will sometimes see sincere and well-meaning Christians doing things which God never intended them to do, in the matter of separation from the world, and h ne ly believing that they are in the path of duty. Their mistakes often do great harm. They give occasion to the wicked to ridicule all religion, and supply them with an excuse for having none. They cause the way of truth to be evil spoken of, and add to the offence of the cross. I think it a plain duty to make a few remarks on the subject. We must never forget that it is possible to be very much in earnest, and to think we are "doing God service," when in reality we are making some great mistake. There is such a thing as "zeal not according to knowledge." (John xvi. 2, Rom. x. 2.) There are few things about which it is so important to pray for a right judgment and sanctified common sense, as about separation from the world.

(*a*) When St. Paul said, "Come out and be separate," he did not mean that Christians ought to give up all worldly callings, trades, professions, and business. He did not forbid men to be soldiers, sailors, lawyers, doctors, merchants, bankers, shop-keepers, or tradesmen. There is not a word in the New Testament to justify such a line of conduct. Cornelius the centurion, Luke the physician, Zenas the lawyer, are examples to the contrary. Idleness is in itself a sin. A lawful calling is a remedy against temptation. "If any man will not work, neither shall he eat." (2 Thess. iii. 10.) To give up any business of life, which is not necessarily sinful, to the wicked and the devil, from fear of getting harm from it, is lazy, cowardly conduct. The right plan is to carry our religion into our business, and not to give up business under the specious pretence that it interferes with our religion.

(b) When St. Paul said, "Come out and be separate," he did not mean that Christians ought to decline all intercourse with unconverted people, and refuse to go into their society. There is no warrant for such conduct in the New Testament. Our Lord and His disciples did not refuse to go to a marriage feast, or to sit at meat at a Pharisee's table. St. Paul does not say, "If any of them that believe not bid you to a feast," you must not go, but only tells us how to behave if we do go. (1 Cor. x. 27.) Moreover, it is a dangerous thing to begin judging people too closely, and settling who are converted and who are not, and what society is godly and what ungodly. We are sure to make mistakes. Above all, such a course of life would cut us off from many opportunities of doing good. If we carry our Master with us wherever we go, who can tell but we may "save some," and get no harm? (1 Cor. ix. 22.)

(c) When St. Paul says, "Come out and be separate," he did not mean that Christians ought to take no interest in anything on earth except religion. To neglect science, art, literature, and politics,—to read nothing which is not directly spiritual,—to know nothing about what is going on among mankind, and never to look at a newspaper,—to care nothing about the government of one's country, and to be utterly indifferent as to the persons who guide its counsels and make its laws,—all this may seem very right and proper in the eyes of some people. But I take leave to think that it is an idle, selfish neglect of duty. St. Paul knew the value of good government, as one of the main helps to our "living a quiet and peaceable life in godliness and honesty." (1 Tim. ii. 2.) St. Paul was not ashamed to read heathen writers, and to quote their words in his speeches and writings. St. Paul did not think it beneath him to show an acquaintance with the laws and customs and callings of the world, in the illustrations he gave from them. Christians who plume themselves on their ignorance of secular things are precisely the Christians who bring religion into contempt. I knew the case of a blacksmith who would not come to hear his clergyman preach the Gospel, until he found out that he knew the properties of iron. Then he came.

(d) When St. Paul said, "Come out and be separate," he did not mean that Christians should be singular, eccentric, and peculiar in their dress, manners, demeanour, and voice. Anything which attracts notice in these matters is most objectionable, and ought to be carefully avoided. To wear clothes of such a colour, or made in such a fashion, that when you go into company every eye is fixed on you, and you are the object of general observation, is an enormous mistake. It gives occasion to the wicked to ridicule religion, and looks self-righteous and affected. There is not the slightest proof that our Lord and His apostles, and Priscilla, and Persis, and their companions, did not dress and behave just like others in their own ranks of life. On the other hand, one of the many charges our Lord brings against the Pharisees was that of "making broad their phylacteries, and enlarging the borders of their garments," so as to be "seen of men." (Matt. xxiii. 5.) True sanctity and sanctimoniousness are entirely different things. Those who try to show their unworldliness by wearing conspicuously ugly clothes, or by speaking in a whining, snuffling voice, or by affecting an unnatural slavishness, humility, and gravity of manner, miss their mark altogether, and only give occasion to the enemies of the Lord to blaspheme.

(e) When St. Paul said, "Come out and be separate," he did not mean that Christians ought to retire from the company of mankind, and shut themselves up in solitude. It is one of the crying errors of the Church of Rome to suppose that eminent holiness is to be attained by such practices. It is the unhappy delusion of the whole army of monks, nuns, and hermits. Separation of this kind is not according to the mind of Christ. He says distinctly in His last prayer, "I pray not that Thou shouldest take them out of the world, but that Thou shouldest keep them from the evil." (John xvii. 15.) There is not a word in the Acts or Epistles to recommend such a separation. True believers are always represented as mixing in the world, doing their duty in it, and glorifying God by patience, meekness, purity, and courage in their several positions, and not by cowardly desertion of them. Moreover, it is foolish to suppose that we can keep the world and the devil out of our hearts by going into holes and corners. True religion and unworldliness are best seen, not in timidly forsaking the post which God has allotted to us, but in manfully standing our ground, and showing the power of grace to overcome evil.

(ƒ) Last, but not least, when St. Paul said, "Come out and be separate," he did not mean that Christians ought to withdraw from every Church in which there are unconverted members, or to refuse to worship in company with any who are not believers, or to keep away from the Lord's table if any ungodly people go up to it. This is a very common but a very grievous mistake. There is not a text in the New Testament to justify it, and it ought to be condemned as a pure invention of man. Our Lord Jesus Christ Himself deliberately allowed Judas Iscariot to be an apostle for three years, and gave him the Lord's Supper. He has taught us, in the parable of the wheat and tares, that converted and unconverted will be " together till the harvest," and cannot be divided. (Matt. xiii. 30.) In His Epistles to the Seven Churches, and in all St. Paul's Epistles, we often see faults and corruptions mentioned and reproved ; but we are never told that they justify desertion of the assembly, or neglect of ordinances. In short, we must not look for a perfect Church, a perfect congregation, and a perfect company of communicants, until the marriage supper of the Lamb. If others are unworthy Churchmen, or unworthy partakers of the Lord's Supper, the sin is theirs and not ours: we are not their judges. But to separate ourselves from Church assemblies, and deprive ourselves of Christian ordinances, because others use them unworthily, is to take up a foolish, unreasonable, and unscriptural position. It is not the mind of Christ, and it certainly is not St. Paul's idea of separation from the world.

I commend these six points to the calm consideration of all who wish to understand the subject of separation from the world. About each and all of them far more might be said than I have space to say in this paper. About each and all of them I have seen so many mistakes made, and so much misery and unhappiness caused by those mistakes, that I want to put Christians on their guard. I want them not to take up positions hastily, in the zeal of their first love, which they will afterwards be obliged to give up.

I leave this part of my subject with two pieces of advice, which I offer especially to young Christians.

I advise them, for one thing, if they really desire to come out from the world, to remember that the shortest path is not always the path of duty. To quarrel with all our unconverted relatives, to "cut" all our old friends, to withdraw entirely from mixed society, to live an exclusive life, to give up every act of courtesy and civility in order that we may devote ourselves to the direct work of Christ,—all this may seem very right, and may satisfy our consciences and save us trouble. But I venture a doubt whether it is not often a selfish, lazy, self-pleasing line of conduct, and whether the true cross and true line of duty may not be to deny ourselves, and adopt a very different course of action.

I advise them, for another thing, if they want to come out from the world, to watch against a sour, morose, ungenial, gloomy, unpleasant, bearish demeanour, and never to forget that there is such a thing as " winning without the Word." (1 Peter iii. 1.) Let them strive to show unconverted people that their principles, whatever may be thought of them, make them cheerful, amiable, good-tempered, unselfish, considerate for others, and ready to take an interest in everything that is innocent and of good report. In short, let there be no needless separation between us and the world. In many things, as I shall soon show, we must be separate; but let us take care that it is separation of the right sort. If the world is offended by such separation we cannot help it. But let us never give the world occasion to say that our separation is foolish, senseless, ridiculous, unreasonable, uncharitable, and unscriptural.

III. In the third place, I shall try to show *what true separation from the world really is.*

I take up this branch of my subject with a very deep sense of its difficulty. That there is a certain line of conduct which all true Christians ought to pursue with respect to "the world, and the things of the world," is very evident. The texts already quoted make that plain. The key to the solution of that question lies in the word "separation." But in what separation consists it is not easy to show. On some points it is not hard to lay down particular rules; on others it is impossible to do more than state general principles, and leave every one to apply them according to his position in life. This is what I shall now attempt to do.

(*a*) First and foremost, he that desires to "come out from the world, and be separate," *must steadily and habitually refuse to be guided by the world's standard of right and wrong.*

The rule of the bulk of mankind is to go with the stream, to do as others, to follow the fashion, to keep in with the common opinion, and to set your watch by the town-clock. The true Christian will never be content with such a rule as that. He will simply ask, What saith the Scripture? What is written in the Word of God? He will maintain firmly that nothing can be right which God says is wrong, and that the customs and opinions of his neighbours can never make that to be a trifle which God calls serious, or that to be no sin which God calls sin. He will never think lightly of such sins as drinking, swearing, gambling, lying, cheating, swindling, or breach of the seventh commandment, because they are common, and many say, "Where is the mighty harm?" That miserable argument,—"Everybody thinks so, everybody says so, everybody does it, everybody will be there,"—goes for nothing with him. Is it condemned or approved by the Bible? That is his only question. If he stands alone in the parish, or town, or congregation, he will not go against the Bible. If he has to come out from the crowd, and take a position by himself, he will not flinch from it rather than disobey the Bible. This is genuine Scriptural separation.

(b) He that desires to "come out from the world and be separate," *must be very careful how he spends his leisure time.*

This is a point which at first sight appears of little importance. But the longer I live, the more I am persuaded that it deserves most serious attention. Honourable occupation and lawful business are a great safeguard to the soul, and the time that is spent upon them is comparatively the time of our least danger. The devil finds it hard to get a hearing from a busy man. But when the day's work is over, and the time of leisure arrives, then comes the hour of temptation.

I do not hesitate to warn every man who wants to live a Christian life, to be very careful how he spends his evenings. Evening is the time when we are naturally disposed to unbend after the labours of the day; and evening is the time when the Christian is too often tempted to lay aside his armour, and consequently brings trouble on his soul. "Then cometh the devil," and with the devil the world. Evening is the time when the poor man is tempted to go to the public-house, and fall into sin. Evening is the time when the tradesman too often goes to the Inn parlour, and sits for hours hearing and seeing things which do him no good. Evening is the time which the higher classes choose for dancing, card playing, and the like; and consequently never get to bed till late at night. If we love our souls, and would not become worldly, let us mind how we spend our evenings. Tell me how a man spends his evenings, and I can generally tell what his character is.

The true Christian will do well to make it a settled rule never to *waste* his evenings. Whatever others may do, let him resolve always to make time for quiet, calm thought,—for Bible-reading and prayer. The rule will prove a hard one to keep. It may bring on him the charge of being unsocial and over strict. Let him not mind this. Anything of this kind is better than habitual late hours in company, hurried prayers, slovenly Bible reading, and a bad conscience. Even if he stands alone in his parish or town let him not depart from his rule. He will find himself in a minority, and be thought a peculiar man. But this is genuine Scriptural separation.

(c) He that desires to "come out from the world and be separate," must *steadily and habitually determine not to be swallowed up and absorbed in the business of the world.*

A true Christian will strive to do his duty in whatever station or position he finds himself, and to do it well. Whether statesman, or merchant, or banker, or lawyer, or doctor, or tradesman, or farmer, he will try to do his work so that no one can find occasion for fault in him. But he will not allow it to get between him and Christ. If he finds his business beginning to eat up his Sundays, his Bible-reading, his private prayer, and to bring clouds between him and heaven, he will say, "Stand back! There is a limit. Hitherto thou mayest go, but no further. I cannot sell my soul for place, fame, or gold." Like Daniel, he will make time for his communion with God, whatever the cost may be. Like Havelock, he will deny himself anything rather than lose his Bible-reading and his prayers. In all this he will find he stands almost alone. Many will laugh at him, and tell him they get on well enough without being so strict and particular. He will heed it not. He will resolutely hold the world at arm's length, whatever present loss or sacrifice it may seem to entail. He will choose rather to be less rich and prosperous in this world, than not to prosper about his soul. To stand alone in this way, to run counter to the ways of others, requires immense self denial. But this is genuine Scriptural separation.

(d) He that desires to "come out from the world and be separate" must steadily *abstain from all amusements and recreations which are inseparably connected with sin.*

This is a hard subject to handle, and I approach it with pain. But I do not think I should be faithful to Christ, and faithful to my office as a minister, if I did not speak very plainly about it, in considering such a matter as separation from the world.

Let me, then, say honestly, that I cannot understand how any one who makes any pretence to real vital religion can allow himself to attend races and theatres. Conscience, no doubt, is a strange thing, and every man must judge for himself and use his liberty. One man sees no harm in things which another regards with abhorrence as evil. I can only give my own opinion for what it is worth, and entreat my readers to consider seriously what I say.

That to look at horses running at full speed is in itself

perfectly harmless, no sensible man will pretend to deny. That many plays, such as Shakespeare's, are among the finest productions of the human intellect, is equally undeniable. But all this is beside the question. The question is whether horse-racing and theatres, as they are now conducted, in England, are not inseparably bound up with things that are downright wicked. I assert without hesitation that they are so bound up. I assert that the breach of God's commandments so invariably accompanies the race and the play, that you cannot go to the amusement without helping sin.

I entreat all professing Christians to remember this, and to take heed what they do. I warn them plainly that they have no right to shut their eyes to facts which every intelligent person knows, for the mere pleasure of seeing a horse-race, or listening to good actors or actresses. I warn them that they must not talk of separation from the world, if they can lend their sanction to amusements which are invariably connected with gambling, betting, drunkenness, and fornication. These are the things "which God will judge."—"The end of these things is death." (Heb. xiii. 4; Rom. vi. 21.)

Hard words these, no doubt! But are they not true? It may seem to your relatives and friends very strait-laced, strict, and narrow, if you tell them you cannot go to the races or the theatre with them. But we must fall back on first principles. Is the world a danger to the soul, or is it not? Are we to come out from the world, or are we not? These are questions which can only be answered in one way.

If we love our souls we must have nothing to do with amusements which are bound up with sin. Nothing short of this can be called genuine scriptural separation from the world.*

---

* See Note, page 310.

(e) He that desires to "come out from the world, and be separate," must be *moderate in the use of lawful and innocent recreations.*

No sensible Christian will ever think of condemning all recreations. In a world of wear and tear like that we live in, occasional unbending and relaxation are good for all. Body and mind alike require seasons of lighter occupation, and opportunities of letting off high spirits, and especially when they are young. Exercise itself is a positive necessity for the preservation of mental and bodily health. I see no harm in cricket, rowing, running, and other manly athletic recreations. I find no fault with those who play at chess and such-like games of skill. We are all fearfully and wonderfully made. No wonder the poet says,—

> "Strange that a harp of thousand strings
> Should keep in tune so long ! "

Anything which strengthens nerves, and brain, and digestion, and lungs, and muscles, and makes us more fit for Christ's work, so long as it is not in itself sinful, is a blessing, and ought to be thankfully used. Anything which will occasionally divert our thoughts from their usual grinding channel, in a healthy manner, is a good and not an evil.

But it is the excess of these innocent things which a true Christian must watch against, if he wants to be separate from the world. He must not devote his whole heart, and soul, and mind, and strength, and time to them, as many do, if he wishes to serve Christ. There are hundreds of lawful things which are good in moderation, but bad when taken in excess: healthful medicine in small quantities,—downright poison when swallowed down in huge doses. In nothing is this so true as it is in the matter of recreations. The use of them is one thing, and the abuse of them is another. The Christian who uses them must know when to stop, and how to say "Hold: enough!"—Do they interfere with his private religion? Do they take up too much of his thoughts and attention? Have they a secularizing effect on his soul? Have they a tendency to pull him down to earth? Then let him hold hard and take care. All this will require courage, self-denial, and firmness. It is a line of conduct which will often bring on us the ridicule and contempt of those who know not what moderation is, and who spend their lives in making trifles serious things and serious things trifles. But if we mean to come out from the world we must not mind this. We must be "temperate" even in lawful things, whatever others may think of us. This is genuine Scriptural separation.

(*f*) Last, but not least, he that desires to "come out from the world and be separate" must be *careful how he allows himself in friendships, intimacies, and close relationships with worldly people.*

We cannot help meeting many unconverted people as long as we live. We cannot avoid having intercourse with them, and doing business with them, unless "we go out of the world." (1 Cor. v. 10.) To treat them with the utmost courtesy, kindness, and charity, whenever we do meet them, is a positive duty. But acquaintance is one thing, and intimate friendship is quite another. To seek their society without cause, to choose their company, to cultivate intimacy with them, is very dangerous to the soul. Human nature is so constituted that we cannot be much with other people without effect on our own character. The old proverb will never fail to prove true: "Tell me with whom a man chooses to live, and I will tell you what he is." The Scripture says expressly, "He that walketh with wise men shall be wise; but a companion of fools shall be destroyed." (Prov. xiii. 20.) If then a Christian, who desires to live consistently, chooses for his friends those who either do not care for their souls, or the Bible,

or God, or Christ, or holiness, or regard them as of
secondary importance, it seems to me impossible for him
to prosper in his religion. He will soon find that their
ways are not his ways, nor their thoughts his thoughts, nor
their tastes his tastes; and that, unless they change, he
must give up intimacy with them. In short, there must
be separation. Of course such separation will be painful.
But if we have to choose between the loss of a friend and
the injury of our souls, there ought to be no doubt in our
minds. If friends will not walk in the narrow way with
us, we must not walk in the broad way to please them.
But let us distinctly understand that to attempt to keep
up close intimacy between a converted and an unconverted
person, if both are consistent with their natures, is to
attempt an impossibility.

The principle here laid down ought to be carefully
remembered by all unmarried Christians in the choice of
a husband or wife. I fear it is too often entirely forgotten.
Too many seem to think of everything except religion in
choosing a partner for life, or to suppose that it will come
somehow as a matter of course. Yet when a praying,
Bible-reading, God-fearing, Christ-loving, Sabbath-keeping
Christian marries a person who takes no interest whatever
in serious religion, what can the result be but injury to
the Christian, or immense unhappiness? Health is not
infectious, but disease is. As a general rule, in such cases,
the good go down to the level of the bad, and the bad do
not come up to the level of the good. The subject is a
delicate one, and I do not care to dwell upon it. But this
I say confidently to every unmarried Christian man or
woman,—if you love your soul, if you do not want to
fall away and backslide, if you do not want to destroy
your own peace and comfort for life, resolve never to
marry any person who is not a thorough Christian,
whatever the resolution may cost you. You had better
die than marry an unbeliever. Stand to this resolution,

and let no one ever persuade you out of it. Depart from this resolution, and you will find it almost impossible to "come out and be separate." You will find you have tied a mill-stone round your own neck in running the race towards heaven; and, if saved at last, it will be "so as by fire." (1 Cor. iii. 15.)

I offer these six general hints to all who wish to follow St. Paul's advice, and to come out from the world and be separate. In giving them, I lay no claim to infallibility; but I believe they deserve consideration and attention. I do not forget that the subject is full of difficulties, and that scores of doubtful cases are continually arising in a Christian's course, in which it is very hard to say what is the path of duty, and how to behave. Perhaps the following bits of advice may be found useful.—In all doubtful cases we should first pray for wisdom and sound judgment. If prayer is worth anything, it must be specially valuable when we desire to do right, but do not see our way.—In all doubtful cases let us often try ourselves by recollecting the eye of God. Should I go to such and such a place, or do such and such a thing, if I really thought God was looking at me ?—In all doubtful cases let us never forget the second advent of Christ and the day of judgment. Should I like to be found in such and such company, or employed in such and such ways ?— Finally, in all doubtful cases let us find out what the conduct of the holiest and best Christians has been under similar circumstances. If we do not clearly see our own way, we need not be ashamed to follow good examples. I throw out these suggestions for the use of all who are in difficulties about disputable points in the matter of separation from the world. I cannot help thinking that they may help to untie many knots, and solve many problems.

IV. I shall now conclude the whole subject by trying to *show the secrets of real victory over the world.*

To come out from the world of course is not an easy thing. It cannot be easy so long as human nature is what it is, and a busy devil is always near us. It requires a constant struggle and exertion; it entails incessant conflict and self-denial; it often places us in exact opposition to members of our own families, to relations and neighbours; it sometimes obliges us to do things which give great offence, and bring on us ridicule and petty persecution. It is precisely this which makes many hang back and shrink from decided religion. They know they are not right; they know that they are not so "thorough" in Christ's service as they ought to be, and they feel uncomfortable and ill at ease. But the fear of man keeps them back. And so they linger on through life with aching, dissatisfied hearts,—with too much religion to be happy in the world, and too much of the world to be happy in their religion. I fear this is a very common case, if the truth were known.

Yet there are some in every age who seem to get the victory over the world. They come out decidedly from its ways, and are unmistakably separate. They are independent of its opinions, and unshaken by its opposition. They move on like planets in an orbit of their own, and seem to rise equally above the world's smiles and frowns. And what are the secrets of their victory? I will set them down.

(a) The first secret of victory over the world is a *right heart*. By that I mean a heart renewed, changed and sanctified by the Holy Ghost,—a heart in which Christ dwells, a heart in which old things have passed away, and all things become new. The grand mark of such a heart is the bias of its tastes and affections. The owner of such a heart no longer likes the world, and the things of the world, and therefore finds it no trial or sacrifice to give them up. He has no longer any appetite for the company, the conversation, the amusements, the occupations, the books which he once loved, and to "come out" from them seems natural to him. Great indeed is the expulsive power of a new principle! Just as the new spring-buds in a beech hedge push off the old leaves and make them quietly fall to the ground, so does the new heart of a believer invariably affect his tastes and likings, and make him drop many things which he once loved and lived in, because he now likes them no more. Let him that wants to "come out from the world and be separate," make sure first and foremost that he has got a new heart. If the heart is really right, everything else will be right in time. "If thine eye be single, thy whole body shall be full of light." (Matt. vi. 22.) If the affections are not right, there never will be right action.

(b) The second secret of victory over the world is a *lively practical faith* in unseen things. What saith the Scripture? "This is the victory that overcometh the world, even our faith." (1 John v. 4.) To attain and keep up the habit of looking steadily at invisible things, as if they were visible,—to set before our minds every day, as grand realities, our souls, God, Christ, heaven, hell, judgment, eternity,—to cherish an abiding conviction that what we do not see is just as real as what we do see, and ten thousand times more important,—this, this is one way to be conquerors over the world. This was the faith which made the noble army of saints, described in the eleventh chapter of Hebrews, obtain such a glorious testimony from the Holy Ghost. They all acted under a firm persuasion that they had a real God, a real Saviour, and a real home in heaven, though unseen by mortal eyes. Armed with this faith, a man regards this world as a shadow compared to the world to come, and cares little for its praise or blame, its enmity or its rewards. Let him that wants to come out from the world and be separate, but shrinks and hangs back for fear of the things seen, pray and strive to have this faith. "All things are possible to him that believes." (Mark ix. 23.) Like Moses, he will find it possible to forsake Egypt, seeing Him that is invisible. Like Moses, he will not care what he loses and who is displeased, because he sees afar off, like one looking through a telescope, a substantial recompense of reward. (Heb. xi. 26.)

(c) The third and last secret of victory over the world, is to attain and cultivate the *habit of boldly confessing Christ* on all proper occasions. In saying this I would not be mistaken. I want no one to blow a trumpet before him, and thrust his religion on others at all seasons. But I do wish to encourage all who strive to come out from the world to show their colours, and to act and speak out like men who are not ashamed to serve Christ. A steady, quiet assertion of our own principles, as Christians, —an habitual readiness to let the children of the world see that we are guided by other rules than they are, and do not mean to swerve from them,—a calm, firm, courteous maintenance of our own standard of things in every company,—all this will insensibly form a habit within us, and make it comparatively easy to be a separate man. It will be hard at first, no doubt, and cost us many a struggle; but the longer we go on, the easier will it be. Repeated acts of confessing Christ will produce habits. Habits once formed will produce a settled character. Our characters once known, we shall be saved much trouble. Men will know what to expect from us, and will count it no strange thing if they see us living the lives of separate peculiar people. He that grasps the nettle most firmly will always be less hurt than the man who touches it with a trembling hand. It is a great thing to be able to say "No" decidedly, but courteously, when asked to do anything which conscience says is wrong. He that shows his colours boldly from the first, and is never ashamed to let men see "whose he is and whom he serves," will soon find that he has overcome the world, and will be let alone. Bold confession is a long step towards victory.

It only remains for me now to conclude the whole subject with a few short words of application. The danger of the world ruining the soul, the nature of true separation from the world, the secrets of victory over the world, are all before the reader of this paper. I now ask him to give me his attention for the last time, while I try to say something directly for his personal benefit.

(1) My first word shall be *a question*. Are you overcoming the world, or are you overcome by it? Do you know what it is to come out from the world and be separate, or are you yet entangled by it, and conformed to it? If you have any desire to be saved, I entreat you to answer this question.

If you know nothing of "separation," I warn you affectionately that your soul is in great danger. The world passeth away; and they who cling to the world, and think only of the world, will pass away with it to everlasting ruin. Awake to know your peril before it be too late. Awake and flee from the wrath to come. The time is short. The end of all things is at hand. The shadows are lengthening. The sun is going down. The night cometh when no man can work. The great white throne will soon be set. The judgment will begin. The books will be opened. Awake, and come out from the world while it is called to-day.

Yet a little while, and there will be no more worldly occupations and worldly amusements,—no more getting money and spending money,—no more eating, and drinking, and feasting, and dressing, and ball-going, and theatres, and races, and cards, and gambling. What will you do when all these things have passed away for ever? How can you possibly be happy in an eternal heaven, where holiness is all in all, and worldliness has no place? Oh consider these things, and be wise! Awake, and break the chains which the world has thrown around you. Awake, and flee from the wrath to come.

(2) My second word shall be *a counsel*. If you want to come out from the world, but know not what to do, take the advice which I give you this day. Begin by applying direct, as a penitent sinner, to our Lord Jesus Christ, and put your case in His hands. Pour out your heart before Him. Tell Him your whole story, and keep nothing back. Tell Him that you are a sinner wanting to be saved from the world, the flesh, and the devil, and entreat Him to save you.

That blessed Saviour "gave Himself for us that He might deliver us from this present evil world." (Gal. i. 2.) He knows what the world is, for He lived in it thirty and three years. He knows what the difficulties of a man are, for He was made man for our sakes, and dwelt among men. High in heaven, at the right hand of God, He is able to save to the uttermost all who come to God by Him,—able to keep us from the evil of the world while we are still living in it,—able to give us power to become the sons of God,—able to keep us from falling,—able to make us more than conquerors. Once more I say, Go direct to Christ with the prayer of faith, and put yourself wholly and unreservedly in His hands. Hard as it may seem to you now to come out from the world and be separate, you shall find that with Jesus nothing is impossible. You, even you, shall overcome the world.

(3) My third and last word shall be *encouragement*. If you have learned by experience what it is to come out from the world, I can only say to you, Take comfort, and persevere. You are in the right road; you have no cause to be afraid. The everlasting hills are in sight. Your salvation is nearer than when you believed. Take comfort and press on.

No doubt you have had many a battle, and made many

a false step. You have sometimes felt ready to faint, and been half disposed to go back to Egypt. But your Master has never entirely left you, and He will never suffer you to be tempted above that you are able to bear. Then persevere steadily in your separation from the world, and never be ashamed of standing alone. Settle it firmly in your mind that the most decided Christians are always the happiest, and remember that no one ever said at the end of his course that he had been too holy, and lived too near to God.

Hear, last of all, what is written in the Scriptures of truth:

"Whosoever shall confess Me before men, him shall the Son of man also confess before the angels of God." (Luke xii. 8.)

"There is no man that hath left house, or brethren, or sisters, or father, or mother, or wife, or children, or lands, for my sake, and the gospel's,

"But he shall receive an hundred-fold now in this time, houses, and brethren, and sisters, and mothers, and children, and lands, with persecutions; and in the world to come eternal life." (Mark x. 29, 30.)

"Cast not away therefore your confidence, which hath great recompense of reward.

"For ye have need of patience, that, after ye have done the will of God, ye might receive the promise.

"For yet a little while, and He that shall come will come, and will not tarry." (Heb. x. 35—37.)

Those words were written and spoken for our sakes. Let us lay hold on them, and never forget them. Let us persevere to the end, and never be ashamed of coming out from the world, and being separate. We may be sure it brings its own reward.

NOTE.

THOUGHTFUL and intelligent readers will probably observe that, under the head of worldly amusements, I have said nothing about ball-going and card-playing. They are delicate and difficult subjects, and many classes of society are not touched by them. But I am quite willing to give my opinion, and the more so because I do not speak of them without experience in the days of my youth.

(a) Concerning *ball-going*, I only ask Christians to judge the amusement by its tendencies and accompaniments. To say there is anything morally wrong in the mere bodily act of dancing would be absurd. David danced before the ark. Solomon said, "There is a time to dance." (Eccle. iii. 4.) Just as it is natural to lambs and kittens to frisk about, so it seems natural to young people, all over the world, to jump about to a lively tune of music. If dancing were taken up for mere exercise, if dancing took place at early hours, and men only danced with men, and women with women, it would be needless and absurd to object to it. But everybody knows that this is not what is meant by modern ball-going. This is an amusement which involves very late hours, extravagant dressing, and an immense amount of frivolity, vanity, jealousy, unhealthy excitement, and vain conversation. Who would like to be found in a modern ball-room when the Lord Jesus Christ comes the second time? Who that has taken much part in balls, as I myself once did, before I knew better, can deny that they have a most dissipating effect on the mind, like opium-eating and dram-drinking on the body? I cannot withhold my opinion that ball-going is one of those worldly amusements which "war against the soul," and which it is wisest and best to give up. And as for those parents who urge their sons and daughters, against their wills and inclinations, to go to balls, I can only say that they are taking on themselves a most dangerous responsibility, and risking great injury to their children's souls.

(b) Concerning *card-playing*, my judgment is much the same. I ask Christian people to try it by its tendencies and consequences. Of course it would be nonsense to say there is positive wickedness in an innocent game of cards, for diversion, and not for money. I have known instances of old people of lethargic and infirm habit of body, unable to work or read, to whom cards in an evening were really useful, to keep them from drowsiness, and preserve their health. But it is vain to shut our eyes to facts. If masters and mistresses once begin to play cards in the parlour, servants are likely to play cards in the kitchen ; and then comes in a whole train of evils. Moreover, from simple card-playing to desperate gambling there is but a chain of steps. If parents teach young people that there is no harm in the first step, they must never be surprised if they go on to the last.

I give this opinion with much diffidence. I lay no claim to infallibility. Let every one be persuaded in his own mind. But, considering all things, it is my deliberate judgment that the Christian who wishes to keep his soul right, and to "come out from the world," will do wisely to have nothing to do with card-playing. It is a habit which seems to grow on some people so much that it becomes at last a necessity, and they cannot live without it. "Madam," said Romaine to an old lady at Bath, who declared she could not do without her cards,—"Madam, if this is the case, cards are your god, and your god is a very poor one." Surely in doubtful matters like these it is well to give our souls the benefit of the doubt, and to refrain.

(c) Concerning *field-sports*, I admit that it is not easy to lay down a strict rule. I cannot go the length of some, and say that galloping across country, or shooting grouse, partridges, or pheasants, or catching salmon or trout, are in themselves positively sinful occupations, and distinct marks of an unconverted heart. There are many persons, I know, to whom violent out-door exercise and complete diversion of mind are absolute necessities, for the preservation of their bodily and mental health. But in all these matters the chief question is one of degree. Much depends on the company men are thrown into, and the extent to which the thing is carried. The great danger lies in excess. It is possible to be *intemperate* about hunting and shooting as well as about drinking. We are commanded in Scripture to be "temperate in all things," if we would so run as to obtain ; and those who are addicted to field-sports should not forget this rule.

The question, however, is one about which Christians must be careful in expressing an opinion, and moderate in their judgments. The man who can neither ride, nor shoot, nor throw a fly, is hardly qualified to speak dispassionately about such matters. It is cheap and easy work to condemn others for doing things which you cannot do yourself, and are utterly unable to enjoy ! One thing only is perfectly certain,—all intemperance or excess is sin. The man who is wholly absorbed in field-sports, and spends all his years in such a manner that he seems to think God only created him to be a "hunting, shooting, and fishing animal," is a man who at present knows very little of Scriptural Christianity. It is written, "Where your treasure is, there will your heart be also." (Matt. vi. 21.)

XIII

RICHES AND POVERTY

" There was a certain rich man, which was clothed in purple and
fine linen, and fared sumptuously every day:
" And there was a certain beggar named Lazarus, which was laid at
his gate, full of sores,
" And desiring to be fed with the crumbs which fell from the rich
man's table: moreover, the dogs came and licked his sores.
" And it came to pass that the beggar died, and was carried by the
angels into Abraham's bosom: the rich man also died, and was
buried;
" And in hell he lift up his eyes, being in torments, and seeth
Abraham afar off, and Lazarus in his bosom."—
Luke xvi. 19—23.

THERE are probably few readers of the Bible who are not
familiar with the parable of the rich man and Lazarus.
It is one of those passages of Scripture which leave an
indelible impression on the mind. Like the parable of the
Prodigal Son, once read it is never forgotten.

The reason of this is clear and simple. The whole
parable is a most vividly painted picture. The story, as
it goes on, carries our senses with it with irresistible power.
Instead of readers, we become lookers on. We are witnesses of all the events described. We see. We hear.
We fancy we could almost touch. The rich man's
banquet,—the purple,—the fine linen,—the gate,—the
beggar lying by it,—the sores,—the dogs,—the crumbs,—

the two deaths,—the rich man's burial,—the ministering
angels,—the bosom of Abraham,—the rich man's fearful
waking up,—the fire,—the gulf,—the hopeless remorse,—
all, all stand out before our eyes in bold relief, and stamp
themselves upon our minds. This is the perfection of
language. This is the attainment of the famous Arabian
standard of eloquence.—"He speaks the best who turns
the ear into an eye."

But, after all, it is one thing to admire the masterly
composition of this parable, and quite another to receive
the spiritual lessons it contains. The eye of the intellect
can often see beauties while the heart remains asleep,
and sees nothing at all. Hundreds read Pilgrim's Progress
with deep interest, to whom the struggle for the celestial
city is foolishness. Thousands are familiar with every
word of the parable before us this day, who never consider
how it comes home to their own case. Their conscience
is deaf to the cry which ought to ring in their ears as they
read,—"Thou art the man." Their heart never turns to
God with the solemn inquiry,—"Lord, is this my picture?
—Lord, is it I?"

I invite my readers this day to consider the leading
truths which this parable is meant to teach us. I purposely
omit to notice any part of it but that which stands at the
head of this paper. May the Holy Ghost give us a
teachable spirit, and an understanding heart, and so
produce lasting impressions on our souls!

I. Let us observe, first of all, *how different are the
conditions which God allots to different men.*

The Lord Jesus begins the parable by telling us of a
rich man and a beggar. He says not a word in praise
either of poverty or of riches. He describes the circumstances of a wealthy man and the circumstances of a poor
man; but He neither condemns the temporal position of
one, nor praises that of the other.

The contrast between the two men is painfully striking. Look on this picture, and on that.

Here is one who possessed abundance of this world's good things. "He was clothed in purple and fine linen, and fared sumptuously every day."

Here is another who has literally nothing. He is a friendless, diseased, half-starved pauper. "He lies at the rich man's gate full of sores," and begs for crumbs.

Both are children of Adam. Both came from the same dust, and belonged to one family. Both are living in the same land and subjects of the same government. And yet how different is their condition!

But we must take heed that we do not draw lessons from the parable which it was never meant to teach. The rich are not always bad men, and do not always go to hell. The poor are not always good men, and do not always go to heaven. We must not rush into the extreme of supposing that it is sinful to be rich. We must not run away with the idea that there is anything wicked in the difference of condition here described, and that God intended all men to be equal. There is nothing in our Lord Jesus Christ's words to warrant any such conclusion. He simply describes things as they are often seen in the world, and as we must expect to see them.

Universal equality is a very high-sounding expression, and a favourite idea with visionary men. Many in every age have disturbed society by stirring up the poor against the rich, and by preaching up the popular doctrine that all men ought to be equal. But so long as the world is under the present order of things this universal equality cannot be attained. Those who declaim against the vast inequality of men's lots will doubtless never be in want of hearers; but so long as human nature is what it is, this inequality cannot be prevented.

So long as some are wise and some are foolish,—some strong and some weak,—some healthy and some diseased,

—some lazy and some diligent,—some provident and some improvident;—so long as children reap the fruit of their parent's misconduct;—so long as sun, and rain, and heat, and cold, and wind, and waves, and drought, and blight, and storms, and tempests are beyond man's control,—so long there always will be some rich and some poor. All the political economy in the world will never make the poor altogether "cease out of the land." (Deut. xv. 11.)

Take all the property in England by force this day, and divide it equally among the inhabitants. Give every man above twenty years old an equal portion. Let all take share and share alike, and begin the world over again. Do this, and see where you would be at the end of fifty years. You would just have come round to the point where you began. You would just find things as unequal as before. Some would have worked, and some would have been idle. Some would have been always careless, and some always scheming. Some would have sold, and others would have bought. Some would have wasted, and others would have saved. And the end would be that some would be rich and others poor.

Let no man listen to those vain and foolish talkers who say that all men were meant to be equal. They might as well tell you that all men ought to be of the same height, weight, strength, and cleverness,—or that all oak trees ought to be of the same shape and size,—or that all blades of grass ought to be of the same length.

Settle it in your mind that the main cause of all the suffering you see around you is sin. Sin is the grand cause of the enormous luxury of the rich, and the painful degradation of the poor,—of the heartless selfishness of the highest classes, and the helpless poverty of the lowest. Sin must be first cast out of the world. The hearts of all men must be renewed and sanctified. The devil must be bound. The Prince of Peace must come down and take His great power and reign. All this must be before there ever can be universal happiness, or the gulf be filled up which now divides the rich and poor.

Beware of expecting a millennium to be brought about by any method of government, by any system of education, by any political party. Labour might and main to do good to all men. Pity your poorer brethren, and help every reasonable endeavour to raise them from their low estate. Slack not your hand from any endeavour to increase knowledge, to promote morality, to improve the temporal condition of the poor. But never, never forget that you live in a fallen world, that sin is all around you, and that the devil is abroad. And be very sure that the rich man and Lazarus are emblems of two classes which will always be in the world until the Lord comes.

II. Let us observe, in the next place, that *a man's temporal condition is no test of the state of his soul.*

The rich man in the parable appears to have been the world's pattern of a prosperous man. If the life that now is were all, he seems to have had everything that heart could wish. We know that he was "clothed in purple and fine linen, and fared sumptuously every day." We need not doubt that he had everything else which money could procure. The wisest of men had good cause for saying, "Money answereth all things." "The rich hath many friends." (Eccles. x. 19; Prov. xiv. 20.)

But who that reads the story through can fail to see that in the highest and best sense the rich man was pitiably *poor?* Take away the good things of this life, and he had nothing left,—nothing after death,—nothing beyond the grave,—nothing in the world to come. With all his riches he had no "treasure laid up in heaven." With all his purple and fine linen he had no garment of righteousness. With all his boon companions he had no Friend and Advocate at God's right hand. With all his sumptuous fare he had never tasted the bread of life.

With all his splendid palace he had no home in the eternal world. Without God, without Christ, without faith, without grace, without pardon, without holiness, he lives to himself for a few short years, and then goes down hopelessly into the pit. How hollow and unreal was all his prosperity! Judge what I say,—*The rich man was very poor.*

Lazarus appears to have been one who had literally nothing in the world. It is hard to conceive a case of greater misery and destitution than his. He had neither house, nor money, nor food, nor health, nor, in all probability, even clothes. His picture is one that can never be forgotten. He "lay at the rich man's gate, covered with sores." He desired to be "fed with the crumbs that fell from the rich man's table." Moreover, the dogs came and "licked his sores." Verily the wise man might well say, "The poor is hated even of his neighbour." "The destruction of the poor is their poverty." (Prov. xiv. 20; x. 15.)

But who that reads the parable to the end can fail to see that in the highest sense Lazarus was not poor, but *rich ?* He was a child of God. He was an heir of glory. He possessed durable riches and righteousness. His name was in the book of life. His place was prepared for Him in heaven. He had the best of clothing,—the righteousness of a Saviour. He had the best of friends,—God Himself was his portion. He had the best of food,—he had meat to eat the world knew not of. And, best of all, he had these things for ever. They supported him in life. They did not leave him in the hour of death. They went with him beyond the grave. They were his to eternity. Surely in this point of view we may well say, not "poor Lazarus," but "rich Lazarus."

We should do well to measure all men by God's standard,—to measure them not by the amount of their income, but by the condition of their souls. When the

Lord God looks down from heaven and sees the children of men, He takes no account of many things which are highly esteemed by the world. He looks not at men's money, or lands, or titles. He looks only at the state of their souls, and reckons them accordingly. Oh, that you would strive to do likewise! Oh, that you would value grace above titles, or intellect, or gold! Often, far too often, the only question asked about a man is, "How much is he worth?" It would be well for us all to remember that every man is pitiably poor until he is rich in faith, and rich toward God. (James ii. 5.)

Wonderful as it may seem to some, all the money in the world is worthless in God's balances, compared to grace! Hard as the saying may sound, I believe that a converted beggar is far more important and honourable in the sight of God than an unconverted king. The one may glitter like the butterfly in the sun for a little season, and be admired by an ignorant world; but his latter end is darkness and misery for ever. The other may crawl through the world like a crushed worm, and be despised by every one who sees him; but his latter end is a glorious resurrection and a blessed eternity with Christ. Of him the Lord says, "I know thy poverty (but thou art rich)." (Rev. ii. 9.)

King Ahab was ruler over the ten tribes of Israel. Obadiah was nothing more than a servant in his household. Yet who can doubt which was most precious in God's sight, the servant or the king?

Ridley and Latimer were deposed from all their dignities, cast into prison as malefactors, and at length burnt at the stake. Bonner and Gardiner, their perse-cutors, were raised to the highest pitch of ecclesiastical greatness, enjoyed large incomes, and died unmolested in their beds. Yet who can doubt which of the two parties was on the Lord's side?

Baxter, the famous divine, was persecuted with savage

malignity, and condemned to a long imprisonment by a most unjust judgment. Jeffreys, the Lord Chief Justice, who sentenced him, was a man of infamous character, without either morality or religion. Baxter was sent to jail and Jeffreys was loaded with honours. Yet who can doubt which was the good man of the two, the Lord Chief Justice or the author of the "Saint's Rest"?

We may be very sure that riches and worldly greatness are no certain marks of God's favour. They are often, on the contrary, a snare and hindrance to a man's soul. They make him love the world and forget God. What says Solomon? "Labour not to be rich." (Prov. xxiii. 4.) What says St. Paul? "They that *will* be rich, fall into temptation and a snare, and into many foolish and hurtful lusts, which drown men in destruction and perdition." (1 Tim. vi. 9.)

We may be no less sure that poverty and trial are no certain proof of God's anger. They are often blessings in disguise. They are always sent in love and wisdom. They often serve to wean man from the world. They teach him to set his affections on things above. They often show the sinner his own heart. They often make the saint fruitful in good works. What says the book of Job? "Happy is the man whom God correcteth; therefore despise not thou the chastening of the Almighty." (Job v. 17.) What says St. Paul? "Whom the Lord loveth He chasteneth." (Heb. xii. 6.)

One great secret of happiness in this life is to be of a patient, contented spirit. Strive daily to realize the truth that this life is not the place of reward. The time of retribution and recompense is yet to come. Judge nothing hastily before that time. Remember the words of the wise man: "If thou seest the oppression of the poor, and violent perverting of judgment and justice in a province, marvel not at the matter: for He that is higher than the highest regardeth, and there be higher than they." (Eccles. v. 8.)

Yes! there is a day of judgment yet to come. That day shall put all in their right places. At last there shall be seen a mighty difference "between him that serveth God, and him that serveth Him not." (Malachi iii. 18.) The children of Lazarus and the children of the rich mar shall at length be seen in their true colours, and every on shall receive according to his works.

III. Let us observe, in the next place, how *all lasses alike come to the grave.*

The rich man in the parable died, and Lazaru died also. Different and divided as they were in their lives, they had both to drink of the same cup at the last. Both went to the house appointed for all living. Both went to that place where rich and poor meet together. Dust they were, and unto dust they returned. (Gen. iii. 19.)

This is the lot of all men. It will be our own, unless the Lord shall first return in glory. After all our scheming, and contriving, and planning, and studying,—after all our inventions, and discoveries, and scientific attainments,—there remains one enemy we cannot conquer and disarm, and that is death. The chapter in Genesis which ecords the long lives of Methuselah and the rest who lived before the flood, winds up the simple story of each by two expressive words: "he died." And now, after 4,800 years, what more can be said of the greatest among ourselves? The histories of Marlborough, and Washington, and Napoleon, and Wellington, arrive at just the same humbling conclusion. The end of each, after all his greatness is just this,—"he died."

Death is a mighty leveller. He spares none, he waits for none, and stands on no ceremony. He will not tarry till you are ready. He will not be kept out by moats, and doors, and bars, and bolts. The Englishman boasts that his home is his castle, but with all his boasting, he cannot exclude death. An Austrian nobleman forbade death and the smallpox to be named in his presence.   But, named or not named, it matters little, in God's appointed hour death will come.

One man rolls easily along the road in the easiest and handsomest carriage that money can procure.   Another toils wearily along the path on foot.   Yet both are sure to meet at last in the same home.

One man, like Absalom, has fifty servants to wait upon him and do his bidding.   Another has none to lift a finger to do him a service.   But both are travelling to a place where they must lie down alone.

One man is the owner of hundreds of thousands. Another has scarce a shilling that he can call his own property.   Yet neither one nor the other can carry one farthing with him into the unseen world.

One man is the possessor of half a county.   Another has not so much as a garden of herbs.   And yet two paces of the vilest earth will be amply sufficient for either of them at the last.

One man pampers his body with every possible delicacy, and clothes it in the richest and softest apparel.   Another has scarce enough to eat, and seldom enough to put on. Yet both alike are hurrying on to a day when "ashes to ashes, and dust to dust," shall be proclaimed over them, and fifty years hence none shall be able to say, "This was the rich man's bone, and this the bone of the poor."

I know that these are ancient things.   I do not deny it for a moment.   I am writing stale old things that all men *know*.   But I am also writing things that all men do not *feel*.   Oh, no! if they did feel them they would not speak and act as they do.

You wonder sometimes at the tone and language of ministers of the Gospel.   You marvel that we press upon you immediate decision.   You think us extreme, and extravagant, and ultra in our views, because we urge upon you to close with Christ,—to leave nothing uncertain,—to

make sure that you are born again and ready for heaven.
You hear, but do not approve. You go away, and say to
one another,—"The man means well, but he goes too far."

But do you not see that the reality of death is continually forbidding us to use other language? We see him
gradually thinning our congregations. We miss face after
face in our assemblies. We know not whose turn may
come next. We only know that as the tree falls there
it will lie, and that "after death comes the judgment."
We *must* be bold and decided, and uncompromising in
our language. We would rather run the risk of offending
some, than of losing any. We would aim at the standard
set up by old Baxter:—

> "I'll preach as though I ne'er should preach again,
> And as a dying man to dying men!"

We would realize the character given by Charles II. of
one of his preachers: "That man preaches as though death
was behind his back. When I hear him I cannot go to
sleep."

Oh, that men would learn to live as those who may one
day die! Truly it is poor work to set our affections on a
dying world and its shortlived comforts, and for the sake
of an inch of time to lose a glorious immortality! Here
we are toiling, and labouring, and wearying ourselves
about trifles, and running to and fro like ants upon a heap;
and yet after a few years we shall all be gone, and another
generation will fill our place. Let us live for eternity.
Let us seek a portion that can never be taken from us.
And let us never forget John Bunyan's golden rule: "He
that would live well, let him make his dying day his
company-keeper."

IV. Let us observe, in the next place, *how precious a
believer's soul is in the sight of God.*

The rich man, in the parable, dies and is buried.

Perhaps he had a splendid funeral,—a funeral proportioned to his expenditure while he was yet alive. But we hear nothing further of the moment when soul and body were divided. The next thing we hear of is that he is in *hell*.

The poor man, in the parable, dies also. What manner of burial he had we know not. A pauper's funeral among ourselves is a melancholy business. The funeral of Lazarus was probably no better. But this we do know,—that the moment Lazarus dies he is carried by the angels into Abraham's bosom,—carried to a place of rest, where all the faithful are waiting for the resurrection of the just.

There is something to my mind very striking, very touching, and very comforting in this expression of the parable. I ask your especial attention to it. It throws great light on the relation of all sinners of mankind who believe in Christ, to their God and Father. It shows a little of the care bestowed on the least and lowest of Christ's disciples, by the King of kings.

No man has such friends and attendants as the believer, however little he may think it. Angels rejoice over him in the day that he is born again of the Spirit. Angels minister to him all through life. Angels encamp around him in the wilderness of this world. Angels take charge of his soul in death, and bear it safely home. Yes! vile as he may be in his own eyes, and lowly in his own sight, the very poorest and humblest believer in Jesus is cared for by his Father in heaven, with a care that passeth knowledge. The Lord has become his Shepherd, and he can "want nothing." (Ps. xxiii. 1.) Only let a man come unfeignedly to Christ, and be joined to Him, and he shall have all the benefits of a covenant ordered in all things and sure.

Is he laden with many sins? Though they be as scarlet they shall be white as snow.

Is his heart hard and prone to evil? A new heart shall be given to him, and a new spirit put in him.

Is he weak and cowardly? He that enabled Peter to confess Christ before his enemies shall make him bold.

Is he ignorant? He that bore with Thomas' slowness shall bear with him, and guide him into all truth.

Is he alone in his position? He that stood by Paul when all men forsook him shall also stand by his side.

Is he in circumstances of special trial? He that enabled men to be saints in Nero's household shall also enable him to persevere.

The very hairs of his head are all numbered. Nothing can harm him without God's permission. He that hurteth him, hurteth the apple of God's eye, and injures a brother and member of Christ Himself.

His trials are all wisely ordered. Satan can only vex him, as he did Job, when God permits him. No temptation can happen to him above what he is able to bear. All things are working together for his good.

His steps are all ordered from grace to glory. He is kept on earth till he is ripe for heaven, and not one moment longer. The harvest of the Lord must have its appointed proportion of sun and wind, of cold and heat, of rain and storm. And then when the believer's work is done, the angels of God shall come for him, as they did for Lazarus, and carry him safe home.

Alas! the men of the world little think whom they are despising, when they mock Christ's people. They are mocking those whom angels are not ashamed to attend upon. They are mocking the brethren and sisters of Christ Himself. Little do they consider that these are they for whose sakes the days of tribulation are shortened. These are they by whose intercession kings reign peacefully. Little do they reck that the prayers of men like Lazarus have more weight in the affairs of nations than hosts of armed men.

Believers in Christ, who may possibly read these pages, you little know the full extent of your privileges and possessions. Like children at school, you know not half that your Father is doing for your welfare. Learn to live by faith more than you have done. Acquaint yourselves with the fulness of the treasure laid up for you in Christ even now. This world, no doubt, must always be a place of trial while we are in the body. But still there are comforts provided for the brethren of Lazarus which many never enjoy.

V. Observe, in the last place, *what a dangerous and soul-ruining sin is the sin of selfishness.*

You have the rich man, in the parable, in a hopeless state. If there was no other picture of a lost soul in hell in all the Bible you have it here. You meet him in the beginning, clothed in purple and fine linen. You part with him at the end, tormented in the everlasting fire.

And yet there is nothing to show that this man was a murderer, or a thief, or an adulterer, or a liar. There is no reason to say that he was an atheist, or an infidel, or a blasphemer. For anything we know, he attended to all the ordinances of the Jewish religion. But we do know that he was lost for ever!

There is something to my mind very solemn in this thought. Here is a man whose outward life in all probability was correct. At all events we know nothing against him. He dresses richly; but then he had money to spend on his apparel. He gives splendid feasts and entertainments; but then he was wealthy, and could well afford it. We read nothing recorded against him that might not be recorded of hundreds and thousands in the present day, who are counted respectable and good sort of people. And yet the end of this man is that he goes to hell. Surely this deserves serious attention.

(*a*) I believe it is meant to teach us *to beware of living only for ourselves.* It is not enough that we are able to say, "I live correctly. I pay every one his due. I discharge all the relations of life with propriety. I attend to all the outward requirements of Christianity." There remains behind another question, to which the Bible requires an answer. "To whom do you live? to yourself or to Christ? What is the great end, aim, object, and ruling motive in your life?" Let men call the question extreme if they please. For myself, I can find nothing short of this in St. Paul's words: "He died for all, that they which live should not henceforth live unto themselves, but unto Him which died for them and rose again." (2 Cor. v. 15.) And I draw the conclusion, that if, like the rich man, we live only to ourselves, we shall ruin our souls.

(b) I believe, further, that this passage is meant to teach us *the damnable nature of sins of omission.* It does not seem that it was so much the things the rich man did, but the things he left undone, which made him miss heaven. Lazarus was at his gate, and he let him alone. But is not this exactly in keeping with the history of the judgment, in the twenty-fifth of St. Matthew? Nothing is said there of the sins of commission of which the lost are guilty. How runs the charge?—"I was an hungered, and ye gave me no meat: I was thirsty, and ye gave me no drink: I was a stranger, and ye took me not in: naked, and ye clothed me not: sick, and in prison, and ye visited me not." (Matt. xxv. 42, 43.) The charge against them is simply that they did not do certain things. On this their sentence turns. And I draw the conclusion again, that, except we take heed, sins of omission may ruin our souls. Truly it was a solemn saying of good Archbishop Usher, on his death-bed: "Lord, forgive me all my sins, but specially my sins of omission."

(c) I believe, further, that the passage is meant to teach us that *riches bring special danger with them.* Yes! riches, which the vast majority of men are always seeking after, —riches for which they spend their lives, and of which they make an idol,—riches entail on their possessors immense spiritual peril! The possession of them has a very hardening effect on the soul. They chill. They freeze. They petrify the inward man. They close the eye to the things of faith. They insensibly produce a tendency to forget God.

And does not this stand in perfect harmony with all the language of Scripture on the same subject? What says our Lord? "How hardly shall they that have riches enter into the kingdom of God! It is easier for a camel to go through the eye of a needle, than for a rich man to enter the kingdom of God!" (Mark x. 23, 25.) What says St. Paul? "The love of money is the root of all evil; which while some coveted after, they have erred from the faith, and pierced themselves through with many sorrows." (1 Tim vi. 10.) What can be more striking than the fact that the Bible has frequently spoken of money as a most fruitful cause of sin and evil? For money Achan brought defeat on the armies of Israel, and death on himself. For money Balaam sinned against light, and tried to curse God's people. For money Delilah betrayed Sampson to the Philistines. For money Gehazi lied to Naaman and Elisha, and became a leper. For money Ananias and Sapphira became the first hypocrites in the early Church, and lost their lives. For money Judas Iscariot sold Christ, and was ruined eternally. Surely these facts speak loudly.

Money, in truth, is one of the most *unsatisfying* of possessions. It takes away some cares, no doubt; but it brings with it quite as many cares as it takes away. There is trouble in the getting of it. There is anxiety in the keeping of it. There are temptations in the use of it. There is guilt in the abuse of it. There is sorrow in the losing of it. There is perplexity in the disposing of it. Two-thirds of all the strifes, quarrels, and lawsuits in the world, arise from one simple cause,—*money!*

Money most certainly is one of the most *ensnaring and*

heart-changing of possessions. It seems desirable at a distance. It often proves a poison when in our hand. No man can possibly tell the effect of money on his soul, if it suddenly falls to his lot to possess it. Many an one did run well as a poor man, who forgets God when he is rich.

I draw the conclusion that those who have money, like the rich man in the parable, ought to take double pains about their souls. They live in a most unhealthy atmosphere. They have double need to be on their guard.

(*d*) I believe, not least, that the passage is meant to *stir up special carefulness about selfishness in these last days.* You have a special warning in 2 Tim. iii. 1, 2: "In the last days perilous times shall come: for men shall be lovers of their own selves, covetous." I believe we have come to the last days, and that we ought to beware of the sins here mentioned, if we love our souls.

Perhaps we are poor judges of our own times. We are apt to exaggerate and magnify their evils, just because we see and feel them. But, after every allowance, I doubt whether there ever was more need of warnings against selfishness than in the present day. I am sure there never was a time when all classes in England had so many comforts and so many temporal good things. And yet I believe there is an utter disproportion between men's expenditure on themselves and their outlay on works of charity and works of mercy. I see this in the miserable one guinea subscriptions to which many rich men confine their charity. I see it in the languishing condition of many of our best religious Societies, and the painfully slow growth of their annual incomes. I see it in the small number of names which appear in the list of contributions to any good work. There are, I believe, thousands of rich people in this country who literally give away nothing at all. I see it in the notorious fact, that few, even of those who give, give anything proportioned to their means. I see all this, and mourn over it. I regard it as the selfishness and covetousness predicted as likely to arise in "the last days."

I know that this is a painful and delicate subject. But it must not on that account be avoided by the minister of Christ. It is a subject for the times, and it needs pressing home. I desire to speak to myself, and to all who make any profession of religion. Of course I cannot expect worldly and utterly ungodly persons to view this subject in Bible light. To them the Bible is no rule of faith and practice. To quote texts to them would be of little use.

But I do ask all professing Christians to consider well what Scripture says against covetousness and selfishness, and on behalf of liberality in giving money. Is it for nothing that the Lord Jesus spoke the parable of the rich fool, and blamed him because he was not "rich towards God"? (Luke xii. 21.) Is it for nothing that in the parable of the sower He mentions the "deceitfulness of riches" as one reason why the seed of the Word bears no fruit? (Matt. xiii. 22.) Is it for nothing that He says, "Make to yourselves friends of the mammon of unrighteousness"? (Luke xvi. 9.) Is it for nothing that He says, "When thou makest a dinner or a supper, call not thy friends, nor thy brethren, neither thy kinsmen, nor thy rich neighbours; lest they also bid thee again, and a recompense be made thee. But when thou makest a feast, call the poor, the maimed, the lame, the blind: and thou shalt be blessed; for they cannot recompense thee; for thou shalt be recompensed at the resurrection of the just"? (Luke xiv. 14.) Is it for nothing that He says, "Sell that ye have and give alms; provide yourselves bags which wax not old, a treasure in the heavens that faileth not, where no thief approacheth, neither moth corrupteth"? (Luke xii. 33.) Is it for nothing that He says, "It is more blessed to give than to receive"? (Acts xx. 35.) Is it for nothing that He warns us against the example of the priest

and Levite, who saw the wounded traveller, but passed by
on the other side? Is it for nothing that He praises the
good Samaritan, who denied himself to show kindness to a
stranger? (Luke x. 34.) Is it for nothing that St. Paul
classes covetousness with sins of the grossest description,
and denounces it as idolatry? (Coloss. iii. 5.) And is
there not a striking and painful difference between this
language and the habits and feeling of society about
money? I appeal to any one who knows the world. Let
him judge what I say.

I only ask my reader to consider calmly the passages of
Scripture to which I have referred. I cannot think they
were meant to teach nothing at all. That the habits of
the East and our own are different, I freely allow. That
some of the expressions I have quoted are figurative, I
freely admit. But still, after all, a principle lies at the
bottom of all these expressions. Let us take heed that
this principle is not neglected. I wish that many a
professing Christian in this day, who perhaps dislikes
what I am saying, would endeavour to write a commen-
tary on these expressions, and try to explain to himself
what they mean.

To know that alms-giving cannot atone for sin is well.
To know that our good works cannot justify us is excellent.
To know that we may give all our goods to feed the poor,
and build hospitals and cathedrals, without any real charity,
is most important. But let us beware lest we go into the
other extreme, and because our money cannot save us, give
away no money at all.

Has any one money who reads these pages? Then "take
heed and beware of covetousness." (Luke xii. 15.) Remember you carry weight in the race towards heaven. All
men are naturally in danger of being lost for ever, but you
are doubly so because of your possessions. Nothing is said
to put out fire so soon as earth thrown upon it. Nothing I
am sure has such a tendency to quench the fire of religion

us the possession of money. It was a solemn message which Buchanan, on his death-bed, sent to his old pupil, James I.: "He was going to a place where few kings and great men would come." It is possible, no doubt, for you to be saved as well as others. With God nothing is impossible. Abraham, Job, and David were all rich, and yet saved. But oh, take heed to yourself! Money is a good servant, but a bad master. Let that saying of our Lord's sink down into your heart: "How hardly shall they that have riches enter into the kingdom of God." (Mark x. 23.) Well said an old divine: "The surface above gold mines is generally very barren." Well might old Latimer begin one of his sermons before Edward VI. by quoting three times over our Lord's words: "Take heed and beware of covetousness," and then saying, "What if I should say nothing else these three or four hours?" There are few prayers in our Litany more wise and more necessary than that petition, "In all time of our *wealth*, good Lord deliver us."

Has any one little or no money who reads these pages? Then do not envy those who are richer than yourself. Pray for them. Pity them. Be charitable to their faults. Remember that high places are giddy places, and be not too hasty in your condemnation of their conduct. Perhaps if you had their difficulties you would do no better yourself. Beware of the "love of money." It is the "root of all evil." (1 Tim. vi. 10.) A man may love money over-much without having any at all. Beware of the love of self. It may be found in a cottage as well as in a palace. And beware of thinking that poverty alone will save you. If you would sit with Lazarus in glory, you must not only have fellowship with him in suffering, but in grace.

Does any reader desire to know the remedy against that love of self which ruined the rich man's soul, and cleaves to us all by nature, like our skin? I tell him plainly there is only one remedy, and I ask Him to mark well what that remedy is. It is not the fear of hell. It is not the hope of heaven. It is not any sense of duty. Oh, no! The disease of selfishness is far too deeply rooted to yield to such secondary motives as these. Nothing will ever cure it but an experimental knowledge of Christ's redeeming love. You must know the misery and guilt of your own estate by nature. You must experience the power of Christ's atoning blood sprinkled upon your conscience, and making you whole. You must taste the sweetness of peace with God through the mediation of Jesus, and feel the love of a reconciled Father shed abroad in your heart by the Holy Ghost.

Then, and not till then, the mainspring of selfishness will be broken. *Then,* knowing the immensity of your debt to Christ, you will feel that nothing is too great and too costly to give to Him. Feeling that you have been loved much when you deserved nothing, you will heartily love in return, and cry, "What shall I render unto the Lord for all His benefits?" (Ps. cxvi. 12.) Feeling that you have freely received countless mercies, you will think it a privilege to do anything to please Him to whom you owe all. Feeling that you have been "bought with a price," and are no longer your own, you will labour to glorify God with body and spirit, which are His. (1 Cor. vi. 20.)

Yes: I repeat it this day. I know no *effectual* remedy for the love of self, but a believing apprehension of the love of Christ. Other remedies may palliate the disease: this alone will heal it. Other antidotes may hide its deformity: this alone will work a perfect cure.

An easy, good-natured temper may cover over selfishness in one man. A love of praise may conceal it in a second. A self-righteous asceticism and an affected spirit of self-denial may keep it out of sight in a third. But nothing will ever cut up selfishness by the roots but the love of Christ revealed in the mind by the Holy Ghost, and felt in the heart by simple faith. Once let a man see the full meaning of the words, "Christ loved me and gave Himself for me," and then he will delight to give himself to Christ, and all that he has to His service. He will live to Him, not in order that he may be secure, but because he is secure already. He will work for Him, not that he may have life and peace, but because life and peace are his own already.

Go to the cross of Christ, all you that want to be delivered from the power of selfishness. Go and see what a price was paid there to provide a ransom for your soul. Go and see what an astounding sacrifice was there made, that a door to eternal life might be provided for poor sinners like you. Go and see how the Son of God gave Himself for you, and learn to think it a small thing to give yourself to Him.

The disease which ruined the rich man in the parable may be cured. But oh, remember, there is only one real remedy! If you would not live to yourself you must live to Christ. See to it that this remedy is not only known, but applied,—not only heard of, but used.

(1) And now let me conclude all *by urging on every reader of these pages, the great duty of self-inquiry.*

A passage of Scripture like this parable ought surely to raise in many an one great searchings of heart.—"What am I? Where am I going? What am I doing? What is likely to be my condition after death? Am I prepared to leave the world? Have I any home to look forward to in the world to come? Have I put off the old man and put on the new? Am I really one with Christ, and a pardoned soul?" Surely such questions as these may well be asked when the story of the rich man and Lazarus has been heard. Oh, that the Holy Ghost may incline many a reader's heart to ask them!

(2) In the next place, *I invite* all readers who desire to have their souls saved, and have no good account to give

of themselves at present, to seek salvation while it can be found. I do entreat you to apply to Him by whom alone man can enter heaven and be saved,—even Jesus Christ the Lord. He has the keys of heaven. He is sealed and appointed by God the Father to be the Saviour of all that will come to Him. Go to Him in earnest and hearty prayer, and tell Him your case. Tell Him that you have heard that "He receiveth sinners," and that you come to Him as such. (Luke xv. 2.) Tell Him that you desire to be saved by Him in His own way, and ask Him to save you. Oh, that you may take this course without delay! Remember the hopeless end of the rich man. Once dead there is no more change.

(3) Last of all, *I entreat* all professing Christians to encourage themselves in habits of liberality towards all causes of charity and mercy. Remember that you are God's stewards, and give money liberally, freely, and without grudging, whenever you have an opportunity. You cannot keep your money for ever. You must give account one day of the manner in which it has been expended. Oh, lay it out with an eye to eternity while you can!

I do not ask rich men to leave their situations in life, give away all their property, and go into the workhouse. This would be refusing to fill the position of a steward for God. I ask no man to neglect his worldly calling, and to omit to provide for his family. Diligence in business is a positive Christian duty. Provision for those dependent on us is proper Christian prudence. But I ask all to look around continually as they journey on, and to remember the poor,—the poor in body and the poor in soul. Here we are for a few short years. How can we do most good with our money while we are here? How can we so spend it as to leave the world somewhat happier and somewhat holier when we are removed? Might we not abridge some of our luxuries?

Might we not lay out less upon ourselves, and give more to Christ's cause and Christ's poor? Is there none we can do good to? Are there no sick, no poor, no needy, whose sorrows we might lessen, and whose comforts we might increase? Such questions will never fail to elicit an answer from some quarter. I am thoroughly persuaded that the income of every religious and charitable Society in England might easily be multiplied tenfold, if English Christians would give in proportion to their means.

There are none surely to whom such appeals ought to come home with such power as professing believers in the Lord Jesus. The parable of the text is a striking illustration of our position by nature, and our debt to Christ. We all lay, like Lazarus, at heaven's gate, sick unto the death, helpless, and starving. Blessed be God! we were not neglected, as he was. Jesus came forth to relieve us. Jesus gave Himself for us, that we might have hope and live. For a poor Lazarus-like world He came down from heaven, and humbled Himself to become a man. For a poor Lazarus-like world He went up and down doing good, caring for men's bodies as well as souls, until He died for us on the cross.

I believe that in giving to support works of charity and mercy, we are doing that which is according to Christ's mind,—and I ask readers of these pages to begin the habit of giving, if they never began it before; and to go on with it increasingly, if they have begun.

I believe that in offering a warning against worldliness and covetousness, I have done no more than bring forward a warning specially called for by the times, and I ask God to bless the consideration of these pages to many souls.

XIV

THE BEST FRIEND

" This is my friend."—CANT. v. 16.

A FRIEND is one of the greatest blessings on earth. Tell me not of money: affection is better than gold; sympathy is better than lands. He is the poor man who has no friends.

This world is full of sorrow because it is full of sin. It is a dark place. It is a lonely place. It is a disappointing place. The brightest sunbeam in it is a friend. Friendship halves our troubles and doubles our joys.

A real friend is scarce and rare. There are many who will eat, and drink, and laugh with us in the sunshine of prosperity. There are few who will stand by us in the days of darkness,—few who will love us when we are sick, helpless, and poor,—few, above all, who will care for our souls.

Does any reader of this paper want a real friend? I write to recommend one to your notice this day. I know of One "who sticketh closer than a brother." (Prov. xviii. 24.) I know of One who is ready to be your friend for time and for eternity, if you will receive Him. Hear me, while I try to tell you something about Him.

The friend I want you to know is Jesus Christ. Happy is that family in which Christ has the foremost place! Happy is that person whose chief friend is Christ!

I. Do we want *a friend in need?* Such a friend is the Lord Jesus Christ.

Man is the neediest creature on God's earth, because he is a sinner. There is no need so great as that of sinners: poverty, hunger, thirst, cold, sickness, all are nothing in comparison. Sinners need pardon, and they are utterly unable to provide it for themselves; they need deliverance from a guilty conscience and the fear of death, and they have no power of their own to obtain it. This need the Lord Jesus Christ came into the world to relieve. "He came into the world to save sinners." (1 Tim. i. 15.)

We are all by nature poor dying creatures. From the king on his throne to the pauper in the workhouse, we are all sick of a mortal disease of soul. Whether we know it or not, whether we feel it or not, we are all dying daily. The plague of sin is in our blood. We cannot cure ourselves: we are hourly getting worse and worse. All this the Lord Jesus undertook to remedy. He came into the world "to bring in health and cure;" He came to deliver us "from the second death;" He came "to abolish death, and bring life and immortality to light through the Gospel." (Jer. xxxiii. 6; Rev. ii. 11; 2 Tim. i. 10.)

We are all by nature imprisoned debtors. We owed our God ten thousand talents, and had nothing to pay. We were wretched bankrupts, without hope of discharging ourselves. We could never have freed ourselves from our load of liabilities, and were daily getting more deeply involved. All this the Lord Jesus saw, and undertook to remedy. He engaged to "ransom and redeem us;" He came to "proclaim liberty to the captives, and the opening of the prison to them that are bound;" "He came to redeem us from the curse of the law." (Hos. xiii. 14; Isai. lxi. 1; Gal. iii. 13.)

We were all by nature shipwrecked and cast away. We could never have reached the harbour of everlasting life. We were sinking in the midst of the waves, shiftless hopeless, helpless, and powerless; tied and bound by the chain of our sins, foundering under the burden of our own guilt, and like to become a prey to the devil. All this the Lord Jesus saw and undertook to remedy. He came down from heaven to be our mighty "helper;" He came to "seek and to save that which was lost;" and to "deliver us from going down into the pit." (Psalm lxxxix. 19; Luke xix. 10; Job xxxiii. 24.)

Could we have been saved without the Lord Jesus Christ coming down from heaven? It would have been impossible, so far as our eyes can see. The wisest men of Egypt, and Greece, and Rome never found out the way to peace with God. Without the friendship of Christ we should all have been lost for evermore in hell.

Was the Lord Jesus Christ obliged to come down to save us? Oh, no! no! It was His own free love, mercy, and pity that brought Him down. He came unsought and unasked because He was gracious.

Let us think on these things. Search all history from the beginning of the world,—look round the whole circle of those you know and love: you never heard of such friendship among the sons of men. There never was such a real friend in need as Jesus Christ.

II. Do you want *a friend in deed?* Such a friend is the Lord Jesus Christ.

The true extent of a man's friendship must be measured by his deeds. Tell me not what he says, and feels, and wishes; tell me not of his words and letters: tell me rather what he does. "Friendly is that friendly does."

The doings of the Lord Jesus Christ for man are the grand proof of His friendly feeling towards him. Never were there such acts of kindness and self-denial as those which He has performed on our behalf. He has not loved us in word only but in deed.

For our sakes He took our nature upon Him, and was

born of a woman. He who was very God, and equal with the Father, laid aside for a season His glory, and took upon Him flesh and blood like our own. The almighty Creator of all things became a little babe like any of us, and experienced all our bodily weaknesses and infirmities, sin only excepted. "Though He was rich He became poor, that we through His poverty might be rich." (2 Cor. viii. 9.)

For our sakes He lived thirty-three years in this evil world, despised and rejected of men, a man of sorrows, and acquainted with grief. Though He was King of kings, He had not where to lay His head: though He was Lord of lords, He was often weary, and hungry, and thirsty, and poor. "He took on Him the form of a servant, and humbled Himself." (Philipp. iii. 7, 8.)

For our sakes He suffered the most painful of all deaths, even the death of the cross. Though innocent, and without fault, He allowed Himself to be condemned, and found guilty. He who was the Prince of Life was led as a lamb to the slaughter, and poured out His soul unto death. He "died for us." (1 Thess. v. 10.)

Was He obliged to do this? Oh, no! He might have summoned to His help more than twelve legions of angels, and scattered His enemies with a word. He suffered voluntarily and of His own free will, to make atonement for our sins. He knew that nothing but the sacrifice of His body and blood could ever make peace between sinful man and a holy God. He laid down His life to pay the price of our redemption: He died that we might live; He suffered that we might reign; He bore shame that we might receive glory. "He suffered for sins, the just for the unjust, that He might bring us to God." "He was made sin for us, who knew no sin: that we might be made the righteousness of God in Him." (1 Peter iii. 18; 2 Cor. v. 21.)

Such friendship as this passes man's understanding.

Friends who would die for those who love them, we may
have heard of sometimes. But who can find a man who
would lay down his life for those that hate him ? Yet
this is what Jesus has done for us. "God commendeth
His love towards us, in that while we were yet sinners,
Christ died for us." (Rom. v. 8.)

Ask all the tribes of mankind, from one end of the
world to the other, and you will nowhere hear of a deed
like this. None was ever so high and stooped down so
low as Jesus the Son of God : none ever gave so costly a
proof of his friendship ; none ever paid so much and
endured so much to do good to others. Never was there
such a friend in deed as Jesus Christ !

III. Do we want *a mighty and powerful friend* ?
Such a friend is Jesus Christ.

Power to help is that which few possess in this world.
Many have will enough to do good to others, but no power.
They feel for the sorrows of others, and would gladly
relieve them if they could : they can weep with their
friends in affliction, but are unable to take their grief
away. But though man is weak, Christ is strong,—though
the best of our earthly friends is feeble, Christ is almighty :
"All power is given unto Him in heaven and earth."
(Matt. xxviii. 18.) No one can do so much for those whom
He befriends as Jesus Christ. Others can befriend their
bodies a little : He can befriend both body and soul.
Others can do a little for them in time : He can be a
friend both for time and eternity.

(*a*) He is *able to pardon* and save the very chief of
sinners. He can deliver the most guilty conscience from
all its burdens, and give it perfect peace with God. He
can wash away the vilest stains of wickedness, and make a
man whiter than snow in the sight of God. He can
clothe a poor weak child of Adam in everlasting righteousness, and give him a title to heaven that can never be

overthrown. In a word, He can give any one of us peace, hope, forgiveness, and reconciliation with God, if we will only trust in Him. "The blood of Jesus Christ cleanseth from all sin." (1 John i. 7.)

(b) He is *able to convert* the hardest of hearts, and create in man a new spirit. He can take the most thoughtless and ungodly people, and give them another mind by the Holy Ghost which He puts in them. He can cause old things to pass away, and all things to become new. He can make them love the things which they once hated, and hate the things which they once loved. "He can give them power to become the sons of God." "If any man be in Christ, he is a new creature." (John i. 12; 2 Cor. v. 17.)

(c) He is *able to preserve* to the end all who believe in Him, and become His disciples. He can give them grace to overcome the world, the flesh and the devil, and fight a good fight at the last. He can lead them on safely in spite of every temptation, carry them home through a thousand dangers, and keep them faithful, though they stand alone and have none to help them. "He is able to save them to the uttermost that come unto God by Him." (Heb. vii. 25.)

(d) He is *able to give* those that love Him the best of gifts. He can give them in life inward comforts, which money can never buy,—peace in poverty, joy in sorrow, patience in suffering. He can give them in death bright hopes, which enable them to walk through the dark valley without fear. He can give them after death a crown of glory, which fadeth not away, and a reward compared to which the Queen of England has nothing to bestow.

This is power indeed: this is true greatness; this is real strength. Go and look at the poor Hindoo idolater, seeking peace in vain by afflicting his body; and, after fifty years of self-imposed suffering, unable to find it. Go and look at the benighted Romanist, giving money to his priest to pray for his soul, and yet dying without comfort. Go and look at rich men, spending thousands in search of happiness, and yet always discontented and unhappy. Then turn to Jesus, and think what He can do, and is daily doing for all who trust Him. Think how He heals all the broken-hearted, comforts all the sick, cheers all the poor that trust in Him, and supplies all their daily need. The fear of man is strong, the opposition of this evil world is mighty, the lusts of the flesh rage horribly, the fear of death is terrible, the devil is a roaring lion seeking whom he may devour; but Jesus is stronger than them all. Jesus can make us conquerors over all these foes. And then say whether it be not true, that there never was so mighty a friend as Jesus Christ.

IV. Do we want *a loving and affectionate friend?* Such a friend is Jesus Christ.

Kindness is the very essence of true friendship. Money and advice and help lose half their grace, if not given in a loving manner. What kind of love is that of the Lord Jesus toward man? It is called, "A love that passeth knowledge." (Ephes. iii. 19.)

Love shines forth in His *reception of sinners.* He refuses none that come to Him for salvation, however unworthy they may be. Though their lives may have been most wicked, though their sins may be more in number than the stars of heaven, the Lord Jesus is ready to receive them, and give them pardon and peace. There is no end to His compassion: there are no bounds to His pity. He is not ashamed to befriend those whom the world casts off as hopeless. There are none too bad, too filthy, and too much diseased with sin, to be admitted into His home. He is willing to be the friend of any sinner: He has kindness and mercy and healing medicine for all. He has long proclaimed this to be His rule: "Him that cometh unto Me I will in no wise cast out." (John vi. 37.)

Love shines forth in His *dealings with sinners,* after they have believed in Him and become His friends. He is very patient with them, though their conduct is often very trying and provoking. He is never tired of hearing their complaints, however often they may come to Him. He sympathizes deeply in all their sorrows. He knows what pain is: He is "acquainted with grief." (Is. liii. 3.) In all their afflictions He is afflicted. He never allows them to be tempted above what they are able to bear: He supplies them with daily grace for their daily conflict. Their poor services are acceptable to Him: He is as well pleased with them as a parent is with his child's endeavours to speak and walk. He has caused it to be written in His book, that "He taketh pleasure in His people," and that "He taketh pleasure in them that fear Him." (Ps. cxlvii. 11 ; cxlix. 4.)

There is no love on earth that can be named together with this! We love those in whom we see something that deserves our affection, or those who are our bone or our flesh: the Lord Jesus loves sinners in whom there is no good thing. We love those from whom we get some return for our affection: the Lord Jesus loves those who can do little or nothing for Him, compared to what He does for them. We love where we can give some reason for loving: the great Friend of sinners draws His reasons out of His own everlasting compassion. His love is purely disinterested, purely unselfish, purely free. Never, never was there so truly loving a friend as Jesus Christ.

V. Do we want *a wise and prudent friend?* Such a friend is the Lord Jesus Christ.

Man's friendship is sadly blind. He often injures those he loves by injudicious kindness: he often errs in the counsel he gives; he often leads his friends into trouble by bad advice, even when he means to help them. He some- times keeps them back from the way of life, and entangles them in the vanities of the world, when they have well nigh escaped. The friendship of the Lord Jesus is not so: it always does us good, and never evil.

The Lord Jesus *never spoils* His friends by extravagant indulgence. He gives them everything that is really for their benefit; He withholds nothing from them that is really good; but He requires them to take up their cross daily and follow Him. He bids them endure hardships as good soldiers: He calls on them to fight the good fight against the world, the flesh, and the devil. His people often dislike it at the time, and think it hard; but when they reach heaven they will see it was all well done.

The Lord Jesus *makes no mistakes* in managing His friends' affairs. He orders all their concerns with perfect wisdom: all things happen to them at the right time, and in the right way. He gives them as much of sickness and as much of health, as much of poverty and as much of riches, as much of sorrow and as much of joy, as He sees their souls require. He leads them by the right way to bring them to the city of habitation. He mixes their bitterest cups like a wise physician, and takes care that they have not a drop too little or too much. His people often misunderstand His dealings; they are silly enough to fancy their course of life might have been better ordered: but in the resurrection-day they will thank God that not their will, but Christ's was done.

Look round the world and see the harm which people are continually getting from their friends. Mark how much more ready men are to encourage one another in worldliness and levity, than to provoke to love and good works. Think how often they meet together, not for the better, but for the worse,—not to quicken one another's souls in the way to heaven, but to confirm one another in the love of this present world. Alas, there are thousands who are wounded unexpectedly in the house of their friends!

And then turn to the great Friend of sinners, and see how different a thing is His friendship from that of man. Listen to Him as He walks by the way with His disciples; mark how He comforts, reproves, and exhorts with perfect wisdom. Observe how He times His visits to those He loves, as to Mary and Martha at Bethany. Hear how He converses, as He dines on the shore of the sea of Galilee: "Simon, son of Jonas, lovest thou Me?" (John xxi. 16.) His company is always sanctifying. His gifts are always for our soul's good; His kindness is always wise; His fellowship is always to edification. One day of the Son of Man is better than a thousand in the society of earthly friends: one hour spent in private communion with Him, is better than a year in kings' palaces. Never, never was there such a wise friend as Jesus Christ.

VI. Do we want *a tried and proved friend?* Such a friend is Jesus Christ.

Six thousand years have passed away since the Lord Jesus began His work of befriending mankind. During that long period of time He has had many friends in this world. Millions on millions, unhappily, have refused His offers and been miserably lost for ever; but thousands on thousands have enjoyed the mighty privilege of His friendship and been saved. He has had great experience.

(*a*) He has had friends of *every rank and station* in life. Some of them were kings and rich men, like David, and Solomon, and Hezekiah, and Job; some of them were very poor in this world, like the shepherds of Bethlehem, and James, and John, and Andrew: but they were all alike Christ's friends.

(*b*) He has had friends *of every age* that man can pass through. Some of them never knew Him till they were advanced in years, like Manasseh, and Zacchæus, and probably the Ethiopian Eunuch. Some of them were His friends even from their earliest childhood, like Joseph, and Samuel, and Josiah, and Timothy. But they were all alike Christ's friends.

(c) He has had friends *of every possible temperament and disposition.* Some of them were simple plain men, like Isaac; some of them were mighty in word and deed, like Moses; some of them were fervent and warm-hearted, like Peter; some of them were gentle and retiring spirits, like John; some of them were active and stirring, like Martha; some of them loved to sit quietly at His feet, like Mary; some dwelt unknown among their own people, like the Shunamite; some have gone everywhere and turned the world upside down, like Paul. But they were all alike Christ's friends.

(d) He has had friends *of every condition in life.* Some of them were married, and had sons and daughters; like Enoch; some of them lived and died unmarried, like Daniel and John the Baptist; some of them were often sick, like Lazarus and Epaphroditus; some of them were strong to labour, like Persis, and Tryphena, and Tryphosa; some of them were masters, like Abraham and Cornelius; some of them were servants, like the saints in Nero's household; some of them had bad servants, like Elisha; some of them had bad masters like Obadiah; some of them had bad wives and children, like David. But they were all alike Christ's friends.

(e) He has had friends *of almost every nation, and people, and tongue.* He has had friends in hot countries and in cold; friends among nations highly civilized, and friends among the simplest and rudest tribes. His book of life contains the names of Greeks and Romans, of Jews and Egyptians, of bond and of free. There are to be found on its lists reserved Englishmen and cautious Scotchmen, impulsive Irishmen and fiery Welchmen, volatile Frenchmen and dignified Spaniards, refined Italians and solid Germans, rude Africans and refined Hindoos, cultivated Chinese and half-savage New Zealanders. But they were all alike Christ's friends.

All these have made trial of Christ's friendship, and proved it to be good. They all found nothing wanting when they began: they all found nothing wanting as they went on. No lack, no defect, no deficiency was ever found by any one of them in Jesus Christ. Each found his own soul's wants fully supplied; each found every day, that in Christ there was enough and to spare. Never, never was there a friend so fully tried and proved as Jesus Christ.

VII. Last, but not least, do we want *an unfailing friend?* Such a friend is the Lord Jesus Christ.

The saddest part of all the good things of earth is their instability. Riches make themselves wings and flee away; youth and beauty are but for a few years; strength of body soon decays; mind and intellect are soon exhausted. All is perishing. All is fading. All is passing away. But there is one splendid exception to this general rule, and that is the friendship of Jesus Christ.

The Lord Jesus is *a friend who never changes.* There is no fickleness about Him: those whom He loves, He loves unto the end. Husbands have been known to forsake their wives; parents have been known to cast off their children; human vows and promises of faithfulness have often been forgotten. Thousands have been neglected in their poverty and old age, who were honoured by all when they were rich and young. But Christ never changed His feelings towards one of His friends. He is "the same yesterday, to-day, and for ever." (Heb. xiii. 8.)

The Lord Jesus *never goes away from His friends.* There is never a parting and good-bye between Him and His people. From the time that He makes His abode in the sinner's heart, He abides in it for ever. The world is full of leave-takings and departures: death and the lapse of time break up the most united family; sons go forth to make their way in life; daughters are married, and leave their father's house for ever. Scattering, scattering, scattering, is the yearly history of the happiest home. How many we have tearfully watched as they drove away from our doors, whose pleasant faces we have never seen again! How many we have sorrowfully followed to the grave, and then come back to a cold, silent, lonely, and blank fireside! But, thanks be to God, there is One who never leaves His friends! The Lord Jesus is He who has said, "I will never leave thee nor forsake thee." (Heb. xiii. 5.)

The Lord Jesus *goes with His friends wherever they go.* There is no possible separation between Him and those whom He loves. There is no place or position on earth, or under the earth, that can divide them from the great Friend of their souls. When the path of duty calls them far away from home, He is their companion; when they pass through the fire and water of fierce tribulation, He is with them; when they lie down on the bed of sickness, He stands by them and makes all their trouble work for good; when they go down the valley of the shadow of death, and friends and relatives stand still and can go no further, He goes down by their side. When they wake up in the unknown world of Paradise, they are still with Him; when they rise with a new body at the judgment day, they will not be alone. He will own them for His friends, and say, "They are mine: deliver them and let them go free." He will make good His own words: "I am with you alway, even unto the end of the world." (Matt. xxviii. 20.)

Look round the world, and see how failure is written on all men's schemes. Count up the partings, and separations, and disappointments, and bereavements which have happened under your own knowledge. Think what a privilege it is that there is One at least who never fails, and in whom no one was ever disappointed! Never, never was there so unfailing a friend as Jesus Christ.

And now, suffer me to conclude this paper with a few plain words of application. I know not who you are or in what state your soul may be; but I am sure that the words I am about to say deserve your serious attention. Oh, that this paper may not find you heedless of spiritual things! Oh, that you may be able to give a few thoughts to Christ!

(1) Know then, for one thing, that I call upon you to *consider solemnly whether Christ is your Friend and you are His.*

There are thousands on thousands, I grieve to say, who are not Christ's friends. Baptized in His name, outward members of His Church, attendants on His means of grace, —all this they are, no doubt. But they are not Christ's *friends.* Do they hate the sins which Jesus died to put away? No.—Do they love the Saviour who came into the world to save them? No.—Do they care for the souls which were so precious in His sight? No.—Do they delight in the word of reconciliation? No.—Do they try to speak with the Friend of sinners in prayer? No.—Do they seek close fellowship with Him? No.—Oh, reader, is this your case? How is it with you? Are you or are you not one of Christ's friends?

(2) Know, in the next place, that *if you are not one of Christ's friends, you are a poor miserable being.*

I write this down deliberately. I do not say it without thought. I say that if Christ be not your friend, you are a poor, miserable being.

You are in the midst of a failing, sorrowful world, and you have no real source of comfort, or refuge for a time of need. You are a dying creature, and you are not ready to die. You have sins, and they are not forgiven. You are going to be judged, and you are not prepared to meet God:

you might be, but you refuse to use the one only Mediator and Advocate. You love the world better than Christ. You refuse the great Friend of sinners, and you have no friend in heaven to plead your cause. Yes: it is sadly true! You are a poor, miserable being. It matters nothing what your income is: without Christ's friendship you are very poor.

(3) Know, in the third place, that *if you really want a friend, Christ is willing to become your friend.*

He has long wanted you to join His people, and He now invites you by my hand. He is ready to receive you, all unworthy as you may feel, and to write your name down in the list of His friends. He is ready to pardon all the past, to clothe you with righteousness, to give you His Spirit, to make you His own dear child. All He asks you to do is to come to Him.

He bids you come with all your sins; only acknowledging your vileness, and confessing that you are ashamed. Just as you are,—waiting for nothing,—unworthy of anything in yourself,—Jesus bids you come and be His friend.

Oh, come and be wise! Come and be safe. Come and be happy. Come and be Christ's friend.

(4) Know, in the last place, that *if Christ is your friend, you have great privileges, and ought to walk worthy of them.*

Seek every day to have closer communion with Him who is your Friend, and to know more of His grace and power. True Christianity is not merely the believing a certain set of dry abstract propositions: it is to live in daily personal communication with an actual living person —Jesus the Son of God. "To me," said Paul, "to live is Christ." (Phil. i. 21.)

Seek every day to glorify your Lord and Saviour in all your ways. "He that hath a friend should show himself friendly" (Prov. xviii. 24), and no man surely is under such mighty obligations as the friend of Christ. Avoid everything which would grieve your Lord. Fight hard against besetting sins, against inconsistency, against backwardness to confess Him before men. Say to your soul, whenever you are tempted to that which is wrong, "Soul, soul, is this thy kindness to thy Friend?"

Think, above all, of the mercy which has been shown thee, and learn to rejoice daily in thy Friend! What though thy body be bowed down with disease? What though thy poverty and trials be very great? What though thine earthly friends forsake thee, and thou art alone in the world? All this may be true: but if thou art in Christ thou hast a Friend, a mighty Friend, a loving Friend, a wise Friend, a Friend that never fails. Oh, think, think much upon thy friend!

Yet a little time and thy Friend shall come to take thee home, and thou shalt dwell with Him for ever. Yet a little time and thou shalt see as thou hast been seen, and know as thou hast been known. And then thou shalt hear assembled worlds confess, that HE IS THE RICH AND HAPPY MAN WHO HAS HAD CHRIST FOR HIS FRIEND.

XV

SICKNESS

"He whom Thou lovest is sick."—JOHN xi. 3.

THE chapter from which this text is taken is well known to all Bible readers. In life-like description, in touching interest, in sublime simplicity, there is no writing in existence that will bear comparison with that chapter. A narrative like this is to my own mind one of the great proofs of the inspiration of Scripture. When I read the story of Bethany, I feel "There is something here which the infidel can never account for."—"This is nothing else but the finger of God."

The words which I specially dwell upon in this chapter are singularly affecting and instructive. They record the message which Martha and Mary sent to Jesus when their brother Lazarus was sick: "Lord, behold he whom Thou lovest is sick." That message was short and simple. Yet almost every word is deeply suggestive.

Mark the child-like faith of these holy women. They turned to the Lord Jesus in their hour of need, as the frightened infant turns to its mother, or the compass-needle turns to the Pole. They turned to Him as their Shepherd, their almighty Friend, their Brother born for adversity. Different as they were in natural temperament, the two sisters in this matter were entirely agreed. Christ's help was their first thought in the day of trouble.

Christ was the refuge to which they fled in the hour of need. Blessed are all they that do likewise!

Mark the simple humility of their language about Lazarus. They call Him "He whom Thou lovest." They do not say, "He who loves Thee, believes in Thee, serves Thee," but "He whom Thou lovest." Martha and Mary were deeply taught of God. They had learned that Christ's love towards us, and not our love towards Christ, is the true ground of expectation, and true foundation of hope. Blessed, again, are all they that are taught likewise! To look inward to our love towards Christ is painfully unsatisfying: to look outward to Christ's love towards us is peace.

Mark, lastly, the touching circumstance which the message of Martha and Mary reveals: "He whom Thou lovest is sick." Lazarus was a good man, converted, believing, renewed, sanctified, a friend of Christ, and an heir of glory. And yet Lazarus was sick! Then sickness is no sign that God is displeased. Sickness is intended to be a blessing to us, and not a curse. "All things work together for good to them that love God, and are called according to His purpose." "All things are yours,—life, death, things present, or things to come: for ye are Christ's; and Christ is God's." (Rom. viii. 28; 1 Cor. iii. 22.) Blessed, I say again, are they that have learned this! Happy are they who can say, when they are ill, "This is my Father's doing. It must be well."

I invite the attention of my readers to the subject of sickness. The subject is one which we ought frequently to look in the face. We cannot avoid it. It needs no prophet's eye to see sickness coming to each of us in turn one day. "In the midst of life we are in death." Let us turn aside for a few moments, and consider sickness as Christians. The consideration will not hasten its coming, and by God's blessing may teach us wisdom.

In considering the subject of sickness, three points

appear to me to demand attention. On each I shall say a few words.

I. The *universal prevalence* of sickness and disease.

II. The *general benefits* which sickness confers on mankind.

III. The *special duties* to which sickness calls us.

I. The *universal prevalence of sickness.*

I need not dwell long on this point. To elaborate the proof of it would only be multiplying truisms, and heaping up common-places which all allow.

Sickness is everywhere. In Europe, in Asia, in Africa, in America; in hot countries and in cold, in civilized nations and in savage tribes,—men, women, and children sicken and die.

Sickness is among all classes. Grace does not lift a believer above the reach of it. Riches will not buy exemption from it. Rank cannot prevent its assaults. Kings and their subjects, masters and servants, rich men and poor, learned and unlearned, teachers and scholars, doctors and patients, ministers and hearers, all alike go down before this great foe. "The rich man's wealth is his strong city." (Prov. xviii. 11.) The Englishman's house is called his castle; but there are no doors and bars which can keep out disease and death.

Sickness is of every sort and description. From the crown of our head to the sole of our foot we are liable to disease. Our capacity of suffering is something fearful to contemplate. Who can count up the ailments by which our bodily frame may be assailed? Who ever visited a museum of morbid anatomy without a shudder? "Strange that a harp of thousand strings should keep in tune so long." It is not, to my mind, so wonderful that men should die so soon, as it is that they should live so long.

Sickness is often one of the most humbling and distressing trials that can come upon man. It can turn the strongest into a little child, and make him feel "the grasshopper a burden." (Eccles. xii. 5.) It can unnerve the boldest, and make him tremble at the fall of a pin. We are "fearfully and wonderfully made." (Psalm cxxxix. 14.) The connection between body and mind is curiously close. The influence that some diseases can exercise upon the temper and spirits is immensely great. There are ailments of brain, and liver, and nerves, which can bring down a Solomon in mind to a state little better than that of a babe. He that would know to what depths of humiliation poor man can fall, has only to attend for a short time on sick-beds.

Sickness is not preventible by anything that man can do. The average duration of life may doubtless be somewhat lengthened. The skill of doctors may continually discover new remedies, and effect surprising cures. The enforcement of wise sanitary regulations may greatly lower the death-rate in a land. But, after all,—whether in healthy or unhealthy localities,—whether in mild climates or in cold,—whether treated by homœopathy or allopathy,—men will sicken and die. "The days of our years are three-score years and ten; and if by reason of strength they be four-score years, yet is their strength labour and sorrow; for it is soon cut off, and we fly away." (Psalm xc. 10.) That witness is indeed true. It was true 3300 years ago.—It is true still.

Now what can we make of this great fact,—the universal prevalence of sickness? How shall we account for it? What explanation can we give of it? What answer shall we give to our inquiring children when they ask us, "Father, why do people get ill and die?" These are grave questions. A few words upon them will not be out of place.

Can we suppose for a moment that God created sickness

and disease at the beginning? Can we imagine that He who formed our world in such perfect order was the Former of needless suffering and pain? Can we think that He who made all things "very good," made Adam's race to sicken and to die? The idea is, to my mind, revolting. It introduces a grand imperfection into the midst of God's perfect works. I must find another solution to satisfy my mind.

The only explanation that satisfies me is that which the Bible gives. Something has come into the world which has dethroned man from his original position, and stripped him of his original privileges. Something has come in, which, like a handful of gravel thrown into the midst of machinery, has marred the perfect order of God's creation. And what is that *something*? I answer, in one word, It is sin. "Sin has entered into the world, and death by sin." (Rom. v. 12.) Sin is the cause of all the sickness, and disease, and pain, and suffering, which prevail on the earth. They are all a part of that curse which came into the world when Adam and Eve ate the forbidden fruit and fell. There would have been no sickness, if there had been no fall. There would have been no disease, if there had been no sin.

I pause for a moment at this point, and yet in pausing I do not depart from my subject. I pause to remind my readers that there is no ground so untenable as that which is occupied by the Atheist, the Deist, or the unbeliever in the Bible. I advise every young reader of this paper, who is puzzled by the bold and specious arguments of the infidel, to study well that most important subject,—the *Difficulties of Infidelity*. I say boldly that it requires far more credulity to be an infidel than to be a Christian. I say boldly, that there are great broad patent facts in the condition of mankind, which nothing but the Bible can explain, and that one of the most striking of these facts is the universal prevalence of pain, sickness, and disease.

In short, one of the mightiest difficulties in the way of Atheists and Deists, is the body of man.

You have doubtless heard of Atheists. An Atheist is one who professes to believe that there is no God, no Creator, no First Cause, and that all things came together in this world by mere chance.—Now shall we listen to such a doctrine as this? Go, take an Atheist to one of the excellent surgical schools of our land, and ask him to study the wonderful structure of the human body. Show him the matchless skill with which every joint, and vein, and valve, and muscle, and sinew, and nerve, and bone, and limb, has been formed. Show him the perfect adaptation of every part of the human frame to the purpose which it serves. Show him the thousand delicate contrivances for meeting wear and tear, and supplying daily waste of vigour. And then ask this man who denies the being of a God, and a great First Cause, if all this wonderful mechanism is the result of chance? Ask him if it came together at first by luck and accident? Ask him if he so thinks about the watch he looks at, the bread he eats, or the coat he wears? Oh, no! Design is an insuperable difficulty in the Atheist's way. *There is a God.*

You have doubtless heard of Deists. A Deist is one who professes to believe that there is a God, who made the world and all things therein. But He does not believe the Bible. "A God, but no Bible!—a Creator, but no Christianity!" This is the Deist's creed.—Now, shall we listen to this doctrine? Go again, I say, and take a Deist to an hospital, and show him some of the awful handiwork of disease. Take him to the bed where lies some tender child, scarce knowing good from evil, with an incurable cancer. Send him to the ward where there is a loving mother of a large family in the last stage of some excruciating disease. Show him some of the racking pains and agonies to which flesh is heir, and ask him to account for them. Ask this man, who believes there is a great and

wise God who made the world, but cannot believe the
Bible,—ask him how he accounts for these traces of
disorder and imperfection in his God's creation. Ask this
man, who sneers at Christian theology and is too wise to
believe the fall of Adam,—ask him upon his theory to
explain the universal prevalence of pain and disease in the
world. You may ask in vain! You will get no satisfactory
answer. Sickness and suffering are insuperable difficulties
in the Deist's way. *Man has sinned, and therefore man
suffers.* Adam fell from his first estate, and therefore
Adam's children sicken and die.

The universal prevalence of sickness is one of the
indirect evidences that the Bible is true. The Bible
explains it. The Bible answers the questions about it
which will arise in every inquiring mind. No other
systems of religion can do this. They all fail here. They
are silent. They are confounded. The Bible alone looks
the subject in the face. It boldly proclaims the fact that
man is a fallen creature, and with equal boldness proclaims
a vast remedial system to meet his wants. I feel shut up
to the conclusion that the Bible is from God. Christianity
is a revelation from heaven. "Thy word is truth." (John
xvii. 17.)

Let us stand fast on the old ground, that the Bible, and
the Bible only, is God's revelation of Himself to man. Be
not moved by the many new assaults which modern
scepticism is making on the inspired volume. Heed not
the hard questions which the enemies of the faith are
fond of putting about Bible difficulties, and to which
perhaps you often feel unable to give an answer. Anchor
your soul firmly on this safe principle,—that the whole
book is God's truth. Tell the enemies of the Bible that,
in spite of all their arguments, there is no book in the
world which will bear comparison with the Bible,—none
that so thoroughly meets man's wants,—none that explains
so much of the state of mankind. As to the hard things

in the Bible, tell them you are content to wait. You find enough plain truth in the book to satisfy your conscience and save your soul. The hard things will be cleared up one day. What you know not now, you will know hereafter.

II. The second point I propose to consider is *the general benefits which sickness confers on mankind.*

I use that word "benefits" advisedly. I feel it of deep importance to see this part of our subject clearly. I know well that sickness is one of the supposed weak points in God's government of the world, on which sceptical minds love to dwell.—"Can God be a God of love, when He allows pain? Can God be a God of mercy, when He permits disease? He might prevent pain and disease; but He does not. How can these things be?" Such is the reasoning which often comes across the heart of man.

I reply to all such reasoners, that their doubts and questionings are most unreasonable. They might us well doubt the existence of a Creator, because the order of the universe is disturbed by earthquakes, hurricanes, and storms. They might as well doubt the providence of God, because of the horrible massacres of Delhi and Cawnpore. All this would be just as reasonable as to doubt the mercy of God, because of the presence of sickness in the world.

I ask all who find it hard to reconcile the prevalence of disease and pain with the love of God, to cast their eyes on the world around them, and to mark what is going on. I ask them to observe the extent to which men constantly submit to present loss for the sake of future gain,—present sorrow for the sake of future joy,—present pain for the sake of future health. The seed is thrown into the ground, and rots: but we sow in the hope of a future harvest. The boy is sent to school amidst many tears: but we send him in the hope of his getting future wisdom. The father of a family undergoes some fearful surgical operation: but he bears it, in the hope of future health.—I ask men to apply this great principle to God's government of the world. I ask them to believe that God allows pain, sickness, and disease, not because He loves to vex man, but because He desires to benefit man's heart, and mind, and conscience, and soul, to all eternity.

Once more I repeat, that I speak of the "benefits" of sickness on purpose and advisedly. I know the suffering and pain which sickness entails. I admit the misery and wretchedness which it often brings in its train. But I cannot regard it as an unmixed evil. I see in it a wise permission of God. I see in it a useful provision to check the ravages of sin and the devil among men's souls. If man had never sinned I should have been at a loss to discern the benefit of sickness. But since sin is in the world, I can see that sickness is a good. It is a blessing quite as much as a curse. It is a rough schoolmaster, I grant. But it is a real friend to man's soul.

(a) Sickness helps to *remind men of death.* The most live as if they were never going to die. They follow business, or pleasure, or politics, or science, as if earth was their eternal home. They plan and scheme for the future, like the rich fool in the parable, as if they had a long lease of life, and were not tenants at will. A heavy illness sometimes goes far to dispel these delusions. It awakens men from their day-dreams, and reminds them that they have to die as well as to live. Now this I say emphatically is a mighty good.

(b) Sickness helps to *make men think seriously of God,* and their souls, and the world to come. The most in their days of health can find no time for such thoughts. They dislike them. They put them away. They count them troublesome and disagreeable. Now a severe disease has sometimes a wonderful power of mustering and rallying these thoughts, and bringing them up before the eyes of a man's soul. Even a wicked king like Benhadad, when

sick, could think of Elisha. (2 Kings viii. 8.) Even
heathen sailors, when death was in sight, were afraid, and
"cried every man to his god." (Jonah i. 5.) Surely anything that helps to make men think is a good.

(c) Sickness helps to *soften men's hearts*, and teach them
wisdom. The natural heart is as hard as a stone. It can
see no good in anything which is not of this life, and no
happiness excepting in this world. A long illness sometimes goes far to correct these ideas. It exposes the
emptiness and hollowness of what the world calls "good"
things, and teaches us to hold them with a loose hand.
The man of business finds that money alone is not everything the heart requires. The woman of the world finds
that costly apparel, and novel-reading, and the reports of
balls and operas, are miserable comforters in a sick room.
Surely anything that obliges us to alter our weights and
measures of earthly things is a real good.

(d) Sickness helps to *level and humble us*. We are all
naturally proud and high-minded. Few, even of the
poorest, are free from the infection. Few are to be found
who do not look down on somebody else, and secretly
flatter themselves that they are "not as other men." A
sick bed is a mighty tamer of such thoughts as these. It
forces on us the mighty truth that we are all poor worms,
that we "dwell in houses of clay," and are "crushed before
the moth" (Job iv. 19), and that kings and subjects, masters
and servants, rich and poor, are all dying creatures, and will
soon stand side by side at the bar of God. In the sight
of the coffin and the grave it is not easy to be proud.
Surely anything that teaches that lesson is good.

(e) Finally, sickness helps *to try men's religion*, of what
sort it is. There are not many on earth who have no
religion at all. Yet few have a religion that will bear
inspection. Most are content with traditions received
from their fathers, and can render no reason of the hope
that is in them. Now disease is sometimes most useful to

a man in exposing the utter worthlessness of his soul's foundation. It often shows him that he has nothing solid under his feet, and nothing firm under his hand. It makes him find out that, although he may have had a form of religion, he has been all his life worshipping "an unknown God." Many a creed looks well on the smooth waters of health, which turns out utterly unsound and useless on the rough waves of the sick bed. The storms of winter often bring out the defects in a man's dwelling, and sickness often exposes the gracelessness of a man's soul. Surely anything that makes us find out the real character of our faith is a good.

I do not say that sickness confers these benefits on all to whom it comes. Alas, I can say nothing of the kind! Myriads are yearly laid low by illness, and restored to health, who evidently learn no lesson from their sick beds, and return again to the world. Myriads are yearly passing through sickness to the grave, and yet receiving no more spiritual impression from it than the beasts that perish. While they live they have no feeling, and when they die there are "no bands in their death." (Psalm lxxiii. 4.) These are awful things to say. But they are true. The degree of deadness to which man's heart and conscience may attain, is a depth which I cannot pretend to fathom.

But does sickness confer the benefits of which I have been speaking on only a few? I will allow nothing of the kind. I believe that in very many cases sickness produces impressions more or less akin to those of which I have just been speaking. I believe that in many minds sickness is God's "day of visitation," and that feelings are continually aroused on a sick bed which, if improved, might, by God's grace, result in salvation. I believe that in heathen lands sickness often paves the way for the missionary, and makes the poor idolater lend a willing ear to the glad tidings of the Gospel. I believe that in our own land sickness is one of the greatest aids to the minister

of the Gospel, and that sermons and counsels are often
brought home in the day of disease which we have
neglected in the day of health. I believe that sickness is
one of God's most important subordinate instruments in
the saving of men, and that though the feelings it calls
forth are often temporary, it is also often a means whereby
the Spirit works effectually on the heart. In short, I
believe firmly that the sickness of men's bodies has often
led, in God's wonderful providence, to the salvation of
men's souls.

I leave this branch of my subject here. It needs no
further remark. If sickness can do the things of which I
have been speaking (and who will gainsay it?), if sickness
in a wicked world can help to make men think of God and
their souls, then sickness confers benefits on mankind.

We have no right to murmur at sickness, and repine at
its presence in the world. We ought rather to thank God
for it. It is God's witness. It is the soul's adviser. It is
an awakener to the conscience. It is a purifier to the
heart. Surely I have a right to tell you that sickness is
a blessing and not a curse,—a help and not an injury,—a
gain and not a loss,—a friend and not a foe to mankind.
So long as we have a world wherein there is sin, it is a
mercy that it is a world wherein there is sickness.

III. The third and last point which I propose to
consider, is *the special duties which the prevalence of
sickness entails on each one of ourselves.*

I should be sorry to leave the subject of sickness
without saying something on this point. I hold it to be
of cardinal importance not to be content with generalities
in delivering God's message to souls. I am anxious to
impress on each one into whose hands this paper may fall,
his own personal responsibility in connection with the
subject. I would fain have no one lay down this paper
unable to answer the questions,—"What practical lesson

have I learned? What, in a world of disease and death, what ought I to do?"

(a) One paramount duty which the prevalence of sickness entails on man, is that of *living habitually prepared to meet God.* Sickness is a remembrancer of death. Death is the door through which we must all pass to judgment. Judgment is the time when we must at last see God face to face. Surely the first lesson which the inhabitant of a sick and dying world should learn should be to prepare to meet his God.

When are you prepared to meet God? Never till your iniquities are forgiven, and your sin covered! Never till your heart is renewed, and your will taught to delight in the will of God! You have many sins. If you go to church your own mouth is taught to confess this every Sunday. The blood of Jesus Christ can alone cleanse those sins away. The righteousness of Christ can alone make you acceptable in the sight of God. Faith, simple childlike faith, can alone give you an interest in Christ and His benefits. Would you know whether you are prepared to meet God? Then where is your faith?—Your heart is naturally unmeet for God's company. You have no real pleasure in doing His will. The Holy Ghost must transform you after the image of Christ. Old things must pass away. All things must become new. Would you know whether you are prepared to meet God? Then, where is your grace? Where are the evidences of your conversion and sanctification?

I believe that this, and nothing less than this, is preparedness to meet God. Pardon of sin and meetness for God's presence,—justification by faith and sanctification of the heart,—the blood of Christ sprinkled on us, and the Spirit of Christ dwelling in us,—these are the grand essentials of the Christian religion. These are no mere words and names to furnish bones of contention for wrangling theologians. These are sober, solid, substantial realities. To live in the actual possession of these things, in a world full of sickness and death, is the first duty which I press home upon your soul.

(b) Another paramount duty which the prevalence of sickness entails on you, is that of *living habitually ready to bear it patiently.* Sickness is no doubt a trying thing to flesh and blood. To feel our nerves unstrung, and our natural force abated,—to be obliged to sit still and be cut off from all our usual avocations,—to see our plans broken off and our purposes disappointed,—to endure long hours, and days, and nights of weariness and pain,—all this is a severe strain on poor sinful human nature. What wonder if peevishness and impatience are brought out by disease! Surely in such a dying world as this we should study patience.

How shall we learn to bear sickness patiently, when sickness comes to our turn? We must lay up stores of grace in the time of health. We must seek for the sanctifying influence of the Holy Ghost over our unruly tempers and dispositions. We must make a real business of our prayers, and regularly ask for strength to endure God's will as well as to do it. Such strength is to be had for the asking: "If ye shall ask anything in my name, I will do it for you." (John xiv. 14.)

I cannot think it needless to dwell on this point. I believe the passive graces of Christianity receive far less notice than they deserve. Meekness, gentleness, long-suffering, faith, patience, are all mentioned in the Word of God as fruits of the Spirit. They are passive graces which specially glorify God. They often make men think, who despise the active side of the Christian character. Never do these graces shine so brightly as they do in the sick room. They enable many a sick person to preach a silent sermon, which those around him never forget. Would you adorn the doctrine you profess? Would you make your Christianity beautiful in the eyes of others? Then take the hint I give you this day. Lay up a store of patience against the time of illness. Then, though your sickness be not to death, it shall be for the " glory of God." (John xi. 4.)

(c) One more paramount duty which the prevalence of sickness entails on you, is that of *habitual readiness to feel with and help your fellow-men*. Sickness is never very far from us. Few are the families who have not some sick relative. Few are the parishes where you will not find some one ill. But wherever there is sickness, there is a call to duty. A little timely assistance in some cases,—a kindly visit in others,—a friendly inquiry,—a mere expression of sympathy, may do a vast good. These are the sort of things which soften asperities, and bring men together, and promote good feeling. These are ways by which you may ultimately lead men to Christ and save their souls. These are good works to which every professing Christian should be ready. In a world full of sickness and disease we ought to " bear one another's burdens," and be " kind one to another." (Gal. vi. 2; Ephes. iv. 32.)

These things, I dare say, may appear to some little and trifling. They must needs be doing something great, and grand, and striking, and heroic! I take leave to say that conscientious attention to these little acts of brotherly-kindness is one of the clearest evidences of having " the mind of Christ." They are acts in which our blessed Master Himself was abundant. He was ever " going about doing good" to the sick and sorrowful. (Acts x. 38.) They are acts to which He attaches great importance in that most solemn passage of Scripture, the description of the last judgment. He says there: "I was sick, and ye visited Me." (Matt. xxv. 36.)

Have you any desire to prove the reality of your charity,—that blessed grace which so many talk of, and so few practise? If you have, beware of unfeeling selfishness and neglect of your sick brethren. Search them out.

Assist them if they need aid. Show your sympathy with them. Try to lighten their burdens. Above all, strive to do good to their souls. It will do you good if it does no good to them. It will keep your heart from murmuring. It may prove a blessing to your own soul. I firmly believe that God is testing and proving us by every case of sickness within our reach. By permitting suffering, He tries whether Christians have any feeling. Beware, lest you be weighed in the balances and found wanting. If you can live in a sick and dying world and not feel for others, you have yet much to learn.

I leave this branch of my subject here. I throw out the points I have named as suggestions, and I pray God that they may work in many minds. I repeat, that habitual preparedness to meet God,—habitual readiness to suffer patiently,—habitual willingness to sympathize heartily,— are plain duties which sickness entails on all. They are duties within the reach of every one. In naming them I ask nothing extravagant or unreasonable. I bid no man retire into a monastery and ignore the duties of his station. I only want men to realize that they live in a sick and dying world, and to live accordingly. And I say boldly, that the man who lives the life of faith, and holiness, and patience, and charity, is not only the most true Christian, but the most wise and reasonable man.

And now I conclude all with four words of practical application. I want the subject of this paper to be turned to some spiritual use. My heart's desire and prayer to God in placing it in this volume is to do good to souls.

(1) In the first place, I offer a *question* to all who read this paper, to which, as God's ambassador, I entreat their serious attention. It is a question which grows naturally out of the subject on which I have been writing. It is a question which concerns all, of every rank, and class, and condition. I ask you, What will you do when you are ill?

The time must come when you, as well as others, must go down the dark valley of the shadow of death. The hour must come when you, like all your forefathers, must sicken and die. The time may be near or far off. God only knows. But whenever the time may be, I ask again, What are you going to do? Where do you mean to turn for comfort? On what do you mean to rest your soul? On what do you mean to build your hope? From whence will you fetch your consolations?

I do entreat you not to put these questions away, Suffer them to work on your conscience, and rest not till you can give them a satisfactory answer. Trifle not with that precious gift, an immortal soul. Defer not the consideration of the matter to a more convenient season. Presume not on a death-bed repentance. The greatest business ought surely not to be left to the last. One dying thief was saved that men might not despair, but only one that none might presume. I repeat the question. I am sure it deserves an answer. "What will you do when you are ill?"

If you were going to live for ever in this world I would not address you as I do. But it cannot be. There is no escaping the common lot of all mankind. Nobody can die in our stead. The day must come when we must each go to our long home. Against that day I want you to be prepared. The body which now takes up so much of your attention—the body which you now clothe, and feed, and warm with so much care,—that body must return again to the dust. Oh, think what an awful thing it would prove at last to have provided for everything except the one thing needful,—to have provided for the body, but to have neglected the soul,—to die, in fact, like Cardinal Beaufort, and "give no sign" of being saved! Once more I press my question on your conscience: "What will you do when you are ill?"

(2) In the next place, I offer *counsel* to all who feel

they need it and are willing to take it,—to all who feel they are not yet prepared to meet God. That counsel is short and simple. Acquaint yourself with the Lord Jesus Christ without delay. Repent, be converted, flee to Christ, and be saved.

Either you have a soul or you have not. You will surely never deny that you have. Then if you have a soul, seek that soul's salvation. Of all gambling in the world, there is none so reckless as that of the man who lives unprepared to meet God, and yet puts off repentance. —Either you have sins or you have none. If you have (and who will dare to deny it ?), break off from those sins, cast away your transgressions, and turn away from them without delay.—Either you need a Saviour or you do not. If you do, flee to the only Saviour this very day, and cry mightily to Him to save your soul. Apply to Christ at once. Seek Him by faith. Commit your soul into His keeping. Cry mightily to Him for pardon and peace with God. Ask Him to pour down the Holy Spirit upon you, and make you a thorough Christian. He will hear you. No matter what you have been, He will not refuse your prayer. He has said, "Him that cometh to Me I will in no wise cast out." (John vi. 37.)

Beware, I beseech you, of a vague and indefinite Christianity. Be not content with a general hope that all is right because you belong to the old Church of England, and that all will be well at last because God is merciful. Rest not, rest not without personal union with Christ Himself. Rest not, rest not till you have the witness of the Spirit in your heart, that you are washed, and sanctified, and justified, and one with Christ, and Christ in you. Rest not till you can say with the apostle, "I know whom I have believed, and am persuaded that He is able to keep that which I have committed to Him against that day." (2 Tim. i. 12.)

Vague, and indefinite, and indistinct religion may do

very well in time of health. It will never do in the day of sickness. A mere formal, perfunctory Churchmembership may carry a man through the sunshine of youth and prosperity. It will break down entirely when death is in sight. Nothing will do then but real heart-union with Christ. Christ interceding for us at God's right hand,—Christ known and believed as our Priest, our Physician, our Friend,—Christ alone can rob death of its sting and enable us to face sickness without fear. He alone can deliver those who through fear of death are in bondage. I say to every one who wants advice, Be acquainted with Christ. As ever you would have hope and comfort on the bed of sickness, be acquainted with Christ. Seek Christ. Apply to Christ.

Take every care and trouble to Him when you are acquainted with Him. He will keep you and carry you through all. Pour out your heart before Him, when your conscience is burdened. He is the true Confessor. He alone can absolve you and take the burden away. Turn to Him first in the day of sickness, like Martha and Mary. Keep on looking to Him to the last breath of your life. Christ is worth knowing. The more you know Him the better you will love Him. Then be acquainted with Jesus Christ.

(3) In the third place, I exhort all true Christians who read this paper to remember how much they may glorify God in the time of sickness, and to *lie quiet in God's hand when they are ill.*

I feel it very important to touch on this point. I know how ready the heart of a believer is to faint, and how busy Satan is in suggesting doubts and questionings, when the body of a Christian is weak. I have seen something of the depression and melancholy which sometimes comes upon the children of God when they are suddenly laid aside by disease, and obliged to sit still. I have marked how prone some good people are to torment themselves with morbid thoughts at such seasons, and to say in their hearts, "God has forsaken me: I am cast out of His sight."

I earnestly entreat all sick believers to remember that they may honour God as much by patient suffering as they can by active work. It often shows more grace to sit still than it does to go to and fro, and perform great exploits. I entreat them to remember that Christ cares for them as much when they are sick as He does when they are well, and that the very chastisement they feel so acutely is sent in love, and not in anger. Above all, I entreat them to recollect the sympathy of Jesus for all His weak members. They are always tenderly cared for by Him, but never so much as in their time of need. Christ has had great experience of sickness. He knows the heart of a sick man. He used to see "all manner of sickness, and all manner of disease" when He was upon earth. He felt specially for the sick in the days of His flesh. He feels for them specially still. Sickness and suffering, I often think, make believers more like their Lord in experience, than health. "Himself took our infirmities, and bare our sicknesses." (Isaiah liii. 3; Matt. viii. 17.) The Lord Jesus was a "Man of sorrows, and acquainted with grief." None have such an opportunity of learning the mind of a suffering Saviour as suffering disciples.

(4) I conclude with a word of *exhortation* to all believers, which I heartily pray God to impress upon their souls. I exhort you to keep up a habit of close communion with Christ, and never to be afraid of "going too far" in your religion. Remember this, if you wish to have "great peace" in your times of sickness.

I observe with regret a tendency in some quarters to lower the standard of practical Christianity, and to denounce what are called "extreme views" about a Christian's daily walk in life. I remark with pain that even religious people will sometimes look coldly on those who withdraw from worldly society, and will censure them as "exclusive, narrow-minded, illiberal, uncharitable, sour-spirited," and the like. I warn every believer in Christ who reads this paper to beware of being influenced by such censures. I entreat him, if he wants light in the valley of death, to "keep himself unspotted from the world," to "follow the Lord very fully," and to walk very closely with God. (James i. 27; Num. xiv. 24.)

I believe that the want of "thoroughness" about many people's Christianity is one secret of their little comfort, both in health and sickness. I believe that the "half-and-half,"—"keep-in-with-everybody" religion, which satisfies many in the present day, is offensive to God, and sows thorns in dying pillows, which hundreds never discover till too late. I believe that the weakness and feebleness of such a religion never comes out so much as it does upon a sick bed.

If you and I want "strong consolation" in our time of need, we must not be content with a bare union with Christ. (Heb. vi. 18.) We must seek to know something of heart-felt, experimental *communion* with Him. Never, never let us forget, that "union" is one thing, and "communion" another. Thousands, I fear, who know what "union" with Christ is, know nothing of "communion."

The day may come when after a long fight with disease, we shall feel that medicine can do no more, and that nothing remains but to die. Friends will be standing by, unable to help us. Hearing, eyesight, even the power of praying, will be fast failing us. The world and its shadows will be melting beneath our feet. Eternity, with its realities, will be looming large before our minds. What shall support us in that trying hour? What shall enable us to feel, "I fear no evil"? (Psalm xxiii. 4.) Nothing, nothing can do it but close communion with Christ.

Christ dwelling in our hearts by faith,—Christ putting His right arm under our heads,—Christ felt to be sitting by our side,—Christ can alone give us the complete victory in the last struggle.

Let us cleave to Christ more closely, love Him more heartily, live to Him more thoroughly, copy Him more exactly, confess Him more boldly, follow Him more fully. Religion like this will always bring its own reward. Worldly people may laugh at it. Weak brethren may think it extreme. But it will wear well. At even time it will bring us light. In sickness it will bring us peace. In the world to come it will give us a crown of glory that fadeth not away.

The time is short. The fashion of this world passeth away. A few more sicknesses, and all will be over. A few more funerals, and our own funeral will take place. A few more storms and tossings, and we shall be safe in harbour. We travel towards a world where there is no more sickness,—where parting, and pain, and crying, and mourning, are done with for evermore. Heaven is becoming every year more full, and earth more empty. The friends ahead are becoming more numerous than the friends astern. "Yet a little time and He that shall come will come, and will not tarry." (Heb. x. 37.) In His presence shall be fulness of joy. Christ shall wipe away all tears from His people's eyes. The last enemy that shall be destroyed is Death. But he shall be destroyed. Death himself shall one day die. (Rev. xx. 14.)

In the meantime let us live the life of faith in the Son of God. Let us lean all our weight on Christ, and rejoice in the thought that He lives for evermore.

Yes: blessed be God! Christ lives, though we may die. Christ lives, though friends and families are carried to the grave. He lives who abolished death, and brought life and immortality to light by the Gospel. He lives who said, "O death, I will be thy plagues: O grave, I will be thy destruction." (Hos. xiii. 14.) He lives who will one day change our vile body, and make it like unto His glorious body. In sickness and in health, in life and in death, let us lean confidently on Him. Surely we ought to say daily with one of old, "Blessed be God for Jesus Christ!"

XVI

THE FAMILY OF GOD

"The whole family in heaven and earth."—EPHES. iii. 15.

THE words which form the title of this paper ought to stir some feelings in our minds at any time. There lives not the man or woman on earth who is not member of some "family." The poorest as well as the richest has his kith and kin, and can tell you something of his "family."

Family gatherings at certain times of the year, such as Christmas, we all know, are very common. Thousands of firesides are crowded then, if at no other time of the year. The young man in town snatches a few days from business, and takes a run down to the old folks at home. The young woman in service gets a short holiday, and comes to visit her father and mother. Brothers and sisters meet for a few hours. Parents and children look one another in the face. How much there is to talk about! How many questions to be asked! How many interesting things to be told! Happy indeed is that fireside which sees gathered round it at Christmas "the whole family!"

Family gatherings are natural, and right, and good. I approve them with all my heart. It does me good to see them kept up. They are one of the very few pleasant things which have survived the fall of man. Next to the grace of God, I see no principle which unites people so much in this sinful world as family feeling. Community of blood is a most powerful tie. It was a fine saying of an American naval officer, when his men insisted on helping the English sailors in fighting the Taku forts in China,—"I cannot help it: blood is thicker than water." I have often observed that people will stand up for their relations, merely because they *are* their relations,—and refuse to hear a word against them,—even when they have no sympathy with their tastes and ways. Anything which helps to keep up family feeling ought to be commended. It is a wise thing, when it can be done, to gather together at Christmas "the whole family."

Family gatherings, nevertheless, are often sorrowful things. It would be strange indeed, in such a world as this, if they were not. Few are the family circles which do not show gaps and vacant places as years pass away. Changes and deaths make sad havoc as time goes on. Thoughts will rise up within us, as we grow older, about faces and voices no longer with us, which no Christmas merriment can entirely keep down. When the young members of the family have once begun to launch forth into the world, the old heads may long survive the scattering of the nest; but after a certain time, it seldom happens that you see together "the whole family."

There is one great family to which I want all the readers of this paper to belong. It is a family despised by many, and not even known by some. But it is a family of far more importance than any family on earth. To belong to it entitles a man to far greater privileges than to be the son of a king. It is the family of which St. Paul speaks to the Ephesians, when he tells them of the "whole family in heaven and earth." It is the family of God.

I ask the attention of every reader of this paper while I try to describe this family, and recommend it to his notice. I want to tell you of the amazing benefits which membership of this family conveys. I want you to be found one of this family, when its gathering shall come at last,—a gathering without separation, or sorrow, or tears. Hear me while, as a minister of Christ, and friend to your soul, I speak to you for a few minutes about "the whole family in heaven and earth:"—

I.   First of all, *what is this family?*

II.   Secondly, *what is its present position?*

III.   Thirdly, *what are its future prospects.*

I wish to unfold these three things before you, and I invite your serious consideration of them. Our family gatherings on earth must have an end one day. Our last earthly Christmas must come. Happy indeed is that Christmas which finds us prepared to meet God!

I.   *What is that family* which the Bible calls "the whole family in heaven and earth"? Of whom does it consist?

The family before us consists of all real Christians,—of all who have the Spirit,—of all true believers in Christ,—of the saints of every age, and Church, and nation, and tongue. It includes the blessed company of all faithful people. It is the same as the election of God,—the household of faith,—the mystical body of Christ,—the bride,—the living temple,—the sheep that never perish,—the Church of the first-born,—the holy Catholic Church. All these expressions are only "the family of God" under other names.

Membership of the family before us does not depend on any earthly connection. It comes not by natural birth, but by new birth. Ministers cannot impart it to their hearers. Parents cannot give it to their children. You may be born in the godliest family in the land, and enjoy the richest means of grace a Church can supply, and yet

never belong to the family of God. To belong to it you
must be born again. None but the Holy Ghost can make
a living member of His family. It is His special office
and prerogative to bring into the true Church such as
shall be saved. They that are born again are born, " not
of blood, nor of the will of the flesh, nor of the will or
man, but of God." (John i. 13.)

Do you ask the reason of this name which the Bible
gives to the company of all true Christians ? Would you
like to know why they are called " a family " ? Listen and
I will tell you.

(a) True Christians are called " a family " because they
have all *one Father*. They are all children of God by faith
in Christ Jesus. They are all born of one Spirit. They are
all sons and daughters of the Lord Almighty. They have
received the Spirit of adoption, whereby they cry, Abba
Father. (Gal. iii. 26; John iii. 8; 2 Cor. vi. 18; Rom.
viii. 15.) They do not regard God with slavish fear, as an
austere Being, only ready to punish them. They look up
to Him with tender confidence, as a reconciled and loving
parent,—as one forgiving iniquity, transgression, and sin, to
all who believe on Jesus,—and full of pity even to the least
and feeblest. The words, " Our Father which art in
heaven," are no mere form in the mouth of true Christians. No wonder they are called God's " family."

(b) True Christians are called " a family," because they
all *rejoice in one name*. That name is the name of their
great Head and Elder Brother, even Jesus Christ the Lord.
Just as a common family name is the uniting link to all
the members of a Highland clan, so does the name of Jesus
tie all believers together in one vast family. As members
of outward visible Churches they have various names and
distinguishing appellations. As living members of Christ,
they all, with one heart and mind, rejoice in one Saviour.
Not a heart among them but feels drawn to Jesus as the
only object of hope. Not a tongue among them but would

tell you that "Christ is all." Sweet to them all is the thought of Christ's death for them on the cross. Sweet is the thought of Christ's intercession for them at the right hand of God. Sweet is the thought of Christ's coming again to unite them to Himself in one glorified company for ever. In fact, you might as well take away the sun out of heaven, as take away the name of Christ from believers. To the world there may seem little in His name. To believers it is full of comfort, hope, joy, rest, and peace. No wonder they are called "a family."

(c) True Christians, above all, are called "a family" because there is so strong *a family likeness* among them. They are all led by one Spirit, and are marked by the same general features of life, heart, taste, and character. Just as there is a general bodily resemblance among the brothers and sisters of a family, so there is a general spiritual resemblance among all the sons and daughters of the Lord Almighty. They all hate sin and love God. They all rest their hope of salvation on Christ, and have no confidence in themselves. They all endeavour to "come out and be separate" from the ways of the world, and to set their affections on things above. They all turn naturally to the same Bible, as the only food of their souls and the only sure guide in their pilgrimage toward heaven: they find it a "lamp to their feet, and a light to their path." (Psa. cxix. 105.) They all go to the same throne of grace in prayer, and find it as needful to speak to God as to breathe. They all live by the same rule, the Word of God, and strive to conform their daily life to its precepts. They have all the same inward experience. Repentance, faith, hope, charity, humility, inward conflict, are things with which they are all more or less acquainted. No wonder they are called "a family."

This family likeness among true believers is a thing that deserves special attention. To my own mind it is one of the strongest indirect evidences of the truth of Christianity

It is one of the greatest proofs of the reality of the work
of the Holy Ghost. Some true Christians live in civilized
countries, and some in the midst of heathen lands. Some
are highly educated, and some are unable to read a letter.
Some are rich and some are poor. Some are Churchmen
and some are Dissenters. Some are old and some are
young. And yet, notwithstanding all this, there is a
marvellous oneness of heart and character among them.
Their joys and their sorrows, their love and their hatred,
their likes and their dislikes, their tastes and their distastes,
their hopes and their fears, are all most curiously alike.
Let others think what they please, I see in all this the
finger of God. His handiwork is always one and the same.
No wonder that true Christians are compared to "a
family."

Take a converted Englishman and a converted Hindoo,
and let them suddenly meet for the first time. I will
engage, if they can understand one another's language,
they will soon find common ground between them, and
feel at home. The one may have been brought up at
Eton and Oxford, and enjoyed every privilege of English
civilization. The other may have been trained in the
midst of gross heathenism, and accustomed to habits, ways,
and manners as unlike the Englishman's as darkness
compared to light. And yet now in half an hour they feel
that they are friends! The Englishman finds that he has
more in common with his Hindoo brother than he has
with many an old college companion or school-fellow!
Who can account for this? How can it be explained?
Nothing can account for it but the unity of the Spirit's
teaching. It is "one touch" of grace (not nature) "that
makes the whole world kin." God's people are in the
highest sense "a family."

This is the family to which I wish to direct the attention
of my readers in this paper. This is the family to which
I want you to belong. I ask you this day to consider it

well, if you never considered it before. I have shown you the Father of the family,—the God and Father of our Lord Jesus Christ. I have shown you the Head and Elder Brother of the family,—the Lord Jesus Himself. I have shown you the features and characteristics of the family. Its members have all great marks of resemblance. Once more I say, consider it well.

Outside this family, remember, there is no salvation. None but those who belong to it, according to the Bible, are in the way that leads to heaven. The salvation of our souls does not depend on union with one Church or separation from another. They are miserably deceived who think that it does, and will find it out to their cost one day, except they awake. No! the life of our souls depends on something far more important. This is life eternal, to be a member of "the whole family in heaven and earth."

II. I will now pass on to the second thing which I promised to consider. *What is the present position* of the whole family in heaven and earth ?

The family to which I am directing the attention of my readers this day is divided into two great parts. Each part has its own residence or dwelling-place. Part of the family is in heaven, and part is on earth. For the present the two parts are entirely separated from one another. But they form one body in the sight of God, though resident in two places ; and their union is sure to take place one day.

Two places, be it remembered, and two only, contain the family of God. The Bible tells us of no third habitation. There is no such thing as purgatory, whatever some Christians may think fit to say. There is no house of purifying, training, or probation for those who are not true Christians when they die. Oh no ! There are but two parts of the family,—the part that is seen and the part that is unseen, the part that is in "heaven" and the part that is,

on "earth." The members of the family that are not in
heaven are on earth, and those that are not on earth are
in heaven. Two parts, and two only! Two places, and
two only! Let this never be forgotten.

Some of God's family are safe *in heaven*. They are at
rest in that place which the Lord Jesus expressly calls
"Paradise." (Luke xxiii. 43.) They have finished their
course. They have fought their battle. They have done
their appointed work. They have learned their lessons.
They have carried their cross. They have passed through
the waves of this troublesome world and reached the
harbour. Little as we know about them, we know that
they are happy. They are no longer troubled by sin and
temptation. They have said good-bye for ever to poverty
and anxiety, to pain and sickness, to sorrow and tears.
They are with Christ Himself, who loved them and gave
Himself for them, and in His company they must needs
be happy. (Phil. i. 23.) They have nothing to fear in
looking back to the past. They have nothing to dread in
looking forward to things to come. Three things only are
lacking to make their happiness complete. These three
are the second advent of Christ in glory, the resurrection
of their own bodies, and the gathering together of all
believers. And of these three things they are sure.

Some of God's family are still *upon earth*. They are
scattered to and fro in the midst of a wicked world, a few
in one place and a few in another. All are more or less
occupied in the same way, according to the measure of
their grace. All are running a race, doing a work, warring
a warfare, carrying a cross, striving against sin, resisting
the devil, crucifying the flesh, struggling against the world,
witnessing for Christ, mourning over their own hearts,
hearing, reading, and praying, however feebly, for the life
of their souls. Each is often disposed to think no cross so
heavy as his own, no work so difficult, no heart so hard.
But each and all hold on their way,—a wonder to the

ignorant world around them, and often a wonder to themselves.

But, however divided God's family may be at present in dwelling-place and local habitation, it is still one family. Both parts of it are still one in character, one in possessions, and one in relation to God. The part in heaven has not so much superiority over the part on earth as at first sight may appear. The difference between the two is only one of degree.

(*a*) Both parts of the family love the same Saviour, and delight in the same perfect will of God. But the part on earth loves with much imperfection and infirmity, and lives by faith, not by sight.—The part in heaven loves without weakness, or doubt, or distraction. It walks by sight and not by faith, and sees what it once believed.

(*b*) Both parts of the family are saints. But the saints on earth are often poor weary pilgrims, who find the "flesh lusting against the spirit and the spirit lusting against the flesh, so that they cannot do the things they would." (Gal. v. 17.) They live in the midst of an evil world, and are often sick of themselves and of the sin they see around them.—The saints in heaven, on the contrary, are delivered from the world, the flesh, and the devil, and enjoy a glorious liberty. They are called "the spirits of just men made perfect." (Heb. xii. 23.)

(*c*) Both parts of the family are alike God's children. But the children in heaven have learned all their lessons, have finished their appointed tasks, have begun an eternal holiday.—The children on earth are still at school. They are daily learning wisdom, though slowly and with much trouble, and often needing to be reminded of their past lessons by chastisement and the rod. Their holidays are yet to come.

(*d*) Both parts of the family are alike God's soldiers. But the soldiers on earth are yet militant. Their warfare is not accomplished. Their fight is not over. They need every day to put on the whole armour of God.—The soldiers in heaven are all triumphant. No enemy can hurt them now. No fiery dart can reach them. Helmet and shield may both be laid aside. They may at last say to the sword of the Spirit, "Rest and be still." They may at length sit down, and need not to watch and stand on their guard.

(2) Last, but not least, both parts of the family are alike safe and secure. Wonderful as this may sound, it is true. Christ cares as much for His members on earth as His members in heaven. You might as well think to pluck the stars out of heaven, as to pluck one saint, however feeble, out of Christ's hand. Both parts of the family are alike secured by "an everlasting covenant ordered in all things and sure." (2 Sam. xxiii. 5.) The members on earth, through the burden of the flesh and the dimness of their faith, may neither see, nor know, nor feel their own safety. But they are safe, though they may not see it. The whole family is "kept by the power of God, through faith unto salvation." (1 Peter i. 5.) The members yet on the road are as secure as the members who have got home. Not one shall be found missing at the last day. The words of the Christian poet shall be found strictly true:—

> "More happy, but not more secure,
> The glorified spirits in heaven."

Before I leave this part of my subject, I ask every reader of this paper to understand thoroughly the present position of God's family, and to form a just estimate of it. Learn not to measure its numbers or its privileges by what you see with your eyes. You see only a small body of believers in this present time. But you must not forget that a great company has got safe to heaven already, and that when all are assembled at the last day they will be "a multitude which no man can number." (Rev. vii. 9.)

You only see that part of the family which is struggling on earth. You must never forget that the greater part of the family has got home and is resting in heaven.—You see the militant part, but not the triumphant. You see the part that is carrying the cross, but not the part which is safe in Paradise. The family of God is far more rich and glorious than you suppose. Believe me, it is no small thing to belong to the "whole family in heaven and earth."

III. I will now pass on to the last thing which I promised to consider.—*What are the future prospects* of the whole family in heaven and earth?

The future prospects of a family! What a vast amount of uncertainty these words open up when we look at any family now in the world! How little we can tell of the things coming on any of us! What a mercy that we do not know the sorrows and trials and separations through which our beloved children may have to pass, when we have left the world! It is a mercy that we do not know "what a day may bring forth," and a far greater mercy that we do not know what may happen in twenty years. (Prov. xxvii. 1.) Alas, foreknowledge of the future pros-pects of our belongings would spoil many a family gathering, and fill the whole party with gloom!

Think how many a fine boy, who is now the delight of his parents, will by and by walk in the prodigal's footsteps, and never return home! Think how many a fair daughter, the joy of a mother's heart, will follow the bent of her self-will after a few years, and insist on some miserably mistaken marriage! Think how disease and pain will often lay low the loveliest of a family circle, and make her life a burden and weariness to herself, if not to others! Think of the endless breaches and divisions arising out of money matters! Alas, there is many a life-long quarrel about a few pounds, between those who once played together in the same nursery! Think of these things. The "future prospects" of many a family which meets together every Christmas are a solemn and serious subject. Hundreds, to say the least, are gathering together for the last time: when they part, they will never meet again.

But, thank God, there is one great family whose "prospects" are very different. It is the family of which I am speaking in this paper, and commending to your attention. The future prospects of the family of God are not uncertain. They are good, and only good,—happy, and only happy. Listen to me, and I will try to set them in order before you.

(a) The members of God's family shall all be *brought safe home* one day. Here upon earth they may be scattered, tried, tossed with tempests, and bowed down with afflictions. But not one of them shall perish. (John x. 28.) The weakest lamb shall not be left to perish in the wilderness: the feeblest child shall not be missing when the muster-roll is brought out at the last day. In spite of the world, the flesh, and the devil, the whole family shall get home. "If, when we were enemies, we were reconciled to God by the death of His Son, much more, being reconciled, we shall be saved by His life." (Rom. v. 10.)

(b) The members of God's family *shall all have glorious bodies* one day. When the Lord Jesus Christ comes the second time, the dead saints shall all be raised and the living shall all be changed. They shall no longer have a vile mortal body, full of weaknesses and infirmities: they shall have a body like that of their risen Lord, without the slightest liability to sickness and pain. They shall no longer be clogged and hindered by an aching frame, when they want to serve God: they shall be able to serve Him night and day without weariness, and to attend upon Him without distraction. The former things will have passed away. That word will be fulfilled, "I make all things new." (Rev. xxi. 5.)

(c) The members of God's family shall all be *gathered into one company* one day. It matters nothing where they have lived or where they have died. They may have been separated from one another both by time and space. One may have lived in tents, with Abraham, Isaac, and Jacob, and another travelled by railway in our own day. One may have laid his bones in an Australian desert, and another may have been buried in an English churchyard. It makes no difference. All shall be gathered together from north and south, and east and west, and meet in one happy assembly, to part no more. The earthly partings of God's family are only for a few days. Their meeting is for eternity. It matters little where we live. It is a time of scattering now, and not of gathering. It matters little where we die. All graves are equally near to Paradise. But it does matter much whether we belong to God's family. If we do we are sure to meet again at last.

(d) The members of God's family shall all be *united in mind and judgment* one day. They are not so now about many little things. About the things needful to salvation there is a marvellous unity among them. About many speculative points in religion, about forms of worship and Church government, they often sadly disagree. But there shall be no disagreement among them one day. Ephraim shall no longer vex Judah, nor Judah Ephraim. Churchmen shall no more quarrel with Dissenters, nor Dissenters with Churchmen. Partial knowledge and dim vision shall be at an end for ever. Divisions and separations, misunderstandings and misconstructions, shall be buried and forgotten. As there shall only be one language, so there shall only be one opinion. At last, after six thousand years of strife and jangling, perfect unity and harmony shall be found. A family shall at length be shown to angels and men in which all are of one mind.

(e) The members of God's family shall all be *perfected*

in holiness one day. They are not literally perfect now, although "complete in Christ." (Col. ii. 10.) Though born again, and renewed after the image of Christ, they offend and fall short in many things. (James iii. 2.) None know it better than they do themselves. It is their grief and sorrow that they do not love God more heartily and serve Him more faithfully. But they shall be completely freed from all corruption one day. They shall rise again at Christ's second appearing without any of the infirmities which cleave to them in their lives. Not a single evil temper or corrupt inclination shall be found in them. They shall be presented by their Head to the Father, without spot, or wrinkle, or any such thing, —perfectly holy and without blemish,—fair as the moon, and clear as the sun. (Eph. v. 27; Cant. v. 10.) Grace, even now, is a beautiful thing, when it lives, and shines, and flourishes in the midst of imperfection. But how much more beautiful will grace appear when it is seen pure, unmixed, unmingled, and alone! And it shall be seen so when Christ comes to be glorified in His saints at the last day.

(*f*) Last, but not least, the members of God's family shall all be *eternally provided for* one day. When the affairs of this sinful world are finally wound up and settled, there shall be an everlasting portion for all the sons and daughters of the Lord almighty. Not even the weakest of them shall be overlooked and forgotten. There shall be something for everyone, according to his measure. The smallest vessel of grace, as well as the greatest, shall be filled to the brim with glory. The precise nature of that glory and reward it would be folly to pretend to describe. It is a thing which eye has not seen, nor mind of man conceived. Enough for us to know that each member of God's family, when he awakes up after His Master's likeness, shall be "satisfied." (Psalm xvii. 15.) Enough, above all, to know that their joy, and glory, and reward shall be for ever. What they receive in the day of the Lord they will never lose. The inheritance reserved for them, when they come of age, is "incorruptible, undefiled, and fadeth not away." (1 Peter i. 4.)

These prospects of God's family are great realities. They are not vague shadowy talk of man's invention. They are real true things, and will be seen as such before long. They deserve your serious consideration. Examine them well.

Look round the families of earth with which you are acquainted, the richest, the greatest, the noblest, the happiest. Where will you find one among them all which can show prospects to compare with those of which you have just heard. The earthly riches, in many a case, will be gone in a hundred years hence. The noble blood, in many a case, will not prevent some disgraceful deed staining the family name. The happiness, in many a case, will be found hollow and seeming. Few, indeed, are the homes which have not a secret sorrow, or "a skeleton in the closet." Whether for present possessions or future prospects, there is no family so well off as "the whole family in heaven and earth." Whether you look at what they have now, or will have hereafter, there is no family like the family of God.

My task is done. My paper is drawing to a close. It only remains to close it with a few words of practical application. Give me your attention for the last time. May God bless what I am going to say to the good of your soul!

(1) I ask you a plain question. Take it with you to every family gathering which you join at any season of the year. Take it with you, and amidst all your happiness make time for thinking about it. It is a simple question, but a solemn one,—*Do you yet belong to the family of God?*

To the family of God, remember! This is the point of my question. It is no answer to say that you are a Protestant, or a Churchman, or a Dissenter. I want to hear of something more and better than that. I want you to have some soul-satisfying and soul-saving religion, —a religion that will give you peace while you live, and hope when you die. To have such peace and hope you must be something more than a Protestant, or a Churchman, or a Dissenter. You must belong to "the family of God." Thousands around you do not belong to it, I can well believe. But that is no reason why you should not.

If you do not yet belong to God's family, I invite you this day to join it without delay. Open your eyes to see the value of your soul, the sinfulness of sin, the holiness of God, the danger of your present condition, the absolute necessity of a mighty change. Open your eyes to see these things, and repent this very day.—Open your eyes to see the great Head of God's family, even Christ Jesus, waiting to save your soul. See how He has loved you, lived for you, died for you, risen again for you, and obtained complete redemption for you. See how He offers you free, full, immediate pardon, if you will believe in Him. Open your eyes to see these things. Seek Christ at once. Come and believe on Him, and commit your soul to His keeping this very day.

I know nothing of your family or past history. I know not where you go to spend your leisure weeks, or what company you are going to be in. But I am bold to say, that if you join the family of God you will find it the best and happiest family in the world.

(2) If you really belong to the whole family in heaven and earth, count up your privileges, and *learn to be more thankful*. Think what a mercy it is to have something which the world can neither give nor take away,—something which makes you independent of sickness or poverty, —something which is your own for evermore. The old

family fireside will soon be cold and tenantless. The old family gatherings will soon be past and gone for ever. The loving faces we now delight to gaze on are rapidly leaving us. The cheerful voices which now welcome us will soon be silent in the grave. But, thank God, if we belong to Christ's family there is a better gathering yet to come. Let us often think of it, and be thankful!

The family gathering of all God's people will make amends for all that their religion now costs them. A meeting where none are missing,—a meeting where there are no gaps and empty places,—a meeting where there are no tears,—a meeting where there is no parting,—such a meeting as this is worth a fight and a struggle. And such a meeting is yet to come to "the whole family in heaven and earth."

In the meantime let us strive to live worthy of the family to which we belong. Let us labour to do nothing that may cause our Father's house to be spoken against. Let us endeavour to make our Master's name beautiful by our temper, conduct, and conversation. Let us love as brethren, and abhor all quarrels. Let us behave as if the honour of "the family" depended on our behaviour.

So living, by the grace of God, we shall make our calling and election sure, both to ourselves and others. So living, we may hope to have an abundant entrance, and to enter harbour in full sail, whenever we change earth for heaven. (2 Peter i. 11.) So living, we shall recommend our Father's family to others, and perhaps by God's blessing incline them to say, "We will go with you."

XVII

OUR HOME!

"Lord, Thou hast been our dwelling-place in all generations."
PSALM XC. 1.

THERE are two reasons why the text which heads this
paper should ring in our hearts with special power. It is
the first verse of a deeply solemn Psalm,—the first bar of
a wondrous piece of spiritual music. How others feel
when they read the ninetieth Psalm I cannot tell. It
always makes me lean back in my chair and think.

For one thing, this ninetieth Psalm is the only Psalm
composed by "Moses, the man of God." * It expresses
that holy man's feelings, as he saw the whole generation
whom he had led forth from Egypt, dying in the wilderness.
Year after year he saw that fearful judgment fulfilling,
which Israel brought on itself by unbelief:—"Your
carcases shall fall in this wilderness; and all that were
numbered of you, according to your whole number, from
twenty years old and upward, which have murmured

---

* I am quite aware that I have no direct authority for this statement,
except the prefatory heading at the beginning of the Psalm. However
ancient those headings may be, it is agreed among learned men that
they were not given by inspiration, and must not be regarded as a part
of God's Word. There is, nevertheless, a curious amount of agreement
among critics, that in the case of this ninetieth Psalm the tradition
about its authorship is not without foundation.

against Me, doubtless ye shall not come into the land."
(Num. xiv. 29.) One after another he saw the heads of
the families whom he had led forth from Egypt, laying
their bones in the desert. For forty long years he saw
the strong, the swift, the wise, the tender, the beautiful,
who had crossed the Red Sea with him in triumph, cut
down and withering like grass. For forty years he saw
his companions continually changing, consuming, and
passing away. Who can wonder that he should say,
"Lord, Thou art our dwelling-place." We are all pilgrims
and strangers upon earth, and there is none abiding.
"Lord, Thou art our home."

For another thing, the ninetieth Psalm forms part of
the Burial Service of the Church of England. Whatever
fault men may find with the Prayer-book, I think no one
can deny the singular beauty of the Burial Service.
Beautiful are the texts which it puts into the minister's
mouth as he meets the coffin at the churchyard gate, and
leads the mourners into God's house. Beautiful is the
chapter from the first Epistle to the Corinthians about the
resurrection of the body. Beautiful are the sentences and
prayers appointed to be read as the body is laid in its
long home. But specially beautiful, to my mind, are the
Psalms which are selected for reading when the mourners
have just taken their places in church. I know nothing
which sounds so soothing, solemnizing, heart-touching, and
moving to man's spirit, at that trying moment, as the
wondrous utterance of the old inspired law-giver: "Lord,
Thou hast been our dwelling-place." "Lord, Thou art our
home."

I want to draw from these words two thoughts that may
do the readers of this paper some good. An English home
is famous all over the world for its happiness and comfort.
It is a little bit of heaven left upon earth. But even an
English home is not for ever. The family nest is sure to
be taken down, and its inmates are sure to be scattered,

Bear with me for a few short minutes, while I try to set before you the best, truest, and happiest home.

I. The first thought that I will offer you is this:—I will show you *what the world is*.

It is a beautiful world in many respects, I freely admit. Its seas and rivers, its sunrises and sunsets, its mountains and valleys, its harvests and its forests, its fruits and its flowers, its days and its nights, all, all are beautiful in their way. Cold and unfeeling must that heart be which never finds a day in the year when it can admire anything in nature! But beautiful as the world is, there are many things in it to remind us that it is not home. It is an inn, a tent, a tabernacle, a lodging, a training school. But it is not home.

(*a*) It is a *changing* world. All around us is continually moving, altering, and passing away. Families, properties, landlords, tenants, farmers, labourers, tradesmen, all are continually on the move. To find the same name in the same dwelling for three generations running is so uncommon, that it is the exception and not the rule. A world so full of change cannot be called home.

(*b*) It is a *trying and disappointing* world. Who ever lives to be fifty years old and does not find to his cost that it is so? Trials in married life and trials in single life,—trials in children and trials in brothers and sisters, —trials in money matters and trials in health,—how many they are! Their name is legion. And not the tenth part of them perhaps ever comes to light. Few indeed are the families which have not "a skeleton in the closet." A world so full of trial and disappointment cannot be called home.

(*c*) It is a *dying* world. Death is continually about us and near us, and meets us at every turn. Few are the family gatherings, when Christmas comes round, in which there are not some empty chairs and vacant places. Few

are the men and women, past thirty, who could not number
a long list of names, deeply cut for ever in their hearts,
but names of beloved ones now dead and gone. Where
are our fathers and mothers? Where are our ministers
and teachers? Where are our brothers and sisters?
Where are our husbands and wives? Where are our
neighbours and friends? Where are the old grey-headed
worshippers, whose reverent faces we remember so well,
when we first went to God's house? Where are the boys
and girls we played with when we went to school? How
many must reply, "Dead, dead, dead! The daisies are
growing over their graves, and we are left alone." Surely
a world so full of death can never be called a home.

(d) It is a *scattering and dividing* world. Families are
continually breaking up, and going in different directions.
How rarely do the members of a family ever meet together again, after the surviving parent is laid in the grave!
The band of union seems snapped, and nothing welds it
again. The cement seems withdrawn from the parts of
the building, and the whole principle of cohesion is lost.
How often some miserable squabble about trinkets, or
some wretched wrangle about money, makes a breach that
is never healed, and, like a crack in china, though riveted,
can never be quite cured! Rarely indeed do those who
played in the same nursery lie down at length in the same
churchyard, or keep peace with one another till they die.
A world so full of division can never be home.

These are ancient things. It is useless to be surprised
at them. They are the bitter fruit of sin, and the sorrowful
consequence of the fall. Change, trial, death, and division,
all entered into the world when Adam and Eve trans-
gressed. We must not murmur. We must not fret. We
must not complain. We must accept the situation in
which we find ourselves. We must each do our best to
lighten the sorrows, and increase the comforts of our position. We must steadily resolve to make the best of

everybody and everything around us. But we must never, never, never, forget that the world is not home.

Are you young? Does all around and before you seem bright, and cheerful, and happy? Do you secretly think in your own mind that I take too gloomy a view of the world? Take care. You will not say so by and by. Be wise betimes. Learn to moderate your expectations. Depend on it, the less you expect from people and things here below the happier you will be.

Are you prosperous in the world? Have death, and sickness, and disappointment, and poverty, and family troubles, passed over your door up to this time, and not come in? Are you secretly saying to yourself, "Nothing can hurt me much. I shall die quietly in my bed, and see no sorrow." Take care. You are not yet in harbour. A sudden storm of unexpected trouble may make you change your note. Set not your affection on things below. Hold them with a very loose hand, and be ready to surrender them at a moment's notice. Use your prosperity well while you have it; but lean not all your weight on it, lest it break suddenly and pierce your hand.

Have you a happy home? Are you going to spend Christmas round a family hearth, where sickness, and death, and poverty, and partings, and quarrellings, have never yet been seen? Be thankful for it: oh, be thankful for it! A really happy Christian home is the nearest approach to heaven on earth. But take care. This state of things will not last for ever. It must have an end; and if you are wise, you will never forget that—"the time is short: it remaineth, that both they that have wives be as though they had none; and they that weep, as though they wept not; and they that rejoice, as though they rejoiced not; and they that buy, as though they possessed not; and they that use this world, as not abusing it; for the fashion of this world passeth away." (1 Cor. vii. 29—31.)

II. The second thought that I will offer you is this: I will show you *what Christ is, even in this life, to true Christians.*

Heaven, beyond doubt, is the final home in which a true Christian will dwell at last. Towards that he is daily travelling: nearer to that he is daily coming. " We know that if our earthly house of this tabernacle were dissolved, we have a building of God, an house not made with hands, eternal in the heavens." (2 Cor. v. 1.) Body and soul united once more, renewed, beautified, and perfected, will live for ever in the Father's great house in heaven. To that home we have not yet come. We are not yet in heaven.

But is there meanwhile no home for our souls? Is there no spiritual dwelling-place to which we may continually repair in this desolate world, and, repairing to it, find rest and peace? Thank God, there is no difficulty in finding an answer to that question. There is a home provided for all labouring and heavy-laden souls, and that home is Christ. To know Christ by faith, to live the life of faith in Him, to abide in Him daily by faith, to flee to Him in every storm of conscience, to use Him as our refuge in every day of trouble, to employ Him as our Priest, Confessor, Absolver, and spiritual Director, every morning and evening in our lives,—this is to be at home spiritually, even before we die. To all sinners of mankind who by faith use Christ in this fashion, Christ is in the highest sense a dwelling-place. They can say with truth, " We are pilgrims and strangers on earth, and yet we have a home."

Of all the emblems and figures under which Christ is set before man, I know few more cheering and comforting than the one before us. Home is one of the sweetest, tenderest words in the English language. Home is the place with which our pleasantest thoughts are closely bound up. All that the best and happiest home is to its inmates, that Christ is to the soul that believes on Him. In the midst of a dying, changing, disappointing world, a true Christian has always something which no power on earth can take away. Morning, noon, and night, he has near him a living Refuge,—a living home for his soul. You may rob him of life, and liberty, and money; you may take from him health, and lands, and house, and friends; but, do what you will, you cannot rob him of his home. Like those humblest of God's creatures which carry their shells on their backs, wherever they are, so the Christian, wherever he goes, carries his home. No wonder that holy Baxter sings,—

> "What if in prison I must dwell,
> May I not then converse with Thee?
> Save me from sin, Thy wrath, and hell,—
> Call me Thy child, and I am free!"

(*a*) No home like Christ! In Him there is *room for all*, and room for all sorts. None are unwelcome guests and visitors, and none are refused admission. The door is always on the latch, and never bolted. The best robe, the fatted calf, the ring, the shoes are always ready for all comers. What though in time past you have been the vilest of the vile, a servant of sin, an enemy of all righteousness, a Pharisee of Pharisees, a Sadducee of Sadducees, a publican of publicans? It matters nothing: there is yet hope. All may be pardoned, forgiven, and forgotten. There is a home and refuge where your soul may be admitted this very day. That home is Christ. "Come unto Me," He cries: "Knock, and it shall be opened unto you." (Matt. xi. 28; vii. 7.)

(*b*) No home like Christ! In Him there is boundless and unwearied *mercy for all*, even after admission. None are rejected and cast forth again after probation, because they are too weak and bad to stay. Oh, no! Whom He receives, them He always keeps. Where He begins, there He

makes a good end. Whom He admits, them He at once
fully justifies. Whom He justifies, them He also sanctifies.
Whom He sanctifies, them He also glorifies. No hopeless
characters are ever sent away from His house. No men
or women are ever found too bad to heal and renew.
Nothing is too hard for Him to do who made the world
out of nothing. He who is Himself the Home, hath said
it, and will stand to it: "Him that cometh unto Me, I
will in no wise cast out." (John vi. 37.)

(c) No home like Christ! In Him there is unvarying
kindness, patience, and gentle dealing for all. He is not
"an austere man," but "meek and lowly in heart." (Matt.
xi. 29.) None who apply to Him are ever treated roughly,
or made to feel that their company is not welcome. A
feast of fat things is always provided for them. The holy
Spirit is placed in their hearts, and dwells in them as in a
temple. Leading, guiding, and instruction are daily provided for them. If they err, they are brought back into
the right way; if they fall, they are raised again; if they
transgress wilfully, they are chastised to make them better.
But the rule of the whole house is love.

(d) No home like Christ! In Him there is *no change.*
From youth to age He loves all who come to Him, and is
never tired of doing them good. Earthly homes, alas, are
full of fickleness and uncertainty. Favour is deceitful.
Courtesy and civility are often on men's lips, while inwardly they are weary of your company and wish you were
gone. You seldom know how long your presence is welcome,
or to what extent your friends really care to see you. But
it is not so with Christ. "He is the same yesterday, and
to-day, and for ever." (Heb. xiii. 8.)

(e) No home like Christ! Communion once begun with
Him shall *never be broken off.* Once joined to the Lord
by faith, you are joined to Him for an endless eternity.
Earthly homes always come to an end sooner or later:
the dear old furniture is sold and dispersed; the dear old

heads of the family are gathered to their fathers; the dear old nest is pulled to pieces. But it is not so with Christ. Faith will at length be swallowed up in sight: hope shall at last be changed into certainty. We shall see one day with our eyes, and no longer need to believe. We shall be moved from the lower chamber to the upper, and from the outer court to the Holy of Holies. But once in Christ, we shall never be out of Christ. Once let our name be placed in the Lamb's book of life, and we belong to a home which shall continue for evermore.

(1) And now, before I conclude, let me ask every reader of this paper a plain question. *Have you got a home for your soul?* Is it safe? Is it pardoned? Is it justified? Is it prepared to meet God? With all my heart I wish you a happy home. But remember my question. Amidst the greetings and salutations of home, amidst the meetings and partings, amidst the laughter and merriment, amidst the joys and sympathies and affections, think, think of my question,—Have you got a home for your soul?

Our earthly homes will soon be closed for ever. Time hastens on with giant strides. Old age and death will be upon us before many years have passed away. Oh, seek an abiding home for the better part of you,—the part that never dies! Before it be too late seek a home for your soul.

Seek Christ, that you may be safe. Woe to the man who is found outside the ark when the flood of God's wrath bursts at length on a sinful world!—Seek Christ, that you may be happy. None have a real right to be cheerful, merry, light-hearted, and at ease, excepting those who have got a home for their souls. Once more I say, Seek Christ without delay.

(2) If Christ is the home of your soul, *accept a friendly caution.* Beware of being ashamed of your home in any place or company.

The man who is ashamed of the home where he was

born, the parents that brought him up when a baby, the brothers and sisters that played with him,—that man, as a general rule, may be set down as a mean and despicable being. But what shall we say of the man who is ashamed of Him who died for him on the cross? What shall we say of the man who is ashamed of his religion, ashamed of his Master, ashamed of his home?

Take care that you are not that man. Whatever others around you please to think, do you never be ashamed of being a Christian. Let them laugh, and mock, and jest, and scoff, if they will. They will not scoff in the hour of death and in the day of judgment. Hoist your flag; show your colours; nail them to the mast. Of drinking, gambling, lying, swearing, Sabbath-breaking, idleness, pride, you may well be ashamed. Of Bible-reading, praying, and belonging to Christ, you have no cause to be ashamed at all. Let those laugh that win. A good soldier is never ashamed of his Queen's colours, and his uniform. Take care that you are never ashamed of your Master. Never be ashamed of your home.

(3) If Christ is the home of your soul, *accept a piece of friendly advice.* Let nothing tempt you to stray away from home.

The world and the devil will often try hard to make you drop your religion for a little season, and walk with them. Your own flesh will whisper that there is no danger in going a little with them, and that it can do you no mighty harm. Take care, I say: take care when you are tempted in this fashion. Take care of looking back, like Lot's wife. Forsake not your home.

There are pleasures in sin no doubt, but they are not real and satisfactory. There is an excitement and short-lived enjoyment in the world's ways, beyond all question, but it is joy that leaves a bitter taste behind it. Oh, no! wisdom's ways alone are ways of pleasantness, and wisdom's paths alone are paths of peace. Cleave to them strictly and turn not aside. Follow the Lamb whithersoever He goes. Stick to Christ and His rule, through evil report and good report. The longer you live the happier you will find His service: the more ready will you be to sing, in the highest sense, "There is no place like home."

(4) If Christ is the home of your soul, *accept a hint about your duty.* Mind that you take every opportunity of telling others about your happiness. Tell them THAT, wherever you are. Tell them that you have a happy home.

Tell them, if they will hear you, that you find Christ a good Master, and Christ's service a happy service. Tell them that His yoke is easy, and His burden is light. Tell them that, whatever the devil may say, the rules of your home are not grievous, and that your Master pays far better wages than the world does! Try to do a little good wherever you are. Try to enlist more inmates for your happy home. Say to your friends and relatives, if they will listen, as one did of old, "Come with us, and we will do you good; for the Lord hath spoken good concerning Israel." (Numbers x. 29.)

XVIII

HEIRS OF GOD

" As many as are led by the Spirit of God, they are the sons of God.

" For ye have not received the spirit of bondage again to fear; but ye have received the Spirit of adoption, whereby we cry, Abba, Father.

" The Spirit itself beareth witness with our spirit, that we are the children of God:

" And if children, then heirs; heirs of God, and joint heirs with Christ; if so be that we suffer with Him, that we may be also glorified together."—(ROMANS viii. 14—17.)

THE people of whom St. Paul speaks in the verses before our eyes are the richest people upon earth. It must needs be so. They are called "heirs of God, and joint heirs with Christ."

The inheritance of these people is the only inheritance *really worth having.* All others are unsatisfying and disappointing. They bring with them many cares. They cannot cure an aching heart, or lighten a heavy conscience. They cannot keep off family troubles. They cannot prevent sicknesses, bereavements, separations, and deaths. But there is no disappointment among the "heirs of God."

The inheritance I speak of is the only inheritance *which can be kept for ever.* All others must be left in the hour of death, if they have not been taken away before. The

owners of millions of pounds can carry nothing with them
beyond the grave. But it is not so with the "heirs of God."
Their inheritance is eternal.

The inheritance I speak of is the only inheritance *which
is within every body's reach.* Most men can never obtain
riches and greatness, though they labour hard for them all
their lives. But glory, honour, and eternal life, are offered
to every man freely, who is willing to accept them on God's
terms. "Whosoever will," may be an "heir of God, and
joint heir with Christ."

If any reader of this paper wishes to have a portion of
this inheritance, let him know that he must be a member
of that one family on earth to which it belongs, and that
is the family of all true Christians. You must become
one of God's children on earth, if you desire to have glory
in heaven. I write this paper in order to persuade you
to become a child of God this day, if you are not one
already. I write it to persuade you to make sure work
that you are one, if at present you have only a vague
hope, and nothing more. None but true Christians are
the children of God! None but the children of God are
heirs of God! Give me your attention, while I try to
unfold to you these things, and to show the lessons contained in the verses which head this page.

I. Let me show *the relation of all true Christians
to God. They are "sons of God."*

II. Let me show *the special evidences of this relation.*
True Christians are "*led by the Spirit.*" They have "*the
Spirit of adoption.*" They have the "*witness of the
Spirit.*" They "*suffer with Christ.*"

III. Let me show *the privileges of this relation.*
True Christians are "*heirs of God, and joint heirs with
Christ.*"

1. First let me show *the relation of all true Christians to God.* They are God's "Sons."

I know no higher and more comfortable word that could have been chosen. To be servants of God,—to be subjects, soldiers, disciples, friends,—all these are excellent titles; but to be the "sons" of God is a step higher still. What says the Scripture? "The servant abideth not in the house for ever, but the Son abideth ever." (John viii. 35.)

To be son of the rich and noble in this world,—to be son of the princes and kings of the earth,—this is commonly reckoned a great temporal advantage and privilege. But to be a son of the King of kings, and Lord of lords, —to be a son of the High and Holy One, who inhabiteth eternity,—this is something far higher. And yet this is the portion of every true Christian.

The son of an earthly parent looks naturally to his father for affection, maintenance, provision, and education. There is a home always open to him. There is a love which, generally speaking, no bad conduct can completely extinguish. All these are things belonging even to the sonship of this world. Think then how great is the privilege of that poor sinner of mankind who can say of God, "He is my Father."

But HOW can sinful men like ourselves become sons of God? When do we enter into this glorious relationship? We are not the sons of God by nature. We were not born so when we came into the world. No man has a natural right to look to God as his Father. It is a vile heresy to say that he has. Men are said to be born poets and painters,—but men are never born sons of God. The Epistle to the Ephesians tells us, "Ye were by nature children of wrath, even as others." (Ephes. ii. 3.) The Epistle of St. John says, "The children of God are manifest, and the children of the devil: whosoever doeth not righteousness is not of God." (1 John iii. 10.) The Catechism of the Church of England wisely follows the doctrine of the Bible, and teaches us to say, "By nature we are born in sin, and children of wrath." Yes : we are all rather children of the devil, than children of God ! Sin is indeed hereditary, and runs in the family of Adam. Grace is anything but hereditary, and holy men have not, as a matter of course, holy sons. How then and when does this mighty change and translation come upon men ? When and in what manner do sinners become the "sons and daughters of the Lord Almighty ? " (2 Cor vi. 18.)

Men become sons of God in the day that the Spirit leads them to believe on Jesus Christ for salvation, and not before.* What says the Epistle to the Galatians ? "Ye are all the children of God by faith in Christ Jesus." (Gal. iii. 26.) What says the first Epistle to the Corinthians ? "Of Him are ye in Christ Jesus." (1 Cor. i. 30.) What says the Gospel of John ? "As many as received Christ, to them gave He power (or privilege) to become the sons of God, even to them that believe on His name." (John i. 12.) Faith unites the sinner to the Son of God, and makes him one of His members. Faith makes him one of those in whom the Father sees no spot, and is well-pleased. Faith marries him to the beloved Son of God, and entitles him to be reckoned among the sons. Faith gives him "fellowship with the Father and the Son." (1 John i. 3.) Faith grafts him into the Father's family, and opens up to him a room in the Father's house. Faith gives him life instead of death, and makes him, instead of being a servant, a son. Show me a man that has this faith, and, whatever be his church or denomination, I say that he is a son of God.

This is one of those points we should never forget. You and I know nothing of a man's sonship *until he believes*. No doubt the sons of God are foreknown and chosen from

---

* The reader will of course understand that I am not speaking now of children who die in infancy, or of persons who live and die idiots.

all eternity, and predestinated to adoption. But, remember, it is not till they are called in due time, and believe,—it is not till then that you and I can be certain they are sons. It is not till they repent and believe, that the angels of God rejoice over them. The angels cannot read the book of God's election: they know not who are "His hidden ones" in the earth. (Ps. lxxxiii. 3.) They rejoice over no man till he believes. But when they see some poor sinner repenting and believing, then there is joy among them,— joy that one more brand is plucked from the burning, and one more son and heir born again to the Father in heaven. (Luke xv. 10.) But once more I say, you and I know nothing certain about a man's sonship to God *until he believes on Christ.*

I warn you to beware of the delusive notion that all men and women are alike children of God, whether they have faith in Christ or not. It is a wild theory which many are clinging to in these days, but one which cannot be proved out of the Word of God. It is a perilous dream, with which many are trying to soothe themselves, but one from which there will be a fearful waking up at the last day.

That God in a certain sense is the universal Father of all mankind, I do not pretend to deny. He is the Great First Cause of all things. He is the Creator of all mankind, and in Him alone, all men, whether Christians or heathens, "live and move and have their being." All this is unquestionably true. In this sense Paul told the Athenians, a poet of their own had truly said, "we are His offspring." (Acts xvii. 28.) But this sonship gives no man a title to heaven. The sonship which we have by creation is one which belongs to stones, trees, beasts, or even to the devils, as much as to us. (Job i. 6.)

That God loves all mankind with a love of pity and compassion, I do not deny. "His tender mercies are over all His works."—"He is not willing that any should perish, but that all should come to repentance."—"He has no pleasure in the death of him that dieth." All this I admit to the full. In this sense our Lord Jesus tells us, " God so loved the world, that He gave His only begotten Son, that whosoever believeth in Him should not perish, but have eternal life." (Ps. cxlv. 9 ; 2 Peter iii. 9 ; Ezek. xviii. 32 ; John iii. 16.)

But that God is a reconciled and pardoning Father to any but the members of His Son Jesus Christ, and that any are members of Jesus Christ who do not believe on Him for salvation,—this is a doctrine which I utterly deny. The holiness and justice of God are both against the doctrine. They make it impossible for sinful men to approach God, excepting through the Mediator. They tell us that God out of Christ is " a consuming fire." (Heb. xii. 29.) The whole system of the new Testament is against the doctrine. That system teaches that no man can claim interest in Christ unless he will receive Him as his Mediator, and believe on Him as his Saviour. Where there is no faith in Christ it is a dangerous error to say that a man may take comfort in God as his Father. God is a reconciled Father to none but the members of Christ.

It is unreasonable to talk of the view I am now upholding as narrow-minded and harsh. The Gospel sets an open door before every man. Its promises are wide and full. Its invitations are earnest and tender. Its requirements are simple and clear. " Only believe on the Lord Jesus Christ, and, whosoever thou art, thou shalt be saved." But to say that proud men, who will not bow their necks to the easy yoke of Christ, and worldly men who are determined to have their own way and their sins,—to say that such men have a right to claim an interest in Christ, and a right to call themselves sons of God, is to say what never can be proved from Scripture. God offers to be their Father ; but He does it on certain distinct terms :—they must draw near to Him through Christ. Christ offers to be their Saviour; but in doing it He makes one simple requirement:—they must commit their souls to Him, and give Him their hearts. They refuse the *terms*, and yet dare to call God their Father! They scorn the *requirement*, and yet dare to hope that Christ will save them! God is to be their Father,—but on their own terms! Christ is to be their Saviour,—but on their own conditions! What can be more unreasonable? What can be more proud? What can be more unholy than such a doctrine as this? Let us beware of it, for it is a common doctrine in these latter days. Let us beware of it, for it is often speciously put forward, and sounds beautiful and charitable in the mouth of poets, novelists, sentimentalists, and tender-hearted women. Let us beware of it, unless we mean to throw aside our Bible altogether, and set up ourselves to be wiser than God. Let us stand fast on the old Scriptural ground: *No sonship to God without Christ! No interest in Christ without faith!*

I would to God there was not so much cause for giving warnings of this kind. I have reason to think they need to be given clearly and unmistakably. There is a school of theology rising up in this day, which appears to me most eminently calculated to promote infidelity, to help the devil, and to ruin souls. It comes to us like Joab to Amasa, with the highest professions of charity, liberality, and love. God is all mercy and love, according to this theology:—His holiness and justice are completely left out of sight! Hell is never spoken of in this theology:—its talk is all of heaven! Damnation is never mentioned:— it is treated as an impossible thing:—all men and women are to be saved! Faith, and the work of the Spirit, are refined away into nothing at all! "Everybody who believes anything has faith! Everybody who thinks anything has the Spirit! Everybody is right! Nobody is wrong! Nobody is to blame for any action he may commit! It is the result of his position It is the effect of circumstances!

He is not accountable for his opinions, any more than for
the colour of his skin! He must be what he is! The
Bible is a very imperfect book! It is old-fashioned!
It is obsolete! We may believe just as much of it as we
please, and no more!"—Of all this theology I warn men
solemnly to beware. In spite of big swelling words about
"liberality," and "charity," and "broad views," and "new
lights," and "freedom from bigotry," and so forth, I do
believe it to be a theology that leads to hell.

(a) *Facts* are directly against the teachers of this theology.
Let them visit Mesopotamia, and see what desolation
reigns where Nineveh and Babylon once stood. Let them
go to the shores of the Dead Sea, and look down into its
mysterious bitter waters. Let them travel in Palestine,
and ask what has turned that fertile country into a
wilderness. Let them observe the wandering Jews, scattered over the face of the world, without a land of their
own, and yet never absorbed among other nations. And
then let them tell us, if they dare, that God is so entirely
a God of mercy and love that He never does and never
will punish sin.

(b) *The conscience of man* is directly against these
teachers. Let them go to the bedside of some dying child of
the world, and try to comfort him with their doctrines. Let
them see if their vaunted theories will calm his gnawing,
restless anxiety about the future, and enable him to depart
in peace. Let them show us, if they can, a few well-
authenticated cases of joy and happiness in death without
Bible promises,—without conversion,—and without that
faith in the blood of Christ, which old-fashioned theology
enjoins. Alas! when men are leaving the world, conscience
makes sad work of the new systems of these latter days.
Conscience is not easily satisfied, in a dying hour, that
there is no such thing as hell.

(c) *Every reasonable conception that we can form of a
future state* is directly against these teachers. Fancy a

heaven which should contain all mankind! Fancy a
heaven in which holy and unholy, pure and impure, good
and bad, would be all gathered together in one confused
mass! What point of union would there be in such a
company? What common bond of harmony and brother-
hood? What common delight in a common service?
What concord, what harmony, what peace, what oneness
of spirit could exist? Surely the mind revolts from the
idea of a heaven in which there would be no distinction
between the righteous and the wicked,—between Pharaoh
and Moses, between Abraham and the Sodomites, between
Paul and Nero, between Peter and Judas Iscariot, between
the man who dies in the act of murder or drunkenness,
and men like Baxter, George Herbert, Wilberforce, and
M'Cheyne! Surely an eternity in such a miserably confused
crowd would be worse than annihilation itself! Surely
such a heaven would be no better than hell!

(d) The *interests of all holiness and morality* are directly
against these teachers. If all men and women alike are
God's children, whatever is the difference between them
in their lives,—and all alike going to heaven, however
different they may be from one another here in the world,
—where is the use of labouring after holiness at all?
What motive remains for living soberly, righteously, and
godly? What does it matter how men conduct themselves,
if all go to heaven, and nobody goes to hell? Surely the
heathen poets and philosophers of Greece and Rome could
tell us something better and wiser than this! Surely a
doctrine which is subversive of holiness and morality,
and takes away all motives to exertion, carries on the face
of it the stamp of its origin. It is of earth, and not of
heaven. It is of the devil, and not of God.

(e) *The Bible* is against these teachers from first to
last. Hundreds of texts might be quoted which are
diametrically opposed to their theories. These texts must
be rejected summarily, if the Bible is to square with their

views. There may be no reason why they should be rejected,—but to suit the theology I speak of they must be thrown away! At this rate the authority of the whole Bible is soon at an end. And what do men give us in its place? Nothing,—nothing at all! They rob us of the bread of life, and do not give us in its stead so much as a stone.

Once more I warn all into whose hands this volume may fall to beware of this theology. I charge you to hold fast the doctrine which I have been endeavouring to uphold in this paper. Remember what I have said, and never let it go. No inheritance of glory without sonship to God! No sonship to God without an interest in Christ! No interest in Christ without your own personal faith! This is God's truth. Never forsake it.

Who now among the readers of this paper *desires to know whether he is a son of God?* Ask yourself this question, and ask it this day,—and ask it as in God's sight, whether you have repented and believed. Ask yourself whether you are experimentally acquainted with Christ, and united to Him in heart. If not you may be very sure you are no son of God. You are not yet born again. You are yet in your sins. Your Father in creation God may be, but your reconciled and pardoning Father God is not. Yes! though Church and world may agree to tell you to the contrary,—though clergy and laity unite in flattering you,—your sonship is worth little or nothing in the sight of God. Let God be true and every man a liar. Without faith in Christ you are no son of God: you are not born again.

Who is there among the readers of this paper who *desires to become a son of God?* Let that person see and feel his sins, and flee to Christ for salvation, and this day he shall be placed among the children.—Only acknowledge thine iniquity, and lay hold on the hand that Jesus holds out to thee this day, and sonship, with all it privileges, is thine own. Only confess thy sins, and bring them unto Christ, and God is "faithful and just to forgive thee thy sins, and cleanse thee from all unrighteousness." (1 John i. 9.) This very day old things shall pass away, and all things become new. This very day thou shalt be forgiven, pardoned, "accepted in the Beloved." (Ephes. i. 6.) This very day thou shalt have a new name given to thee in heaven. Thou didst take up this book a child of wrath. Thou shalt lie down to night a child of God. Mark this, if thy professed desire after sonship is sincere,—if thou art truly weary of thy sins, and hast really something more than a lazy wish to be free,—there is real comfort for thee. It is all true. It is all written in Scripture, even as I have put it down. I dare not raise barriers between thee and God. This day I say, Believe on the Lord Jesus Christ, and thou shalt be " a son," and be saved.

Who is there among the readers of this paper that *is a son of God indeed?* Rejoice, I say, and be exceeding glad of your privileges. Rejoice, for you have good cause to be thankful. Remember the words of the beloved apostle: "Behold what manner of love the Father hath bestowed upon us, that we should be called the sons of God." (1 John iii. 1.) How wonderful that heaven should look down on earth,—that the holy God should set His affections on sinful man, and admit him into His family! What though the world does not understand you! What though the men of this world laugh at you, and cast out your name as evil! Let them laugh if they will. God is your Father. You have no need to be ashamed. The Queen can create a nobleman. The Bishops can ordain clergymen. But Queen, Lords, and Commons,—bishops, priests, and deacons,—all together cannot, of their own power, make one son of God, or one of greater dignity than a son of God. The man that can call God his Father, and Christ his elder brother,—that man may be poor and lowly, yet he never need be ashamed.

II. Let me show, in the second place, *the special evidences of the true Christian's relation to God.*

How shall a man make sure work of his own sonship? How shall he find out whether he is one that has come to Christ by faith and been born again? What are the marks and signs, and tokens, by which the "sons of God" may be known? This is a question which all who love eternal life ought to ask. This is a question to which the verses of Scripture I am asking you to consider, like many others, supply an answer.

(1) The sons of God, for one thing, are all *led by His Spirit.* What says the Scripture which heads this paper? "As many as are led by the Spirit of God, they are the sons of God." (Rom. viii. 14.)

They are all under the leading and teaching of a power which is Almighty, though unseen,—even the power of the Holy Ghost. They no longer turn every man to his own way, and walk every man in the light of His own eyes, and follow every man his own natural heart's desire. The Spirit leads them. The Spirit guides them. There is a movement in their hearts, lives, and affections, which they feel, though they may not be able to explain, and a movement which is always more or less in the same direction.

They are led away from sin,—away from self-righteousness,—away from the world. This is the road by which the Spirit leads God's children. Those whom God adopts He teaches and trains. He shows them their own hearts. He makes them weary of their own ways. He makes them long for inward peace.

They are led to Christ. They are led to the Bible. They are led to prayer. They are led to holiness. This is the beaten path along which the Spirit makes them to travel. Those whom God adopts He always sanctifies. He makes sin very bitter to them. He makes holiness very sweet.

It is the Spirit who leads them to Sinai, and first shows

them the law, that their hearts may be broken. It is He who leads them to Calvary, and shows them the cross, that their hearts may be bound up and healed. It is He who leads them to Pisgah, and gives them distinct views of the promised land, that their hearts may be cheered. When they are taken into the wilderness, and taught to see their own emptiness, it is the leading of the Spirit. When they are carried up to Tabor or Hermon, and lifted up with glimpses of the glory to come, it is the leading of the Spirit. Each and all of God's sons is the subject of these leadings. Each and every one is "willing in the day of the Spirit's power," and yields himself to it. And each and all is led by the right way, to bring him to a city of habitation. (Ps. cx. 3; cvii. 7.)

Settle this down in your heart, and do not let it go. The sons of God are a people "led by the Spirit of God," and always led more or less in the same way. Their experience will tally wonderfully when they compare notes in heaven. This is one mark of sonship.

(2) Furthermore, all the sons of God *have the feelings of adopted children towards their Father in heaven.* What says the Scripture which heads this paper? "Ye have not received the spirit of bondage again to fear, but ye have received the Spirit of adoption, whereby we cry Abba Father." (Rom. viii. 15.)

The sons of God are delivered from that slavish fear of God which sin begets in the natural heart. They are redeemed from that feeling of guilt which made Adam "hide himself in the trees of the garden," and Cain "go out from the presence of the Lord." (Gen. iii. 8; iv. 16.) They are no longer afraid of God's holiness, and justice, and majesty. They no longer feel as if there was a great gulf and barrier between themselves and God, and as if God was angry with them, and must be angry with them, because of their sins. From these chains and fetters of the soul the sons of God are delivered.

Their feelings towards God are now those of peace and confidence. They see Him as a Father reconciled in Christ Jesus. They look on Him as a God whose attributes are all satisfied by their great Mediator and Peacemaker, the Lord Jesus,—as a God who is "just, and yet the Justifier of every one that believeth on Jesus." (Rom. iii. 26.) As a Father, they draw near to Him with boldness: as a Father, they can speak to Him with freedom. They have exchanged the spirit of bondage for that of liberty, and the spirit of fear for that of love. They know that God is holy, but they are not afraid : they know that they are sinners, but they are not afraid. Though holy, they believe that God is completely reconciled : though sinners, they believe they are clothed all over with Jesus Christ. Such is the feeling of the sons of God.

I allow that some of them have this feeling more vividly than others. Some of them carry about scraps and remnants of the old spirit of bondage to their dying day. Many of them have fits and paroxysms of the old man's complaint of fear returning upon them at intervals. But very few of the sons of God could be found who would not say, if cross-examined, that since they knew Christ they have had very different feelings towards God from what they ever had before. They feel as if something like the old Roman form of adoption had taken place between themselves and their Father in heaven. They feel as if He had said to each one of them, "Wilt thou be my son?" and as if their hearts had replied, "I will."

Let us try to grasp this also, and hold it fast. The sons of God are a people who feel towards God in a way that the children of the world do not. They feel no more slavish fear towards Him : they feel towards Him as a reconciled parent. This, then, is another mark of sonship.

(3) But, again, the sons of God *have the witness of the Spirit in their consciences.* What says the Scripture which heads this paper? "The Spirit itself beareth wit-

ness with our spirit, that we are the children of God."
(Rom. viii. 16.)

The sons of God have got something within their hearts
which tells them there is a relationship between themselves
and God. They feel something which tells them that old
things are passed away, and all things become new: that
guilt is gone, that peace is restored, that heaven's door is
open, and hell's door is shut. They have, in short, what
the children of the world have not,—a felt, positive,
reasonable hope. They have what Paul calls the "seal"
and "earnest" of the Spirit. (2 Cor. i. 22; Eph. i. 13.)

I do not for a moment deny that this witness of the
Spirit is exceedingly various in the extent to which the
sons of God possess it. With some it is a loud, clear,
ringing, distinct testimony of conscience: "I am Christ's,
and Christ is mine." With others it is a little, feeble,
stammering whisper, which the devil and the flesh often
prevent being heard. Some of the children of God speed
on their course towards heaven under the full sails of
assurance. Others are tossed to and fro all their voyage,
and will scarce believe they have got faith. But take the
least and lowest of the sons of God. Ask him if he will
give up the little bit of religious hope which he has
attained? Ask him if he will exchange his heart, with
all its doubts and conflicts, its fightings and fears,—ask
him if he will exchange that heart for the heart of the
downright worldly and careless man? Ask him if he
would be content to turn round and throw down the
things he has got hold of, and go back to the world?
Who can doubt what the answer would be? "I cannot
do that," he would reply. "I do not know whether I have
faith, I do not feel sure I have got grace; but I have got
something within me I would not like to part with." And
what is that "*something*"? I will tell you.—It is the
witness of the Spirit.

Let us try to understand this also. The sons of God

have the witness of the Spirit in their consciences. This is another mark of sonship.

(4) One thing more let me add. All the sons of God *take part in suffering with Christ.* What says the Scripture which heads this paper? " If children, then heirs, heirs of God and joint heirs with Christ, if so be that we suffer with Him." (Rom. viii. 17.)

All the children of God have a cross to carry. They have trials, troubles, and afflictions to go through for the Gospel's sake. They have trials from the world,—trials from the flesh,—and trials from the devil. They have trials of feeling from relations and friends,—hard words, hard treatment, and hard judgment. They have trials in the matter of character ;— slander, misrepresentation, mockery, insinuation of false motives,—all these often rain thick upon them. They have trials in the matter of worldly interests. They have often to choose whether they will please man and lose glory, or gain glory and offend man. They have trials from their own hearts. They have each generally their own thorn in the flesh,—their own home-devil, who is their worst foe. This is the experience of the sons of God.

Some of them suffer more, and some less. Some of them suffer in one way, and some in another. God measures out their portions like a wise physician, and cannot err. But never, I believe, was there one child of God who reached paradise without a cross.

Suffering is the diet of the Lord's family. " Whom the Lord loveth He chasteneth."—" If ye be without chastisement, then are ye bastards, and not sons."—"Through much tribulation we must enter the kingdom of God."—"All that will live godly in Christ Jesus shall suffer persecution." (Heb. xii. 6, 8 ; Acts xiv. 22 ; 2 Tim. iii. 12.) When Bishop Latimer was told by his landlord that he had never had a trouble, " Then," said he, " God cannot be here."

Suffering is a part of the process by which the sons of

God are sanctified. They are chastened to wean them from the world, and make them partakers of God's holiness. The Captain of their salvation was "made perfect through suffering," and so are they. (Heb. ii. 10; xii. 10.) There never yet was a great saint who had not either great afflictions or great corruptions. Well said Philip Melancthon: "Where there are no cares there will generally be no prayers."

Let us try to settle this down into our hearts also. The sons of God have all to bear a cross. A suffering Saviour generally has suffering disciples. The Bridegroom was a man of sorrows. The Bride must not be a woman of pleasures and unacquainted with grief. Blessed are they that mourn! Let us not murmur at the cross. This also is a sign of sonship.

I warn men never to suppose that they are sons of God except they have the scriptural marks of sonship. Beware of a sonship without evidences. Again I say, Beware. When a man has no leading of the Spirit to show me, no spirit of adoption to tell of, no witness of the Spirit in his conscience, no cross in his experience,—is this man a son of God? Whatever others may think I dare not say so! His spot is "not the spot of God's children." (Deut. xxxii. 5.) He is no heir of glory.

Tell me not that you have been baptized and taught the catechism of the Church of England, and therefore must be a child of God. I tell you that the parish register is not the book of life. I tell you that to be styled a child of God, and called regenerate in infancy by the faith and charity of the Prayer-book, is one thing; but to be a child of God in deed, another thing altogether. Go and read that catechism again. It is the "death unto sin and the new birth unto righteousness," which makes men *children of grace*. Except you know these by experience, you are no son of God.

Tell me not that you are a member of Christ's Church, and so must be a son. I answer that the sons of the

Church are not necessarily the sons of God. Such sonship is not the sonship of the eighth of Romans. That is the sonship you must have if you are to be saved.

And now, I doubt not some reader of this paper will want to know if he may not be saved without the witness of the Spirit.

I answer, If you mean by the witness of the Spirit, the full assurance of hope,—You may be so saved, without question. But if you want to know whether a man can be saved without *any* inward sense, or knowledge, or hope of salvation, I answer, that ordinarily He cannot. I warn you plainly to cast away all indecision as to your state before God, and to make your calling sure. Clear up your position and relationship. Do not think there is anything praiseworthy in always doubting. Leave that to the Papists. Do not fancy it wise and humble to be ever living like the borderers of old time, on the "debateable ground." "Assurance," said old Dod, the puritan, "may be attained: and what have we been doing all our lives, since we became Christians, if we have not attained it?"

I doubt not some true Christians who read this paper will think their evidence of sonship is too small to be good, and will write bitter things against themselves. Let me try to cheer them. Who gave you the feelings you possess? Who made you hate sin? Who made you love Christ? Who made you long and labour to be holy? Whence did these feelings come? Did they come from nature? There are no such products in a natural man's heart.—Did they come from the devil? He would fain stifle such feelings altogether.— Cheer up, and take courage. Fear not, neither be cast down. Press forward, and go on. There is hope for you after all. Strive. Labour. Seek. Ask. Knock. Follow on. You shall yet see that you are "sons of God."

III. Let me show, in the last place, *the privileges of the true Christian's relation to God.*

Nothing can be conceived more glorious than the prospects of the sons of God. The words of Scripture which head this paper contain a rich mine of good and comfortable things. "If we are children," says Paul, "we are heirs, heirs of God, and joint heirs with Christ,—to be glorified together with Him." (Rom. viii. 17.)

True Christians then are "heirs."—Something is prepared for them all which is yet to be revealed.

They are "heirs of God."—To be heirs of the rich on earth is something. How much more then is it to be son and heir of the King of kings!

They are "joint heirs with Christ." They shall share in His majesty, and take part in His glory. They shall be glorified together with Him.

And this, we must remember, is for *all* the children. Abraham took care to provide for all his children, and God takes care to provide for His. None of them are disinherited. None will be cast out. None will be cut off. Each shall stand in his lot, and have a portion, in the day when the Lord brings many sons to glory.

Who can tell the full nature of the inheritance of the saints in light? Who can describe the glory which is yet to be revealed and given to the children of God? Words fail us. Language falls short. Mind cannot conceive fully, and tongue cannot express perfectly, the things which are comprised in the glory yet to come upon the sons and daughters of the Lord Almighty. Oh, it is indeed a true saying of the Apostle John: "It doth not yet appear what we shall be." (1 John iii. 2.)

The very Bible itself only lifts a little of the veil which hangs over this subject. How could it do more? We could not thoroughly understand more if more had been told us. Our mental constitution is as yet too earthly,— our understanding is as yet too carnal to appreciate more if we had it. The Bible generally deals with the subject in negative terms and not in positive assertions. It describes

what there will not be in the glorious inheritance, that
thus we may get some faint idea of what there will be.
It paints the *absence* of certain things, in order that we
may drink in a little the blessedness of the things *present*.
It tells us that the inheritance is "incorruptible, undefiled,
and fadeth not away." It tells us that "the crown of glory
fadeth not away." It tells us that the devil is to be
"bound," that there shall be "no more night and no more
curse," that "death shall be cast into the lake of fire,"
that "all tears shall be wiped away," and that the
inhabitant shall no more say, "I am sick." And these are
glorious things indeed. No corruption!—No fading!—
No withering!—No devil!—No curse of sin!—No sorrow!
—No tears!—No sickness!—No death! Surely the cup
of the children of God will indeed run over! (1 Pet. i. 4;
v. 4; Rev. **xx.** 2; xxi. 25; xxii. 3; xx. 14; xxi. 4; Is.
xxxiii. 24.)

But there are positive things told us about the glory
yet to come upon the heirs of God, which ought not to
be kept back. There are many sweet, pleasant, and
unspeakable comforts in their future inheritance, which
all true Christians would do well to consider. There
are cordials for fainting pilgrims in many words and
expressions of Scripture, which you and I ought to lay
up against time of need.

(*a*) Is *knowledge* pleasant to us now? Is the little that
we know of God and Christ, and the Bible precious to our
souls, and do we long for more? We shall have it perfectly in glory. What says the Scripture? "Then shall
I know even as also I am known." (1 Cor. xiii. 12.)
Blessed be God, there will be no more disagreements among
believers! Episcopalians and Presbyterians,—Calvinists
and Arminians,—Millennarians and Anti-millennarians,—
friends of Establishments and friends of the Voluntary
system,—advocates of infant baptism and advocates of
adult baptism,—all will at length see eye to eye. The

former ignorance will have passed away. We shall marvel to find how childish and blind we have been.

(*b*) Is *holiness* pleasant to us now ? Is sin the burden and bitterness of our lives ? Do we long for entire conformity to the image of God ? We shall have it perfectly in glory. What says the Scripture ? "Christ gave Himself for the Church," not only that He might sanctify it on earth, but also "that He might present it to Himself a glorious Church, not having spot or wrinkle, or any such thing." (Ephes. v. 27.) Oh, the blessedness of an eternal good-bye to sin ! Oh, how little the best of us do at present ! Oh, what unutterable corruption sticks, like birdlime, to all our motives, all our thoughts, all our words, all our actions ! Oh, how many of us, like Naphtali, are goodly in our words, but, like Reuben, unstable in our works ! Thank God, all this shall be changed. (Gen. xlix. 4, 21.)

(*c*) Is *rest* pleasant to us now ? Do we often feel "faint though pursuing ?" (Judges viii. 4.) Do we long for a world in which we need not to be always watching and warring ? We shall have it perfectly in glory. What saith the Scripture ? "There remaineth a rest for the people of God." (Heb. iv. 9.) The daily, hourly conflict with the world, the flesh, and the devil, shall at length be at an end. The enemy shall be bound. The warfare shall be over. The wicked shall at last cease from troubling. The weary shall at length be at rest. There shall be a great calm.

(*d*) Is *service* pleasant to us now ? Do we find it sweet to work for Christ, and yet groan being burdened by a feeble body ? Is our spirit often willing, but hampered and clogged by the poor weak flesh ? Have our hearts burned within us, when we have been allowed to give a cup of cold water for Christ's sake, and have we sighed to think what unprofitable servants we are ? Let us take comfort. We shall be able to serve perfectly in glory, and without weariness. What saith the Scripture ?

"They serve Him day and night in His temple." (Rev. vii. 15.)

(e) Is *satisfaction* pleasant to us now? Do we find the world empty? Do we long for the filling up of every void place and gap in our hearts? We shall have it perfectly in glory. We shall no longer have to mourn over cracks in all our earthen vessels, and thorns in all our roses, and bitter dregs in all our sweet cups. We shall no longer lament with Jonah over withered gourds. We shall no longer say with Solomon, "All is vanity and vexation of spirit." We shall no longer cry with aged David, "I have seen an end of all perfection." What saith the Scripture? "I shall be satisfied when I awake with Thy likeness." (Eccles. i. 14; Ps. cxix. 96; xvii. 15.)

(f) Is *communion with the saints* pleasant to us now? Do we feel that we are never so happy as when we are with the "excellent of the earth?" Are we never so much at home as in their company? (Ps. xvi. 3.) We shall have it perfectly in glory. What saith the Scripture? "The Son of man shall send His angels, and they shall gather out of His kingdom all they that offend, and them which work iniquity." "He shall send His angels with a great sound of a trumpet, and they shall gather together His elect from the four winds." (Matt. xiii. 41; xxiv. 31.) Praised be God! We shall see all the saints of whom we have read in the Bible, and in whose steps we have tried to walk. We shall see apostles, prophets, patriarchs, martyrs, reformers, missionaries, and ministers, of whom the world was not worthy. We shall see the faces of those we have known and loved in Christ on earth, and over whose departure we shed bitter tears. We shall see them more bright and glorious than they ever were before. And, best of all, we shall see them without hurry and anxiety, and without feeling that we only meet to part again. In the coming glory there is no death, no parting, no farewell.

(g) Is *communion with Christ* pleasant to us now? Do

we find His name precious to us? Do we feel our hearts
burn within us at the thought of His dying love? We shall
have perfect communion with Him in glory. "We shall ever
be with the Lord." (1 Thess. iv. 17.) We shall be with Him
in paradise. (Luke xxiii. 43.) We shall see His face in the
kingdom. These eyes of ours will behold those hands
and feet which were pierced with nails, and that head
which was crowned with thorns. Where He is, there will
the sons of God be. When He comes, they will come
with Him. When He sits down in His glory, they shall
sit down by His side. Blessed prospect indeed! I am
a dying man in a dying world. All before me is dark.
The world to come is a harbour unknown. But Christ is
there, and that is enough. Surely if there is rest and
peace in following Him by faith on earth, there will be
far more rest and peace when we see Him face to face.
If we have found it good to follow the pillar of cloud and
fire in the wilderness, we shall find it a thousand times
better to sit down in our eternal inheritance, with our
Joshua, in the promised land.

If any one among the readers of this paper is not yet
among the sons and heirs, I do pity you with all my heart!
How much you are missing! How little true comfort you
are enjoying! There you are, struggling on, and toiling
in the fire, and wearying yourself for mere earthly ends,
—seeking rest and finding none,—chasing shadows and
never catching them,—wondering why you are not happy,
and yet refusing to see the cause,—hungry, and thirsty,
and empty, and yet blind to the plenty within your reach.
Oh, that you were wise! Oh, that you would hear the
voice of Jesus, and learn of Him!

If you are one of those who are sons and heirs, you may
well rejoice and be happy. You may well wait, like the
boy Patience in Pilgrim's Progress: your best things are
yet to come. You may well bear crosses without murmuring: your light affliction is but for a moment. "The

sufferings of this present time are not worthy to be
compared to the glory which is to be revealed."—"When
Christ our life appears, then you also shall appear with
Him in glory." (Rom. viii. 18; Colos. iii. 4.) You may
well not envy the transgressor and his prosperity. You
are the truly rich. Well said a dying believer in my own
parish: "I am more rich than I ever was in my life."
You may say as Mephibosheth said to David: "Let the
world take all, my king is coming again in peace." (2
Sam. xix. 30.) You may say as Alexander said when he
gave all his riches away, and was asked what he kept for
himself: "I have hope." You may well not be cast down
by sickness: the eternal part of you is safe and provided
for, whatever happens to your body. You may well look
calmly on death: it opens a door between you and your
inheritance. You may well not sorrow excessively over
the things of the world,—over partings and bereavements,
over losses and crosses: the day of gathering is before
you. Your treasure is beyond reach of harm. Heaven is
becoming every year more full of those you love, and
earth more empty. Glory in your inheritance. It is all
yours if you are a son of God: "If we are children, then
we are heirs."

(1) And now, in concluding this paper, *let me ask every
one who reads it Whose child are you?* Are you the child
of nature or the child of grace? Are you the child of the
devil or the child of God? You cannot be both at once.
Which are you?

Settle the question without delay, for you must die at
last either one or the other. Settle it, for it can be
settled, and it is folly to leave it doubtful. Settle it,
for time is short, the world is getting old, and you are
fast drawing near to the judgment seat of Christ. Settle
it, for death is nigh, the Lord is at hand, and who can tell
what a day might bring forth? Oh, that you would never

rest till the question is settled! Oh, that you may never feel satisfied till you can say, "I have been born again: I am a son of God!"

(2) *If you are not a son and heir of God, let me entreat you to become one without delay.* Would you be rich? There are unsearchable riches in Christ. Would you be noble? You shall be a king. Would you be happy? You shall have a peace which passeth understanding, and which the world can never give and never take away. Oh, come out, and take up the cross and follow Christ! Come out from among the thoughtless and worldly, and hear the word of the Lord: "I will receive you, and will be a Father unto you, and ye shall be my sons and daughters, saith the Lord almighty." (2 Cor. vi. 18.)

(3) *If you are a son of God, I beseech you to walk worthy of your Father's house.* I charge you solemnly to honour Him in your life; and above all to honour Him by implicit obedience to all His commands, and hearty love to all His children. Labour to travel through the world like a child of God and heir to glory. Let men be able to trace a family likeness between you and Him that begat you. Live a heavenly life. Seek things that are above. Do not seem to be building your nest below. Behave like a man who seeks a city out of sight, whose citizenship is in heaven, and who would be content with many hardships till he gets home.

Labour *to feel like a son of God* in every condition in which you are placed. Never forget you are on your Father's ground so long as you are here on earth. Never forget that a Father's hand sends all your mercies and crosses. Cast every care on Him. Be happy and cheerful in Him. Why indeed art thou ever sad if thou art the King's son? Why should men ever doubt, when they look at you, whether it is a pleasant thing to be one of God's children?

Labour *to behave towards others like a son of God.* Be

blameless and harmless in your day and generation. Be a "peacemaker among all you know." (Matt. v. 9.) Seek for your children sonship to God, above everything else: seek for them an inheritance in heaven, whatever else you do for them. No man leaves his children so well provided for as he who leaves them sons and heirs of God.

Persevere in your Christian calling, if you are a son of God, and press forward more and more. Be careful to lay aside every weight, and the sin which most easily besets you. Keep your eyes steadily fixed on Jesus. Abide in Him. Remember that without Him you can do nothing, and with Him you can do all things. (John xv. 5; Philip. iv. 13.) Watch and pray daily. Be steadfast, unmoveable, and always abounding in the work of the Lord. Settle it down in your heart that not a cup of cold water given in the name of a disciple shall lose its reward, and that every year you are so much nearer home.

"Yet a little time and He that shall come will come, and will not tarry." (Heb. x. 37.) Then shall be the glorious liberty, and the full manifestation of the sons of God. (Rom. viii. 19, 21.) Then shall the world acknowledge that they were the truly wise. Then shall the sons of God at length come of age, and be no longer heirs in expectancy, but heirs in possession. Then shall they hear with exceeding joy those comfortable words: "Come, ye blessed of my Father, inherit the kingdom prepared for you from the foundation of the world." (Matt. xxv. 34.) Surely that day will make amends for all!

XIX

THE GREAT GATHERING

"Now we beseech you, brethren, by the coming of our Lord Jesus Christ, and by our gathering together unto Him."—2 Thess. ii. 1.

THE text which heads this page contains an expression which deserves no common attention. That expression is,—"Our gathering together."

"Our gathering together!" Those three words touch a note which ought to find a response in every part of the world. Man is by nature a social being: he does not like to be alone. Go where you will on earth, people generally like meeting together, and seeing one another's faces. It is the exception, and not the rule, to find children of Adam who do not like "gathering together."

For example, Christmas is peculiarly a time when English people "gather together." It is the season when family meetings have become almost a national institution. In town and in country, among rich and among poor, from the palace to the workhouse, Christmas cheer and Christmas parties are proverbial things. It is the one time in the twelvemonth with many for seeing their friends at all. Sons snatch a few days from London business to run down and see their parents; brothers get leave of absence from the desk to spend a week with their sisters; friends accept long-standing invitations, and contrive to pay a visit to their friends; boys rush home from school, and glory in the warmth and comfort of the old house. Business for a little space comes to a standstill: the weary wheels of incessant labour seem almost to cease revolving for a few hours. In short, from the Isle of Wight to Berwick-on-Tweed, and from the Land's End to the North Foreland, there is a general spirit of "gathering together."

Happy is the land where such a state of things exists! Long may it last in England, and never may it end! Poor and shallow is that philosophy which sneers at Christmas gatherings. Cold and hard is that religion which pretends to frown at them, and denounces them as wicked. Family affection lies at the very roots of well-ordered society. It is one of the few good things which have survived the fall, and prevent men and women from being mere devils. It is the secret oil on the wheels of our social system which keeps the whole machine going, and without which neither steam nor fire would avail. Anything which helps to keep up family affection and brotherly love is a positive good to a country. May the Christmas day never arrive in England when there are no family meetings and no gatherings together!

But earthly gatherings after all have something about them that is sad and sorrowful. The happiest parties sometimes contain uncongenial members: the merriest meetings are only for a very short time. Moreover, as years roll on, the hand of death makes painful gaps in the family circle. Even in the midst of Christmas merriment we cannot help remembering those who have passed away. The longer we live, the more we feel to stand alone. The old faces will rise before the eyes of our minds, and the old voices will sound in our ears, even in the midst of holiday mirth and laughter. People do not talk much of such things; but there are few that do not feel them. We need not intrude our inmost thoughts on others, and especially when all around us are bright and happy. But there are not many, I suspect, who reach middle age, who would not admit, if they spoke the truth, that there are sorrowful things inseparably mixed up with a Christmas party. In short, there is no unmixed pleasure about any earthly "gathering."

But is there no better "gathering" yet to come? Is there no bright prospect in our horizon of an assembly which shall far outshine the assemblies of Christmas and New Year,—an assembly in which there shall be joy without sorrow, and mirth without tears? I thank God that I can give a plain answer to these questions; and to give it is the simple object of this paper. I ask my readers to give me their attention for a few minutes, and I will soon show them what I mean.

I. There is a "gathering together" of true Christians which is to come. *What is it, and when shall it be?*

The gathering I speak of shall take place at the end of the world, in the day when Christ returns to earth the second time. As surely as He came the first time, so surely shall He come the second time. In the clouds of heaven He went away, and in the clouds of heaven He shall return. Visibly, in the body, He went away, and visibly, in the body, He will return. And the very first thing that Christ will do will be to "gather together" His people. "He shall send His angels with a great sound of a trumpet, and they shall gather together His elect from the four winds, from one end of heaven to the other." (Matt. xxiv. 31.)

The *manner* of this "gathering together" is plainly revealed in Scripture. The dead saints shall all be raised, and the living saints shall all be changed. It is written, "The sea shall give up the dead which are in it, and death and hell shall give up the dead that are in them."—"The dead in Christ shall rise first. Those which are alive and

remain shall be caught up together with them in the
clouds, to meet the Lord in the air."—"We shall not all
sleep, but we shall all be changed, in a moment, in the
twinkling of an eye, at the last trump: for the trumpet
shall sound, and the dead shall be raised incorruptible,
and we shall be changed." (Rev. xx. 13; 1 Thess. iv. 16,
17; 1 Cor. xv. 51, 52.) And then, when every member of
Christ is found, and not one left behind, when soul and
body, those old companions, are once more reunited, then
shall be the grand "gathering together."

The *object* of this "gathering together" is as clearly
revealed in Scripture as its manner. It is partly for the
final reward of Christ's people: that their complete justification from all guilt may be declared to all creation; that
they may receive the "crown of glory which fadeth not
away," and the "kingdom prepared before the foundation
of the world;" that they may be admitted publicly into the
joy of their Lord.—It is partly for the safety of Christ's
people, that, like Noah in the ark and Lot in Zoar, they
may be hid and covered before the storm of God's judgment
comes down on the wicked; that when the last plagues
are falling on the enemies of the Lord, they may be
untouched, as Rahab's family in the fall of Jericho, and
unscathed as the three children in the midst of the fire.
The saints have no cause to fear the day of gathering,
however fearful the signs that may accompany it. Before
the final crash of all things begins, they shall be hidden
in the secret place of the Most High. The grand gathering
is for their safety and their reward. "Fear not ye," shall
the angel-reapers say, "for ye seek Jesus which was
crucified."—"Come, my people," shall their Master say:
"enter thou into thy chambers, and shut thy doors about
thee: hide thyself as it were for a little moment, until the
indignation be overpast." (Matt. xxviii. 5; Isa. xxvi. 20.)

(*a*) This gathering will be a *great* one. All children of
God who have ever lived, from Abel the first saint down to

the last born in the day that our Lord comes,—all of every age, and nation, and church, and people, and tongue,—all shall be assembled together. Not one shall be overlooked or forgotten. The weakest and feeblest shall not be left behind. Now, when "scattered," true Christians seem a little flock; then, when "gathered," they shall be found a multitude which no man can number.

(b) This gathering will be a *wonderful* one. The saints from distant lands, who never saw each other in the flesh, and could not understand each other's speech if they met, shall all be brought together in one harmonious company. The dwellers in Australia shall find they are as near heaven, and as soon there, as the dwellers in England. The believers who died five thousand years ago, and whose bones are mere dust, shall find their bodies raised and renewed as quickly as those who are alive when the trumpet sounds. Above all, miracles of grace will be revealed. We shall see some in heaven who we never expected would have been saved at all. The confusion of tongues shall at length be reversed, and done away. The assembled multitude will cry with one heart and in one language, "What hath God wrought!" (Num. xxiii. 23.)

(c) This gathering shall be a *humbling* one. It shall make an end of bigotry and narrow-mindedness for ever. The Christians of one denomination shall find themselves side by side with those of another denomination. If they would not tolerate them on earth, they will be obliged to tolerate them in heaven. Churchmen and Dissenters, who will neither pray together nor worship together now, will discover to their shame that they must praise together hereafter to all eternity. The very people who will not receive us at their ordinances now, and keep us back from their Table, will be obliged to acknowledge us before our Master's face, and to let us sit down by their side. Never will the world have seen such a complete overthrow of sectarianism, party spirit, unbrotherliness, religious jeal-

ousy, and religious pride. At last we shall all be completely
"clothed with humility." (1 Pet. v. 5.)

This mighty, wonderful "gathering together," is the
gathering which ought to be often in men's thoughts. It
deserves consideration: it demands attention. Gatherings
of other kinds are incessantly occupying our minds, political gatherings, scientific gatherings, gatherings for
pleasure, gatherings for gain. But the hour comes, and
will soon be here, when gatherings of this kind will be
completely forgotten. One thought alone will swallow up
men's minds: that thought will be, "Shall I be gathered
with Christ's people into a place of safety and honour, or
be left behind to everlasting woe?" LET US TAKE
CARE THAT WE ARE NOT LEFT BEHIND.

II. *Why is this "gathering together" of true Christians
a thing to be desired?* Let us try to get an answer to
that question.

St. Paul evidently thought that the gathering at the
last day was a cheering object which Christians ought to
keep before their eyes. He classes it with that second
coming of our Lord, which he says elsewhere believers
love and long for. He exalts it in the distant horizon as
one of those "good things to come," which should animate
the faith of every pilgrim in the narrow way. Not only,
he seems to say, will each servant of God have rest, and a
kingdom, and a crown; he will have besides a happy
"gathering together." Now, where is the peculiar blessedness of this gathering? Why is it a thing that we ought
to look forward to with joy, and expect with pleasure?
Let us see,

(1) For one thing, the "gathering together" of all true
Christians will be a *state of things totally unlike their
present condition.* To be scattered, and not gathered,
seems the rule of man's existence now. Of all the
millions who are annually born into the world, how few

continue together till they die ! Children who draw their
first breath under the same' roof, and play by the same
fireside, are sure to be separated as they grow up, and to
draw their last breath far distant from one another.—The
same law applies to the people of God. They are spread
abroad like salt, one in one place and one in another, and
never allowed to continue long side by side. It is doubtless good for the world that it is so. A town would be a very
dark place at night if all the lighted candles were crowded
together into one room.—But, good as it is for the world,
it is no small trial to believers. Many a day they feel
desolate and alone; many a day they long for a little more
communion with their brethren, and a little more com-
panionship with those who love the Lord! Well, they
may look forward with hope and comfort. The hour is
coming when they shall have no lack of companions. Let
them lift up their heads and rejoice. There will be a
"gathering together" by and by.

(2) For another thing, the gathering together of all true
Christians will be *an assembly entirely of one mind.*
There are no such assemblies now. Mixture, hypocrisy,
and false profession, creep in everywhere. Wherever
there is wheat there are sure to be tares. Wherever there
are good fish there are sure to be bad. Wherever there
are wise virgins there are sure to be foolish. There is
no such thing as a perfect Church now. There is a Judas
Iscariot at every communion table, and a Demas in every
Apostolic company; and wherever the "sons of God" come
together Satan is sure to appear among them. (Job i. 6.)
But all this shall come to an end one day. Our Lord shall
at length present to the Father a perfect Church, "having
neither spot nor wrinkle, nor any such thing." (Eph. v. 27.)
How glorious such a Church will be ! To meet with half-a-
dozen believers together now is a rare event in a Christian's
year, and one that cheers him like a sunshiny day in
winter: it makes him feel his heart burn within him, as

the disciples felt on the way to Emmaus. But how much more joyful will it be to meet a "multitude that no man can number!" To find too, that all we meet are at last of one opinion and one judgment, and see eye to eye,—to discover that all our miserable controversies are buried for ever, and that Calvinists no longer hate Arminians, nor Arminians Calvinists, Churchmen no longer quarrel with Dissenters, nor Dissenters with Churchmen,—to join a company of Christians in which there is neither jarring, squabbling, nor discord,—every man's graces fully developed, and every man's besetting sins dropped off like beech-leaves in spring,—all this will be happiness indeed! No wonder that St. Paul bids us look forward.

(3) For another thing, the gathering together of true Christians will be *a meeting at which none shall be absent*. The weakest lamb shall not be left behind in the wilderness: the youngest babe that ever drew breath shall not be overlooked or forgotten. We shall once more see our beloved friends and relatives who fell asleep in Christ, and left us in sorrow and tears,—better, brighter, more beautiful, more pleasant than ever we found them on earth. We shall hold communion with all the saints of God who have fought the good fight before us, from the beginning of the world to the end. Patriarchs and Prophets, Apostles and Fathers, Martyrs and Missionaries, Reformers and Puritans, all the host of God's elect shall be there. If to read their words and works has been pleasant, how much better shall it be to see them! If to hear of them, and be stirred by their example, has been useful, how much more delightful to talk with them, and ask them questions! To sit down with Abraham, Isaac, and Jacob, and hear how they kept the faith without any Bible,—to converse with Moses, and Samuel, and David, and Isaiah, and Daniel, and hear how they could believe in a Christ yet to come,—to converse with Peter, and Paul, and Lazarus, and Mary, and Martha, and listen to their wondrous tale of what their Master did for

them,—all this will be sweet indeed! No wonder that St. Paul bids us look forward.

(4) In the last place, the gathering of all true Christians shall be *a meeting without a parting.* There are no such meetings now. We seem to live in an endless hurry, and can hardly sit down and take breath before we are off again. "Good-bye" treads on the heels of "How do you do?" The cares of this world, the necessary duties of life, the demands of our families, the work of our various stations and callings,—all these things appear to eat up our days, and to make it impossible to have long quiet times of communion with God's people. But, blessed be God, it shall not always be so. The hour cometh, and shall soon be here, when "good-bye" and "farewell" shall be words that are laid aside and buried for ever. When we meet in a world where the former things have passed away, where there is no more sin and no more sorrow,—no more poverty and no more money,—no more work of body or work of brains,—no more need of anxiety for families,— no more sickness, no more pain, no more old age, no more death, no more change,—when we meet in that endless state of being, calm, and restful, and unhurried,—who can tell what the blessedness of the change will be? I cannot wonder that St. Paul bids us look up and look forward.

I lay these things before all who read this paper, and ask their serious attention to them. If I know anything of a Christian's experience, I am sure they contain food for reflection. This, at least, I say confidently: the man who sees nothing much in the second coming of Christ and the public "gathering" of Christ's people,—nothing happy, nothing joyful, nothing pleasant, nothing desirable,—such a man may well doubt whether he himself is a true Christian and has got any grace at all.

(1) *I ask you a plain question.* Do not turn away

from it and refuse to look it in the face. Shall you be gathered by the angels into God's home when the Lord returns, or shall you be left behind?

One thing, at any rate, is very certain. There will only be two parties of mankind at the last great day: those who are on the right hand of Christ, and those who are on the left;—those who are counted righteous, and those who are wicked;—those who are safe in the ark, and those who are outside;—those who are gathered like wheat into God's barn, and those who are left behind like tares to be burned. Now, what will your portion be?

Perhaps you do not know yet. You cannot say. You are not sure. You hope the best. You trust it will be all right at last: but you won't undertake to give an opinion. Well! I only hope you will never rest till you do know. The Bible will tell you plainly who are they that will be gathered. Your own heart, if you deal honestly, will tell you whether you are one of the number. Rest not, rest not, till you know!

How men can stand the partings and separations of this life if they have no hope of anything better,—how they can bear to say "good-bye" to sons and daughters, and launch them on the troublesome waves of this world, if they have no expectation of a safe "gathering" in Christ at last,—how they can part with beloved members of their families, and let them journey forth to the other side of the globe, not knowing if they shall ever meet happily in this life or a life to come,—how all this can be, completely baffles my understanding I can only suppose that the many never think, never consider, never look forward. Once let a man begin to think, and he will never be satisfied till he has found Christ and is safe.

(2) *I offer you a plain means of testing your own soul's condition*, if you want to know your own chance of being gathered into God's home. Ask yourself what kind of gatherings you like best here upon earth? Ask

yourself whether you really love the assembling together of God's people?

How could that man enjoy the meeting of true Christians in heaven who takes no pleasure in meeting true Christians on earth? How can that heart which is wholly set on balls, and races, and feasts, and amusements, and worldly assemblies, and thinks earthly worship a weariness —how can such a heart be in tune for the company of saints, and saints alone? The thing is impossible. It cannot be.

Never, never let it be forgotten, that our tastes on earth are a sure evidence of the state of our hearts; and the state of our hearts here is a sure indication of our position hereafter. Heaven is a prepared place for a prepared people. He that hopes to be gathered with saints in heaven while he only loves the gathering of sinners on earth is deceiving himself. If he lives and dies in that state of mind he will find at last that he had better never have been born.

(3) If you are a true Christian, *I exhort you to be often looking forward.* Your good things are yet to come. Your redemption draweth nigh. The night is far spent. The day is at hand. Yet a little time, and He whom you love and believe on will come, and will not tarry. When He comes, He will bring His dead saints with Him and change His living ones. Look forward! There is a "gathering together" yet to come.

The morning after a shipwreck is a sorrowful time. The joy of half-drowned survivors, who have safely reached the land, is often sadly marred by the recollection of shipmates who have sunk to rise no more. There will be no such sorrow when believers gather together round the throne of the Lamb. Not one of the ship's company shall be found absent. "Some on boards, and some on broken pieces of the ship,—all will get safe to shore at last." (Acts xxvii. 44.) The great waters and raging waves shall swallow none of God's elect. When the sun rises they shall be seen all safe, and "gathered together."

Even the day after a great victory is a sorrowful time. The triumphant feelings of the conquerors are often mingled with bitter regrets for those who fell in action, and died on the field. The list of "killed, wounded, and missing," breaks many a heart, fills many a home with mourning, and brings many a grey head sorrowing to the grave. The great Duke of Wellington often said, "there was but one thing worse than a victory, and that was a defeat." But, thanks be to God, there will be no such sorrow in heaven! The soldiers of the great Captain of our salvation shall all answer to their names at last. The muster-roll shall be as complete after the battle as it was before. Not one believer shall be "missing" in the great "gathering together."

Does Christmas, for instance, bring with it sorrowful feelings and painful associations? Do tears rise unbidden in your eyes when you mark the empty places round the fireside? Do grave thoughts come sweeping over your mind, even in the midst of your children's mirth, when you recollect the dear old faces and much loved voices of some that sleep in the churchyard? Well, look up and look forward! The time is short. The world is growing old. The coming of the Lord draweth nigh. There is yet to be a meeting without parting, and a gathering without separation. Those believers whom you laid in the grave with many tears are in good keeping: you will yet see them again with joy. Look up! I say once more. Lay hold by faith on the "coming of our Lord Jesus Christ, and our gathering together unto Him." Believe it, think of it, rest on it. It is all true.

Do you feel lonely and desolate as every December comes round? Do you find few to pray with, few to praise with, few to open your heart to, few to exchange experience with? Do you learn increasingly, that heaven is

becoming every year more full and earth more empty?
Well, it is an old story. You are only drinking a cup
which myriads have drunk before. Look up and look
forward. The lonely time will soon be past and over:
you will have company enough by and by. "When you
wake up after your Lord's likeness you shall be satisfied."
(Ps. xvii. 15.) Yet a little while and you shall see a
congregation that shall never break up, and a sabbath that
shall never end. "The coming of our Lord Jesus Christ,
and our gathering together unto Him," shall make amends
for all.

XX

THE GREAT SEPARATION

" Whose fan is in His hand, and He will throughly purge His floor, and gather His wheat into the garner ; but He will burn up the chaff with unquenchable fire."—MATT. iii. 12.

THE verse of Scripture which is now before our eyes contains words which were spoken by John the Baptist. They are a prophecy about our Lord Jesus Christ, and a prophecy which has not yet been fulfilled. They are a prophecy which we shall all see fulfilled one day, and God alone knows how soon.

I invite every reader of this paper to consider seriously the great truths which this verse contains. I invite you to give me your attention, while I unfold them, and set them before you in order. Who knows but this text may prove a word in season to your soul ? Who knows but this text may help to make this day the happiest day in your life ?

I. Let me show, in the first place, *the two great classes into which mankind may be divided.*

There are only two classes of people in the world in the sight of God, and both are mentioned in the text which begins this paper. There are those who are called *the wheat*, and there are those who are called *the chaff*.

Viewed with the eye of man, the earth contains many different sorts of inhabitants. Viewed with the eye of

God it only contains two. Man's eye looks at the outward appearance:—this is all he thinks of. The eye of God looks at the heart:—this is the only part of which He takes any account. And tried by the state of their hearts, there are but two classes into which people can be divided:—either they are wheat, or they are chaff.

Who are the wheat in the world? This is a point which demands special consideration.

The wheat means all men and women who are believers in the Lord Jesus Christ,—all who are led by the Holy Spirit,—all who have felt themselves sinners, and fled for refuge to the salvation offered in the Gospel,—all who love the Lord Jesus and live to the Lord Jesus, and serve the Lord Jesus,—all who have taken Christ for their only confidence, and the Bible for their only guide, and regard sin as their deadliest enemy, and look to heaven as their only home. All such, of every Church, name, nation, people, and tongue,—of every rank, station, condition, and degree,—all such are God's "wheat."

Show me people of this kind anywhere, and I know what they are. I know not that they and I may agree in all particulars, but I see in them the handiwork of the King of kings, and I ask no more. I know not whence they came, and where they found their religion; but I know where they are going, and that is enough for me. They are the children of my Father in heaven. They are part of His "wheat."

All such, though sinful and vile, and unworthy in their own eyes, are the precious part of mankind. They are the sons and daughters of God the Father. They are the delight of God the Son. They are the habitation of God the Spirit. The Father beholds no iniquity in them:—they are the members of His dear Son's mystical body: in Him He sees them, and is well-pleased. The Lord Jesus discerns in them the fruit of His own travail and work upon the cross, and is well satisfied. The Holy

Ghost regards them as spiritual temples which He Himself has reared, and rejoices over them. In a word, they are the "wheat" of the earth.

Who are the chaff in the world? This again is a point which demands special attention.

The chaff means all men and women who have no saving faith in Christ, and no sanctification of the Spirit, whosoever they may be. Some of them perhaps are infidels, and some are formal Christians. Some are sneering Sadducees, and some self-righteous Pharisees. Some of them make a point of keeping up a kind of Sunday religion, and others are utterly careless of everything except their own pleasure and the world. But all alike, who have the two great marks already mentioned—*no faith and no sanctification,*—all such are "chaff." From Paine and Voltaire to the dead Churchman who can think of nothing but outward ceremonies,—from Julian and Porphyry to the unconverted admirer of sermons in the present day,—all, all are standing in one rank before God: all, all are "chaff."

They bring no glory to God the Father. "They honour not the Son, and so do not honour the Father that sent Him." (John v. 23.) They neglect that mighty salvation which countless millions of angels admire. They disobey that Word which was graciously written for their learning. They listen not to the voice of Him who condescended to leave heaven and die for their sins. They pay no tribute of service and affection to Him who gave them "life, and breath, and all things." And therefore God takes no pleasure in them. He pities them, but He reckons them no better than "chaff."

Yes! you may have rare intellectual gifts and high mental attainments: you may sway kingdoms by your counsel, move millions by your pen, or keep crowds in breathless attention by your tongue; but if you have never submitted yourself to the yoke of Christ, and never honoured His Gospel by heartfelt reception of it, you are nothing in His sight. Natural gifts without grace are like a row of cyphers without an unit before them : they look big, but they are of no value. The meanest insect that crawls is a nobler being than you are : it fills its place in creation, and glorifies its Maker with all its power, and you do not. You do not honour God with heart, and will, and intellect, and members, which are all His. You invert His order and arrangement, and live as if time was of more importance than eternity, and body better than soul. You dare to neglect God's greatest gift,—His own incarnate Son. You are cold about that subject which fills all heaven with hallelujahs. And so long as this is the case you belong to the worthless part of mankind. You are the "chaff" of the earth.

Let this thought be graven deeply in the mind of every reader of this paper, whatever else he forgets. Remember there are only two sorts of people in the world. There are wheat, and there are chaff.

There are many nations in Europe. Each differs from the rest. Each has its own language, its own laws, its own peculiar customs. But God's eye divides Europe into two great parties,—the wheat and the chaff.

There are many classes in England. There are peers and commoners,—farmers and shopkeepers,—masters and servants,—rich and poor. But God's eye only takes account of two orders,—the wheat and the chaff.

There are many and various minds in every congregation that meets for religious worship. There are some who attend for a mere form, and some who really desire to meet Christ,—some who come there to please others, and some who come to please God,—some who bring their hearts with them and are not soon tired, and some who leave their hearts behind them, and reckon the whole service weary work. But the eye of the Lord Jesus only sees two divisions in the congregation,—the wheat and the chaff.

There were millions of visitors to the Great Exhibition of 1851. From Europe, Asia, Africa, and America,—from North and South, and East and West,—crowds came together to see what skill and industry could do. Children of our first father Adam's family, who had never seen each other before, for once met face to face under one roof. But the eye of the Lord only saw two companies thronging that large palace of glass,—the wheat and the chaff.

I know well the world dislikes this way of dividing professing Christians. The world tries hard to fancy there are *three* sorts of people, and not *two*. To be very good and very strict does not suit the world:—they cannot, will not be saints. To have no religion at all does not suit the world:—it would not be respectable.—"Thank God," they will say, "we are not so bad as that." But to have religion enough to be saved, and yet not go into extremes,—to be sufficiently good, and yet not be peculiar,—to have a quiet, easy-going, moderate kind of Christianity, and go comfortably to heaven after all,—this is the world's favourite idea. There is a third class,—a safe middle class,—the world fancies, and in this middle class the majority of men persuade themselves they will be found.

I denounce this notion of a middle class, as an immense and soul-ruining delusion. I warn you strongly not to be carried away by it. It is as vain an invention as the Pope's purgatory. It is a refuge of lies,—a castle in the air,—a Russian ice-palace,—a vast unreality,—an empty dream. This middle class is a class of Christians nowhere spoken of in the Bible.

There were two classes in the day of Noah's flood, those who were inside the ark, and those who were without;— two in the parable of the Gospel-net, those who are called the good fish, and those who are called the bad;—two in the parable of the ten virgins, those who are described as wise, and those who are described as foolish;—two in the account of the judgment day, the sheep and the goats;— two sides of the throne, the right hand and the left;—two abodes when the last sentence has been passed, heaven and hell.

And just so there are only two classes in the visible Church on earth,—those who are in the state of nature, and those who are in the state of grace,—those who are in the narrow way, and those who are in the broad,—those who have faith, and those who have not faith,—those who have been converted, and those who have not been converted,—those who are with Christ, and those who are against Him,—those who gather with Him, and those who scatter abroad,—those who are "wheat," and those who are "chaff." Into these two classes the whole professing Church of Christ may be divided. Beside these two classes there is none.

See now what cause there is for self-inquiry. Are you among the wheat, or among the chaff? Neutrality is impossible. Either you are in one class, or in the other. Which is it of the two?

You attend church, perhaps. You go to the Lord's table. You like good people. You can distinguish between good preaching and bad. You think Popery false, and oppose it warmly. You think Protestantism true, and support it cordially. You subscribe to religious Societies. You attend religious meetings. You sometimes read religious books. It is well: it is very well. It is good: it is all very good. It is more than can be said of many. But still this is not a straightforward answer to my question.—Are you wheat or are you chaff?

Have you been born again? Are you a new creature? Have you put off the old man, and put on the new? Have you ever felt your sins, and repented of them? Are you looking simply to Christ for pardon and life eternal? Do you love Christ? Do you serve Christ? Do you loathe heart-sins, and fight against them? Do you long for perfect holiness, and follow hard after it? Have you come out from the world? Do you delight in the Bible? Do you wrestle in prayer? Do you love Christ's people? Do you try to do good to the world? Are you vile in your own eyes, and willing to take the lowest place? Are you a Christian in business, and on week-days, and by your own fireside? Oh, think, think, think on these things, and then perhaps you will be better able to tell the state of your soul.

I beseech you not to turn away from my question, however unpleasant it may be. Answer it, though it may prick your conscience, and cut you to the heart. Answer it, though it may prove you in the wrong, and expose your fearful danger. Rest not, rest not, till you know how it is between you and God. Better a thousand times find out that you are in an evil case, and repent betimes, than live on in uncertainty, and be lost eternally.

II. Let me show, in the second place, *the time when the two great classes of mankind shall be separated.*

The text at the beginning of this paper foretells a separation. It says that Christ shall one day do to His professing Church what the farmer does to his corn. He shall winnow and sift it. He "shall throughly purge His floor." And then the wheat and the chaff shall be divided.

There is no separation yet. Good and bad are now all mingled together in the visible Church of Christ. Believers and unbelievers,—converted and unconverted,—holy and unholy,—all are to be found now among those who call themselves Christians. They sit side by side in our assemblies. They kneel side by side in our pews. They listen side by side to our sermons. They sometimes come up side by side to the Lord's table, and receive the same bread and wine from our hands.

But it shall not always be so. Christ shall come the

second time with His fan in His hand. He shall purge
His Church, even as He purified the temple. And then
the wheat and the chaff shall be separated, and each shall
go to its own place.

(a) Before Christ comes *separation is impossible*. It is
not in man's power to effect it. There lives not the
minister on earth who can read the hearts of every one in
his congregation. About some he may speak decidedly;—
he cannot about all. Who have oil in their lamps, and
who have not,—who have grace as well as profession,—
and who have profession only and no grace,—who are
children of God, and who of the devil,—all these are
questions which in many cases we cannot accurately decide.
The winnowing fan is not put into our hands.

Grace is sometimes so weak and feeble, that it looks
like nature. Nature is sometimes so plausible and well-
dressed, that it looks like grace. I believe we should
many of us have said that Judas was as good as any of the
Apostles; and yet he proved a traitor. I believe we should
have said that Peter was a reprobate when he denied his
Lord; and yet he repented immediately, and rose again.
We are but fallible men. "We know in part and we
prophesy in part." (1 Cor. xiii. 9.) We scarcely understand our own hearts. It is no great wonder if we cannot
read the hearts of others.

But it will not always be so. There is One coming who
never errs in judgment, and is perfect in knowledge.
Jesus shall purge His floor. Jesus shall sift the chaff
from the wheat. I wait for this. Till then I will lean to
the side of charity in my judgments. I would rather
tolerate much chaff in the Church than cast out one
grain of wheat. He shall soon come "who has His fan in
His hand," and then the certainty about every one shall
be known.

(b) Before Christ comes it is useless to *expect to see a
perfect Church*. There cannot be such a thing. The

wheat and the chaff, in the present state of things, will always be found together. I pity those who leave one Church and join another, because of a few faults and unsound members. I pity them, because they are fostering ideas which can never be realized. I pity them, because they are seeking that which cannot be found. I see "chaff" everywhere. I see imperfections and infirmities of some kind in every communion on earth. I believe there are few tables of the Lord, if any, where all the communicants are converted. I often see loud-talking professors exalted as saints. I often see holy and contrite believers set down as having no grace at all. I am satisfied if men are too scrupulous, they may go fluttering about, like Noah's dove, all their days, and never find rest.

Does any reader of this paper desire a perfect Church? You must wait for the day of Christ's appearing. Then, and not till then, you will see a "glorious Church, not having spot or wrinkle or any such thing." (Eph. v. 27.) Then, and not till then, the floor will be purged.

(c) Before Christ comes it is vain to *look for the conversion of the world.* How can it be, if He is to find wheat and chaff side by side in the day of His second coming? I believe some Christians expect that missions will fill the earth with the knowledge of Christ, and that little by little sin will disappear, and a state of perfect holiness gradually glide in. I cannot see with their eyes. I think they are mistaking God's purposes, and sowing for themselves bitter disappointment. I expect nothing of the kind. I see nothing in the Bible, or in the world around me, to make me expect it. I have never heard of a single congregation entirely converted to God, in England or Scotland, or of anything like it.—And why am I to look for a different result from the preaching of the Gospel in other lands? I only expect to see a few raised up as *witnesses* to Christ in every nation, some in one place and some in another. Then I expect the Lord Jesus will come in glory, with His fan in His hand. And when He has purged His floor, and not till then, His kingdom will begin.

No separation and no perfection till Christ comes! This is my creed. I am not moved when the infidel asks me why all the world is not converted, if Christianity is really true. I answer, It was never promised that it would be so in the present order of things. The Bible tells me that believers will always be few,—that corruptions and divisions and heresies will always abound, and that when my Lord returns to earth He will find plenty of chaff.

No perfection till Christ comes! I am not disturbed when men say, "Make all the people good Christians at home before you send missionaries to the heathen abroad." I answer, If I am to wait for that, I may wait for ever. When we have done all at home, the Church will still be a mixed body,—it will contain some wheat and much chaff.

But Christ will come again. Sooner or later there shall be a separation of the visible Church into two companies, and fearful shall that separation be. The wheat shall make up one company. The chaff shall make up another. The one company will be all godly. The other company will be all ungodly. Each shall be by themselves, and a great gulf between, that none can pass. Blessed indeed shall the righteous be in that day! They shall shine like stars, no longer obscured with clouds. They shall be beautiful as the lily, no longer choked with thorns. (Cant. ii. 2.) Wretched indeed will the ungodly be! How corrupt will corruption be when left without one grain of salt to season it! How dark will darkness be when left without one spark of light! Ah, it is not enough to respect and admire the Lord's people! You must belong to them, or you will one day be parted from them for ever. There will be no chaff in heaven. Many, many are the families where one will be taken and another left. (Luke xvii. 34.)

Who is there now among the readers of this paper that loves the Lord Jesus Christ in sincerity? If I know anything of the heart of a Christian, your greatest trials are in the company of worldly people,—your greatest joys in the company of the saints. Yes! there are many weary days, when your spirit feels broken and crushed by the earthly tone of all around you,—days when you could cry with David, "Woe is me that I dwell in Mesech, and have my habitation in the tents of Kedar." (Ps. cxx. 5.) And yet there are hours when your soul is so refreshed and revived by meeting some of God's dear children, that it seems like heaven on earth. Do I not speak to your heart? Are not these things true? See then how you should long for the time when Christ shall come again. See how you should pray daily that the Lord would hasten His kingdom, and say to Him, "Come quickly, Lord Jesus." (Rev. xxii. 20.) Then, and not till then, shall be a pure unmixed communion. Then, and not till then, the saints shall all be together, and shall go out from one another's presence no more. Wait a little. Wait a little. Scorn and contempt will soon be over. Laughter and ridicule shall soon have an end. Slander and misrepresentation will soon cease. Your Saviour shall come and plead your cause. And then, as Moses said to Korah, "the Lord will show who are His." * (Num. xvi. 5.)

Who is there among the readers of this paper that knows his heart is not right in the sight of God? See how you should fear and tremble at the thought of Christ's appearing. Alas, indeed for the man that lives and dies with nothing better than a cloak of religion! In

---

* "This is certain,—when the elect are all converted, then Christ will come to judgment. As he that rows a boat stays till all the passengers are taken into his boat, and then he rows away ; so Christ stays till all the elect are gathered in, and then He will hasten away to judgment."— *Thomas Watson.* 1660

the day when Christ shall purge His floor, you will be shown up and exposed in your true colours. You may deceive ministers, and friends, and neighbours,—but you cannot deceive Christ. The paint and varnish of a heartless Christianity will never stand the fire of that day. The Lord is a God of knowledge, and by Him actions are weighed. You will find that the eye which saw Achan and Gehazi, has read your secrets, and searched out your hidden things. You will hear that awful word, "Friend, how camest thou in hither, not having a wedding garment?" (Matt. xxii. 12.) Oh, tremble at the thought of the day of sifting and separation! Surely hypocrisy is a most losing game. Surely it never answers to act a part. Surely it never answers, like Ananias and Sapphira, to pretend to give God something, and yet to keep back your heart. It all fails at last. Your joy is but for a moment. Your hopes are no better than a dream. Oh, tremble, tremble: tremble and repent!

III. Let me show, in the third place, *the portion which Christ's people shall receive when He comes to purge His floor.*

The text at the beginning of this paper tells us that, in good and comfortable words. It tells us that Christ shall "gather His wheat into the garner."

When the Lord Jesus comes the second time, He shall collect His believing people into a place of safety. He will send His angels and gather them from every quarter. The sea shall give up the dead that are in it, and the graves the dead that are in them, and the living shall be changed. Not one poor sinner of mankind who has ever laid hold on Christ by faith shall be wanting in that company. Not one single grain of wheat shall be missing and left outside, when judgments fall upon a wicked world. There shall be a garner for the wheat of the earth, and into that garner all the wheat shall be brought.

It is a sweet and comfortable thought, that "the Lord taketh pleasure in His people" and "careth for the righteous." (Ps. cxlix. 4; 1 Pet. v. 7.) But how much the Lord cares for them, I fear is little known, and dimly seen. Believers have their trials, beyond question, and these both many and great. The flesh is weak. The world is full of snares. The cross is heavy. The way is narrow. The companions are few. But still they have strong consolations, if their eyes were but open to see them. Like Hagar, they have a well of water near them, even in the wilderness, though they often do not find it out. Like Mary, they have Jesus standing by their side, though often they are not aware of it for very tears. (Gen. xxi. 19; John xx. 14.)

Bear with me while I try to tell you something about Christ's care for poor sinners that believe in Him. Alas, indeed, that it should be needful! But we live in a day of weak and feeble statements. The danger of the state of nature is feebly exposed. The privileges of the state of grace are feebly set forth. Hesitating souls are not encouraged. Disciples are not established and confirmed. The man out of Christ is not rightly alarmed. The man in Christ is not rightly built up. The one sleeps on, and seldom has his conscience pricked. The other creeps and crawls all his days, and never thoroughly understands the riches of his inheritance. Truly this is a sore disease, and one that I would gladly help to cure. Truly it is a melancholy thing that the people of God should never go up to mount Pizgah, and never know the length and breadth of their possessions. To be brethren of Christ, and sons of God by adoption,—to have full and perfect forgiveness, and the renewing of the Holy Ghost,—to have a place in the book of life, and a name on the breast-plate of the Great High Priest in heaven,—all these are glorious things indeed. But still they are not the whole of a believer's portion. They are upper springs indeed, but still there are nether springs beside.

(*a*) The Lord *takes pleasure in His believing people.*
Though black in their own eyes, they are comely and
honourable in His. They are all fair. He sees "no spot"
in them. (Cant. iv. 7.) Their weaknesses and shortcomings
do not break off the union between Him and them. He
chose them, knowing all their hearts. He took them for
his own, with a perfect understanding of all their debts,
liabilities, and infirmities, and He will never break His
covenant and cast them off. When they fall, He will raise
them again. When they wander, He will bring them back.
Their *prayers* are pleasant to Him. As a father loves the
first stammering efforts of his child to speak, so the Lord
loves the poor feeble petitions of His people. He endorses
them with His own mighty intercession, and gives them
power on high. Their *services* are pleasant to Him. As
a father delights in the first daisy that his child picks up
and brings him, even so the Lord is pleased with the weak
attempts of His people to serve Him. Not a cup of cold
water shall lose its reward. Not a word spoken in love
shall ever be forgotten. The Holy Ghost inspired St. Paul
to tell the Hebrews of Noah's faith, but not of his drunkenness,—of Rahab's faith, but not of her lie. It is a
blessed thing to be God's wheat!

(*b*) The Lord *cares for His believing people in their lives.*
Their dwelling-place is well known. The street called
"straight," where Judas dwelt, and Paul lodged,—the house
by the sea-side, where Peter prayed, were all familiar to
their Lord. None have such attendants as they have :—
angels rejoice when they are born again ; angels minister
to them ; and angels encamp around them. None have such
food ;—their bread is given them and their water is sure, and
they have meat to eat of which the world knows nothing.
None have such company as they have : the Spirit dwelleth
with them ; the Father and the Son come to them, and
make their abode with them. (John xiv. 23.) Their steps
are all ordered from grace to glory : they that persecute

them persecute Christ Himself, and they that hurt them
hurt the apple of the Lord's eye. Their trials and temptations are all measured out by a wise Physician :—not a
grain of bitterness is ever mingled in their cup that is not
good for the health of their souls. Their temptations,
like Job's, are all under God's control.—Satan cannot
touch a hair of their head without their Lord's permission,
nor even tempt them above that which they shall be able
to bear. "As a father pitieth his own children, so does
the Lord pity them that fear Him." He never afflicts them
willingly. (Ps. ciii. 13; Lam. iii. 33.) He leads them by the
right way. He withholds nothing that is really for their
good. Come what will, there is always a "needs-be." When
they are placed in the furnace, it is that they may be
purified. When they are chastened, it is that they may
become more holy. When they are pruned, it is to make
them more fruitful. When they are transplanted from
place to place, it is that they may bloom more brightly.
All things are continually working together for their good.
Like the bee, they extract sweetness even out of the
bitterest flowers.

(c) The Lord *cares for His believing people in their
deaths.* Their times are all in the Lord's hand. The hairs
of their heads are all numbered, and not one can ever fall to
the ground without their Father. They are kept on earth
till they are ripe and ready for glory, and not one moment
longer. When they have had sun and rain enough, wind
and storm enough, cold and heat enough,—when the ear
is perfected,—then, and not till then, the sickle is put in.
They are all immortal till their work is done. There is
not a disease that can loosen the pins of their tabernacle,
until the Lord gives the word. A thousand may fall at
their right hand, but there is not a plague that can touch
them till the Lord sees good. There is not a physician
that can keep them alive, when the Lord gives the word.
When they come to their death-bed, the everlasting arms

are round about them, and make all their bed in their sickness. When they die, they die like Moses, "according to the word of the Lord," at the right time, and in the right way. (Deut. xxxiv. 5.) And when they breathe their last, they fall asleep in Christ, and are at once carried, like Lazarus, into Abraham's bosom. Yes! it is a blessed thing to be Christ's wheat! When the sun of other men is setting, the sun of the believer is rising. When other men are laying aside their honours, he is putting his on. Death locks the door on the unbeliever, and shuts him out from hope. But death opens the door to the believer, and lets him into paradise.

(*d*) And the Lord *will care for His believing people in the dreadful day of His appearing.* The flaming fire shall not come nigh them. The voice of the Archangel and the trump of God shall proclaim no terrors to their ears. Sleeping or waking, quick or dead, mouldering in the coffin, or standing at the post of daily duty,—believers shall be secure and unmoved. They shall lift up their heads with joy when they see redemption drawing nigh. They shall be changed, and put on their beautiful garments in the twinkling of an eye. They shall be "caught up to meet the Lord in the air." (1 Thess. iv. 17.) Jesus will do nothing to a sin-laden world till all his people are safe. There was an ark for Noah when the flood began. There was a Zoar for Lot when the fire fell on Sodom. There was a Pella for early Christians when Jerusalem was besieged. There was a Zurich for English reformers when Popish Mary came to the throne. And there will be a garner for all the wheat of the earth in the last day. Yes! it is a blessed thing to be Christ's wheat!

I often wonder at the miserable faithlessness of those among us who are believers. Next to the hardness of the unconverted heart, I call it one of the greatest wonders in the world. I wonder that with such mighty reasons for confidence we can still be so full of doubts. I marvel, above all things, how any can deny the doctrine that Christ's people persevere unto the end, and can fancy that He who loved them so as to die for them upon the cross, will ever let them be cast away. I cannot think so. I do not believe the Lord Jesus will ever lose one of His flock. He will not let Satan pluck away from Him so much as one sick lamb. He will not allow one bone of His mystical body to be broken. He will not suffer one jewel to fall from His crown. He and His bride have been once joined in an everlasting covenant, and they shall never, never be put asunder. The trophies won by earthly conquerors have often been wrested from them, and carried off; but this shall never be said of the trophies of Him who triumphed for us on the cross. "My sheep," He says, "shall never perish." (John x. 28.) I take my stand on that text. I know not how it can be evaded. If words have any meaning, the perseverance of Christ's people is there.

I do not believe, when David had rescued the lamb from the paws of the lion, that he left it weak and wounded to perish in the wilderness. I cannot believe when the Lord Jesus has delivered a soul from the snare of the devil that He will ever leave that soul to take his chance, and wrestle on in his own feebleness, against sin, the devil, and the world.

I dare be sure, if you were present at a shipwreck, and seeing some helpless child tossing on the waves were to plunge into the sea and save him at the risk of your own life,—I dare be sure you would not be content with merely bringing that child safe to shore. You would not lay him down when you had reached the land, and say, "I will do no more. He is weak,—he is insensible,—he is cold: it matters not. I have done enough,—I have delivered him from the waters: he is not drowned." You would not do it. You would not say so. You would not treat that child in such a manner. You would lift him in your arms;

you would carry him to the nearest house; you would try to bring back warmth and animation; you would use every means to restore health and vigour: you would never leave him till his recovery was a certain thing.

And can you suppose the Lord Jesus Christ is less merciful and less compassionate? Can you think He would suffer on the cross and die, and yet leave it uncertain whether believers in Him would be saved? Can you think He would wrestle with death and hell, and go down to the grave for our sakes, and yet allow our eternal life to hang on such a thread as our poor miserable endeavours.

Oh, no: He does not do so! He is a perfect and complete Saviour. Those whom He loves, He loves unto the end. Those whom He washes in His blood He never leaves nor forsakes. He puts His fear into their hearts, so that they shall not depart from Him. Where He begins a work, there He also finishes. All whom He plants in His "garden inclosed" on earth, He transplants sooner or later into paradise. All whom He quickens by His Spirit He will also bring with Him when He enters His kingdom. There is a garner for every grain of the wheat. All shall appear in Zion before God.

From false grace man may fall, and that both finally and foully. I never doubt this. I see proof of it continually. From true grace men never do fall totally. They never did, and they never will. If they commit sin, like Peter, they shall repent and rise again. If they err from the right way, like David, they shall be brought back. It is not any strength or power of their own that keeps them from apostacy. They are kept because the power, and love, and promises of the Trinity are all engaged on their side. The election of God the Father shall not be fruitless; the intercession of God the Son shall not be ineffectual; the love of God the Spirit shall not be labour in vain. The Lord "shall keep the feet of His saints." (1 Sam. ii. 9.) They shall all be more than conquerors, through Him that loved them. They all shall conquer, and none die eternally.*

If you have not yet taken up the cross and become Christ's disciple, you little know what privileges you are missing. Peace with God now and glory hereafter,—the everlasting arms to keep you by the way, and the garner of safety in the end,—all these are freely offered to you without money and without price. You may say that Christians have tribulations;—you forget that they have also consolations. You may say they have peculiar sorrows;—you forget they have also peculiar joys. You see but half the Christian life. You see not all. You see the warfare; —but not the meat and the wages. You see the tossing and conflict of the outward part of Christianity; you see not the hidden treasures which lie deep within. Like Elisha's servant, you see the enemies of God's children; but you do not, like Elisha, see the chariots and horses of fire which protect them. Oh, judge not by outward appearances! Be sure that the least drop of the water of life is better than all the rivers of the world. Remember the garner and the crown. Be wise in time.

If you feel that you are a weak disciple, think not that weakness shuts you out from any of the privileges of which I have been speaking. Weak faith is true faith, and weak grace is true grace; and both are the gift of Him who never gives in vain. Fear not, neither be discouraged. Doubt not, neither despair. Jesus will never "break the bruised reed, nor quench the smoking flax." (Isa. xlii. 3.)

---

* "Blessed for ever and ever be that mother's child whose faith hath made him the child of God. The earth may shake, the pillars of the world may tremble under us, the countenance of the heaven may be appalled, the sun may lose his light, the moon her beauty, the stars their glory: but concerning the man that trusteth in God,—what is there in the world that shall change his heart, overthrow his faith, alter his affection towards God, or the affection of God to him?"— *Richard Hooker*, 1585.

The babes in a family are as much loved and thought of as the elder brothers and sisters. The tender seedlings in a garden are as diligently looked after as the old trees. The lambs in the flock are as carefully tended by the good shepherd as the old sheep. Oh, rest assured it is just the same in Christ's family, in Christ's garden, in Christ's flock! All are loved. All are tenderly thought of. All are cared for. And all shall be found in His garner at last.

IV. Let me show, in the last place, the *portion which remains for all who are not Christ's people.*

The text at the beginning of this paper describes this in words which should make our ears tingle: Christ shall "burn up the chaff with fire unquenchable."

When the Lord Jesus Christ comes to purge His floor, He shall punish all who are not His disciples with a fearful punishment. All who are found impenitent and unbelieving,—all who have held the truth in unrighteousness,—all who have clung to sin, stuck to the world, and set their affections on things below,—all who are without Christ,—all such shall come to an awful end. Christ shall "burn up the chaff."

Their punishment shall be *most severe.* There is no pain like that of burning. Put your finger in the candle for a moment, if you doubt this, and try. Fire is the most destructive and devouring of all elements. Look into the mouth of a blast-furnace, and think what it would be to be there. Fire is of all elements most opposed to life. Creatures can live in air, and earth, and water; but nothing can live in fire. Yet fire is the portion to which the Christless and unbelieving will come. Christ will "burn up the chaff with fire."

Their punishment shall be *eternal.* Millions of ages shall pass away, and the fire into which the chaff is cast shall still burn on. That fire shall never burn low and become dim. The fuel of that fire shall never waste away and be consumed. It is "unquenchable fire."

Alas, these are sad and painful things to speak of! I have no pleasure in dwelling on them. I could rather say with the Apostle Paul, as I write, "I have great heaviness and continual sorrow." (Rom. ix. 2.) But they are things written for our learning, and it is good to consider them. They are a part of that Scripture which is "all profitable," and they ought to be heard. Painful as the subject of hell is, it is one about which I dare not, cannot, must not be silent. Who would desire to speak of hell-fire if God had not spoken of it? When God has spoken of it so plainly, who can safely hold his peace?

I dare not shut my eyes to the fact that a deep-rooted infidelity lurks in men's minds on the subject of hell. I see it oozing out in the utter apathy of some: they eat, and drink, and sleep, as if there was no wrath to come. I see it creeping forth in the coldness of others about their neighbours' souls: they show little anxiety to pluck brands from the fire. I desire to denounce such infidelity with all my might. Believing that there are "terrors of the Lord," as well as the "recompense of reward," I call on all who profess to believe the Bible, to be on their guard.

(a) I know that some do not believe there is any hell at all. They think it impossible there can be such a place. They call it inconsistent with the mercy of God. They say it is too awful an idea to be really true. The devil of course rejoices in the views of such people. They help his kingdom mightily. They are preaching up his own favourite doctrine: "Ye shall not surely die." (Gen. iii. 4.)

(b) I know, furthermore, that some do not believe that hell is eternal. They tell us it is incredible that a compassionate God will punish men for ever. He will surely open the prison doors at last. This also is a mighty help to the devil's cause. "Take your ease," he whispers to sinners: "if you do make a mistake, never mind, it is not for ever." A wicked woman was overheard in the streets of London saying to a bad companion, "Come along: who is afraid? Some parsons say there is no hell."

(c) I know also that some believe there is a hell, but never allow that anybody is going there. All people, with them, are good as soon as they die,—all were sincere,—all meant well,—and all, they hope, got to heaven. Alas, what a common delusion is this! I can well understand the feeling of the little girl who asked her mother where all the wicked people were buried, "for she found no mention on the grave-stones of any except the good."

(d) And I know very well that some believe there is a hell, and never like it to be spoken of. It is a subject that should always be kept back, in their opinion. They see no profit in bringing it forward, and are rather shocked when it is mentioned. This also is an immense help to the devil. "Hush, hush!" says Satan, "say nothing about hell." The fowler wishes to hear no noise when he lays his snares. The wolf would like the shepherd to sleep while he prowls round the fold. The devil rejoices when Christians are silent about hell.

All these notions are the opinions of man. But what is it to you and me what man thinks in religion? Man will not judge us at the last day. Man's fancies and traditions are not to be our guide in this life. There is but one point to be settled: "What says the Word of God?"

(a) Do you believe the Bible? Then depend upon it, *hell is real and true.* It is true as heaven,—as true as justification by faith,—as true as the fact that Christ died upon the cross,—as true as the Dead Sea. There is not a fact or doctrine which you may not lawfully doubt if you doubt hell. Disbelieve hell, and you unscrew, unsettle, and unpin everything in Scripture. You may as well throw your Bible away at once. From "no hell" to "no God" there is but a series of steps.

(b) Do you believe the Bible? Then depend upon it,

hell will have inhabitants. The wicked shall certainly be turned into hell, and all the people that forget God. "These shall go away into everlasting punishment." (Matt. xxv. 46.) The same blessed Saviour who now sits on a throne of grace, will one day sit on a throne of judgment, and men will see there is such a thing as "the wrath of the Lamb." (Rev. vi. 16.) The same lips which now say, "Come: come unto Me!" will one day say, "Depart, ye cursed!" Alas, how awful the thought of being condemned by Christ Himself, judged by the Saviour, sentenced to misery by the Lamb!

(c) Do you believe the Bible? Then depend upon it, *hell will be intense and unutterable woe.* It is vain to talk of all the expressions about it being only figures of speech. The pit, the prison, the worm, the fire, the thirst, the blackness, the darkness, the weeping, the gnashing of teeth, the second death,—all these may be figures of speech if you please. But Bible figures mean something, beyond all question, and here they mean something which man's mind can never fully conceive. The miseries of mind and conscience are far worse than those of the body. The whole extent of hell, the present suffering, the bitter recollection of the past, the hopeless prospect of the future, will never be thoroughly known except by those who go there.

(d) Do you believe the Bible? Then depend upon it, *hell is eternal.* It must be eternal, or words have no meaning at all. For ever and ever—everlasting—unquenchable—never-dying,—all these are expressions used about hell, and expressions that cannot be explained away. It must be eternal, or the very foundations of heaven are cast down. If hell has an end, heaven has an end too. They both stand or fall together.—It must be eternal, or else every doctrine of the Gospel is undermined. If a man may escape hell at length without faith in Christ, or sanctification of the Spirit, sin is no longer an infinite evil, and there was no such great need for Christ making an atonement. And where is there warrant for saying that hell can ever change a heart, or make it fit for heaven?—It must be eternal, or hell would cease to be hell altogether. Give a man hope, and he will bear anything. Grant a hope of deliverance, however distant, and hell is but a drop of water. Ah, these are solemn things! Well said old Caryl: "FOR EVER is the most solemn saying in the Bible." Alas, for that day which will have no to-morrow,—that day when men shall seek death and not find it, and shall desire to die, but death shall flee from them! Who shall dwell with devouring fire? Who shall dwell with everlasting burnings? (Rev. ix. 6; Isa. xxxiii. 14.)

(e) Do you believe the Bible? Then depend upon it, *hell is a subject that ought not to be kept back.* It is striking to observe the many texts about it in Scripture. It is striking to observe that none say so much about it as our Lord Jesus Christ, that gracious and merciful Saviour; and the apostle John, whose heart seems full of love. Truly it may well be doubted whether we ministers speak of it as much as we ought. I cannot forget the words of a dying hearer of Mr. Newton's: "Sir, you often told me of Christ and salvation: why did you not oftener remind me of hell and danger?"

Let others hold their peace about hell if they will;—I dare not do so. I see it plainly in Scripture, and I must speak of it. I fear that thousands are on that broad way that leads to it, and I would fain arouse them to a sense of the peril before them. What would you say of the man who saw his neighbour's house in danger of being burned down, and never raised the cry of "Fire"? What ought to be said of us as ministers, if we call ourselves watchmen for souls, and yet see the fires of hell raging in the distance, and never give the alarm? Call it bad taste, if you like, to speak of hell. Call it charity to make things pleasant, and speak smoothly, and soothe men with a constant lullaby of peace. From such notions of taste and charity may I ever be delivered! My notion of charity is to warn men plainly of danger. My notion of taste in the ministerial office is to declare all the counsel of God. If I never spoke of hell, I should think I had kept back something that was profitable, and should look on myself as an accomplice of the devil.

I beseech every reader of this paper, in all tender affection, to beware of false views of the subject on which I have been dwelling. Beware of new and strange doctrines about hell and the eternity of punishment. Beware of manufacturing a God of your own,—a God who is all mercy, but not just,—a God who is all love, but not holy,—a God who has a heaven for everybody, but a hell for none, —a God who can allow good and bad to be side by side in time, but will make no distinction between good and bad in eternity. Such a God is an idol of your own, as really as Jupiter or Moloch,—as true an idol as any snake or crocodile in an Egyptian temple,—as true an idol as was ever moulded out of brass or clay. The hands of your own fancy and sentimentality have made him. He is not the God of the Bible, and besides the God of the Bible there is no God at all. Your heaven would be no heaven at all. A heaven containing all sorts of characters indiscriminately would be miserable discord indeed. Alas, for the eternity of such a heaven! there would be little difference between it and hell. There is a hell! There is a fire for the chaff! Take heed lest you find it out, to your cost, too late.

Beware of being wise above that which is written. Beware of forming fanciful theories of your own, and then trying to make the Bible square in with them. Beware of making selections from your Bible to suit your taste,— refusing, like a spoilt child, whatever you think bitter,— seizing, like a spoilt child, whatever you think sweet. What is all this but taking Jehoiakim's penknife? (Jer. xxxvi. 23.) What does it amount to but telling God, that you, a poor short-lived worm, know what is good for you better than He. It will not do: it will not do. You must take the Bible as it is. You must read it all, and believe it all. You must come to the reading of it in the spirit of a little child. Dare not to say, "I believe this verse, for I like it. I reject that, for I do not like it. I receive this, for I can understand it. I refuse that, for I cannot reconcile it with my views." Nay, but, O man, "who art thou that repliest against God?" (Rom. ix. 20.) By what right do you talk in this way? Surely it were better to say over every chapter in the Word, "Speak, Lord, for thy servant heareth."—If men would do this, they would never deny hell, the chaff, and the fire.

And now, let me say four things in conclusion, and then I have done. I have shown the two great classes of mankind, the wheat and the chaff.—I have shown the separation which will one day take place.—I have shown the safety of the Lord's people.—I have shown the fearful portion of the Christless and unbelieving.—I commend these things to the conscience of every reader of this paper, as in the sight of God.

(1) First of all, settle it down in your mind that the things of which I have been speaking are *all real and true.*

I do believe that many never see the great truths of religion in this light. I firmly believe that many never listen to the things they hear from ministers as realities. They regard it all, like Gallio, as a matter of "names and words," and nothing more; a huge shadow,—a formal part-acting,—a vast sham. The last novel, the latest news from France, India, Australia, Turkey, or New York,—all these are things they realize: they feel interested and excited about them. But as to the Bible, and heaven, and the kingdom of Christ, and the judgment day,—these are subjects that they hear unmoved: they do not really believe them. If Layard had dug up at Nineveh anything damaging the truth and authority of the Old Testament Scriptures, it would not have interfered with their peace for an hour.

If you have unhappily got into this frame of mind, I charge you to cast it off for ever. Whether you mean to hear or forbear, awaken to a thorough conviction that the things I have brought before you are real and true. The wheat, the chaff, the separation, the garner, the fire,—all these are great realities,—as real as the sun in heaven,—as real as the paper which your eyes behold. For my part, I believe in heaven, and I believe in hell. I believe in a coming judgment. I believe in a day of sifting. I am not ashamed to say so. I believe them all, and therefore write as I do. Oh, take a friend's advice,—live as if these things were true.

(2) Settle it down in your mind, in the second place, that the things of which I write *concern yourself.* They are your business, your affair, and your concern.

Many, I am satisfied, never look on religion as a matter that concerns themselves. They attend on its outward part, as a decent and proper fashion. They hear sermons. They read religious books. They have their children christened. But all the time they never ask themselves, "What is all this to me?" They sit in our churches like spectators in a theatre or court of law. They read our writings as if they were reading a report of an interesting trial, or of some event far away. But they never say to themselves, "I am the man."

If you have this kind of feeling, depend upon it it will never do. There must be an end of all this if ever you are to be saved. You are the man I write to, whoever you may be who reads this paper. I write not specially to the rich. I write not specially to the poor. I write to everybody who will read, whatever his rank may be. It is on your soul's account that I am pleading, and not another's. You are spoken of in the text that begins this paper. You are this very day either among the "wheat" or among the "chaff." Your portion will one day either be the garner or the fire. Oh, that men were wise, and would lay these things to heart! Oh, that they would not trifle, dally, linger, live on half-and-half Christians, meaning well, but never acting boldly, and at last awake when it is too late!

(3) Settle it down in your mind, in the third place, that if you are willing to be one of the wheat of the earth, *the Lord Jesus Christ is willing to receive you.*

Does any man suppose that Jesus is not willing to see His garner filled? Do you think He does not desire to bring many sons to glory? Oh, but you little know the depth of His mercy and compassion, if you can think such a thought! He wept over unbelieving Jerusalem. He mourns over the impenitent and the thoughtless in the present day. He sends you invitations by my mouth this hour. He invites you to hear and live, to forsake the way of the foolish and go in the paths of understanding. "As I live," He says, "I have no pleasure in the death of him that dieth. Turn ye, turn ye: why will ye die?" (Ezek. xviii. 32.)

Oh, if you never came to Christ for life before, come to Him this very day! Come to Him with the penitent's prayer for mercy and grace. Come to Him without delay. Come to Him while the subject of this paper is still fresh on you mind. Come to Him before another sun rises on the earth, and let the morning find you a new creature.

If you are determined to have the world, and the things of the world,—its pleasures and its rewards,—its follies and its sins;—if you must have your own way, and cannot give up anything for Christ and your soul;—if this be your case, there is but one end before you. I fairly warn you,—I plainly tell you:—You will sooner or later come to the unquenchable fire.

But if any man is willing to be saved, the Lord Jesus Christ stands ready to save him. "Come unto Me," He says, "weary soul, and I will give you rest. Come, guilty and sinful soul, and I will give you free pardon. Come, lost and ruined soul, and I will give you eternal life." (Matt. xi. 28.)

Let that passage be a word in season. Arise and call upon the Lord. Let the angels of God rejoice over one more saved soul. Let the courts of heaven hear the good tidings that one more lost sheep is found.

(4) Settle it down in your mind, last of all, that if you have committed your soul to Christ, *Christ will never allow that soul to perish.*

The everlasting arms are round about you. Lean back in them and know your safety. The same hand that was nailed to the cross is holding you. The same wisdom that framed the heavens and the earth is engaged to maintain your cause. The same power that redeemed the twelve tribes from the house of bondage is on your side. The same love that bore with and carried Israel from Egypt to Canaan is pledged to keep you. Yes! they are well kept whom Christ keeps ! Our faith may repose calmly on such a bed as Christ's omnipotence.

Take comfort, doubting believer. Why are you cast down ? The love of Jesus is no summer-day fountain : no man ever yet saw its bottom. The compassion of Jesus is a fire that never yet burned low : the cold, grey ashes of that fire have never yet been seen. Take comfort. In your own heart you may find little cause for rejoicing. But you may always rejoice in the Lord.

You say your faith is so small. But where is it said that none shall be saved except their faith be great ? And after all, "Who gave thee any faith at all ?" The very fact that you have any faith is a token for good.

You say your sins are so many. But where is the sin, or the heap of sins, that the blood of Jesus cannot wash away? And after all, "Who told thee thou hadst any sins?" That feeling never came from thyself. Blessed indeed is that mother's child who really knows and feels that he is a sinner.

Take comfort, I say once more, if you have really come to Christ. Take comfort, and know your privileges. Cast every care on Jesus. Tell every want to Jesus. Roll every burden on Jesus: sins,—unbelief,—doubts,—fears, —anxieties,—lay them all on Christ. He loves to see you doing so. He loves to be employed as your High Priest. He loves to be trusted. He loves to see His people ceasing from the vain effort to carry their burdens for themselves.

I commend these things to the notice of every one into whose hands this volume may fall. Only be among Christ's "wheat" now, and then, in the great day of separation, as sure as the Bible is true, you shall be in Christ's "garner" hereafter.

XXI

ETERNITY!

"The things which are seen are temporal; but the things which are not seen are eternal."—2 Cor. iv. 18.

A SUBJECT stands out on the face of this text which is one of the most solemn and heart-searching in the Bible. That subject is *eternity.**

The subject is one of which the wisest man can only take in a little. We have no eyes to see it fully, no line to fathom it, no mind to grasp it; and yet we must not refuse to consider it. There are star-depths in the heavens above us, which the most powerful telescope cannot pierce;

---

* The following pages contain the *substance* of a sermon which I preached, by invitation, in the nave of Peterborough Cathedral, on the fourth Sunday in Advent, 1877,—the *substance* and not the precise words. The plain truth is, that the sermon was not intended for publication. It was preached from notes, and was one of those popular addresses which will not bear close reporting. A style of language which satisfies the ear when listened to, will seldom satisfy the mind when read. On receiving a manuscript report from the publisher, I soon found that it would require far more labour to condense, correct, paragraph, punctuate, and prepare the sermon for the press, than to write it out roughly from my own notes and recollection. From want of time I had no alternative but to adopt this course, or to object altogether to publication. The result is that the reader has before him the matter, order, heads, arrangement, and principal thoughts of my sermon, but not, I repeat, the precise words.

yet it is well to look into them and learn something, if we cannot learn everything. There are heights and depths about the subject of eternity which mortal man can never comprehend; but God has spoken of it, and we have no right to turn away from it altogether.

The subject is one which we must never approach without the Bible in our hands. The moment we depart from "God's Word written," in considering eternity and the future state of man, we are likely to fall into error. In examining points like these we have nothing to do with preconceived notions as to what is God's character, and what *we think* God ought to be, or ought to do with man after death.* We have only to find out what is written. What saith the Scripture? What saith the Lord? It is wild work to tell us that we ought to have "noble thoughts about God," independent of, and over and above, Scripture. Natural religion soon comes to a standstill here. The noblest thoughts about God which we have a right to hold are the thoughts which He has been pleased to reveal to us in His "written Word."

I ask the attention of all into whose hands this paper may fall, while I offer a few suggestive thoughts about eternity. As a mortal man I feel deeply my own insufficiency to handle this subject. But I pray that God the Holy Ghost, whose strength is made perfect in weakness, may bless the words I speak, and make them seeds of eternal life in many minds.

I. The first thought which I commend to the attention of my readers is this:—*We live in a world where all things are temporal and passing away.*

---

* "What sentence can we expect from a judge, who at the same time that he calls in witnesses and pretends to examine them, makes a declaration that however, let them say what they will, the cause is so absurd, is so unjust, that no evidence will be sufficient to prove it?"—*Horbery,* vol. ii. p. 137.

That man must be blind indeed who cannot realize this. Everything around us is decaying, dying, and coming to an end. There is a sense no doubt in which "matter" is eternal. Once created, it will never entirely perish. But ·in a popular practical sense, there is nothing undying about us except our souls. No wonder the poet says:—

> "Change and decay in all around I see:
> O Thou that changest not, abide with me!"

We are all going, going, going, whether high or low, gentle or simple, rich or poor, old or young. We are all going, and shall soon be gone.

Beauty is only temporal. Sarah was once the fairest of women, and the admiration of the Court of Egypt; yet a day came when even Abraham, her husband, said, "Let me bury my dead out of my sight." (Gen. xxiii. 4.)—Strength of body is only temporal. David was once a mighty man of valour, the slayer of the lion and the bear, and the champion of Israel against Goliath; yet a day came when even David had to be nursed and ministered to in his old age like a child.—Wisdom and power of brain are only temporal. Solomon was once a prodigy of knowledge, and all the kings of the earth came to hear his wisdom; yet even Solomon in his latter days played the fool exceedingly, and allowed his wives to "turn away his heart." (1 Kings xi. 2.)

Humbling and painful as these truths may sound, it is good for us all to realize them and lay them to heart. The houses we live in, the homes we love, the riches we accumulate, the professions we follow, the plans we form, the relations we enter into,—they are only for a time. "The things seen are temporal." "The fashion of this world passeth away." (1 Cor. vii. 31.)

The thought is one which ought to rouse every one who is living only for this world. If his conscience is not utterly seared, it should stir in him great searchings of heart. Oh, take care what you are doing! Awake to see things in their true light before it be too late. The things you live for now are all temporal and passing away. The pleasures, the amusements, the recreations, the merry-makings, the profits, the earthly callings, which now absorb all your heart and drink up all your mind, will soon be over. They are poor ephemeral things which cannot last. Oh, love them not too well; grasp them not too tightly; make them not your idols! You cannot keep them, and you must leave them. Seek first the kingdom of God, and then everything else shall be added to you. "Set your affections on things above, not on things on the earth." Oh, you that love the world, be wise in time! Never, never forget that it is written, "The world passeth away, and the lust thereof; but he that doeth the will of God abideth for ever." (Col. iii. 2; 1 John ii. 17.)

The same thought ought to cheer and comfort every true Christian. Your trials, crosses, and conflicts, are all temporal. They will soon have an end; and even now they are working for you "a far more exceeding and eternal weight of glory." (2 Cor. iv. 17.) Take them patiently : bear them quietly : look upward, forward, onward, and far beyond them. Fight your daily fight under an abiding conviction that it is only for a little time, and that rest is not far off. Carry your daily cross with an abiding recollection that it is one of the "things seen" which are temporal. The cross shall soon be exchanged for a crown, and you shall sit down with Abraham, Isaac, and Jacob in the kingdom of God.

II. The second thought which I commend to the attention of my readers is this :— *We are all going towards a world where everything is eternal.*

That great unseen state of existence which lies behind the grave, is for ever. Whether it be happy or miserable, whether it be a condition of joy or sorrow, in one respect it is utterly unlike this world,—it is for ever. *There* at any rate will be no change and decay, no end, no good-bye, no mornings and evenings, no alteration, no annihilation. Whatever there is beyond the tomb, when the last trumpet has sounded, and the dead are raised, will be endless, everlasting, and eternal. "The things unseen are eternal."

We cannot fully realize this condition. The contrast between now and then, between this world and the next, is so enormously great that our feeble minds will not take it in. The consequences it entails are so tremendous, that they almost take away our breath, and we shrink from looking at them. But when the Bible speaks plainly we have no right to turn away from a subject, and with the Bible in our hands we shall do well to look at the "things which are eternal."

Let us settle it then in our minds, for one thing, that the *future happiness* of those who are saved is eternal. However little we may understand it, it is something which will have no end: it will never cease, never grow old, never decay, never die. At God's "right hand are pleasures for evermore." (Ps. xvi. 11.) Once landed in paradise, the saints of God shall go out no more. The inheritance is "incorruptible, undefiled, and fadeth not away." They shall "receive a crown of glory that fadeth not away." (1 Pet. i. 4; v. 4.) Their warfare is accomplished; their fight is over; their work is done. They shall hunger no more, neither thirst any more. They are travelling on towards an "eternal weight of glory," towards a home which shall never be broken up, a meeting without a parting, a family gathering without a separation, a day without night. Faith shall be swallowed up in sight, and hope in certainty. They shall see as they have been seen, and know as they have been known, and "be for ever with the Lord." I do not wonder that the apostle Paul adds, "Comfort one another with these words." (1 Thess. iv. 17, 18.)

Let us settle it, for another thing, in our minds, that the *future misery* of those who are finally lost is eternal. This is an awful truth, I am aware, and flesh and blood naturally shrink from the contemplation of it. But I am one of those who believe it to be plainly revealed in Scripture, and I dare not keep it back in the pulpit. To my eyes eternal future happiness and eternal future misery appear to stand side by side. I fail to see how you can distinguish the duration of one from the duration of the other. If the joy of the believer is for ever, the sorrow of the unbeliever is also for ever. If heaven is eternal, so likewise is hell. It may be my ignorance, but I know not how the conclusion can be avoided.

I cannot reconcile the non-eternity of punishment with the *language of the Bible*. Its advocates talk loudly about love and charity, and say that it does not harmonize with the merciful and compassionate character of God. But what saith the Scripture? Who ever spoke such loving and merciful words as our Lord Jesus Christ? Yet His are the lips which three times over describe the consequence of impenitence and sin, as "the worm that never dies and the fire that is not quenched." He is the Person who speaks in one sentence of the wicked going away into "everlasting punishment" and the righteous into "life eternal." (Mark ix. 43—48; Matt. xxv. 46.)*— Who does not remember the Apostle Paul's words about charity? Yet he is the very Apostle who says, the wicked

---

* "If God had intended to have told us that the punishment of wicked man shall have no end, the languages wherein the Scriptures are written do hardly afford fuller and more certain words than those that are used in this case, whereby to express a duration without end; and likewise, which is almost a peremptory decision of the thing, the duration of the punishment of wicked men is in the very same sentence expressed by the very same word which is used for the duration of happiness of the righteous."—*Archbishop Tillotson on Hell Torments.* See *Horbery*, vol. ii. p. 42.

"shall be punished with everlasting destruction." (2 Thess.
i. 9.)—Who does not know the spirit of love which runs
through all St. John's Gospel and Epistles? Yet the
beloved Apostle is the very writer in the New Testament
who dwells most strongly, in the book of Revelation, on
the reality and eternity of future woe. What shall we say
to these things? Shall we be wise above that which is
written? Shall we admit the dangerous principle that
words in Scripture do not mean what they appear to mean?
Is it not far better to lay our hands on our mouths and
say, "Whatever God has written must be true." "Even
so, Lord God Almighty, true and righteous are Thy judgments." (Rev. xvi. 7.)

I cannot reconcile the non-eternity of punishment with
the *language of our Prayer-book*. The very first petition
in our matchless Litany contains this sentence, "From
everlasting damnation, good Lord, deliver us." — The
Catechism teaches every child who learns it, that whenever we repeat the Lord's Prayer we desire our Heavenly
Father to "keep us from our ghostly enemy and from
everlasting death."—Even in our Burial Service we pray
at the grave side, "Deliver us not into the bitter pains of
eternal death."—Once more I ask, "What shall we say to
these things?" Shall our congregations be taught that
even when people live and die in sin we may hope for
their happiness in a remote future? Surely the common
sense of many of our worshippers would reply, that if this
is the case Prayer-book words mean nothing at all.

I lay no claim to any peculiar knowledge of Scripture.
I feel daily that I am no more infallible than the Bishop
of Rome. But I must speak according to the light which
God has given to me; and I do not think I should do
my duty if I did not raise a warning voice on this subject,
and try to put Christians on their guard. Six thousand
years ago sin entered into the world by the devil's daring
falsehood,—"Ye shall not surely die." (Gen. iii. 4.) At

the end of six thousand years the great enemy of man-kind is still using his old weapon, and trying to persuade men that they may live and die in sin, and yet at some distant period may be finally saved. Let us not be ignorant of his devices. Let us walk steadily in the old paths. Let us hold fast the old truth, and believe that as the happiness of the saved is eternal, so also is the misery of the lost.*

(a) Let us hold it fast *in the interest of the whole system of revealed religion.* What was the use of God's Son becoming incarnate, agonizing in Gethsemane, and dying on the cross to make atonement, if men can be finally saved without believing on Him? Where is the slightest proof that saving faith in Christ's blood can ever begin after death? Where is the need of the Holy Ghost, if sinners are at last to enter heaven without conversion and renewal of heart? Where can we find the smallest evidence that any one can be born again, and have a new heart, if he dies in an unregenerate state? If a man may escape eternal punishment at last, without faith in Christ or sanctification of the Spirit, sin is no longer an infinite evil, and there was no need for Christ making an atonement.

(b) Let us hold it fast *for the sake of holiness and morality.* I can imagine nothing so pleasant to flesh and blood as the specious theory that we may live in sin, and yet escape eternal perdition; and that although we "serve divers lusts and pleasures" while we are here, we shall somehow or other all get to heaven hereafter! Only tell

---

* "There is nothing that Satan more desires than that we should believe that he does not exist, and that there is no such a place as hell, and no such things as eternal torments. He whispers all this into our ears, and he exults when he hears a layman, and much more when he hears a clergyman, deny these things, for then he hopes to make them and others his victims."—*Bishop Wordsworth's Sermons on Future Rewards and Punishments,* p. 36.

the young man who is "wasting his substance in riotous living" that there is heaven at last even for those who live and die in sin, and he is never likely to turn from evil. Why should he repent and take up the cross, if he can get to heaven at last without trouble?

(c) Finally, let us hold it fast, *for the sake of the common hopes of all God's saints.* Let us distinctly understand that every blow struck at the eternity of punishment is an equally heavy blow at the eternity of reward. It is impossible to separate the two things. No ingenious theological definition can divide them. They stand or fall together. The same language is used, the same figures of speech are employed, when the Bible speaks about either condition. Every attack on the duration of hell is also an attack on the duration of heaven.* It is a deep and true saying, "With the sinner's fear our hope departs.'

I turn from this part of my subject with a deep sense of its painfulness. I feel strongly with Robert M'Cheyne, that "it is a hard subject to handle lovingly." But I turn from it with an equally deep conviction that if we believe the Bible we must never give up anything which it contains. From hard, austere, and unmerciful theology, good Lord, deliver us! If men are not saved it is because they "will not come to Christ." (John v. 40.) But we must not be wise above that which is written. No morbid love of liberality, so called, must induce us to reject anything which God has revealed about eternity. Men sometimes talk exclusively about God's mercy and love and compassion, as if He had no other attributes, and leave out of

---

* "If the punishment of the wicked is only temporary, such will also be the happiness of the righteous, which is repugnant to the whole teaching of Scripture; but if the happiness of the righteous will be everlasting (who will be equal to the angels, and their bodies will be like the body of Christ), such also will be the punishment of the wicked."— *Bishop Wordsworth's Sermon on Future Rewards and Punishments, p.* 31.

sight entirely His holiness and His purity, His justice and His unchangeableness, and His hatred of sin. Let us beware of falling into this delusion. It is a growing evil in these latter days. Low and inadequate views of the unutterable vileness and filthiness of sin, and of the unutterable purity of the eternal God, are fertile sources of error about man's future state. Let us think of the mighty Being with whom we have to do, as he Himself declared His character to Moses, saying, "The Lord, the Lord God, merciful and gracious, long-suffering and abundant in goodness and truth, keeping mercy for thousands, forgiving iniquity, and transgression and sin." But let us not forget the solemn clause which concludes the sentence: "And *that will by no means clear the guilty*." (Exod. xxxiv. 6, 7.) Unrepented sin is an eternal evil, and can never cease to be sin; and He with whom we have to do is an eternal God.

The words of Psalm cxlv. are strikingly beautiful: "The Lord is gracious, and full of compassion; slow to anger, and of great mercy. The Lord is good to all: and His tender mercies are over all His works.—The Lord upholdeth all that fall, and raiseth up all those that be bowed down.—The Lord is righteous in all His ways, and holy in all His works. The Lord is nigh unto all them that call upon Him, to all that call upon Him in truth.—The Lord preserveth all them that love Him." Nothing can exceed the mercifulness of this language! But what a striking fact it is that the passage goes on to add the following solemn conclusion, "*All the wicked will He destroy*." (Psalm cxlv. 8—20.)

III. The third thought which I commend to the attention of my readers is this:—*Our state in the unseen world of eternity depends entirely on what we are in time.*

The life that we live upon earth is short at the very

best, and soon gone. "We spend our days as a tale that
is told."—"What is our life? It is a vapour: so soon
passeth it away, and we are gone." (Psalm xc. 9; James
iv. 14.) The life that is before us when we leave this
world is an endless eternity, a sea without a bottom, and
an ocean without a shore. "One day in Thy sight,"
eternal God, "is as a thousand years, and a thousand years
as one day." (2 Pet. iii. 8.) In that world time shall be no
more.—But short as our life is here, and endless as it will
be hereafter, it is a tremendous thought that eternity
hinges upon time. Our lot after death depends, humanly
speaking, on what we are while we are alive. It is written,
God "will render to every man according to his deeds: to
them who by patient continuance in well-doing seek for
glory and honour and immortality, eternal life: but to
them that are contentious, and do not obey the truth, but
obey unrighteousness, indignation and wrath." (Rom.
ii. 6, 7.)

We ought never to forget, that we are all, while we live,
in a state of probation. We are constantly sowing seeds
which will spring up and bear fruit, every day and hour
in our lives. There are eternal consequences resulting
from all our thoughts and words and actions, of which we
take far too little account. "For every idle word that
men speak they shall give account in the day of judgment." (Matt. xii. 36.) Our thoughts are all numbered,
our actions are weighed. No wonder that St. Paul says,
"He that soweth to the flesh shall of the flesh reap corruption; but he that soweth to the Spirit shall of the
Spirit reap life everlasting." (Gal. vi. 8.) In a word,
what we sow in life we shall reap after death, and reap to
all eternity.

There is no greater delusion than the common idea
that it is possible to live wickedly, and yet rise again
gloriously; to be without religion in this world, and yet
to be a saint in the next. When the famous Whitefield

revived the doctrine of conversion last century, it is reported that one of his hearers came to him after a sermon and said,—"It is all quite true, sir. I hope I shall be converted and born again one day, but not till after I am dead." I fear there are many like him. I fear the false doctrine of the Romish *purgatory* has many secret friends even within the pale of the Church of England! However carelessly men may go on while they live, they secretly cling to the hope that they shall be found among the saints when they die. They seem to hug the idea that there is some cleansing, purifying effect produced by death, and that, whatever they may be in this life, they shall be found "meet for the inheritance of the saints" in the life to come. But it is all a delusion.*

"Life is the time to serve the Lord,
    The time to insure the great reward."

The Bible teaches plainly, that as we die, whether converted or unconverted, whether believers or unbelievers, whether godly or ungodly, so shall we rise again when the last trumpet sounds. There is no repentance in the grave: there is no conversion after the last breath is drawn. Now is the time to believe in Christ, and to lay hold on eternal life. Now is the time to turn from darkness unto light, and to make our calling and election sure. The night cometh when no man can work. As the tree falls, there it will lie. If we leave this world impenitent and unbelieving, we shall rise the same in the resurrection

---

* "The Scripture never represents the state of future misery, as a state of purgation and purification, or anything like analogous to a state of trial, where men may fit and qualify themselves for some better state of existence: but always as a state of retribution, punishment, and righteous vengeance, in which God's justice (a perfection of which some men seem to render no account) vindicates the power of His majesty, His government, and His love, by punishing those who have despised them."—*Horbery*, vol. ii. p. 183.

morning, and find it had been "good for us if we had
never been born." *

I charge every reader of this paper to remember this,
and to make a good use of time. Regard it as the stuff
of which life is made, and never waste it or throw it
away. Your hours and days and weeks and months and
years have all something to say to an eternal condition
beyond the grave. What you sow in life you are sure to
reap in a life to come. As holy Baxter says, it is "now or
never." Whatever we do in religion must be done now.

Remember this in your use of all the means of grace,
from the least to the greatest. Never be careless about
them. They are given to be your helps toward an eternal
world, and not one of them ought to be thoughtlessly
treated or lightly and irreverently handled. Your daily
prayers and Bible-reading, your weekly behaviour on the
Lord's day, your manner of going through public worship,
—all, all these things are important. Use them all as one
who remembers eternity.

Remember it, not least, whenever you are tempted to
do evil. When sinners entice you, and say, "It is only a
little one,"—when Satan whispers in your heart, "Never
mind : where is the mighty harm ? Everybody does so,"
—then look beyond time to a world unseen, and place in
the face of the temptation the thought of eternity. There
is a grand saying recorded of the martyred Reformer,
Bishop Hooper, when one urged him to recant before he
was burned, saying, "Life is sweet and death is bitter."

---

* "This life is the time of our preparation for our future state. Our
souls will continue for ever what we make them in this world. Such a
taste and disposition of mind as a man carries with him out of this life,
he shall retain in the next. It is true, indeed, heaven perfects those
holy and virtuous dispositions which are begun here ; but the other
world alters no man as to his main state. He that is filthy will be filthy
still ; and he that is unrighteous will be unrighteous still."—*Archbishop
Tillotson's Sermon on Phil.* iii. 20. (See *Horbrey*, vol. ii. p. 133.)

" True," said the good Bishop, " quite true ! But eternal life is more sweet, and eternal death is more bitter."

IV. The last thought which I commend to the attention of my readers is this:—*The Lord Jesus Christ is the great Friend to whom we must all look for help, both for time and eternity.*

The purpose for which the eternal Son of God came into the world can never be declared too fully, or proclaimed too loudly. He came to give us hope and peace while we live among the "things seen, which are temporal," and glory and blessedness when we go into the "things unseen, which are eternal." He came to "bring life and immortality to light," and to "deliver those who, through fear of death, were all their life-time subject to bondage." (2 Tim. i. 10 ; Heb. ii. 15.) He saw our lost and bankrupt condition, and had compassion on us. And now, blessed be His name, a mortal man may pass through "things temporal" with comfort, and look forward to "things eternal" without fear.

These mighty privileges our Lord Jesus Christ has purchased for us at the cost of His own precious blood. He became our Substitute, and bore our sins in His own body on the cross, and then rose again for our justification. "He suffered for sins, the just for the unjust, that He might bring us unto God." He was made sin for us who knew no sin, that we poor sinful creatures might have pardon and justification while we live, and glory and blessedness when we die. (1 Peter ii. 24 ; iii. 18 ; 2 Cor. v. 21.)

And all that our Lord Jesus Christ has purchased for us He offers freely to every one who will turn from his sins, come to Him, and believe. "I am the light of the world," He says : "he that followeth Me shall not walk in darkness, but shall have the light of life."—"Come unto Me, all ye that labour and are heavy laden, and I will give you rest."—"If any man thirst, let him come unto Me

and drink."—"Him that cometh unto Me I will in no
wise cast out."—And the terms are as simple as the offer
is free: "Believe on the Lord Jesus Christ and thou shalt
be saved."—"Whosoever believeth on Him shall not perish
but have eternal life." (John viii. 12; Matt. xi. 28;
John vii. 37; vi. 37; Acts xvi. 31; John iii. 16.)

He that has Christ, has life. He can look round him
on the "things temporal," and see change and decay on
every side without dismay. He has got treasure in heaven,
which neither rust nor moth can corrupt, nor thieves break
through and steal. He can look forward to the "things
eternal," and feel calm and composed. His Saviour has
risen, and gone to prepare a place for him. When he
leaves this world he shall have a crown of glory, and be
for ever with his Lord. He can look down even into the
grave, as the wisest Greeks and Romans could never do,
and say, "Oh, death, where is thy sting? oh, grave, where
is thy victory? oh, eternity, where are thy terrors?"
(1 Cor. xv. 55.)

Let us all settle it firmly in our minds that the only
way to pass through "things seen" with comfort, and look
forward to "things unseen" without fear, is to have Christ
for our Saviour and Friend, to lay hold on Christ by faith,
to become one with Christ and Christ in us, and while we
live in the flesh to live the life of faith in the Son of God.
(Gal. ii. 20.) How vast is the difference between the state
of him who has faith in Christ, and the state of him who
has none! Blessed indeed is that man or woman who can
say, with truth, "I trust in Jesus: I believe." When
Cardinal Beaufort lay upon his death-bed, our mighty
poet describes King Henry as saying, "He dies, but gives
no sign." When John Knox, the Scotch Reformer, was
drawing to his end, and unable to speak, a faithful servant
asked him to give some proof that the Gospel he had
preached in life gave him comfort in death, by raising his
hand. He heard; and raised his hand toward heaven

three times, and then departed. Blessed, I say again, is he that believes! He alone is rich, independent, and beyond the reach of harm. If you and I have no comfort amidst things temporal, and no hope for the things eternal, the fault is all our own. It is because we "will not come to Christ, that we may have life." (John v. 40.)

I leave the subject of eternity here, and pray that God may bless it to many souls. In conclusion, I offer to every one who reads this volume some food for thought, and matter for self-examination.

(1) First of all, how are you *using your time?* Life is short and very uncertain. You never know what a day may bring forth. Business and pleasure, money-getting and money-spending, eating and drinking, marrying and giving in marriage,—all, all will soon be over and done with for ever. And you, what are you doing for your immortal soul? Are you wasting time, or turning it to good account? Are you preparing to meet God?

(2) Secondly, where *shall you be in eternity?* It is coming, coming, coming very fast upon us. You are going, going, going very fast into it. But where will you be? On the right hand or on the left, in the day of judgment? Among the lost or among the saved? Oh, rest not, rest not till your soul is insured! Make sure work: leave nothing uncertain. It is a fearful thing to die unprepared, and fall into the hands of the living God.

(3) Thirdly, would you be *safe for time and eternity?* Then seek Christ, and believe in Him. Come to Him just as you are. Seek Him while He may be found, call upon Him while He is near. There is still a throne of grace. It is not too late. Christ waits to be gracious: He invites you to come to Him. Before the door is shut and the judgment begins, repent, believe, and be saved.

(4) Lastly, *would you be happy?* Cling to Christ, and live the life of faith in Him. Abide in Him, and live

near to Him.   Follow Him with heart and soul and mind
and strength, and seek to know Him better every day.
So doing you shall have great peace while you pass through
" things temporal," and in the midst of a dying world shall
" never die."   (John xi. 26.)   So doing, you shall be able
to look forward to " things eternal " with unfailing
confidence, and to feel and " know that if our earthly
house of this tabernacle be dissolved we have a building
of God, a house not made with hands, eternal in the
heavens."   (2 Cor. v. 1.)

P. S.

SINCE preaching the above Sermon I have read Canon
Farrar's volume, " Eternal Hope."   With much that this
book contains I cannot at all agree.   Anything that comes
from the pen of such a well-known writer of course deserves
respectful consideration.   But I must honestly confess,
after reading " Eternal Hope," that I see no reason to
withdraw anything I have said in my Sermon on "Eternity,"
and that I laid down the volume with regret and dissatisfaction, unconvinced and unshaken in my opinions.

I can find nothing new in Canon Farrar's statements.
He says hardly anything that has not been said before,
and refuted before.   To all who wish to examine fully the
subject of the reality and eternity of future punishment,
I venture to recommend some works which are far less
known than they ought to be, and which appear to me far
sounder, and more Scriptural, than " Eternal Hope."   These
are " Horbery's Enquiry into the Scripture Doctrine of
the Duration of Future Punishment," " Girdlestone's
Dies Iræ," the Rev. C. F. Childe's " Unsafe Anchor," and
the Rev. Flavel Cook's " Righteous Judgment."   " Bishop
Pearson on the Creed," under the head " Resurrection,"

and "*Hodge's Systematic Theology*," vol. iii. p. 868 will also repay a careful perusal.

The plain truth is, that there are vast difficulties bound up with the subject of the future state of the wicked, which Canon Farrar seems to me to leave untouched. The amazing mercifulness of God, and the awfulness of supposing that many around us will be lost eternally, he has handled fully and with characteristic rhetoric. No doubt the compassions of God are unspeakable. He is "not willing that any should perish." He "would have all men to be saved." His love in sending Christ into the world to die for sinners is an inexhaustible subject.—But this is only one side of God's character, as we have it revealed in Scripture. His character and attributes need to be looked at all round. The infinite holiness and justice of an eternal God,—His hatred of evil, manifested in Noah's flood and at Sodom, and in the destruction of the seven nations of Canaan,—the unspeakable vileness and guilt of sin in God's sight,—the wide gulf between natural man and his perfect Maker,—the enormous spiritual change which every child of Adam must go through, if he is to dwell for ever in God's presence,—and the utter absence of any intimation in the Bible that this change can take place after death,—all, all these are points which seem to me comparatively put on one aside, or left alone, in Canon Farrar's volume. My mind demands satisfaction on these points before I can accept the views advocated in "Eternal Hope," and that satisfaction I fail to find in the book.

The position that Canon Farrar has taken up was first formally advocated by Origen, a Father who lived in the third century after Christ. He boldly broached the opinion that future punishment would be only temporary; but his opinion was rejected by almost all his contemporaries. Bishop Wordsworth says,—" The Fathers of the Church in Origen's time and in the following centuries, among whom were many to whom the original language of the New Testament was their mother tongue, and who *could not be misled by translations,* examined minutely the opinion and statements of Origen, and agreed for the most part in rejecting and condemning them. Irenæus, Cyril of Jerusalem, Chrysostom, Basil, Cyril of Alexandria, and others of the Eastern Church, and Tertullian, Cyprian, Lactantius, Augustine, Gregory the Great, Bede, and many more of the Western Church, were unanimous in teaching that the joys of the righteous and the punishments of the wicked will not be temporary, but everlasting."

"Nor was this all. The Fifth General Council, held at Constantinople under the Emperor Justinian, in 553, A.D. examined the tenets of Origen, and passed a synodical decree condemnatory of them. And for a thousand years after that time there was an unanimous consent in Christendom in this sense." (Bishop Wordsworth's "Sermons," p. 34.)

Let me add to this statement the fact that the eternity of future punishment has been held by almost all the greatest theologians from the time of the Reformation down to the present day. It is a point on which Lutherans, Calvinists, and Arminians, Episcopalians, Presbyterians, and Independents have always, with a few exceptions, been of one mind. Search the writings of the most eminent and learned Reformers, search the works of the Puritans, search the few literary remains of the men who revived English Christianity in the eighteenth century, and, as a rule, you will always get one harmonious answer. Within the last few years, no doubt, the "non-eternity of future punishment" has found several zealous advocates. But up to a comparatively modern date, I unhesitatingly assert, the supporters of Canon Farrar's views have always been an extremely small minority among orthodox Christians. That fact is, at any rate, worth remembering.

As to the *difficulties* besetting the old or common view of future punishment, I admit their existence, and I do not pretend to explain them. But I always expect to find many mysteries in revealed religion, and I am not stumbled by them. I see other difficulties in the world which I cannot solve, and I am content to wait for their solution. What a mighty divine has called, "The mystery of God, the great mystery of His suffering vice and confusion to prevail,"—the origin of evil,—the permission of cruelty, oppression, poverty, and disease,—the allowed sickness and death of infants before they know good from evil,—the future prospects of the heathen who never heard the Gospel,—the times of ignorance which God has winked at,—the condition of China, Hindostan, and Central Africa, for the last 1800 years,—all these things are to my mind great knots which I am unable to untie, and depths which I have no line to fathom. But I wait for light, and I have no doubt all will be made plain. I rest in the thought that I am a poor ignorant mortal, and that God is a Being of infinite wisdom, and is doing all things well. "Shall not the Judge of all the earth do right." (Gen. xviii. 25.) It is a wise sentence of Bishop Butler: "All shadow of injustice, and indeed all harsh appearances in the various economy of God, would be lost, if we would keep in mind that every merciful allowance shall be made, and no more shall be required of any one, than what might have been equitably expected of him from the circumstances in which he was placed, and not what might have been expected from him had he been placed in other circumstances." ("Analogy," part ii. ch. vi. p. 425. Wilson's edition.) It is a grand saying of Elihu, in Job, "Touching the Almighty, we cannot find Him out: He is excellent in power, and in judgment, and in plenty of justice: He will not afflict." (Job xxxvii. 23.)

It may be perfectly true that many Romish divines,

and even some Protestants, have made extravagant and
offensive statements about the bodily sufferings of the lost
in another world. It may be true that those who believe
in eternal punishment have occasionally misunderstood or
mistranslated texts, and have pressed figurative language too
far. But it is hardly fair to make Christianity responsible
for the mistakes of its advocates. It is an old saying
that "Christian errors are infidel arguments." Thomas
Aquinas, and Dantè, and Milton, and Boston, and Jonathan
Edwards were not inspired and infallible, and I decline to
be answerable for all they may have written about the
physical torments of the lost. But after every allowance,
admission, and deduction, there remains, in my humble
opinion, a mass of Scripture evidence in support of the
doctrine of eternal punishment, which can never be explained away, and which no revision or new translation of
the English Bible will ever overthrow.* That there are
degrees of misery as well as degrees of glory in the future
state, that the condition of some who are lost will be far
worse than that of others, all this is undeniable. But that
the punishment of the wicked will ever have an end, or
that length of time alone can ever change a heart, or that
the Holy Spirit ever works on the dead, or that there is
any purging, purifying process beyond the grave, by which
the wicked will be finally fitted for heaven, these are
positions which I maintain it is utterly impossible to prove
by texts of Scripture. Nay, rather, there are texts of
Scripture which teach an utterly different doctrine. "It
is surprising," says Horbery, "if hell be such a state of
purification, that it should always be represented in
Scripture as a place of punishment." (Vol. ii. p. 223.)
"Nothing," says Girdlestone, "but clear statements of
Scripture could justify us in holding, or preaching to

---

* Horbery alone alleges and examines no less than one hundred and
three texts, on his side, in his reply to Whiston.

ungodly men, the doctrine of repentance after death; and not one clear statement on this subject is to be found." ("Dies Iræ," p. 269.) If we once begin to invent doctrines which we cannot prove by texts, or to refuse the evidence of texts in Scripture because they land us in conclusions we do not like, we may as well throw aside the Bible altogether, and discard it as the judge of controversy.

The favourite argument of some, that no religious doctrine can be true which is rejected by the "common opinion" and popular feeling of mankind,—that any texts which contradict this common popular feeling must be wrongly interpreted,—and that therefore eternal punishment cannot be true, because the inward feeling of the multitude revolts against it,—this argument appears to me alike most dangerous and unsound. It is *dangerous*, because it strikes a direct blow at the authority of Scripture as the only rule of faith. Where is the use of the Bible, if the "common opinion" of mortal man is to be regarded as of more weight than the declarations of God's Word?—It is *unsound*, because it ignores the great fundamental principle of Christianity,—that man is a fallen creature, with a corrupt heart and understanding, and that in spiritual things his judgment is worthless. There is a veil over our hearts. "The natural man receiveth not the things of the Spirit of God, for they are foolishness to him." (1 Cor. ii. 14.) To say, in the face of such a text, that any doctrine which the majority of men dislike, such as eternal punishment, *must* therefore be untrue, is simply absurd! The "common opinion" is more likely to be wrong than right! No doubt Bishop Butler has said, "If in revelation there be found any passage the seeming meaning of which is contrary to natural religion, we may most certainly conclude such seeming meaning not to be the real one." But those who triumphantly quote these words would do well to observe the sentence which immediately follows: "But it is not any degree of a presumption against an interpretation of Scripture, that such an interpretation contains a doctrine which the light of nature cannot discover." ("Analogy," part i. chap. ii. p. 358. Wilson's edition.)

After all, what the "common feeling" or opinion of the majority of mankind is about the duration of future punishment, is a question which admits of much doubt. Of course we have no means of ascertaining: and it signifies little either way. In such a matter the only point is, What saith the Scripture? But I have a strong suspicion, if the world could be polled, that we should find the greater part of mankind believed in eternal punishment! About the opinion of the Greeks and Romans at any rate there can be little dispute. If anything is clearly taught in the stories of their mythology it is the endless nature of the sufferings of the wicked. Bishop Butler says, "Gentile writers, both moralist and poetic, speak of the future punishment of the wicked, both as to duration and degree, in a like manner of expression and description as the Scripture does." ("Analogy," part i. chap. ii. p. 218.) The strange and weird legends of Tantalus, Sisyphus, Ixion, Prometheus, and the Danaides, have all one common feature about them. In each case the punishment is eternal! This is a fact worth noticing. It is worth what it is worth. But it shows, at all events, that the opponents of eternal punishment should not talk too confidently about the "common opinion of mankind."

As to the doctrine of the *Annihilation of the Wicked*, to which many adhere, it appears to me so utterly irreconcilable with our Lord Jesus Christ's words about "the resurrection of damnation," and "the worm that never dies, and the fire that is not quenched," and St. Paul's words about "the resurrection of the unjust" (John v. 29; Mark ix. 43—48; Acts xxiv. 15), that until those words can be proved to form no part of inspired Scripture it seems to me mere waste of time to argue about it.

The favourite argument of the advocates of this doctrine, that "death, dying, perishing, destruction," and the like, are phrases which can only mean "cessation of existence," is so ridiculously weak that it is scarcely worth noticing. Every Bible reader knows that God said to Adam, concerning the forbidden fruit, "In the day thou eatest thereof thou shalt surely *die*." (Gen. ii. 17.) But every well-taught Sunday scholar knows that Adam did not "cease to exist," when he broke the commandment. He died spiritually, but he did not cease to be!—So also St. Peter says of the flood: "The world that then was, being overflowed with water, *perished*." (2 Peter iii. 6.) Yet, though temporarily drowned, it certainly did not cease to be; and when the water was dried up Noah lived on it again.

It only remains for me now to add one more last word, by way of information. Those who care to investigate the meaning of the words "eternal" and "everlasting," as used in Scripture, will find the subject fully and exhaustively considered in *Girdlestone's "Old Testament Synonyms,"* ch. 30, p. 495; and in the same writer's *"Dies Iræ,"* ch. 10 and 11, p. 128.